Shakespeare's History Plays

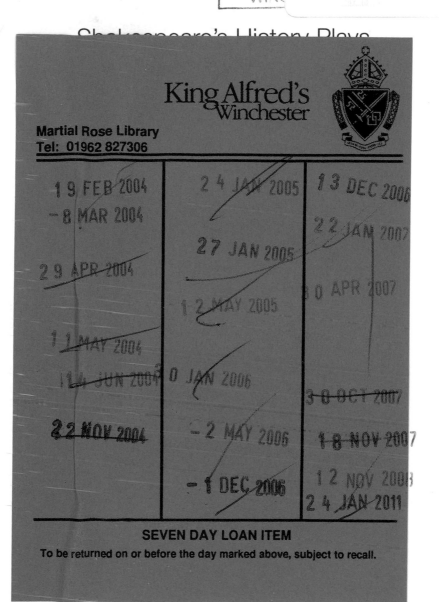

LONGMAN CRITICAL READERS

GENERAL EDITOR

STAN SMITH

Research Professor in Literary Studies, The Nottingham Trent University

TITLES AVAILABLE

Shakespeare's

History Plays

EDITED AND INTRODUCED BY

R.J.C. WATT

An imprint of **Pearson Education**

London • New York • Toronto • Sydney • Tokyo • Singapore • Hong Kong • Cape Town
Madrid • Paris • Amsterdam • Munich • Milan

PEARSON EDUCATION LIMITED

Head Office:
Edinburgh Gate
Harlow CM20 2JE
Tel: +44 (0)1279 623623
Fax: +44 (0)1279 431059

London Office:
128 Long Acre
London WC2E 9AN
Tel: +44 (0)20 7447 2000
Fax: +44 (0)20 7447 2170
Website: www.history-minds.com

First published in Great Britain in 2002

© Pearson Education Limited 2002

The right of R. J. C. Watt to be identified as Author
of this Work has been asserted by him in accordance
with the Copyright, Designs and Patents Act 1988.

ISBN 0 582 41831 3

British Library Cataloguing in Publication Data
A CIP catalogue record for this book can be obtained from the British Library

Library of Congress Cataloging in Publication Data
A CIP catalog record for this book can be obtained from the Library of Congress

10 9 8 7 6 5 4 3 2
07 06 05 04 03

Typeset in 9/12pt Stone Serif by Graphicraft Limited, Hong Kong
Printed and bound in Malaysia, PA

The Publisher's policy is to use paper manufactured from sustainable forests.

Contents

Acknowledgements

W e are grateful to the following for permission to reproduce copyright material:

Blackwell Publishing Ltd for an extract from *Shakespeare and the Popular Voice* by Annabel Patterson; English Literary Renaissance for an extract from 'Wildehirissheman: colonialist representation in Shakespeare's *Henry V*' by David J. Baker published in *English Literary Renaissance* 22 (1992); Oxford University Press and The Regents of the University of California and the University of California Press for an extract from *Faultlines: Cultural Materialism and the Politics of Dissident Reading* by Alan Sinfield (with John Dollimore); Pearson Education Limited for extracts from *Shakespeare Recycled: The Making of Historical Drama* by Graham Holderness (Harvester Wheatsheaf 1992), *Shakespeare* by Kiernan Ryan (Harvester Wheatsheaf 1995), and *Will Power: Essays on Shakespearean Authority* by Richard Wilson (Harvester Wheatsheaf 1993); Routledge Inc., part of The Taylor & Francis Group, for 'A tale of two Branaghs: *Henry V*, ideology and the Mekong Agincourt' by Chris Fitter published in *Shakespeare Left and Right* ed. Ivo Kamps © 1991, and an extract from *Shakespeare's Ghost Writers* by Marjorie Garber © 1987; Taylor & Francis Books Ltd for extracts from *Engendering a Nation: A Feminist Account of Shakespeare's English Histories* by Jean E. Howard and Phyllis Rackin, *Stages of History: Shakespeare's English Chronicles* by Phyllis Rackin, and *Desire and Anxiety: Circulations of Sexuality in Shakespearean Drama* by Valerie Traub; and Verso for 'Topical ideology: witches, amazons and Shakespeare's John of Arc' by Gabriele Bernhard Jackson published in *Shakespeare and Gender: A History* ed. Deborah E. Barker and Ivo Kamps.

Introduction

The theoretically-informed criticism of recent decades has perhaps had more impact on the history plays than on any other part of Shakespeare's work. Critical interpretations have been revolutionised since the break-up of a humanist consensus which dominated thinking in the mid-twentieth century. A largely conservative view of the history plays has been comprehensively swept away by New Historicism and cultural materialism, by feminist and gender-based studies, by psychoanalytical and post-colonial criticism, and by a more rigorous and self-aware political criticism.

The problematising of the concept of history itself is one feature that characterises recent work and sets it apart from what went before. In post-modernism particularly, the past comes to be seen as always already mediated, constituted as a text and in texts rather than objective, factual and unproblematically knowable. In consequence, 'history' has been largely replaced by 'histories' and 'story' has ceased to be history's less authoritative cousin. Such developments place Shakespeare's histories at the centre of one of the most interesting and important cultural shifts of our times. Moreover, as is now widely recognised, Shakespeare is the site of constant interpretative struggles for the cultural prestige which goes with his name. This too has made the history plays a frequent focus of contention, since they can be recruited to partisan accounts of Britishness or Englishness – supposedly quintessential national values and identity – and hence to all kinds of contemporary arguments ranging from the politics of education or the content of curricula to images of monarchy on film and television. The history plays are hotly contested cultural property.

The aim of this volume is to present a selection of the best critical essays of recent decades on the history plays in order to illustrate the variety and energy of recent approaches to the plays, and to situate the essays in their context in order to indicate some of the major trends in recent criticism of the plays. This introduction traces the main outlines of the changing debate, assessing the contribution of each of the movements in literary theory – Foucauldian, Marxist, New Historicist/ cultural materialist, and feminist among others – which have had the biggest impact on readings of the history plays and enabled an invigorated criticism. This volume is concerned with the theoretically-informed criticism of recent years; yet in order to understand the ideas which that criticism reacts against (ideas which still retain cultural power, as we shall see) it is necessary briefly to survey earlier views of the history plays, views which exercised a remarkable influence over much of the second half of the twentieth century.

BATTLES LONG AGO

In 1944 E. M. W. Tillyard published his book *Shakespeare's History Plays*. In it he treats history as if it were an extended Morality play, an expression of a fundamentally religious scheme 'by which events evolve under a law of justice and under the ruling of God's Providence, and of which Elizabeth's England was the acknowledged outcome' (Tillyard, 1966, p. 325). The course of history is equated with 'nature's course'. That course is distorted by a crime, Henry Bolingbroke's usurpation of Richard II's throne, and the plays are seen as recounting a long struggle to restore the true course. Although the 'perfect king' Henry V, 'by his politic wisdom and his piety postpones the day of reckoning', the 'curse' imposed by the usurpation is then realised in the time of Henry VI in 'the dreaded form of a child being king' (pp. 67, 66). The final crisis and resolution come in *Richard III*: with the removal of the monster Richard at the end of the play, 'God had guided England into her haven of Tudor prosperity' (p. 210). This makes of history 'a dramatic and philosophical sweep' (p. 65) and makes the plays an embodiment of the 'Tudor myth' – the idea propagated by Henry VII that 'the union of the two houses of York and Lancaster through his marriage with the York heiress was the providential and happy ending of an organic piece of history' (p. 36). Although Tillyard from time to time avoided naively identifying Shakespeare with these beliefs, claiming that they were the prevalent beliefs of the time which Shakespeare merely adopted for the purposes of the drama, the distinction often collapses, so that Shakespeare appears in Tillyard's account to be an apologist or propagandist for the Tudor regime.

As a complement to his account of the Tudor Myth, Tillyard had written a separate short book *The Elizabethan World Picture* (1943): theirs, he said, was a theory of the cosmos in which everything had its allotted place in a 'vast chain of being', a strict hierarchy which 'stretched from the foot of God's throne to the meanest of inanimate objects' (Tillyard, 1976, p. 33). Through a system of correspondences, each element in the hierarchy was organised as a microcosmic reflection of the larger elements above it; hence a human society should be organised to exhibit the 'order' which characterises the universe itself, ruled by a sovereign who occupies the same place in the human hierarchy as God does in the cosmos and who is therefore to be seen as God's agent or image upon earth. Hence Tillyard can present 'political order' as 'a part of a larger cosmic order' (p. 7). 'Order' is a key idea: for Tillyard the plays present disorder as an abhorrent departure from a natural state of order. He believed that what Shakespeare 'minded most about' was 'England, her past history and her present glory'. Rebellion of any kind is wickedness; monarchy is to be venerated, its 'sanctity' is to be 'heightened'; rulers are to be treated with 'the spirit of worship'.[1]

Some of the major objections to Tillyard's view of the history plays should by now be obvious. They include his monarchism and his monolithic view of culture. Whether he was aware of it or not, his interpretation of the histories was shaped by a conservative and nationalist politics of the 1940s. This produces a Shakespeare who is politically orthodox and conservative, an exponent of Order and an apologist for the Tudor regime. Tillyard makes out Shakespeare's period to be much more homogeneous than recent critics claim. They would argue, not that Tillyard was wrong to identify a strong insistence on order in the period, but that he overlooked the fact that that very insistence on order was in response to disorder and fears of it.

Although Tillyard's view had its critics throughout the period of its dominance, the reaction against him began to gather strength in the 1970s. Some writers, such as H. A. Kelly (1970), challenged his view of the plays as a providential sequence and argued that 'Elizabethan culture must have been more divided and contentious' than Tillyard's unitary model of the Elizabethan World Picture and the Tudor Myth acknowledged. The overthrow of the Tillyardian view, when it came, marked a fall from innocence. The exposure of his conservative assumptions brought many to realise that, as Hugh Grady puts it, 'literary criticism, far from being what it appears, a disinterested inquiry into the meaning and value of an accepted canon of master-works, is instead a complexly overdetermined discourse shaped by politics, aesthetics, and institutional discipline'.[2] By around 1980, instead of arguing against Tillyard, criticism began to leave him behind, with the arrival of the New Historicism in the work of Stephen Greenblatt and others.

All this, it might be thought, scarcely matters now. Every critic in this volume has more modern ideas to pursue than replaying the overthrow of the Tillyardian ascendancy. But in other ways, Tillyard's legacy, adapted or even inverted, still colours assumptions. He made the plays seem political, as they still are for numer-ous critics, though not in his sense, since to him 'politics' described a process of 'having made good nationally' (1966, p. 148) and 'history' meant the history of ideas – he would certainly not have regarded either history or politics as encom-passing anything so vulgar as the actions of a group of London cloth workers, as does Richard Wilson in his essay In this volume (Chapter 2). Moreover, Tillyard saw the plays as reflecting the concerns of Shakespeare's contemporary world. Hence, as we shall discuss below, a number of modern critics have chosen to see the plays instead as conscious acts of historiography, serious attempts to interpret the past, not merely about the 1590s in disguise.

For Tillyard, Prince Hal was Shakespeare's 'perfect ruler' (1966, p. 296). One might therefore expect that, after Hal's ascent to the throne, *Henry V* would be the crowning patriotic glory in Tillyard's scheme. In fact, he regarded the play as 'con-structed without intensity' and showing 'a great falling off in quality' (pp. 317, 311). The character of Henry V, 'the man who knew exactly what he wanted and went for it with utter singleness of heart' (p. 318), is uninteresting to Tillyard, and he regards him as failing to embody 'any wide political idea' or 'principle' (p. 310). Projecting his own view on to Shakespeare, Tillyard says 'the man of action is not his real hero'.[3] His dismissal of *Henry V* as relatively uninteresting, a view which remained influential for several decades, is one context in which we can see the enormous recent intensification of interest in that play. But though Tillyard shied away from the warrior-king, others were ready to propagate him. The making of Laurence Olivier's 1944 film of *Henry V* as a 'trailer for D-Day' is a story that has now been re-told well and often.

Ideas continue to persist and circulate at a diminished level in a culture for years after they have been challenged, like background radiation long after a nuclear explosion. These particular ideas, though intellectually long since rejected, have as much cultural and economic power as ever. As Lisa Jardine has said, 'The nationalistic Shakespeare "industry" – the commercial exploitation of the image of Shakespeare, and his history plays in particular as quintessentially British, now a main plank in the "propaganda" version of Shakespeare's cultural centrality – is in the direct line of descent from this war era Shakespeare/Harry.'[4] The history plays have proved part of the staple diet at the Royal Shakespeare Company in Stratford. The screened adaptations in particular, from Olivier's wartime *Henry V* via Orson Welles to Kenneth Branagh's highly popular *Henry V* of 1989, have taken on major cultural significance in the twentieth century. Images and representations of monarchy are a topical issue for our period as they were for Shakespeare. Chris Fitter's essay in this volume, 'A Tale of Two Branaghs: *Henry V*, Ideology, and the Mekong Agincourt' (Chapter 9), looks at the politics of monarchical representation in film. Fitter argues that although Branagh's version is often grittier than Olivier's, it is every bit as concerned to turn the play into a glorification of monarchy. Whereas Olivier's treatment had the compelling justification of contributing to wartime morale, Branagh had no such excuse in his rush to adopt Hollywood values and to re-spray yet again the fading British monarchy. For as Curtis Breight has shown, in a revealing essay complementing Fitter's but not included in this volume, Branagh maintained a close personal association with the heir to the British throne during the making of the film (Breight, 1998).

Hugh Grady argues that Tillyard's vision of Shakespeare's history plays was really just

a version of the great teleological historical pattern that dominated much of nineteenth-century thought – the pattern, for example, codified by Hegel's celebrated and notorious diagnosis of Napoleon as an embodiment of Reason marching through history leading to the glorious denouement of the Prussian constitutional monarchy; of the positivist vision of a progressive accumulation of scientific knowledge completing Enlightenment and ushering in a new golden age; of the triumph of Democracy and Liberty as the West spread its enlightened institutions into the backward regions of the planet; of the popular version of Darwin according to which Nature reached its *telos* in the culminating production of man; of those parts of Marx and Engels, canonised by both Second and Third Internationals, in which the inevitable outcome of the contradictions of capitalism is a proletarian revolution which produces the complete emancipation of the human race.[5]

In thus imposing a teleology upon the plays, Grady argues, Tillyard was 'borrowing a form from the larger culture and reading it back into Shakespeare'. The tendency to construct such master-narratives has been tempered in recent years, as many feminist, historicist and materialist critics have written of those elements in the plays which *resist* the dominant, such as characters marginalised by gender, nationality or class. The result is a plurality of concurrent and conflicting 'histories' rather than a single 'history'. This change of outlook, which we might call the pluralising of histories, is readily available to critics drawing on theories which stress opposition and conflict as the dynamic of historical and cultural change – theories ultimately Hegelian and Marxist in origin, but which (unlike the master-narratives Grady describes) are more interested in the processes of conflict and change than in their supposed abolition in some future utopia.

PROVIDENCE AND HUMANISM

In the beginning, it was assumed that God made history. That is, divine providence was held to foresee and plan all that occurred. That providential view was being overthrown in Shakespeare's time by the Machiavellian view that human beings, not God, are in control of events, the agents of historical causation. The conflict between these two theories of history can be seen as underlying much of the excitement of the history plays. The overthrow of a providential by a Machiavellian view happened all over again in the third quarter of the twentieth century, when Tillyard's grand scheme of history was dismantled, again placing man (though seldom woman), rather than God, at the centre of things. But that movement of the 1960s and 1970s may now itself be seen as the last hurrah of a humanism dating back to the Renaissance – a focus on 'man' as the centre of value and meaning – which has been comprehensively attacked since then.

The above summary is, of course, an over-simplification. Yet it can provide a skeletal context in which to view many aspects of the critical debate of the last half-century. For example, it can help explain the difficulty our period may have in estimating the importance attached to the individual figure in the plays: it can be hard to retain our sense that the anti-providential emphasis on 'man' as historical agent was radical in Shakespeare's time when to us, four hundred years on, it has come to seem a stultifying orthodoxy overdue for challenge. In other words, we are looking at a period when humanist ideas were radically new, from our own vantage-point where they have newly been rejected.

The diffuse but powerful set of old humanist assumptions from the post-war decades can be illustrated by way of a few examples from John Wilders' book *The Lost Garden: A View of Shakespeare's English and Roman History Plays* (1978). It saw the plays as organised illustrations of great 'themes', with chapter titles such as 'Time and Change' or 'Dilemma and Discovery'. Such work placed emphasis on moral problems and on personal tragedies seen within the framework of a 'history' which was relatively unproblematic and a self which was autonomous (and male). The political process was seen in terms of the ethical challenges and duties faced by kingly or patrician individuals in public life. Wilders stated that his object of investigation was 'the mind which created all the history plays' (p. ix); that that mind 'was guided by certain largely unchanging assumptions'; and that those assumptions amounted to 'a view of human nature' which has remained constant, applicable 'irrespective of the historical period he chose to depict'. These points could almost stand as a summary of everything that has been rejected in the period since Wilders wrote. The same can be said of Wilders' claim that the distinguishing mark of any Shakespeare history play is its ability 'to portray the continuing life of a nation' (p. 7). Just what the 'life of a nation' means is illuminated elsewhere when we are told that 'politics is a family affair' (p. 3): this is true only if your family happens to be that of the monarch. So the 'life of a nation', that supposedly inclusive unity, has shrunk to the interests of a single family with whom we are supposed to identify. We may also note that adjective 'continuing', with its implicit valuing of stability; and note too the assumed unity of '*a*' (single) nation. These are also assumptions which have since been contested by all sorts of critics, feminist,

Marxist, cultural-materialist, or New Historicist, who would point to divisions or conflicts within that supposedly unified nation – conflicts between genders, between class and class, between rulers and ruled, between monarchy and barony, among others. The 'nation' turns out to be at the very least a number of nations yoked together. As Alan Sinfield and Jonathan Dollimore pointedly observe in their essay in this volume, 'The jokes [in *Henry V*] about the way Fluellen pronounces the English language have, apparently, for Elizabethan audiences and many since, been an adequate way of handling the repression of Welsh language and culture' (Chapter 12, p. 214). Recent work argues that the plays are concerned with the *emergence* of ideas of a nation. 'A nation', then, is no longer something fundamental to the plays which can be taken for granted, but something contested, emergent, produced; an overlapping series of partial or fragmentary identities and allegiances.

Modern theory thus challenges humanism, the idea urged by common sense that, as Catherine Belsey puts it, ' "man" is the origin and source of meaning, of action, and of history'.[6] Hence there is an acute issue for representations of action (plays) which are also versions of history: they are likely to be at the heart of theory's challenge to humanism on both counts. Do plays identify human beings, generally or individually, as the origin of the actions they depict? Yet in Shakespeare the issue is of further interest because the plays may be proposing just that character-centred view, in their rejection of providence: that it is people, not God, who make things happen.

In drama the relation between the individual and history centres on character and event. In the nineteenth century, a character-based literary criticism and a 'great man' theory of historical causation were closely allied. On this view, which still survives residually, plays are important because they delineate character; character is important because it gives rise to historical action. The close conjunction can be seen in Thomas Carlyle, principal exponent of the 'great man' theory of history, who began his lectures 'On Heroes and Hero-Worship' in 1840 with the claim that 'Universal History . . . is at bottom the History of . . . Great Men', and went on to assert that 'it is in . . . Portrait-painting, delineating of men and things, especially of men, that Shakespeare is great'.[7] Drama by its nature focuses on individuals, and drama about historic or heroic events may tend to glamorise them. Fortunately, however, drama also has some immunity from the crude view that history is simply the result of the doings of heroes, if only because drama invariably represents conflict among a plurality of characters. We may also recall Aristotle's insistence that, far from dramatic action being a product of character, what we call character is simply a by-product of action.

ESSENCES

Essentialism is the assumption that human beings have a timeless essence, usually called 'human nature', which is often portrayed as stubbornly immune to change. This old humanist view was, and still is, frequently invoked in support of highly conservative political.positions. Literary criticism has helped challenge essentialism, offering instead a view of the self as a construct, contingent upon circumstances and culture. Shakespeare's historical plays can undoubtedly be read in this anti-essentialist way, showing how the self is neither stable nor autonomous. A related issue is the rise of individualism in (and since) the Renaissance, and again the plays may be seen as not uncritical of the cult of the individual. For example, the egregious Machiavel Richard III is a monster; Coriolanus, who strives vainly to be 'author of himself', is a political misfit at best and a menace to humanity at worst; and Richard II, who begins the play insouciantly contemptuous of others, as if an entirely self-sufficient personality, finds that after his loss of the crown he has lost his sense of identity too, becoming 'nothing'. In such ways and many others the plays support, indeed demand, those modern readings which see the self not as a perfected essence but as a construct contingent on its relations and its circumstances, one which is at times as radically unstable as anything in Ovid's *Metamorphoses*, that favourite Elizabethan text.

As suggested above, the assumption that coherent characters are central to drama may be better seen as a legacy of classic nineteenth-century realism rather than something intrinsic to the plays. So, as Gabriele Bernhard Jackson shows in the essay which opens this volume, the tangle of contradictions in the presentation of Joan of Arc in *Henry VI Part 1* is far more convincingly explained as ideological (through examining the various Elizabethan reactions to the 'strong woman') than by invoking a notion of 'character as coherent selfhood'. She studies the uneasy parallels between Queen Elizabeth and Joan of Arc, women who act like men, exposing contemporary anxieties about female rule and dominance.[8] Her work is part of a significant recent trend to re-value the *Henry VI* plays, once dismissed as inferior.

Graham Holderness in turn argues that the protean variety of Falstaff's dramatic roles, and even his command of widely divergent languages and discourses, 'bear no coherent relation to what we call "character", but operate only as part of a specific relation between actor and audience'. Hence Falstaff may be seen 'as a collective rather than an individual being' (Chapter 7, p. 135). Holderness's essay may be seen as one intermediate stage in the overthrow of Falstaff. The overthrow came to seem necessary because for at least a century Falstaff had been 'Shakespeare's greatest comic creation', a triumph of delightfully roguish character portrayal, as well as a licensed rebel, a lord of misrule who is thankfully singular, safely contained and easily neutralised. Holderness sets about the demolition of this 'character', and other critics, such as Valerie Traub (Chapter 6 in this volume), have continued the dethronement by re-inventing Falstaff as a woman (or, more accurately, as a sexually ambiguous figure).[9] Traub's book *Desire and Anxiety: Circulations of Sexuality in Shakespearean Drama* (1992) takes a psychoanalytical approach to Hal's progress, tracing his move away from Falstaff's 'female' body and the maternal towards the sexual mastery displayed in his wooing of Katherine. By the 1990s, other critics simply seemed scarcely interested in Falstaff any longer.

FROM HISTORY TO HISTORIOGRAPHY

If 'history' can notoriously mean both 'what happened' and 'what is written about what happened', the term historiography unambiguously refers to the latter: the writing of history, and the theories and assumptions with which history is written. Several modern critics, including Phyllis Rackin, Paola Pugliatti and Graham Holderness, have attempted to show that Shakespeare should be taken seriously as a historiographer. In her book *Stages of History* (1991), Rackin discusses the move away from a providential view of history and identifies 'three great innovations, all originating in Italy' which 'were changing English historiography during the second half of the sixteenth century – a new interest in causation, a recognition of anachronism, and a questioning of textual authority' (p. 5). She claims that what happens in this period is the emergence of historiography itself – the beginning of an awareness that there is more than one way of writing any history, or as she says, 'the recognition that history was not necessarily identical with historiography' (p. 13). Her essay in this volume argues the case for Shakespeare's part in this process (Chapter 4).

This stress on Shakespeare as a fascinated theoretician of historical writing may or may not be wholly convincing, but it is certainly in contrast with another school of critics. For them, Shakespeare's history plays are not about history at all. Rather, the plays represent the social and political issues, and even particular events, of the years in which Shakespeare wrote them. Accounts of Shakespeare's part in performing *Richard II* complete with its controversial deposition scene the night before the Earl of Essex's actual attempt to overthrow the Queen on 8 February 1601 can still make startling reading. Classic old-historicist studies in this mode, linking the plays to actual contemporary events, are now less favoured than they once were. Instead there is a tendency to see the plays as not merely touching on specific events but representing key conflicts in Shakespeare's period. Richard Wilson's work is an attempt to apply history in this way, one that tries to be better grounded than the 'free-floating anecdote' approach of most New Historicists. His 1986 essay 'A Mingled Yarn: Shakespeare and the Cloth Workers' (Chapter 2) argues that the modern bourgeois liking for political compromise is not a good perspective from which to interpret Shakespeare, and sheds new light on *Henry VI Part 2*. Annabel Patterson's book *Shakespeare and the Popular Voice* (1989) is the most sustained challenge to the notion of Shakespeare as anti-democratic, hierarchist and a supporter of the Elizabethan order. For Patterson, Shakespeare began as a cautious believer in the Elizabethan settlement before moving towards political scepticism and then to a mature radicalism. She and Wilson have disagreed sharply over the way we should interpret the Cade rebellion in *Henry VI Part 2*: see the headnotes to their respective essays. The question as to whether Shakespeare supported the common people or despised them is still wide open to debate.[10]

A NEW HISTORICISM

'Historicism' is also a somewhat slippery term, and many critics of quite opposing schools would see themselves as historicists in some sense. Tillyard and several other writers of the mid-twentieth century held that Shakespeare's plays should be interpreted via the ideas of their period (the difficulty with that approach being, as we have seen, that our accounts of the ideas of a past period tend to bear a striking resemblance to the ideas of our own period.) Another strand of criticism which attempts to see the plays as topical, dealing with particular events of the years in which they were written, has been mentioned above. Both these approaches might be called 'old-historicist'.

New Historicism, on the other hand, was principally a phenomenon of the 1980s in the USA. An excellent discussion of its origins and character can be found in the introduction to the volume in the present series, *New Historicism and Renaissance Drama*, edited by Richard Wilson and Richard Dutton (1992). It will suffice here to sketch some of its main features. It drew heavily on the theories of Michel Foucault, particularly his idea that both truth and power are effects of discourse, created in and by language. Even the most inward aspects of the self are seen as discursive, dependent upon a language and even an audience. Such theories have direct implications for interpreting historical drama. For example, in Foucault's view, an objective knowledge of history is impossible, just as no discourse is fully objective or 'true'. This leads to what Wilson and Dutton regard as the defining characteristic of the New Historicism, its awareness of 'the historicity of texts and the textuality of history' (the phrase is from the New Historicist Louis Montrose).[11] Or again, Foucault's view that discourse is linked to power and that both are pervasive and diffused throughout a society can be seen as leading to the frequent New Historicist interest in the Renaissance theatricalisation of power. On this theory, a play may do more than simply reflect or represent aspects of the power of a state or a monarch; rather, by embodying the discourses in which power resides, it may be an instantiation of that power as significant as any other. To quote a well-known remark of Stephen Greenblatt's, 'Theatricality then is not set over against power but is one of power's essential modes.'[12] The common-sense view that 'poetry makes nothing happen', that the writing of fictions is utterly unlike the practical reality of exercising political power, is collapsed by New Historicism, which sees story and history as almost synonymous. In Greenblatt's words, 'one of the highest achievements of power is to impose fictions upon the world and one of its supreme pleasures is to enforce the acceptance of fictions that are known to be fictions'.[13]

Among New Historicism's other characteristics were these. Its approach to literary texts was cultural and anthropological, aiming to produce a 'poetics of culture'. Hence a characteristic procedure of a New Historicist essay was to begin with an anecdote drawn from a sphere of discourse apparently remote from the drama – a journal, a police report, a sermon – and juxtapose it with a literary text in order to reveal cultural connections. It was fascinated by moments of encounter between alien cultures because of their capacity to reveal ideological assumptions manifesting themselves directly as the exercise of power. It attempted to be materialist, 'constantly returning . . . to the material necessities and social pressures that men and women daily confronted'; and it was dialectical, seeing cultural energies as the product of 'unresolved and continuing conflict'.[14]

The best-known New Historicist essay on the *Henry IV* plays and *Henry V*, Stephen Greenblatt's 'Invisible Bullets', is so well known and available in so many places[15] that it would be superfluous to include it again here. A highly original piece of work, it helped constitute the terms of much subsequent debate. It has helped focus attention on nationalism and the marginalisation, or symbolic taming, of the

Welsh, Irish and Scots in *Henry V*, and on the connection between the conquest of France and the wooing of Katherine, 'an invasion graphically figured as a rape'. Central to this and some other New Historicist essays is the thesis that authority is constantly engaged in producing its own radical subversion and powerfully containing that subversion. Hence subversive voices such as Falstaff's do not undermine the order which produced them. The smoothly articulated career of Prince Hal (Greenblatt is fascinated by careers, and his accounts of the fashioning of selves often turn out to be the forging of careers) is a good fit for this subversion/containment thesis: Hal, after all, announces in advance that he is the rebel who will in due course abjure rebelliousness.[16] But it is questionable whether this pattern is really applicable in general to all authority.

Although Greenblatt denies that 'power' is 'monolithic',[17] he does assert that it is 'monological', and since in his view power is embodied in language anyway, the distinction between monological and monolithic may be more apparent than real. Certainly cultural materialists would regard his view of power as too monolithic, insufficiently acknowledging the presence of the voices of the repressed. In fact Greenblatt, in order to demonstrate his thesis that subversion is always contained, has to find a way of denying efficacy to subversive elements while insisting that they exist within the text. His answer is to assert that the voices of the alien, the disempowered, are merely 'recorded' by a play – a view which David Baker's essay in the present volume effectively challenges for reducing the alien to the mechanistic, passing it through power's recording machine (Chapter 11). Other critics have frequently challenged the New Historicist formula by which, in Graham Holderness's words, 'dissent is always already suppressed, subversion always previously contained'.[18] The stress on the inevitability of containment and the invincibility of state power can make the American New Historicists seem as conservative as Tillyard, and as ready as he was to portray Shakespeare as 'complicit with the Elizabethan power structure'.[19] Richard Wilson's attack on New Historicism is even more robust: to him, its talk of the endless and inexhaustible circulation of energy is 'mystification of the market as the Word of God', that is, merely capitalism in disguise.

The moment of New Historicism is now well past. It may be that its European counterpart, cultural materialism, will prove more durable. At its best the New Historicist essay uses its juxtapositions of historical anecdote with play-text to provoke a re-thinking of the play's relation to its historical and cultural milieu. Its weaknesses can include an arbitrariness of juxtaposition, and a formulaic argument which leads predictably to the same conclusion about subversion and containment. Feminist critics have also objected to the New Historicism's 'neglect of gender issues and its concentration on male power relationships'.[20]

CULTURAL MATERIALISM

If American New Historicism sees ideology and power as locked together in mutual reinforcement, its British relative, cultural materialism, seeks to prise them apart. Where New Historicism often concerns itself with the dominant strand in a culture, cultural materialism invokes Raymond Williams's theory that at any moment a culture may contain dominant, residual and emergent strands.[21] This makes it possible to pay attention to dissident voices, to account for contradiction and for change over time, and to avoid the subversion/containment formula. To quote Steven Mullaney:

Hegemonic culture, in Williams' development of Antonio Gramsci's concept, is neither singular nor static, nor is hegemony synonymous with cultural domination; on the contrary, the culture of any given historical period is conceived as a heterogeneous and irreducibly plural social formation, and as a dynamic process of representation and interpretation rather than as a fixed ensemble of meanings and beliefs.[22]

Hence for Mullaney the role of the critic is to 'situate literary texts in relation to the larger social text that is itself an unstable, heterogeneous, continually rehearsed and renegotiated production', bearing in mind that the cultural performances of a society are 'produced not only by its reigning hierarchies or institutions but also by the contestatory, marginal, or residual forces which the dominant culture must endlessly react to and upon in order to maintain its dominance' (p. xii).

Phyllis Rackin has thoughtfully characterised the difference between New Historicism and cultural materialism by likening it to the division in Shakespeare's time between providential and Machiavellian historiographies. On this view, the New Historicists of our era correspond to the providentialists of the Renaissance: both believe in predetermined outcomes; for both, the voice of the elite always triumphs; the only difference is that whereas Renaissance providentialists ascribed these outcomes to God, New Historicists ascribe them to the monarch or ruling interests. One singular, univocal source of authority has been substituted for another. Similarly the cultural materialists of our time may resemble the Machiavellian historiographers of the Renaissance, emphasising the subversive power of popular protest, insisting on human agency rather than the mechanical workings of power apparatuses, discovering 'a polyphonic discourse, where even the voices of the illiterate can never be fully silenced'.[23]

Numerous critics have observed that the New Historicist fascination with the Renaissance theatricalisation of power was a phenomenon which flourished in the heyday of Ronald Reagan, the actor turned President. We can add that the British cultural materialists' more robust and confrontational views about the possibilities of resistance and subversion similarly owe something to the era of Thatcher and the miners' strike and systematic government hostility to universities. For Richard Wilson, 'the classic text is reproduced in our society to authorise the moral claims of market capitalism' (Chapter 2).

Henry V has undergone a bigger change of critical view than any other history play. After Tillyard dismissed it and Olivier brilliantly simplified it into a wartime morale-raiser, it spent the third quarter of the twentieth century often seen as a relatively naive and uninteresting exercise in patriotism, even xenophobia. The patriotic or monarchist view of the play, as already mentioned, still persists in screen versions and as part of the Shakespeare myth, but meanwhile, academic criticism has moved from one extreme to the other. *Henry V* is now written about more than the other plays, and it would be possible to compile a volume like this one on that play alone. And when one critic can call it, with magnificent over-statement, 'undoubtedly the most formidably difficult text in Shakespeare's whole œuvre',[24] we are once again firmly in territory which tells us more about the preoccupations of our own period than those of Shakespeare's time. Cultural materialism in the 1980s produced its own flagship essay on *Henry V* to rival 'Invisible Bullets'. By Jonathan Dollimore and Alan Sinfield, it originally appeared in John Drakakis's influential collection *Alternative Shakespeares* (1985) entitled 'History and Ideology: the Instance of *Henry V*'. It appears in the present volume in its revised, extended version which adds a full discussion of gender roles to its original account of ideology (Chapter 12). Ranging over imperialism, xenophobia, and homosocial ideology, it brings these things together in impressive synthesis.

IDEOLOGY

Ideology is a key concept for many a post-marxist or materialist critic. The term can be over-used and loosely used, but need not be. Fredric Jameson's characterisation is a useful one: 'ideology is not so much "believing" something as it is being cap-able of registering or representing something'.[25] For Sinfield and Dollimore, ideology is 'not just a set of ideas; it is material practice, woven into the fabric of everyday life'. Its principal strategy 'is to legitimate inequality and exploitation by represent-ing the social order that perpetuates these things as immutable and unalterable'. To put it more fully: 'Ideology is composed of those beliefs, practices, and institutions that work to legitimate the social order – especially by the process of representing sectional or class interests as universal ones. This process presupposes that there are other, subordinate cultures that, far from sharing the interests of the dominant one, are in fact being exploited by it' (Chapter 12). As with Richard Wilson, the key move here is to oppose the dominant by denying that it is universal, replacing a single model of culture by a conflictual model and hence a plural one. The aim is to get away from a history written by the victors.

DECONSTRUCTION, PSYCHOANALYSIS, POST-COLONIAL CRITICISM

Deconstruction has had its impact in helping to create the theoretical climate in which the history plays are now seen, challenging the idea that texts have fixed meanings and the idea of an objective past which can be reconstructed without difficulty by the present. Deconstructionist readings of the history plays, however, have not been widely pursued,[26] probably because many critics interested in the history plays think of themselves as historicists in some sense of that term, while deconstructive play can seem to offer scant respect for the actuality of history. Hence Richard Wilson, for example, attacks Derrideans for 'their anti-historicist mystification of Elizabethan language as a deconstructive feast' which, he argues, can only lead to a view of Shakespeare as 'the modern Magna Carta'.

Psychoanalytic criticism, which has made important contributions to the ana-lysis of theatre and film in general, has also often tended towards Shakespearean genres other than the histories: tragedies, romances, the so-called 'problem plays'. As practised by feminist critics, psychoanalytic criticism places emphasis on the role of the mother, regarding differentiation from the mother as the key stage in the individual's psychological development. Kate McLuskie has attacked early feminist psychological criticism for seeing Shakespeare's plays as 'unproblematically mimetic', straightforward representations of the psychology of the 'human heart'; and also for being essentialist, in that it regarded 'the categories male and female' as 'essential, unchanging, definable in modern, commonsense terms'.[27] It is limitations such as these that Valerie Traub, a feminist psychoanalytic critic represented in this volume (Chapter 6), would want to overcome, seeing her own approach as adding a historicist awareness to psychoanalytics and feminism. Elsewhere Traub has criticised feminist critics who over-use a crude concept of patriarchy, treating it as everywhere the same, 'a monolithic, transhistorical entity' instead of (in Traub's view) 'a profoundly historical, hegemonic ideology, continually contested from without and conflicted from within'.[28] Marjorie Garber's essay on *Richard III* is another subtle psychoanalytical account, making an analogy between the distortions of writing and of history and the distortions of the body in the play (Chapter 3).

A post-colonial critical perspective has an obvious purchase on plays which deal with race, nationality and national identity. A central contention of this approach is that, as Ania Loomba puts it, 'the meanings of Shakespeare's plays were both derived from and used to establish colonial authority' (Loomba and Orkin, 1998, p. 1). Where Tillyard propounded the Tudor pattern of history, much subsequent criticism has remained in unacknowledged thrall to its seventeenth-century successor, the Whig view of history. A Protestant, Anglocentric view is still common, one which, even if it avoids the crassness of using 'England' as a synonym for 'Britain', still does not feel obliged to pay any sustained attention to the remainder. The recent rise of post-colonial criticism ensures that such crassness, though it may still exist, no longer goes unchallenged.

FEMINIST AND GENDER-BASED CRITICISM

As recently as 1992 Graham Holderness, a prolific writer on the history plays, could claim that 'in general feminist critics have, for fairly obvious reasons, declined to address Shakespeare's historical drama'.[29] A decade later such a view had become quite untenable. During that period the biggest change in critical perceptions of the history plays was brought about by a proliferation of gender-based and feminist studies.

The relative lack of feminist studies of the history plays before 1990 rested on two things: the belief that women were relatively insignificant in the plays, and the assumption that a feminist criticism should concern itself mainly with examining women's roles and the representation of women. Already in the 1980s, however, Coppélia Kahn's work showed the possibility of extending feminist criticism to examine questions of masculine identity and values. It became clear that a feminism which restricts itself to examining women's roles or the representation of women in general is one which tamely accepts being confined to an area left over after male-dominated criticism has had its say. A more recent view would see a relative scarcity of women's roles as something which makes gender-based study more, not less, possible and necessary. The most recent work, by Jean E. Howard and Phyllis Rackin, *Engendering a Nation: A Feminist Account of Shakespeare's English Histories* (1997), combines two important areas of study by showing how gender issues inform the construction of national identity in the plays. Rackin's earlier book *Stages of History* (1991) contains good chapters on Renaissance historiography, on women and commoners, on subversive females in *King John*, and on the exclusion of women from history. It is represented in this volume by an extract on *Richard II* (Chapter 4).

A post-humanist, anti-essentialist emphasis is one element which gender-based criticism of the histories shares with most other modern critical positions. 'For some time, historical and materialist feminists have argued that it is not possible to talk about women monolithically, as if all women shared a common essence', say Howard and Rackin (1997, p. 39), and they summarise the interconnectedness of gender issues with economics, politics and cultural representations. Nor, we should add, is it possible to talk of women's and men's roles as simple opposites. The ambiguity of gender-crossing roles is everywhere in Shakespeare, if only because his women were created by a man for boy actors.

In any case it is very far from true that all the history plays lack powerful and interesting women characters. If *Henry IV Part 1* is at one extreme, with a minimal female presence, *Richard III* is at the other, with a high proportion of lines spoken by women. More importantly, in the early plays, the women are often extraordinary and strong.[30] The recent achievements of gender-based criticism, focusing in particular on these exceptional women, have been central to the movement that has rescued these early plays from relative neglect. By contrast, the later, supposedly 'greater', plays lack that formidable female interest. It is Jean E. Howard and Phyllis Rackin, in their book *Engendering a Nation*, who theorise that contrast. They show how the egregious women of the early plays (sometimes admirable, sometimes demonised or monstrous, but frequently central) give way to the feminised, domesticated, lamenting or marginal women of the later plays. In doing so Howard and Rackin move far beyond 'women's' issues. They are less interested in examining the images of women which the plays construct and more concerned to show how the plays have helped shape modern ideas, influencing 'the ways we imagine gender and sexual difference, the institution of marriage, and the gulf between "public" and "private" life' (pp. 20–21).

Howard and Rackin's book is not without its weaknesses, often lacking a sense of irony or doubleness of meaning, failing to see how male roles sometimes deconstruct themselves, and missing the scepticism with which the plays view those concepts such as justice and honour which sustain the supposed rightness of patriarchy. Yet theirs is an ambitious attempt to show that gender issues represented in the plays informed the Renaissance construction of national identity and the establishment of the nation-state. They contend that the confining of women to domestic roles, as evidenced in the move from the early to the later history plays, was also a condition of the emergence of the 'modern' itself. They claim links between 'an emergent conception of a nation as defined by its geographical boundaries and an emergent conception of masculine authority based on personal achievement' (p. 47). They see a new mode of history that defines what it is to be English as being an inhabitant of a place rather than a subject of a monarch, and connect this with the wide-ranging representation of locales in the later plays. Throughout the book they draw on the concept of 'residual and emergent versions of national and personal identity' (p. 49). This again is Raymond Williams's development of Gramsci's concept, as already noted, and again it proves fruitful by avoiding a monolithic account of the period, giving due credit to the complexity of the cultural changes described, and enabling an account of the changes between earlier and later history plays. This is just another example of gender-based criticism's ability to synthesise insights from other critical schools. In that, and in its integration of gender with other issues, feminist criticism has become the very opposite of a one-issue approach focused 'only' on women, as its early detractors claimed.

In other ways too feminist criticism has shown itself capable of taking a step beyond the terms of earlier discussion. 'Most of the twentieth-century debates about Shakespeare's history plays', as Phyllis Rackin says, 'center on various, related forms of authority: the authority of the king, the authority of God, the authority of the historical source, of the dominant ideology, of the authorial script'.[31] It is arguable that the critical shift during the last half-century from the old to the New Historicisms has simply permuted these, replacing the authority of God, king, text and source with the authority of a dominant ideology.[32] A mode of reading which could free itself of the search for a guarantor of authoritative meaning sometimes seems as remote as ever. One response to this endless recycling of different forms of authority is that of feminist psychoanalytic criticism, which would oppose 'paternal authority' with 'maternal priority'.[33] Feminist criticism in general seems well placed to recognise the perpetual authority-quest for what it is, so dislodging it as an unexamined source of critical values and also making possible a discussion of the nature of authority in the plays themselves. For the plays contest ideas of authority, and even show the downfall of their kingly protagonists as the result of their mistaken conceptions of authority. As Phyllis Rackin puts it, 'If Richard III thinks he lives in a Machiavellian universe where authority is only another name for power, Richard II thinks he lives in a providential world where authority alone is sufficient to maintain him in office.'[34]

Despite having made a less spectacular start than movements such as American New Historicism, then, feminist and gender-based criticism now seems likely to be more durable and to effect a more profound change in the understanding of the history plays. It has proved able to assimilate other theoretical perspectives, such as historicist, materialist and psychoanalytic, into a synthesis that often makes other approaches look monolithic or formulaic.

CURRENT TRENDS

Current critical trends have their limitations as well as their strengths, and several avenues still await fruitful exploration. One such avenue is religion. Tillyard saw the history plays as politico-religious, endorsing God's order. When the time came to dislodge his views, his opponents chose to redefine the political but play down the religious. Beyond the history plays too, readings of Shakespeare's plays (much cruder than Tillyard's) which distorted them into Christian allegories have been rightly discredited and have given religious interpretations a bad name. Yet it is profoundly true that in the sixteenth and seventeenth centuries in particular, religion was politics, politics were religion; or, as Fredric Jameson observed, 'religious and theological debate is the form, in pre-capitalist societies, in which groups become aware of their political differences and fight them out'.[35] The move away from crude religious interpretation has had the side-effect of deflecting critics from the much more revealing study of religion as ideology, a system inextricable from questions of social organisation, of gender roles and of history.[36] In the 1990s, however, there was an upsurge of interest in the theory that Shakespeare may have spent his 'lost years' before 1592 in Roman Catholic households in Lancashire, effectively receiving his advanced education in a centre of Catholic (even perhaps Jesuit) faith and learning.[37] This can lead to re-examinations of the plays in a search for possible Catholic sympathies. Provided the pitfalls of the biographical fallacy and of too much speculation are avoided, interesting work remains to be done in this area.

· Every revolution brings some losses, however great the gains. One of the weaknesses of the theoretical revolution has been an occasional tendency to travesty the critical past, writing as if benighted folly and supine subservience were almost universal among literary critics at all times until very recently. Shakespeare's enormous cultural prestige means that Shakespeare studies are an intensely contested field, and the institutionalised production of 'readings' has more to do with a struggle for power than a quest for a supposedly disinterested 'knowledge'. We have noted, too, how no period can succeed in reading the past in a way that does not reflect its own preoccupations. Yet before we allow too much sceptical relativism to collapse all critical difference, we should note that one way in which the new critical approaches try to go beyond the old is by making explicit their own political assumptions, even to the point of making a virtue of their obtrusiveness. The criticism which makes its own designs upon the reader as clear as possible is – to that extent at least – more open and honest: take it or leave it.

Another weakness is that critics have tended to rely repeatedly on a relatively narrow range of theorists: Foucault, Althusser, Gramsci, Raymond Williams, Lacan, Bahktin, Derrida, and a handful of others. Further, literary critics have sometimes employed theory untheoretically, taking theoretical ideas from others and applying them pragmatically to literary texts without full reflection upon their own methodology. Both these tendencies can be exemplified by critics of the history plays: very few of them have engaged deeply with modern work in the philosophy of history, from Wilhelm Dilthey and R. G. Collingwood to Hans-Georg Gadamer. Consequently, although Shakespeare's relation to his past has been fruitfully studied in terms of the emergence of Renaissance historiography, it is relatively rare to find an adequate theorising of the issues at stake in our own, or any period's, encounters with the past.

It can be argued that the various 'schools' or 'approaches' of modern theory – psychoanalytic, deconstructionist, feminist and the rest – actually function as 'brands' in consumer-capitalist marketing. By offering marginally differentiated products which come with guarantees about predictable content, ensuring ready recognisability and distinguishability from other critical 'approaches', they cement an ersatz loyalty which is further defined through fierce disagreements with adherents of other brands. Since the titles of periodicals and book series already function as brands, it makes sense to extend branding to the contents. All this is a marketing person's dream but not necessarily the best way to conduct critical enquiry, and the demanding content of many theoretical approaches can be ironically at odds with the simplified schema of the label. The over-production of symbolic goods, a characteristic of post-modern consumer culture, is also reflected in the proliferation of critical readings. On the other hand, the tendency of post-modernism to resemble shopping, allowing us to browse eclectically among the 'variety' of approaches on offer in the cultural-critical supermarket and letting us mix and match styles at will, can permit a valuable synthesis of theoretically-informed approaches, and I have argued above that feminist and gender-based criticism of the history plays has shown itself well able to absorb such other approaches.

Shakespeare's history plays, accounting for nearly one-third of his work as a dramatist, belong to a genre which was, as Paola Pugliatti says, 'perhaps the most short-lived . . . in the whole history of English drama' (1996, p. 3). History plays were written almost exclusively in and around the 1590s, the decade after the Spanish Armada, the later years of Queen Elizabeth's reign. That brief period produced around eighty popular plays on English historical subjects. Soon after 1600, the history play became 'virtually unwritable', hastening into obsolescence along with two other major Elizabethan genres, romantic comedy and Petrarchan poetry. The reasons why the genre arose, flourished and disappeared are far from agreed. The old view that the upsurge in history plays was part of patriotic euphoria caused by the Armada is shaky. 'Why the young playwright would commemorate a great national victory with a penetrating and dispiriting analysis of how England lost her French possessions and collapsed into civil war is not clear.'[38] Such questions about the social origins of literary form are among the most interesting, and the hardest, faced by criticism. Here too there is the possibility of interesting work to be done.

But although history plays fell out of favour in Shakespeare's own day, they have been of deep interest since, and never more so than in the last few decades. What Stephen Greenblatt eloquently says of our relationship to the Renaissance as a whole is also true of our period's relation to the history plays: we see in them

the shaping of crucial aspects of our sense of self and society and the natural world, but we have become uneasy about our whole way of constituting reality. Above all, perhaps, we sense that the culture to which we are as profoundly attached as our face is to our skull is nonetheless a construct, a thing made, as temporary, time-conditioned, and contingent as those vast European empires from whose power Freud drew his image of repression. We sense too that we are situated at the close of the cultural movement initiated in the Renaissance and that the places in which our social and psychological world seems to be cracking apart are those structural joints visible when it was first constructed. In the midst of the anxieties and contradictions attendant upon the threatened collapse of this phase of our civilization, we respond with passionate curiosity and poignancy to the anxieties and contradictions attendant upon its rise.[39]

Shakespeare's history plays are for our times.

NOTES

1. E. M. W. TILLYARD, *Shakespeare's History Plays* (1994); 2nd edn. (Harmondsworth: Penguin, 1966), p. 151 and pp. 72–3.
2. HUGH GRADY, *The Modernist Shakespeare: Critical Texts in a Material World* (Oxford: Clarendon Press, 1991), p. 160.
3. GRAHAM HOLDERNESS has offered a perceptive explanation as to why Tillyard was uninterested in Henry V: he shied away 'from more robust forms of patriotism'; his business was 'not with winning the war but with reconstituting the national culture in expectation of an Allied victory', and so to him 'the play about the nature of "England" is more important than the play about the military victories of a warrior-king' (*Shakespeare Recycled: The Making of Historical Drama* (New York and London: Harvester Wheatsheaf, 1992), p. 28).
4. LISA JARDINE, *Reading Shakespeare Historically* (London and New York: Routledge, 1996), p. 14.
5. Grady, *The Modernist Shakespeare*, pp. 175–6.
6. CATHERINE BELSEY, *Critical Practice* (London: Methuen, 1980), p. 7.
7. THOMAS CARLYLE, *On Heroes, Hero-Worship, and the Heroic in History*, Lecture 1, 5 May 1840, and Lecture 3, 12 May 1840.
8. A further study of Joan and Margaret of Anjou as embodiments of an alien cultural reality is by GERALDO U. DE SOUSA in Chapter 2 of his book *Shakespeare's Cross-Cultural Encounters* (Basingstoke: Macmillan, 1999).
9. Falstaff has occasionally been played by female actresses as far back as the eighteenth century.
10. Besides Patterson and Wilson, there is another distinguished essay on the Cade rebellion by STEPHEN GREENBLATT: 'Murdering Peasants: Status, Genre, and the Representation of Rebellion' in his book *Representing the English Renaissance* (Berkeley, CA: University of California Press, 1988).
11. See LOUIS A. MONTROSE, 'Professing the Renaissance: the Poetics and Politics of Culture', reprinted in K. M. Newton (ed.), *Twentieth-Century Literary Theory: A Reader* (Basingstoke: Macmillan, 2nd edition, 1997), pp. 242–3.
12. STEPHEN GREENBLATT, 'Invisible Bullets', in Richard Wilson and Richard Dutton (eds), *New Historicism and Renaissance Drama* (London and New York: Longman, 1992), p. 98.
13. STEPHEN GREENBLATT, *Renaissance Self-fashioning: From More to Shakespeare* (Chicago and London: University of Chicago Press, 1980), p. 141.
14. Ibid., pp. 5, 8.
15. The essay can be found, among other places, in the Longman Critical Reader volume *New Historicism and Renaissance Drama*, eds RICHARD WILSON AND RICHARD DUTTON (New York and London: Longman, 1992); in *Political Shakespeare: New Essays in Cultural Materialism*, eds JONATHAN DOLLIMORE AND ALAN SINFIELD (Manchester: Manchester University Press, 1985); and in GREENBLATT'S own book *Shakespearean Negotiations: The Circulation of Social Energy in Renaissance England* (Oxford: Clarendon Press, 1988).
16. In his soliloquy which closes Act 1 Scene ii of *Henry IV Part 1*.
17. Stephen Greenblatt, *Shakespearean Negotiations*, p. 37.
18. Holderness, *Shakespeare Recycled*, p. 34.
19. MICHAEL TAYLOR, *Shakespeare Criticism in the Twentieth Century* (Oxford: Oxford University Press, 2001), p. 189.
20. ANN THOMPSON, in her preface to JEAN E. HOWARD AND PHYLLIS RACKIN, *Engendering a Nation: A Feminist Account of Shakespeare's English Histories* (London and New York: Routledge, 1997), p. xiv.
21. RAYMOND WILLIAMS, *Marxism and Literature* (Oxford: Oxford University Press, 1977), pp. 121–7.

22. STEVEN MULLANEY, *The Place of the Stage: License, Play, and Power in Renaissance England* (Ann Arbor, MI: University of Michigan Press, 1988), p. xi.
23. PHYLLIS RACKIN, *Stages of History: Shakespeare's English Chronicles* (London: Routledge, 1991), p. 42.
24. WEIMANN, ROBERT, 'Bifold Authority in Shakespeare's Theatre', *Shakespeare Quarterly* 39 (1988), p. 411.
25. FREDRIC JAMESON, 'Radicalizing Radical Shakespeare: the Permanent Revolution in Shakespeare Studies', in IVO KAMPS (ed.), *Materialist Shakespeare: A History* (London and New York: Verso, 1995), p. 327.
26. A rare example of a deconstructionist reading is MARGUERITE WALLER, 'Usurpation, Seduction, and the Problematics of the Proper: a "Deconstructive", "Feminist" Rereading of the Seductions of Richard and Anne in Shakespeare's *Richard III*', in Margaret W. Ferguson, Maureen Quilligan and Nancy J. Vickers (eds), *Rewriting the Renaissance: The Discourses of Sexual Difference in Early Modern Europe* (Chicago and London: University of Chicago Press, 1986).
27. In Dollimore and Sinfield, *Political Shakespeare*, pp. 89, 90.
28. See VALERIE TRAUB's essay 'Jewels, Statues, and Corpses: Containment of Female Erotic Power in Shakespeare's Plays' in Deborah E. Barker and Ivo Kamps (eds), *Shakespeare and Gender: A History* (London and New York: Verso, 1995).
29. Holderness, *Shakespeare Recycled*, p. 41. GRAHAM HOLDERNESS's *Shakespeare: The Histories* (Basingstoke: Macmillan, 2000) gives due recognition to the rise of feminist criticism of the history plays.
30. A further study of Joan and Margaret of Anjou as embodiments of an alien cultural reality is by GERALDO U. DE SOUSA in Chapter 2 of his book *Shakespeare's Cross-Cultural Encounters*.
31. Rackin, *Stages of History*, pp. 56–7.
32. The New Historicists' frequent focus on the history plays was taken by some feminists as a sign of New Historicism's hostility to feminist approaches. See, for example, CAROL THOMAS NEELY, 'Constructing the Subject: Feminist Practice and the New Renaissance Discourses', *ELR* 18:1 (Winter 1988), pp. 5–18.
33. The phrases are MADELON SPRENGNETHER's in *The Spectral Mother: Freud, Feminism, and Psychoanalysis* (Ithaca, NY: Cornell University Press, 1990), p. xi; quoted by Valerie Traub in her extract in this volume.
34. Rackin, *Stages of History*, p. 67.
35. FREDRIC JAMESON, 'Religion and Ideology: *Paradise Lost*', in *Literature, Politics and Theory: Papers from the Essex Conference 1976–84*, ed. Francis Barker et al. (London: Methuen, 1986), pp. 38–9.
36. Some exceptions to the tendency to underplay the importance of religion are DONNA B. HAMILTON's book *Shakespeare and the Politics of Protestant England* (Hemel Hempstead: Harvester, 1992) which sets *King John* and *Henry VIII* in the context of relations between church and state and of anti-Catholic sentiment in the period; and two essays from STANLEY WELLS (ed.), *Shakespeare Survey* 48 (1995): TOM MCALINDON, 'Pilgrims of Grace: *Henry IV* Historicised' and STEVEN MARX, 'Holy War in *Henry V*'.
37. See E. A. J. HONIGMANN, *Shakespeare: The 'Lost Years'* (Manchester: Manchester University Press, 1985), and RICHARD WILSON, 'Shakespeare and the Jesuits', *Times Literary Supplement*, 19 December 1997, pp. 11–13.
38. J. D. Cox, *Shakespeare and the Dramaturgy of Power* (Princeton: Princeton University Press, 1989), p. 83; also quoted in PAOLA PUGLIATTI, *Shakespeare the Historian* (Basingstoke: Macmillan, 1996), p. 4.
39. Greenblatt, *Renaissance Self-fashioning*, pp. 174–5.

CHAPTER ONE

Topical Ideology: Witches, Amazons, and Shakespeare's Joan of Arc[1]

GABRIELE BERNHARD JACKSON

Jackson's essay exemplifies the recent trend to discover new interest in Shakespeare's early history plays. It combines a scrupulous attention to historical detail with a gender-based approach, bringing them to bear on the presentation of Joan of Arc in *Henry VI Part 1*. One of the play's surprises is the way that Joan is presented as powerful, even admirable, for much of the time, only to be degraded and humiliated at the end. By examining Elizabethan presentations of the strong woman, Jackson offers a way of understanding the reversal in the presentation of Joan which conventional views of her 'character' are powerless to account for: 'the more free play Joan's attractive force is permitted, the more completely she will have to be feminized at the end of the play'.

Glory is like a circle in the water,
Which never ceaseth to enlarge itself
Till by broad spreading it disperse to nought.
With Henry's death the English circle ends;
Dispersed are the glories it included.

1 Henry VI, 1.2.133–37[2]

This wonderfully evocative description of the everything that is nothing, an exact emblem of the rise and disintegration, in Shakespeare's first tetralogy, of one new center of power after another, is assigned to Joan of Arc, the character whom most critics agree in calling a coarse caricature, an exemplar of authorial chauvinism both national and sexual, or at best a foil to set off the chivalric English heroes of *1 Henry VI*. Her portrait, says Geoffrey Bullough in his compilation of Shakespeare's sources, 'goes far beyond anything found in Hall or Holinshed or in the Burgundian chronicler Monstrelet'.[3] Bullough ruefully lauds Shakespeare's mastery in discrediting the entire French cause through Joan; many subsequent critics have shared Bullough's admiration, although not his compunction, over the skill with which Shakespeare delineated an 'epitome of disorder and rebellion' to pit against the 'epitome of order and loyalty', the English hero Talbot: 'She is absolutely corrupt from beginning to end', rejoices the author of one book on Shakespeare's history plays.[4] When the play was presented in 1591 or 1592, English troops were once again in France, once again supporting a claim to the French crown, a claim by another Henry – their religious ally Henry of Navarre. 'A play recalling the gallant deeds of the English in France at an earlier period . . . would be topical', Bullough rightly says.[5]

The portrait of Joan, by this calculus of relation between drama and social context, takes its place among 'English attempts to blacken the reputation of Joan of Arc'[6] – an easy task in the Elizabethan period, when women 'who refuse[d] the place of silent subjection' could, like Shakespeare's Joan in Act 5, be carted to execution as witches.[7] By this reckoning, the character of Joan of Arc becomes a regrettable sign of the times.

Neither the content nor the form of Joan's words about glory easily supports such a reading. Joan's image of the circle in the water is not only the most poetically resonant statement in the play, it is also specifically borne out by the action. The eloquence of her recognition that all human achievement is writ in water, one of the play's thematic pressure points, sorts ill with a lampooned character 'coarse and crude in language and sensibility'.[8] Yet *1 Henry VI* does contrast English chivalry, especially in the figure of heroic Talbot, with the pragmatism of the French, especially Joan, and Act 5 does dispel both Joan's power and her pretensions to divine aid in a series of progressively less dignified scenes.[9]

First she vainly offers diabolical spirits her blood and sexual favors in exchange for continued French success; subsequently captured, she rejects her old father to claim exalted birth; finally, faced with the prospect of death by burning, she claims to be pregnant, shifting her allegation of paternity from one French leader to another in response to her captors' insistence that each of these is a man whose child should not be allowed to live.

Perhaps it is a reflection as much on accepted critical standards of aesthetic unity as on the gullibility of individual critics that several have read this last scene as Joan's admission of sexual activity with the whole French camp. Ridiculous as such a reading is, it does at least integrate Act 5 with what precedes, undercutting Joan's claims to virginity just as her conjuring undercuts her claims to divinity. Such an interpretation of Act 5 makes it synchronic with previous acts in meaning; only the revelation of that meaning is postponed. Similarly, Joan's claims to divine mission which she never mentions again after her introductory speeches in Act 1, become in such an interpretation synchronic with the action which follows them. In the long central section of the drama, according to such a unified interpretation, Joan's prior assertion of godliness struggles against Talbot's repeated assertions of diabolism until Act 5 vindicates Talbot. The unstated premise of this kind of reading is that temporally multiple suggestions of meaning collapse finally into an integrated pattern that transcends the temporal process of dramatic presentation. In this final pattern, all suggested assignments of value are reconciled and each plot line or character allotted its proper plus or minus sign *sub specie unitatis*. The individual incident or dramatic effect has no more final autonomy than a number in a column for addition has in the sum below the line. These assumptions are very clear in Riggs' influential 1971 summation of Joan's character: 'Beneath these postures, Joan is generically an imposter. . . . Hence the scenes in which she is exposed and burnt as a witch, like the stripping of Duessa in *The Faerie Queene*, serve a formal expository purpose that supersedes any need for a controlled, sequacious plot.'[10]

Now of course the typical Shakespearean play does have a very powerful sense of ending, partly brought about by a 'formal expository' resolution of difficult issues. I want to emphasize, however, that it is equally typical of Shakespeare to present unexplained and suggestive discontinuities. One might remember the complete reversal of Theseus' attitude to the lovers in *Midsummer Night's Dream*: having backed up Hermia's coercive father in Act 1 by citing the unalterable law of Athens, Theseus reappears in Act 4 (after a two-act absence) to overrule the same father and the same law with no explanation whatever. A more subtle version of this kind of turnabout occurs when Othello, calmly superior in Act 1 to the accusation that he has used sorcery in his relationship with Desdemona, informs her in Act 3 that the handkerchief which was his first gift to her is a magical talisman. In these instances, the critic's expectation of unity forces interpretive strategy back on unspoken motivations and implicit character development, raising such questions as whether Othello deliberately lied to the senate in Act 1, or when exactly he gave Desdemona the handkerchief. I want to propose that these are unsuitable strategies and questions for a phenomenon that has little to do with unity of character and much to do with the way in which a character is perceived by the audience at a particular moment of dramatic time. I would argue that in Act 1 Othello had not given Desdemona a magic handkerchief as his first gift, but in Act 3 he had. It is a matter of the character's consonance with the key into which the movement of the play has modulated.

This is not the place to make a detailed case for such an interpretive approach or to try to identify for these examples the reasons – external to a concept of character as coherent selfhood – that direct a change in Shakespeare's presentation. Applying such an approach to the problem of Joan's significance, however, permits us to recognize and give individual value to the phases of her portrayal, which, not untypically for Shakespeare, is partially continuous and partially disjunct. The changing presentation allows Joan to perform in one play inconsistent ideological functions that go much beyond discrediting the French cause or setting off by contrast the glories of English chivalry in its dying moments.[11] As Bullough long ago suggested, the play's ideology is topical, but in what way and to what end cannot be answered as simply as he or some of the play's subsequent critics have believed.[12] To characterize its main military hero, Talbot, the play alludes specifically to the contemporaneous French expedition led by Essex, as John Munro first suggested, but it incorporates far more ideologically ambiguous detail than has been recognized. Similarly, for its presentation of Talbot's national and sexual opposites, the three Frenchwomen who are the play's only female characters, it draws heavily on the current controversy about the nature of women and on the interrelated types of the Amazon, the warrior woman, the cross-dressing woman, and the witch, all figures that – for a variety of reasons – were objects of fascination both in England and on the continent at the end of the sixteenth century.

It is now generally accepted that the play dates from 1591/92, when English troops under Essex had been sent to France for the particular purpose of besieging Rouen; the play unhistorically dramatizes that city's recapture from the French. Actually, Rouen had never been retaken; nor was it after this hopeful piece of stage-craft. But the parallel does not remain general and wishful. The play explicitly links Talbot to the current effort through a neatly turned compliment to Queen Elizabeth which has, oddly, been deflected by critics to Essex alone. Bearing away the fallen Talbot and his son, the English messenger declares: 'from their ashes shall be rear'd / A phoenix that shall make all France afeard' (4.7.92–93). The phoenix was one of Elizabeth's emblems; Shakespeare uses it again in *Henry VIII*. She had not up to this time fulfilled the messenger's prediction: early military success against French forces in Scotland had been completely cancelled by a disastrous occupation of Le Havre in 1563. The vaunting compliment can only refer to the most recent French expedition. Its leader – the dashing young popular favorite, Essex – would be an eminently suitable candidate for the role of Talbot redivivus.[13] In 1591 the becalmed campaign was serving as backdrop for his exploits, one of them mimicked by another of the play's departures from its sources. Encamped before Rouen, 'Essex sent a challenge to the Governor of the town daring him to fight either a duel or a tournament', which was, not surprisingly, declined.[14] In *1 Henry VI*, Talbot similarly challenges Joan and her supporters as they stand victorious on the walls of Rouen (2.2.56ff.).[15] He is contemptuously rebuffed by Joan in one of those moments when English chivalry confronts French pragmatism: 'Belike your lordship takes us then for fools, / To try if that our own be ours or no' (3.2.62–63). A critic guided by the play's obvious national sympathies could plausibly feel that Joan's reply, however momentarily amusing, lacks magnanimity.

A closer look at the topical link between Talbot and Essex, however, suggests a more complicated ideological situation. Both the expedition and its leadership were controversial. Henry IV had broken his promise of reinforcements for a first set of troops, sent in 1589, and Elizabeth sent the second army with misgivings, putting the hot-headed Essex in command with a reluctance well justified by the results. 'Where he is or what he doth or what he is to do', she wrote angrily to her other officers, 'we are ignorant.'[16] Halfway through the expedition she ordered her un-controllable deputy home, although he talked her into sending him back. A likely rescripting of this sequence of events appears in Act 3, where Talbot interrupts his conquests to go and visit his sovereign 'with submissive loyalty of heart' (3.4.10) and receives acclaim, reward, and a commission to return to battle (3.4.16–27; 4.1.68–73). In the second of these scenes, Talbot strips a coward of his undeserved Order of the Garter and makes a long speech about the value of 'the sacred name of knight' (4.1.33ff.) – another touchy subject after Essex's temporary recall, for he had just knighted twenty-four of his do-nothing soldiers. Lord Treasurer Burghley kept this news from Her Majesty as long as he could; Elizabeth was notoriously stingy with new titles – holding, in fact, rather the attitude expressed by Shake-speare's Talbot. She had wanted to deny Essex the privilege of dubbing knights, and remarked caustically on hearing of the twenty-four newcomers to fame unsupple-mented by fortune, 'his lordship had done well to have built his almshouses before he had made his knights'.[17]

Are these portions of Talbot's behavior and speech, then, aligned with the latest news from France in order to celebrate Essex?[18] Or do they obliquely defend him by rewriting his indiscretions in more acceptable terms, sympathetically dramatizing the 'real' meaning of his grand gestures? Or do Talbot's loyal actions, on the contrary, undercut the play's apparent endorsement of Essex by showing how a truly great champion acts? The answers are not at all clear.[19] What is evident is that the play situates itself in an area of controversy easily identifiable by its audience, an area of growing ideological conflict in which a 'war party' contested, if it did not openly confront, the Queen's favored policy of negotiation, delay, and minimal expenditure. Far from playing down the controversial aspects of Essex's command, the drama singles them out for re-enactment, but presents them in such a manner that either side could claim the play for its own. In light of the play's tendency to go both ways, Joan's sardonic reply to Talbot's challenge acquires an integrity of its own, sounding surprisingly like the voice of Her caustic Majesty Queen Elizabeth. Is the play, then, lauding chivalry or correcting it? Is it pro-war or not? This irritable reaching after fact and reason that Keats found so uncharacteristic of Shakespeare is not soothed by the parallels between Talbot and Essex or by the tone of Joan's voice. The coexistence of ideologically opposed elements is typical of the play's dramatic nature and foreshadows the mature Shakespeare.

Critical examination of the play's three women has not proceeded on this assumption. The perceived dominance of patrilineal and patriarchal ideology in Shakespeare's era and in the play's action has been the basis of most interpretations, whether feminist or masculinist.[20] The three women have been seen as a trio of temptresses,[21] of threats to male, and particularly English, hegemony and to the chivalric ideal,[22] as incarnations of what Marilyn French calls the 'outlaw feminine principle'.[23] This kind of negative reading, like the purely positive reading of the play's military expedition, has support in the action. All three women are in different ways unconventionally strong and all three threaten the English with losses. Coppélia Kahn's claim that Shakespeare is here exposing, but not sharing in, male anxieties about women is surely counsel of desperation.[24] Fortunately, it is not the only alternative to pathological or paternalistic Shakespeare. Like the positive militaristic reading, with which it is closely connected, the negative misogynist one neglects both the play's topicality and the historical moment's ideological complexity.

The nature of women had long been under discussion in western Europe in a semi-playful controversy that became especially active in sixteenth-century England. Contributors to this controversy buttressed or undercut female claims to virtue by citing *exempla*, worthy or unworthy women chosen from history, the Bible, and legend. As Linda Woodbridge's recent account of this literary sub-genre in England points out, 'The formal controversy did not always appear full-blown, in carefully developed treatises; it was sometimes sketched in cameo, with the names of a few exemplary women stamped on it like a generic signature.'[25] The 1560s had seen a spate of plays about individual *exempla* in the controversy. By the time *1 Henry VI* appeared, the controversy had already been naturalized into narrative fiction by George Pettie's *A petite pallace of . . . pleasure* (1576) and Lyly's best-selling *Euphues* (1578). In these fictional contexts, the old techniques 'could be used to characterize, to comment on the action, even to advance the plot'.[26] *1 Henry VI* incorporates just such a cameo controversy. The play's three women are surrounded by allusions to legendary females which problematize their evaluation. The Countess of Auvergne compares herself to Tomyris, a bloody warrior queen, and is connected by verbal echo with the Queen of Sheba – two entirely opposite figures.[27] Margaret of Anjou is cast in her lover's description of his situation as Helen of Troy (5.5.103ff.), a woman claimed by both attackers and defenders in the controversy. Joan appears amidst a tangle of contradictory allusions: she is among other identifications a Sibyl, an Amazon, Deborah, Helen the mother of Constantine, and Astraea's daughter to the French, but Hecate and Circe to the English. Of the women alluded to in *1 Henry VI*, eleven appear as *exempla* in the formal controversy. The genre itself was tolerant of, not to say dependent upon, divergent evaluations of the same phenomenon: a number of its *exempla*, like Helen of Troy, appeared regularly on both sides, and some writers handily produced treatises both pro and con. It would come as no surprise to readers of the controversy that one man's Sibyl is another man's Hecate.

1 Henry VI should be classed with what Woodbridge calls the 'second flurry of plays centering on prominent *exempla* of the formal controversy', which 'appeared in the late 1580s and 1590s'.[28] Its deployment of these stock figures is as germane to its ideology as its structural alignment of the female characters, but whereas the play's structure points in the direction of synthesis, of the synchronic or temporally transcendent reading, the *exempla* point towards differentiation, the temporally disjunctive reading.

Joan is evaluated by the French choice of *exempla* at the beginning and by the English choice at the end. At all times before Act 5, however, because of the armor she is described as wearing and the military leadership she exercises, she is an example of what the Elizabethans called a virago, a woman strong beyond the conventional expectations for her sex and thus said to be of a masculine spirit.[29] The increasing fascination of such women is evident in the proliferation of Amazons, female warriors, and cross-dressing ladies in the English fiction and drama of the late sixteenth century.

The Amazon and the warrior woman were already established as two of the most valued positive *exempla* of the controversy over women. Joan is identified with both immediately on her entry into the play's action: 'thou art an Amazon', exclaims the Dauphin, 'And fightest with the sword of Deborah' (1.2.104–05). The power of this combination reaches beyond the arena of the formal debate. Spenser had just used it in *The Faerie Queene*, published 1590, in praise of 'the brave atchievements' of women (3.4.1.3): those 'warlike feates . . . Of bold Penthesilee', the Amazon who aided the Trojans, or the blow with which 'stout Debora strake / Proud Sisera' (3.4.2.4–5, 7–8).[30] For him these two fighters define Britomart, his female knight in armor, who in turn defines Queen Elizabeth, 'whose lignage from this lady I derive along' (3.4.3.9). Both Amazons and women warriors already had some degree of British resonance because the Trojans who received Penthesilea's help were the supposed ancestors of the British, while a proud chapter in legendary English history recounted Queen Boadicea's defense of her country against Roman invasion. The evocation of heroines related to England is continued by Joan's association with Saint Helen, the mother of Constantine; though not a warrior, this finder of the remains of the true cross was by popular tradition British.[31] The Dauphin's welcome to Joan is thus calculated to arouse the most unsuitably positive and even possessive associations in an Elizabethan audience.

Elizabethan literature, of course, contained many other Amazons besides Penthesilea; the race had a long and honorable history, derived from such respected authorities as Plutarch, Ovid, and Apollonius of Rhodes.[32] In the sixteenth century Amazons became a topic of current relevance when exploration of the Americas and Africa began bringing reports of Amazonian tribes sighted or credibly heard of.[33] Within a brief period after *1 Henry VI*, both Ralegh (1596) and Hakluyt (1599) would specify the Amazons' exact location. Perhaps because of their increased timeliness, Amazons were also about to become a vogue on stage; they would appear in at least fourteen dramatic productions from 1592 to 1640.[34]

Elizabethan stage Amazons are all either neutral or positive, an evaluative convention generally in line with their ever more frequent mention in Elizabethan non-dramatic literature. On the other hand, *The Faerie Queene* contains an evil Amazon alongside its positive allusions. For the Amazon figure was inherently double: although 'models of female magnanimity and courage' who appeared regularly in lists of the nine female worthies and were venerated both individually and as a race, Amazons were also acknowledged to be, at times, cruel tormentors of men.[35] From the very beginning, then, Joan's ideological function is complicated to the point of self-contradiction: she seems both French and English, both a type of Penthesilea who helps her countrymen in battle and an unspecified Amazon who may embody threats to men – in fact, a representative of the full complexity of late Elizabethan perception of the strong woman.

These contradictions continue for as long as Joan appears in the role of woman warrior. Although she triumphs over the English and so must be negative, she carries with her a long positive tradition reaching back to Plato's assertions that women could and should be trained for martial exercise and to the figure of the armed goddess Minerva. These classical references as well as invocations of the Old Testament Deborah and Judith figured repeatedly in the formal defenses of women. Female military heroism under special circumstances carried the prestigious sanction of Elyot, More, and Hoby, and Joan's actions conform to the pattern they approved as well as to the current literary conventions defining a praiseworthy female warrior. She fights in defense of her country, 'particularly under siege', and converts the Duke of Burgundy to her cause with a simile that likens France to a dying child (3.3.47–9) – defense of her children being a recognized motivation of the virtuous woman fighter.[36] Like Spenser's Britomart and countless others, she deflates male boasts and engages in a validating duel with a would-be lover.

As Spenser's connection of Britomart with Queen Elizabeth suggests, the tradition of the woman warrior acquired particular contemporaneous relevance from her existence. The maiden warrior-goddess Minerva provided an irresistible parallel with the virginal defender of Protestantism, who even before the year of the Armada was called 'for power in armes, / And vertues of the minde Minervaes mate' by Peele in *The Arraignment of Paris* (1584).[37] Deborah, a magistrate as well as her country's savior in war, was also adopted immediately into the growing iconology of Elizabeth: the coronation pageant contained a Deborah, and the name was frequently used thereafter for the queen.[38] Not unexpectedly, Spenser identifies the Trojan-oriented Penthesilea as an analogue of his Belphoebe, the avowed representation of Queen Elizabeth.[39]

In light of these accumulated associations, a Minerva-like French leader who is a Deborah and Amazon, and is also called 'Astraea's daughter' (1.6.4) at a time when Astraea, goddess of justice, was another *alter ego* of Elizabeth, must be reckoned one of the more peculiar phenomena of the Elizabethan stage.[40] But it is likely that Joan was more than peculiar: she was probably sensational. For the odd fact is that despite all the outpouring of Elizabethan literature both cultivated and popular on the subject of Amazons and warrior women, there seems to be only one rather obscure woodcut of real – as opposed to allegorical – armed women to be found in the English printed books, pamphlets, broadsides, and pictorial narrative strips of the entire era, nor had any such personage (as far as I have yet discovered) ever appeared on the stage.[41] Two Amazons that illustrate Mandeville's *Travels* are clad with impeccable feminine respectability. The coronation Deborah (1559), despite the pageant verses' reference to 'the dint of sworde', was equipped with Parliament robes, not with a deadly weapon, as in Spenser's fantasy.[42] Holinshed's Boadicea (1577) had a wide skirt and long hair. What is more, there seem to be no pictures of women in men's clothing of any kind. It looks as though there was an unspoken taboo on such representations – a taboo just beginning to be breached occasionally in the 1570s, when Holinshed included in his *History of Scotland* an illustration of Woada's daughters. In the 1560s come the first mentions of real Elizabethan women wearing articles of real male apparel, though not armor or weapons, a fashion that was soon to grow into a fad. It is not until the 1580s that a very few cross-dressing ladies appear on stage, and not until after *1 Henry VI* that Amazons, women warriors, and girls in male disguise become a triple dramatic vogue. In 1591/92, dressing Joan in armor was a stunning *coup de théâtre*.

It had perhaps been anticipated. Outside the world of the stage lived a connoisseur of theatrical effect as daring as Shakespeare. In 1588, on the eve of the expected Spanish invasion, Queen Elizabeth visited her soldiers in the camp at Tilbury 'habited like an Amazonian Queene, Buskind and plumed, having a golden Truncheon, Gantlet, and Gorget', according to Heywood's later description.[43] Leonel Sharp, afterwards James I's chaplain and in 1588 'waiting upon the Earl of *Leicester* at *Tilbury* Camp', reported as eyewitness that 'the Queen rode through all the Squadrons of her armie, as Armed *Pallas*'[44] – a figure whose iconographic conventions of plumed helmet, spear, and shield coincided with descriptions of Amazon queens.[45] This was the occasion of her famous speech: 'I know I have the bodie, but of a weak and feeble woman, but I have the heart and Stomach of a King, ... and think foul scorn that ... any Prince of Europe should dare to invade the borders of my Realm. ... I my self will take up arms, I my self will be your General.'[46] Whether or not Elizabeth actually wore armor, her review of her troops was a grand gesture of virago-ship, which combined visual uniqueness with enactment of time-honored conventions identifying the woman warrior. It is probably the shadowy double behind the sudden appearance in the French camp of Joan, the puzzlingly Astraea-connected Amazonian, to lead her army against the invaders of her country.[47]

This probability does not make life any easier for the critic of *1 Henry VI*. One could simplify the situation by seeing Joan as a sarcastic version of such a figure, an anti-Elizabeth, a parodic non-virgin whose soldiership (finally) fails. Perhaps that was the point, or one of the points. But such close mirroring is hard to control. It is difficult to keep doubles separate. An obviously parodic presentation of a figure so suggestive might slide over into parody (dare one breathe it?) of the queen herself.[48] At the same time, the strong honorific associations of the Amazon–Deborah–Elizabeth combination exert their own pull in the opposite direction from parody. If Joan, parodied, functions as inferior foil for English chivalry, Joan honored also functions as its superior. It seems likely, then, that Joan in armor is as fair and foul as the traditional double-potentialed Amazon, and that what she says or does is as likely to undercut 'the glorious deeds of the English in France' as to set off their splendor. She is a powerful warrior and a powerful enemy, but also an inverted image of both. Lest this interpretation seem an implausibly modern critical recourse to ambiguity, we should take notice of one elaborate European visual representation in the Elizabethan period of women in armor, Bruegel's *Dulle Griet* or Mad Meg. As described by Natalie Davis in her account of the sociological phenomenon she calls 'women on top', the painting sends a similar double message. It 'makes a huge, armed, unseeing woman, Mad Meg, the emblem of fiery destruction . . . and disorder. Bruegel's painting cuts in more than one way, however. . . . Nearby other armed women are beating grotesque animals from Hell.'[49] This visual oxymoron sorts well with the double-valenced Amazon figure which is the period's prototype of the powerful and active woman.

Amazon, goddess, or queen, the numinous representative of a strength which, in its very transcendence of social convention, becomes salvific is from another perspective a potential subverter of established order and belief, an overturner of values. Nowhere is this clearer than in the disparity between Elizabethan or Jacobean fictions of cross-dressing women and accounts of real ones from the same period. Both attest to the fascination of the time with gender subversion, as does the cross-dressing phenomenon itself. Fiction could delight in Mary Ambree (1584), who avenged her lover's death in battle by putting on armor to lead the English troops, or in Long Meg of Westminster, said to have lived in Henry VIII's reign: she came from the country to work in a London tavern, dressed in men's clothes, fought and defeated obstreperous males, and went with the soldiers to Boulogne, where she achieved victory over the champion of the French and was honored by the king.[50] Long Meg's story was told in two ballads, a play, and several reprintings of her pamphlet life, all between 1590 and about 1650. And no wonder; for when Long Meg had overcome the (Spanish) aggressor Sir James and humiliated him in the tavern by revealing her womanhood, she 'sat in state like her Majesty'.[51] Once again the warrior woman is assimilated to that modern numinous exemplar, Queen Elizabeth. But during the same period, women who really do participate in the growing fashion for wearing men's clothes, including ultimately weapons, are complained against with mounting sarcasm and hysteria. It is one thing to embody, in the encapsulated realm of fiction or of royalty, transcendence of social constraint

– quite another to undermine on the street the customs around which society is organized.[52]

If Joan's initial presentation plays with the numinous aura and royal superiority of the virago, her portrayal in the play's middle section brings to the fore a special form of the virago's potential for subversion.[53] Uncommitted to convention, Joan is also uncommitted to the ethical stereotypes that structure the consciousness of other characters. This is her most threatening and most appealing function. It can be clearly seen in her comment after her eloquent speech has persuaded Burgundy to return to the French: 'Done like a Frenchman! [*Aside.*] – turn and turn again' (3.3.85). Although this is a topical throwaway for the audience, its effect is very like that of early asides by Richard III, or of Falstaff playing first Henry IV and then Hal. It is characteristic of her persistent demystification of cherished idealisms, an ideological iconoclasm that does not spare her own achievements once she has finished with her original claim to divine aid.

Joan's speech constantly invites skepticism at the very moments when values are in need of affirmation, as when Rouen is captured, when Burgundy is about to desert, when Talbot falls. We should recall her sardonic response to Talbot's chivalric challenge – modeled, it is worth remembering, on Essex's conception of chivalry. Her conversion of Burgundy uses a different mode but achieves a similar shift of perspective, suddenly presenting an audience that enjoys 'the gallant deeds of the English in France' with a point of view that sees 'the cities and the towns defac'd / By wasting ruin of the cruel foe' (3.3.45–46) and forces them to look at the enemy 'As looks the mother on her lowly babe / When death doth close his tender dying eyes' (3.3.47–48). This clash of perspectives becomes extreme, and reaches beyond momentary effect, when the issue is the meaning of death itself. After the messenger who is searching for Talbot has recited the hero's titles of honor, performing unawares the eulogistic function of a traditional funeral oration, Joan observes: 'Here is a silly-stately style indeed! / . . . / Him that thou magnifiest with all these titles, / Stinking and fly-blown lies here at our feet' (4.6.72–76). Like the cross-dressing woman she is, Joan perceives as futile convention what representatives of the status quo perceive as a visible sign of inner nature, be it formulaic titles or formulaic clothing. If her view is allowed, honor's a mere scutcheon, as her fellow-subversive Falstaff later agrees. Like Falstaff, Joan must be neutralized on behalf of stable values, but like his, her point of view is too compelling to be forgotten even when her circle in the water disperses in the humiliations of the fifth act. Although Talbot is the play's ostensible hero and nobility's decay its subject, it is Joan who expresses most forcefully both the vanity of all ideologies and an unorthodox *consolatio*. Like the cross-dressing festival ladies of misrule,[54] Joan offers relief from idealistic codes of behavior – and thus from the need to mourn their demise.

The need to neutralize the virago, however, even the admired virago, is as pervasive in the period's writing as the evident fascination with her; indeed, it is probably a tribute to the force that fascination exerted. This hypothesis helps in understanding some oddities in the presentation of the period's literary Amazons and warrior women.

Two sets of stage Amazons have no lines at all, nor any action relevant to the plot. Three more are actually men in disguise.[55] But by far the most popular strategy for neutralizing the manly woman was to feminize her. Hippolyta in both Shakespeare and Beaumont and Fletcher is a bride, while in an Elizabethan translation from the French, she is said to have become so eager to serve Theseus that she licked his wounded shoulder with her tongue.[56] Less crude and more congenial was the ancient story that when Penthesilea had been slain by Achilles, her helmet fell off and revealed her beauty, causing Achilles to fall in love with her – sadly, luckily, too late. Amplified by the addition of a flood of golden hair loosed from the fallen helmet, the incident enriched Spanish and Italian romance and made its way to Elizabethan England, where at least six Amazonians, including Britomart, met with a version of this accident – all of them deliciously powerless to hide from admiring male gaze their quintessential femininity.[57] Holinshed's Boadicea, with her long tresses, and Mandeville's two gowned Amazons present the same feminized picture. Britomart, who sleeps 'Al in her snow-white smocke, with locks unbownd' (3.1.63.7), having overcome her opposite number, the wicked Amazon, immediately changes all the rules of Amazon-land and 'The liberty of women did repeale, / Which they had long usurpt; . . . them restoring / To mens subjection' (5.7.42.5–7). Even robust Long Meg, who looses her hair voluntarily to embarrass her vanquished opponent, returns from her French conquests to recant; having married a soldier who 'had heard of her manhood' and 'was determined to try her' in a combat with staves, she silently accepts 'three or four blows' and then, 'in submission, fell down on her knees, desiring him to pardon her, "For", said she, "it behoves me to be obedient to you; and it shall never be said. . . . Long Meg is her husband's master; and, therefore, use me as you please." '[58] The strength of her subversive attraction can be measured by the violence with which she is reintegrated into conservative ideology. She is too powerful to be wedded in another key.

We may anticipate, then, what those in Shakespeare's audience familiar with the conventions defining the woman warrior must also have anticipated: that the more free play Joan's attractive force is permitted, the more completely she will have to be feminized at the end of the play. Her scenes in Act 5 should be read in light of this expectation, in full acceptance of their radical difference from her earlier behavior. Her conjuring, once established, assigns her to an overwhelmingly female class of malefactors: informed estimates place the proportion of women executed as witches at about 93 per cent.[59] Her rejection of her father reduces to female vanity the serious social claim implicit in her male clothing, for, as a number of recent writers point out, cross-dressing attacks the concept of natural hierarchy on which, for the Elizabethans, social class is built.[60] Her terrified snatching at subterfuges in the face of death would count as peculiarly female behavior; and when, finally, she claims to be pregnant, naming everyone and anyone as a lover, her feminization becomes irreversible. She has lost her helmet forever. Her captors' harsh reactions to her pleas are the equivalent of Long Meg's beating: Warwick's sadistically merciful directions, 'And hark ye, sirs; because she is a maid, / Spare for no faggots, let there be enow' (5.4.55–56) – are followed by York's unequivocal 'Strumpet, . . . / Use no entreaty, for it is in vain' (84–85).

The witch is Joan's last topical role. Executions for witchcraft in England reached peaks in the 1580s and 1590s, high points on a long curve that Belsey considers 'coterminous with the crisis in the definition of women and the meaning of the family'; she notes that in the last two decades of the sixteenth century 'the divorce debate was also reaching a climax'.[61] These events coincide with the beginnings of the vogue for Amazons and women warriors on stage and with the early phases of the fad for cross-dressing. But of all that twenty-year span, 1591 was the year of the witch in England. It brought to London the pamphlet *Newes from Scotland*, a full account of the spectacular treason-cum-sorcery trials King James had supervised there in the winter of 1590–1591, in which large numbers of his subjects were accused of having made a mass pact with the devil in order to raise storms against the ship bringing the King and his bride from Denmark.[62] The pamphlet had political overtones, as did the trials. King James, described to the English by the tract as 'the greatest enemie the Devil hath on earth', was, after all, an aspirant to their throne.[63]

It is not at all clear, however, that James' 'forwardness', as the English ambassador called it in a letter to Burghley,[64] elicited the kind of acclaim that could help us read Joan's treatment by York and Warwick as pro-Jamesian political doctrine. There are indications that his self-interested zeal may have worked the other way. A woman whom, for political reasons, he particularly wanted disemboweled was acquitted. Moreover, it appears that popular opinion in Scotland did not support the political aspects of the prosecution.[65] Perhaps still more serious, 'the picture of himself as the principal target for witches' might easily look foolish, to say no worse, in a more sophisticated country that had never been as harsh or consistent in its punishment of witches as the continent, where James had first acquired his demonological ideas. As Larner says, 'there was a possibility that his new-found interest in witchcraft . . . could . . . damage his image, especially in England'.[66] Although England executed witches, it did not burn or torture them, and one wonders what an English audience made of James' vindictiveness or of Warwick's call for plenty of faggots and extra barrels of pitch for Joan's stake (5.4.56–57).[67] Furthermore, it was absolutely standard practice in both England and Scotland to put off a witch's execution if she was pregnant, as was the woman whose grisly punishment James unsuccessfully urged. Although Joan is only pretending, her captors are at best playing cat and mouse with her as they condemn her supposed child to death anew each time she assigns it a different father. Joan is the butt of the brutal joke here, but it is unlikely that York and Warwick come off unscathed by the negative associations of their total violation of English custom: 'we will have no bastards live. . . . It dies and if it had a thousand lives. . . . Strumpet, thy words condemn thy brat and thee' (5.4.70, 75, 84).

It is altogether difficult to be sure how an Elizabethan audience might have reacted to Joan's punishment. Opinion on witches in 1591 was by no means monolithic. Skepticism about witch-trials was gathering force; on the continent Montaigne had commented as recently as 1588, 'After all, it is putting a very high price on one's conjectures to have a man roasted alive because of them',[68] and at home Reginald Scot had even earlier published his 600-page attack (1584) on 'those same monsterous lies, which have abused all Christendome' and been the undoing of 'these poore women'.[69] Scot's book was clearly labeled as subversive when it was (appropriately) burnt by the hangman. Later, James attacked Scot by name in his own tract *Daemonologie*. This makes it all the more interesting that the portrayal of

Joan divides into a subversively Scot-like main section and a Jamesian demonological coda. In the long middle section of the play already discussed, her triumphs are based simply on boldness, common sense, and resourcefulness. Comically, this supposed witch is the most down-to-earth pragmatist in the play: 'had your watch been good / This sudden mischief never could have fallen' (2.1.58–59). In consequence, Talbot's repeated insistence that she is a witch sounds not dissimilar from the deluded allegations recounted by Reginald Scot. Joan herself, unlike Talbot and the French leaders, never falls back on metaphysical notions about her opponent. Whereas her companions suggest that Talbot is 'a fiend of hell' or a favorite of the heavens (2.1.46–47), Joan simply expresses realistic respect for his prowess and invents several plans to evade it. Her successes are well served by Scot's commentary: 'it is more strange, that we will imagine that to be possible to be doone by a witch, which to nature and sense is impossible; . . . [for in other legal cases] the judge dooth not attend or regard what the accused man saith; or yet would doo: but what is prooved to have beene committed, and naturallie falleth in mans power and will to doo'.[70] Yet in Act 5, Joan appears as a witch engaged in a diabolical compact, a demonological feature never very important in English witch trials but topically responsive to James' recent proceedings.

The presentation of Joan as witch is almost as diverse in its implications as her Amazonian image, of which it is a kind of transformation. The common folk belief in witches with beards, like the tradition of the Amazon's armor, renders visible the concept of a woman who 'exceeds her sex' (1.2.90).[71] Hall calls her 'This wytch or manly woman',[72] as if the two were so close that he could hardly decide between them. A comment by Belsey illuminates this aspect of Joan's witchhood:

The demonization of women who subvert the meaning of femininity is contradictory in its implications. It places them beyond meaning, beyond the limits of what is intelligible. At the same time it endows them with a (supernatural) power which it is precisely the project of patriarchy to deny. On the stage such figures are seen as simultaneously dazzling and dangerous.[73]

Joan's dazzle is of course neutralized by her fifth-act humiliations, but her danger persists in her final curse on England. Quickly, she is taken off to be neutralized more thoroughly at the stake. Her helplessness *vis-à-vis* her male captors may serve to remind us that despite folk belief, there were no Elizabethan pictures of witches with beards or any other kind of power-laden sexual ambiguity.[74] Joan's fate enacts that annihilation fantasized for the cross-dressing woman by the anonymous author of a Jacobean pamphlet: 'Let . . . the powerful Statute of apparell [the sumptuary law] but lift up his Battle-Axe, so as every one may bee knowne by the true badge of their bloud, . . . and then these *Chymera's* of deformitie will bee sent backe to hell, and there burne to Cynders in the flames of their owne malice.'[75] Yet in a final twist of meaning, as we have seen, the terms of Joan's reintegration into conservative ideology recognizably damage her captors' own ideological sanction.

In my reading of *1 Henry VI*, the disjunctive presentation of Joan that shows her first as numinous, then as practically and subversively powerful, and finally as feminized and demonized is determined by Shakespeare's progressive exploitation of the varied ideological potential inherent in the topically relevant figure of the virago. Each of her phases reflects differently upon the chivalric, patriarchal males in the play, especially Talbot, who also have topical referents outside the drama. At no stage is the allocation of value clear-cut.

Neither is the definition of dominant ideology clear-cut in the play's social context. To bring detailed topical considerations into an assessment of the ideology of *1 Henry VI* is to come upon some truisms worth restating: that there is probably more than one opinion on any crucial issue at any time in any society, and that it is often hard to sort out the relationship between views and power. If the queen considers a French expedition disadvantageous but her subordinate succeeds in continuing it, is the dominant ideology war or peace? If pamphleteers complain that women are becoming moral monsters by cross-dressing, but a fad for Amazons arises and women cross-dress more than ever, what is the ideological situation? This kind of uncertainty complicates the concept of subversion, which I have invoked from time to time in my analysis.

Given the multiple uncertainties within the play's milieu and the uncertainties the play itself generates, it becomes strikingly evident that *1 Henry VI*, like so much of Shakespeare's later work, locates itself in areas of ideological discomfort. It uses culturally powerful images ambiguously, providing material for different members of a diverse audience to receive the drama in very different ways. Although one must agree with the critical judgment that in this play 'the individual consciousness never engages in an *agon* with its milieu, and never asks the great questions',[76] the presence of Joan does provide a form of *agon*, if a less profound one than in the great tragedies. Even the ending, with its strategies of neutralization, cannot disqualify the questions raised.

Finally, once the ways in which disturbing ideological positions are neutralized by the play have been made clear, it seems well to point out that the theater is an illusionistic medium, and that to neutralize on stage is not necessarily to neutralize in reality. In fact, it is possible that maintaining the illusion that an ideological tendency can be reliably neutralized may help to enable toleration of threatening ideas.[77]

NOTES

1. Reprinted from DEBORAH E. BARKER AND IVO KAMPS (eds), *Shakespeare and Gender: A History* (London and New York: Verso, 1995).

   This essay was first presented at the 1986 World Shakespeare Conference in Berlin and, in another form, at the Northeast Modern Language Association on 3 April 1987. It shares a common concern about Joan's ideological ambiguity with Leah Marcus, 'Elizabeth', in *Puzzling Shakespeare: Local Reading and its* Discontents (Berkeley: University of California Press, 1988, pp. 51–105), but we arrive at different conclusions. Professor Marcus was kind enough to allow me to read her work while I was completing this essay.

2. Citations are from *The First Part of King Henry VI*, ed. ANDREW S. CAIRNCROSS, *The Arden Shakespeare* (London, 1962).

3. GEOFFREY BULLOUGH, *Narrative and Dramatic Sources of Shakespeare* (New York, 1960), III, 41.

4. ROBERT B. PIERCE, *Shakespeare's Historic Plays: The Family and the State* (Columbus, Oh., 1971), pp. 46–47. In the same spirit, DON M. RICKS identifies the tone she sets as 'treachery, depravity,

and insolence' in *Shakespeare's Emergent Form: A Study of the Structures of the Henry VI Plays* (Logan, Utah, 1968), p. 45. So common is the critical view of Joan as a moral write-off that she is sometimes assigned reprehensible behavior that does not even occur in the text, as when CATHERINE BELSEY remarks that she 'puts heart into the enemy by her rhetoric', in *The Subject of Tragedy: Identity and Difference in Renaissance Drama* (New York, 1985), p. 183. At the very least she is presumed to be the butt of continuous irony (e.g., by DAVID BEVINGTON in 'The Domineering Female in *1 Henry VI*', *Shakespeare Studies 2* [1966], 51–58 and JOHN WILDERS in *The Lost Garden: A View of Shakespeare's English and Roman History Plays* [Totowa, N.J., 1978], p. 36). A signal exception is H. M. RICHMOND in *Shakespeare's Political Plays* (New York, 1967), who allows her 'heroic power' and even some 'magnetism'; he also goes quite against the current of critical commentary by alluding to 'her subtlety and finesse' (p. 23), but he agrees on 'the harshness of the portrait' (p. 22).

5. Bullough, pp. 24–25.
6. LISA JARDINE, *Still Harping on Daughters: Women and Drama in the Age of Shakespeare* (Sussex, 1983), p. 124.
7. Belsey, p. 184.
8. MARILYN FRENCH, *Shakespeare's Division of Experience* (New York, 1981), p. 47.
9. See DAVID RIGGS, who admirably elucidates the play's structure in *Shakespeare's Heroical Histories: Henry VI and Its Literary Tradition* (Cambridge, Mass., 1971), pp. 100ff. On the play's ideology we disagree.
10. Riggs, p. 107. Riggs' view has been more recently affirmed by NORMAN RABKIN, *Shakespeare and the Problem of Meaning* (Chicago, 1981), pp. 88–89 and n. 39. Ricks and David Sundelson also make explicit, in slightly different ways, a criterion of integration to explain the last act: 'her final degeneration in Act V is but a spectacular demonstration of the unsaintliness which has been implicit in her words and behavior all along. There is nothing contradictory, therefore, about the two views of Joan as Pucelle and as "Puzzel" [whore]' (Ricks, p. 46); 'Shakespeare himself seems unable to tolerate any uncertainty about the source of Joan's potency. He resolves the matter with a scene in which she conjures . . . , thus confirming Talbot's explanation' (DAVID SUNDELSON, *Shakespeare's Restorations of the Father* [New Brunswick, N.J., 1983], p. 20).
11. See, e.g., Rabkin, pp. 86–87.
12. Detailed proposals of the play's topicality have been made by T. W. BALDWIN, *On the Literary Genetics of Shakespeare's Plays 1592–1594* (Urbana, Ill., 1959), pp. 324–40. Less extended suggestions of parallels have come from J. DOVER WILSON in the introduction to his edition of *The First Part of King Henry VI* (Cambridge, 1952), pp. xviii–xix; EMRYS JONES, *The Origins of Shakespeare* (Oxford, 1977), pp. 119–26; JOHN MUNRO in *TLS* October 11, 1947; HEREWARD T. PRICE, *Construction in Shakespeare*, University of Michigan Contributions in Modern Philology No. 17 (Ann Arbor, Mich., 1951), pp. 25–26; and ERNEST WILLIAM TALBERT, *Elizabethan Drama and Shakespeare's Early Plays: An Essay in Historical Criticism* (Chapel Hill, N.C., 1963). Leah Marcus offers a most thorough treatment of many of the play's topical allusions that takes full account of their complexity in 'Elizabeth' (see introductory note above).
13. John Munro first interpreted the lines about the phoenix as a reference to Essex. J. Dover Wilson follows suit in his introduction to the play, where he also suggests that 'Talbot was intended to stand as in some sort the forerunner of Essex' (p. xix). T. W. Baldwin, in his study of the play's 'literary genetics', is dubious about Munro's identification but agrees that the allusion is to 'the English armies in France 1589 and following' (p. 334). E. W. Talbert similarly cites Munro and also accepts the play's connection with the Essex expedition (pp. 163–64 and p. 163 n. 6).

14. J. E. NEALE, *Queen Elizabeth I* (Garden City, N.Y., 1957), p. 337.

15. J. Dover Wilson sees the parallel between Talbot's and Essex's challenges, but interprets it simply as a reminiscence of Essex's gallantry (p. xix). He considers the play 'an outlet for the growing sense of exasperation, anger, and even despair which was felt in London at the impending failure of an invasion of France' (p. xvi).

16. Neale, p. 335.

17. Ibid., p. 336. Elizabeth called the campaign 'rather a jest than a victory' and ordered Essex home for good in January 1592 (ibid., p. 337).

18. That a steady stream of ephemera carried bulletins from France to English readers is evident from the entries in the Stationers' Register. The diversity of possible attitudes to the expedition is perhaps suggested by the contrasting titles of two such pieces: an obviously enthusiastic 'ballad of the noble departinge of the right honorable the Erle of ESSEX lieutenant generall of her maiesties forces in Ffraunce and all his gallant companie' (23 July 1591) and a possibly more ominous-sounding 'letter sent from a gentleman of accoumpte concerninge the true estate of the Englishe forces now in Ffraunce under the conduct of the right honorable the Erle of ESSEX' (6 September 1591).

19. The well-known compliment to Essex in *Henry V*, 5, Cho. 30–34, is also ambiguous in light of the sentence that follows it (ll. 34–35). That this passage refers to Essex has been generally accepted, but the identification has been challenged by W. D. Smith. See G. BLAKEMORE EVANS, 'Chronology and Sources', *The Riverside Shakespeare*, ed. G. Blakemore Evans (Boston, 1974), p. 53.

20. E.g. Marilyn French (note 8 above), following L. C. Knights and Northrop Frye, calls the play a search for legitimacy (p. 43). She believes that legitimacy is presented as a strictly masculine principle – 'Shakespeare's women can never attain legitimacy' – although, somewhat confusingly, she also claims that it can contain 'the inlaw feminine principle' (p. 49).

21. Bevington (note 4 above), pp. 51–58.

22. Riggs (note 9 above).

23. French (note 8 above), p. 51.

24. COPPÉLIA KAHN, *Man's Estate: Masculine Identity in Shakespeare* (Berkeley, Cal., 1981), p. 55 and p. 55 n. 11.

25. LINDA WOODBRIDGE, *Women and the English Renaissance: Literature and the Nature of Womankind 1540–1620* (Urbana, Ill., 1984), p. 61. Shakespeare's interest in this controversy is evident not only in his frequent allusions to its *exempla* (Woodbridge cites references, pp. 126–28, and there are many more) but in his use of at least ten of them as characters in his works, four as protagonists. His is an impressive roster even in a period when plays about the controversy's *exempla* were a growth industry (Woodbridge, pp. 126ff.). The four protagonists are Venus, Lucrece, Cressida, and Cleopatra; the other characters, Volumnia in *Coriolanus*, Portia in *Julius Caesar* and Portia in *The Merchant of Venice* (carefully identified, as Woodbridge notes on p. 127, with 'Cato's daughter, Brutus' Portia'), Octavia, Helen of Troy, and Hippolyta (Thisbe should also be mentioned). The maligned and repudiated Mariana in *Measure for Measure*, too, may be a relative of Mariamne, Herod's defamed second wife, another favorite of the controversialists.

26. Woodbridge, pp. 61–62, 66.

27. Cairncross, 2.3.7–10n., and Bevington.

28. Woodbridge, p. 126. Woodbridge's account of the controversy is invaluable. I cannot agree with her, however, that the plays written in and after the later 1580s were probably not influenced by it; her own evidence (and there is more she does not cite) seems to point overwhelmingly the other way. She observes that 'the drama had many other potential sources', which is true but does not

account for the upsurge in plays devoted specifically to *exempla* from the controversy, and she points out that dramatists often treated these *exempla* differently from controversialists – but this objection assumes that to influence is to produce a copy.

29. The term was almost entirely positive and denoted either physical or spiritual prowess. For the virago's 'manly soul', see SIMON SHEPHERD, *Amazons and Warrior Women: Varieties of Feminism in Seventeenth-Century Drama* (Sussex, 1981), pp. 34–35. Various contemporary allusions to the Queen invoked the pun *virgo/virago*, and her 'masculine' spirit was frequently remarked upon with admiration. See WINFRIED SCHLEINER, '*Divina virago*: Queen Elizabeth as an Amazon', *Studies in Philology* 75, 2 (1978), 163–80. I am grateful to Louis Montrose for calling this extremely useful article to my attention.

30. All citations from *The Faerie Queene* will be identified by book, canto, stanza, and line numbers in my text; these refer to EDMUND SPENSER, *The Faerie Queene*, ed. R. E. Neil Dodge (Cambridge, Mass., 1936). Spenser was mistaken; Yael, not Deborah, struck Sisera.

31. I am indebted to F. J. Levy for calling my attention to this fact.

32. Ironically – or as a calculated symbolic counterstatement to the Maid? – Henry VI's Paris coronation pageant included 'la sage Hippolyte' and her sister Menalippe, as well as Penthesilea and Lampeto, as female worthies. See ROBERT WITHINGTON, *English Pageantry: An Historical Outline*, Vol. I (Cambridge, Mass., 1918), pp. 138–39 n. 4. CELESTE TURNER WRIGHT calls attention to Henry's coronation pageant in 'The Amazons in Elizabethan Literature', *Studies in Philology* 37 (July 1940), 437 n. 41 (n.b.: because of a numbering error in this volume, Wright's article begins on the *second* occurrence of p. 437).

33. See ABBY WETTAN KLEINBAUM, 'The Confrontation', in *The War Against the Amazons* (New York, 1983). I appreciate being directed to this book by Daniel Traister, Curator of Rare Books at the University of Pennsylvania.

34. Schleiner (see note 29 above) also identifies as 'Amazons' the female characters in a mock tournament of 1579, presented for the Queen and the Duke of Alençon's representative (p. 179), although her quotation from her source refers only to 'ladies' (pp. 163–64 n. 3). *Tamburlaine* mentions Amazon armies, but they do not appear. Greene's *Alphonsus*, an obvious offspring of *Tamburlaine*, may have preceded *I Henry VI* in presenting visible Amazons as well as a warrior maiden, but this play has never been satisfactorily dated. Rabkin believes it was 'probably written 1587', but does not give his reasons (introduction to ROBERT GREENE, 'Friar Bacon and Friar Bungay', *Drama of the English Renaissance. I: The Tudor Period*, ed. Russell A. Fraser and Norman Rabkin [New York, 1976] p. 357). The play's general derivative quality suggests, however, that Iphigina is more likely to be a daughter of Joan than the reverse. The other productions I know of containing Amazons are 'A Masque of the Amazons . . . played March 3, 1592' (Henslowe's diary, quoted in WILLIAM PAINTER, *The Palace of Pleasure*, ed. Joseph Jacobs, 3 vols. [London, 1890], I, 1xxxi); 'field pastimes with martiall and heroicall exploits' staged for Prince Henry's christening in 1594 (JOHN NICHOLS, *Progresses, Public Processions, &c. of Queen Elizabeth*, 3 vols. [London, 1823], III, 355); *Midsummer Night's Dream*, 1595; Marston's *Antonio and Mellida*, 1602; *Timon of Athens*, ?1605–1609; Jonson's *Masque of Queens*, 1609; Beaumont and Fletcher's *Two Noble Kinsmen*, ?1613, *The Sea Voyage*, 1622, and *Double Marriage*, 1647; the anonymous *Swetnam, the Woman-Hater*, 1620; Heywood's *Iron Age*, 1632; Shirley's dramatization of the *Arcadia*, 1640; and Davenant's *Salmacida Spolia*, 1640. There is a discussion of Fletcher's *Sea Voyage* and some Amazon dramas 1635–1685 in chapter 11 of Jean Elisabeth Gagen, *The New Woman: Her Emergence in English Drama, 1600–1730* (New York, 1954).

For many of these titles and the beginnings of all my information about Amazons, I have relied on the encyclopedic Wright (note 32 above). Her non-chronological organization assumes, however, that the degree of interest in Amazons and writers' attitudes towards them remained stable throughout the period from which she takes her examples (some undated). Her evidence suggests otherwise.

35. Wright, pp. 442–43, 449–54. Wright's data are difficult to get around in chronologically, but it looks as though doubts about the Amazons – including skepticism about their existence – may have increased in England after 1600, although the Amazonian vogue lasted right up to the Civil War.

Although there are Elizabethan accounts of the Amazons' ruthless origins and habits, I do not agree with Shepherd (note 29 above) that the period's overriding feeling was 'Elizabethan distress about Amazons' (p. 14), in support of which view he instances Radigund and the egregious misogynist Knox. Shepherd wants to extrapolate Spenser's opposition between Radigund and Britomart into a pervasive Elizabethan distinction between Amazons and warrior women: 'Against the warrior ideal there is the Amazon' (p. 13). This schema will not hold up in the face of a mass of evidence for Elizabethan Amazon-enthusiasm. Shepherd's own evidence for the Elizabethan period is slender and largely extrapolated from Stuart texts. Although he does say that the negative meaning of Amazon 'coexists with the virtuous usage' (p. 14), this concession, in itself inadequate, is forgotten in his subsequent loosely supported account.

Nor can I agree with Louis Adrian Montrose's implication in his otherwise insightful and imaginative ' "Shaping Fantasies": Figurations of Gender and Power in Elizabethan Culture', *Representations* 1, 2 (Spring 1983), 61–94, that English Renaissance texts about Amazons generally express 'a mixture of fascination and horror' (p. 66). The passages he quotes detail the Amazons' origins and/or customs; others of this type are often flat in tone and delivered without comment, like Mandeville's (1499, rpt. 1568), while some mention no horrors at all. Even the Amazon-shy Spenser compliments the supposed South American tribe: 'Joy on those warlike women, which so long / Can from all men so rich a kingdome hold!' (*F. Q.* 4.11.22.1–2). Although Montrose calls attention to the association sometimes made between Amazons and the destruction of male children, and in some travel books between Amazons and cannibalism, in an equal number of accounts they produce male children for neighboring tribes and are thought of as desirable breeding stock. By far the greatest number of Amazon allusions, moreover, refer to specific Amazons and appear in a positive context. Penthesilea, the hands-down favorite, is always treated with admiration and respect, as is Hippolyta.

My observations are based on the following Tudor texts: Agrippa, trans. Clapham, *The Nobilitie of Woman Kynde*, 1542 (STC 203), p. 360v; Anghiera (Peter Martyr), trans. Eden, *Decades of the Newe World*, 1555, ed. Arber, *The First Three English Books on America*, 1885, pp. 69, 177, 189; Richard Barckley, *The Felicitie of Man*, 1598 (STC 1381), III, 266–68; Boccaccio, *De Claris Mulieribus*, 1534–47, ed. Wright, EETS (London, 1943), pp. 39–42, 66–67, 103–05 and *Tragedies*, trans. Lydgate, 1554 (STC 3178), I, 12; Quintus Curtius, trans. Brende, *History of . . . Alexander*, 1553 (STC 6142), pp. Pii–Piii; Anthony Gibson, trans., *A Womans Woorth*, 1599 (STC 11831), pp. 5, 37v; Richard Madox, *An Elizabethan in 1582: The Diary of Richard Madox . . .* , ed. Elizabeth Story Donno, Hakluyt Society second series No. 47 (London, 1977), p. 183; Sir John Mandeville, *The Voyage and Travel . . .* , 1568 (STC 17250), pp. Gviii verso; Ortuñez de Calahorra, trans. T[yler], *The Mirrour of . . . Knighthood*, 1578 (STC 18859), 26.91 v, 55.219; Hieronimus Osorius, trans. Blandie, *The Five Books of Civill and Christian Nobilitie*, 1576 (STC 18886), II, 25v;

Ovid, trans. Turberville, *Heroycall Epistles*, 1567 (STC 18940.5), p. 23; William Painter, *The Palace of Pleasure*, 1575, ed. Joseph Jacobs, 3 vols. (London, 1890), II, 159–61; Sir Walter Ralegh, *The Discoverie of . . . Guiana*, 1596 (STC 20636), pp. 23–24 and *History of the World*, 1614 (STC 20637), I.4.195–96; William Shakespeare, *King John*, 1594–96, ed. Herschel Baker, in Evans; Sir Philip Sidney, *The Countess of Pembrokes Arcadia*, 1590, ed. Robertson (Oxford, 1973), pp. 21, 36; Edmund Spenser, *The Faerie Queene*, I–III, 1590, IV–VI, 1596 (see note 30); Andre Thevet, *The New Found World*, trans. 1568 (STC 23950), pp. 101–74 *(recte* 103); William Warner, *Albion's England*, 1586 (STC 15759), pp. 25–26; and two accounts of Spanish voyages known in England, those of Francesco Orellana and Gonzalo Pizarro, *Expeditions into the Valley of the Amazons*, trans. and ed. Clements R. Markham, Hakluyt Society (New York, n.d.), pp. 13, 26, 34, 36. I have also found useful Kleinbaum's chapters 'The Net of Fantasy' and 'The Confrontation'.

36. Woodbridge, p. 21.

37. Cited by both Wright and Shepherd.

38. Wright, p. 455.

39. He makes this identification in 1590, just a year and a half after the Armada crisis (see discussion below, in text). Penthesilea was frequently used as a comparison for Elizabeth, especially around this time (see Schleiner [note 29 above], pp. 170–73). The Amazon analogy was still current in 1633, when Phineas Fletcher likened his 'warlike Maid, / *Parthenia*', a recognizable variant of Elizabeth, to Hippolyta in *The Purple Island* 10.27–40 (STC 11092), pp. 141–44.

40. In 'Elizabeth', Leah Marcus also comments on some of Joan's symbolic identities.

41. For information on woodcuts I am most grateful to Ruth Luborsky, who is currently completing a catalogue of all woodcut-illustrated printed English documents in the period, keyed to the STC. For pictorial narratives, I have consulted David Kunzle, *The Early Comic Strip: Narrative Strips and Picture Stories in the European Broadsheet from 1450–1895* (Berkeley, Cal., 1983). I have examined the engraved representations in Arthur M. Hind, *Engraving in England in the Sixteenth and Seventeenth Centuries*, 3 vols. (Vol. III ed. Margery Corbett and Michael Norton) (Cambridge, 1952–64); in Ronald B. McKerrow, *Printers' and Publishers' Devices 1485–1640 in England and Scotland* (London, 1913); in Ronald B. McKerrow and F. S. Ferguson, *Title-page Borders Used in England & Scotland 1485–1640* (London, 1932 [for 1931] [sic]); and in Margery Corbett and Ronald Lightbown, *The Comely Frontispiece: The Emblematic Title-page in England, 1550–1660* (London, 1979).

42. Nichols (note 34 above), II, pp. 53–54.

43. Quoted from Thomas Heywood's *Exemplary Lives*, 1640, by Shepherd (note 29 above), p. 22.

44. Leonel Sharp, Letter to George Villiers, Duke of Buckingham, n.d. [1623–25], *Cabala, Mysteries of State, in Letters of the great Ministers of K. James and K. Charles* (1654), p. 259.

45. Stow in his *Annals* (1615) calls the Queen at Tilbury 'Bellona-like' (quoted by Miller Christy, 'Queen Elizabeth's Visit to Tilbury in 1588', *EHR* 34 [1919], 58), and an anonymous poem of 1600 appeals to her as 'Thou that . . . bearest harnesse, speare, and shielde' (Schleiner [note 29 above], p. 174). Schleiner, who does not know the Sharp letter, calls Heywood's 1640 description 'probably only theatrical imagination' (p. 176). Heywood was drawing on his own dramatic spectacle, created in 1633 when he brought his two-part stage biography of the Queen to its climax with a final Tilbury scene: 'Enter . . . Queen ELIZABETH, completely armed'. See Thomas Heywood, *The Second Part of If You Know Not Me, You Know No Bodie* (1633), in *Thomas Heywood's Dramatic Works*, ed. J. Payne Collier (London, 1853), II, 156; for the date see editorial note [xxiii]. (The 1606 version of the play does not contain this stage direction, but may of course have used the same costume.)

I do not know where Paul Johnson gets his circumstantial description of a white velvet dress, etc, in *Elizabeth I: A Study in Power and Intellect* (London, 1974), p. 320, which Montrose (note 35 above) follows, p. 77. The description is not in any of the sources Johnson cites in his footnote. SUSAN FRYE casts doubt on the reliability of Sharp's account (which includes the speech) in her wonderfully thorough 'The Myth of Elizabeth at Tilbury', *The Sixteenth Century Journal* XXIII, 1 (1992), 95–114. In her view, the 'myth' of armour arose in the early seventeenth century. She does not, however, to my mind, decisively discredit the several evocations of martial accoutrements in poetry contemporaneous with the event (pp. 105–6). Comparing the Sharp speech with two versions of a different purported speech by Elizabeth on this occasion (pp.101–5), Frye comments: 'Elizabeth I may have delivered both speeches, or neither' (p. 104). Probably neither Elizabeth's clothing nor her speech can be settled definitively.

46. Sharp, p. 260. J. E. NEALE, 'Sayings of Queen Elizabeth', *History* n.s. 10 (October 1925), pp. 212–33, considers this speech substantially authentic (pp. 226–27). Sharp, who recounted it soon after 1623, must have received a copy of it in 1588; he relates that at Tilbury he had been 'commanded to re-deliver' the oration to 'all the Armie together, to keep a Publique Fast' (Sharp, p. 259) after Elizabeth's departure.

For evidence that Elizabeth's rhetorical self-presentations often implied androgyny, see LEAH S. MARCUS, 'Shakespeare's Comic Heroines, Elizabeth I, and the Political Uses of Androgyny', in *Women in the Middle Ages and the Renaissance*, ed. Mary Beth Rose (Syracuse, N.Y., 1986).

47. In 'Elizabeth', Leah Marcus notes numerous similarities between Joan and the queen, including the proposed celebration of a saint's day commemorating each woman and the identity in name between two of Joan's supposed lovers and two of Elizabeth's suitors.

48. Leah Marcus, in 'Elizabeth', does interpret Joan as a figure of parody that embodies 'suppressed cultural anxieties' about Elizabeth.

49. NATALIE ZEMON DAVIS, 'Women on Top', *Society and Culture in Early Modern France* (Stanford, Cal., 1975), p. 129.

50. 'The Life of Long Meg of Westminster', *The Old Book Collector's Miscellany*, ed. CHARLES HINDLEY, vol. II (London, 1872). See also Shepherd (note 29 above), pp. 70–71. The outlines of Long Meg's story exhibit striking similarities with the outlines of Joan's; according to Hall, Joan too came from the country and 'was a greate space a chamberleyn in a commen hostrey' (Bullough, p. 56) before going off to lead the army against the English champion and being honored by the Dauphin.

51. Hindley, p. xii, quoted by Shepherd, p. 73. The ballad of Mary Ambree is given in Thomas Percy, *Reliques*, vol. III (1823), pp. 46–51 (series 2, Bk. 2, no. 19). She was a well-known figure, mentioned by Fletcher and Ben Jonson (Percy, p. 46). Long Meg was even more familiar; she is referred to by Lyly, Nashe, Harvey, Deloney, Taylor, Dekker, Jonson, Beaumont and Fletcher, Middleton, and William Gamage's collection of epigrams (see Hindley and Shepherd).

All modern critics who discuss Long Meg give a wrong date of 1582 for the first pamphlet account of her life. This edition's title page and colophon are forged from an unrelated book published 1582; the rest of the text is ca. 1650. See WILLIAM A. JACKSON, ed. *Records of the Court of the Stationers' Company 1602–1640* (London, 1957), pp. 112–13 and n. 6 (this information is incorporated in the STC's revised Vol. II, ed. Katharine Pantzer). The earliest mention I know of Meg's story is the 18 August 1590 entry in the *Stationers' Register* for her life, followed on 27 August the same year by an entry for a ballad about her. On 14 March 1594/95, another ballad is entered. The first extant life would thus become one printed in 1620 (STC 17782.5), followed by further editions in 1635 and 1636 (STC 17783, 17783.3). After these would come the '1582' *(recte* ca. 1650). Hindley, who reprints the 1635 edition, includes in his introduction another reprint, which he believes to be an abridged version (n.d.) of the supposed 1582 text. It does seem to be Elizabethan, for it contains the casual reference to 'Her Majesty'; later, this phrase was economically altered by the printer to 'she sat in her Majesty' (1635; I have not seen the 1620 edition). Thus the life in Hindley's introduction may be the version registered 1590; if so, it is our earliest text.

52. LAWRENCE STONE believes that female cross-dressing was a reflection of the Jacobean court's homosexuality, and that 'The playwrights noticed what was happening and gave it further circulation'; see *The Crisis of the Aristocracy 1558–1641* (Oxford, 1966), pp. 666–67. Given the early beginnings of both real and fictional cross-dressing, however, behavior at the Jacobean court comes much too late to be an explanation.

53. There is contemporaneous evidence for the possibility of regarding Joan as a heroine. Gabriel Harvey in his commonplace book set her between Alexander and her shepherd-analogue David (Shepherd, p. 35). By the 1620s, she was publicly entered among warlike and valorous women in Thomas Heywood's *Gynaikeion* (Jardine [note 6 above], p. 137 n. 66) and admitted to membership in the long-running formal controversy in CHRISTOPHER NEWSTEAD's *An Apology for Women*, a positive *exemplum* after all (Woodbridge [note 25 above], p. 80).

54. Davis (note 49 above), pp. 138–39.

55. The Amazon army in Greene's *Alphonsus* stands by silently while its non-Amazon leader fights; the Amazons in the masque of Shakespeare's *Timon* sing and dance. Since these are early manifestations of the Amazon vogue in drama, their extraneousness probably reflects their initial use as spectacle rather than integrated content. Marston's *Antonio and Mellida*, the anonymous *Swetnam the Woman-Hater*, and Shirley's dramatization of the *Arcadia*, which fall into the later part of the period, contain men disguised as Amazons.

56. ANTHONY GIBSON, trans., *A Womans Woorth (1599)*, cited by Wright (note 32 above), p. 437.

57. Ortuñez's Claridiana (trans. 1585), Spenser's Britomart and Radigund (although the latter's loss of helmet releases no golden hair), Ariosto's Bradamante (trans. 1591), Tasso's Clorinda (trans. 1600), and Phineas Fletcher's Hippolyta (*The Purple Island*, 1633). See Wright, p. 441, and Shepherd, pp. 9–10. Mary Ambree (1584) removes her helmet to astonish the besieging forces; Shepherd says she 'was forced to reveal her true gender to avoid being killed' (p. 222 n. 2), but the tone of the ballad is triumphant. Nevertheless, Ambree does share in the woman warrior's climactic feminization.

58. Hindley (note 50 above), p. xx; quoted in a slightly different form by Shepherd, pp. 71–72.

59. Belsey (note 4 above), p. 185. CHRISTINA LARNER gives the proportion of females among those put on trial for witchcraft in England at close to 95–100% in *Witchcraft and Religion: The Politics of Popular Belief*, ed. Alan Macfarlane (New York, 1984), p. 85. Belsey's figure is taken from earlier work by Larner.

60. Cf. MARY BETH ROSE's comment that cross-dressing women are 'obscuring . . . the badge of their social status as well, and thereby endangering critically the predictable orderliness of social relations' ('Women in Men's Clothing: Apparel and Social Stability in *The Roaring Girl*', *English Literary Renaissance* 14 [1984], 374).

61. Belsey, p. 185. Overall, Belsey is concerned with an extended period of 'crisis' lasting from 1542 to 1736, when the last statute against witchcraft was repealed.

62. This tract, with its new emphasis on the spectacular pact with the Devil, which had not previously been a factor in Scottish witch trials and was never very important in English ones (Larner, pp. 4, 8, 80–81, 88), seems to have evoked a little spate of conjuring dramas in the early 1590s, including *Dr. Faustus* and possibly *Friar Bacon and Friar Bungay* (written between 1589 and 1592).

63. Larner, pp. 69, 9–10, 12.

64. Ibid., p. 12.
65. Ibid., pp. 12–13.
66. Ibid., pp. 14, 4, 10–11, 15.
67. Warwick does say 'That so her torture may be shortened' (5.4.58), but it seems at best a mixed recommendation. As for the usual English treatment of witchcraft, although it sounds sufficiently grim to us, it was 'fairly far down the scale' of intensity compared with that of other countries, sufficiently different to be often called 'unique' by recent investigators, although Larner is not willing to go that far (pp. 70–71).
68. Michel de Montaigne, in *Witchcraft in Europe 1100–1700: A Documentary History*, ed. ALAN C. KORS AND EDWARD PETERS (Philadelphia, 1972), p. 337.
69. Reginald Scot, Kors and Peters, pp. 327, 326.
70. Scot, Kors and Peters, pp. 318–19.
71. This phrase and its variants (sometimes in Latin) were regularly applied to Queen Elizabeth. James' eulogistic inscription on her monument identifies her, typically, as '*super sexum*' (see Schleiner [note 29 above], pp. 172–73).

  On witches' beards, Belsey (p. 186) cites KEITH THOMAS' *Religion and the Decline of Magic* (London, 1971), p. 678. THOMAS ALFRED SPALDING, *Elizabethan Demonology* (London, 1880), p. 99, instances *The Honest Man's Fortune*, *The Honest Whore*, and *The Merry Wives of Windsor* – besides, of course, *Macbeth*, to which both Belsey and Spalding refer.
72. Bullough, p. 61.
73. Belsey, p. 185.
74. For information on pictures of witches, I am again indebted to Ruth Luborsky. Illustrations are also reproduced in Kors, including some of witches with animal heads and limbs, but none with trans-sexual characteristics.
75. *Hic Mulier*, C1v, cited by Rose (note 60 above), p. 375.
76. RONALD S. BERMAN, 'Shakespeare's Conscious Histories', *Dalhousie Review* 41, 4 (Winter 1961–62), 486.
77. The research for this essay has relied greatly on the knowledgeable and generous help of Georgiana Ziegler, curator of the Furness Collection at the University of Pennsylvania, to whom I owe much gratitude.

CHAPTER TWO

A Mingled Yarn: Shakespeare and the Cloth Workers[1]

RICHARD WILSON

The depiction of Jack Cade's rebellion in Act IV of *Henry VI Part 2* poses acute questions for the interpretation of Shakespeare's political drama. The scenes are in part a response to events in the summer of 1592, as the play was being written, when a group of Southwark feltmakers clashed with the guards of the Marshalsea prison. Does Shakespeare's play evoke sympathy for the crowd, the common people, or are they treated with contempt? Both Richard Wilson, in the essay excerpted below, and Annabel Patterson in her book *Shakespeare and the Popular Voice* (1989), tackle this question, and reach opposite conclusions.

Wilson sees Jack Cade as a carnivalesque figure, an early draft for Falstaff, a theme explored in detail in Graham Holderness's essay (Chapter 7). He notes that after Cade, there is no commoner who speaks so much in Shakespearean drama: for Wilson, Shakespeare's contemptuous treatment of Cade marks the playwright's allegiance to an educated urban elite, and his willingness to take part in a 'silencing of the people's voice in the writers' culture of print and profit'. Patterson, on the other hand, has argued that 'there is nothing in *Henry VI, Part 2*, read carefully, that can justify its use as the court of last appeal in a claim for Shakespeare's conservatism'. Quoting from Wilson's essay, Patterson writes 'Instead of the "brazen manipulation of records practised to buttress the regime" of which he has been accused, what Shakespeare provided in 1592 was an opportunity to discriminate: between contrasting attitudes to the popular voice protesting; and between socially useful or abusive styles of its mediation' (*Shakespeare and the Popular Voice*, 1989, p. 51). Patterson clearly has Wilson in mind when she writes: 'By applying the "official platitudes" of their own doctrines to selected parts of the text only, critics have been deaf to the carefully modulated story it tells.' Wilson in turn has responded by attacking Patterson's 'vision of the Bard as a Jeffersonian democrat' (*Will Power*, 1993, p. 17), seeing her as projecting her own politics on to Shakespeare, and regarding the idea of Shakespeare the democrat as an anachronistic myth. Half a century after Tillyard, Shakespeare's politics and his attitude to order and rebellion are still highly controversial.

'The web of our life is of a mingled yarn, good and ill together.'

(All's Well That Ends Well, IV, iii, 68–9)

Shakespeare continues to serve as the poet of 'consensus'. Thus, when the Young Vic Theatre began a series of radical interpretations of his plays in the mid-1980s, the critics savaged the approach as 'Spartish tosh', protesting that this was to tie the texts in 'a political straitjacket', which 'in effect tells Shakespeare what he was writing about'. The productions were 'well-staged, but wrong-headed', and it was 'an atrocity' to expose the young to such 'unashamedly political', 'comic-strip simplifications'. Repelled by drama that was 'A delight to the Race Relations Board', 'Is the theatre the place', gnashed one critic, 'for political statements?'[2] Yet a hundred yards away, on London's South Bank, the National Theatre's *Coriolanus* was simultaneously hailed by the selfsame critics as 'A Triumph', precisely because its director, Peter Hall, had realised what they called 'Shakespeare's burning political relevance'. What they meant was spelt out in *The Daily Telegraph*, where Hall was lauded for a staging that 'transcends logic to underline the political topicality' of a play which was 'about the threat to democracy when workers are misled by troublemakers'. *Coriolanus* was 'a piece for the British 1980s', the critics were agreed, and Hall was to be thanked for 'a totally political reading of the play' in which 'the affairs of the nation were aired with maximum fairness to all sides'. As Michael Billington enthused in *The Guardian*, 'what makes this a great production is that it connects directly with modern Britain to show conviction government and popular anarchy in headlong, nightmare collision'. So, in the year of the Miners' Strike, it seemed that 'the message' of *Coriolanus* was that 'Good government depends on compromise'. And there was a manifest equation between this revelation and the 'greatness' of Hall's interpretation: 'This is the best Shakespeare production to emerge from the National in its 21 years', enthused Billington, 'and the reason is not far to seek. Abandoning the academic approach, Hall champions "the radical middle". This *Coriolanus* belongs as much to the SDP [Social Democratic Party] as the SPQR [Senate and People of Rome].' So it was that mere 'academic' considerations, and even dramatic 'logic', were discarded in the interests of the correct political persuasion. Nor was there any question now of presuming to tell Shakespeare what he was writing about. 'A really magnificent production of this great play' was quite literally one that endorsed the politics of the SDP and Dr David Owen.[3]

The charm of newspaper criticism is that it betrays its ideological bias so blatantly. As Shakespeare's plays are packaged in this way, they typify the process by which the classic text is reproduced in our society to authorise the moral claims of market capitalism. Here the confusion of 'maximum fairness to all sides' with the aims of the managerial elite is comically naive; but when one of the most influential of all Shakespeare interpreters, G. Wilson Knight, can crown his career by citing Cranmer's prophecy from *Henry VIII* as vindication of Mrs Thatcher's Falklands' campaign,[4] it would be wrong to look to academic criticism for more sophistication. In fact, the identification of 'the affairs of the nation' with the priorities of its dominant classes has been the hallmark, and arguably the function, of British Shakespeare criticism since the First World War. Central to this criticism has been the image of Shakespeare's theatre itself as a democratic forum, where the citizens

of England's supposedly organic pre-industrial community met in a classless mutu-
ality which remains a glowing example to the world. A product of the great panic
following the European revolutions of 1917–20, this myth of the democratic Globe
was crucial to those, like F. R. Leavis, who idealised Elizabethan England as a lost
Eden, a socially homogeneous agrarian culture, whose 'people talked, so making
Shakespeare possible'. It was a legend which took definitive shape during the
Second World War, when Alfred Harbage identified the Globe as a cradle of Anglo-
Saxon democracy, the 'theatre of a nation' for which the only price of admission
was 'the possession by each spectator of some spiritual vitality',[5] and Laurence
Olivier imaged it as a cockney picture palace in *Henry V,* the trailer for D-Day. With
its lords and groundlings, this was the concept of the Elizabethan playhouse that
became glued in schools in a thousand papier mâché replicas, and though Andrew
Gurr remarks that it ignores 'the non-play-going 80 per cent of London's popula-
tion', and Ann Jennalie Cook maintains that it distorts the middle-class bias of the
Globe's privileged playgoers, it is a fantasy essential to the stature of the National
Poet, who, because he appealed equally to all classes, wrote for 'democracy', and
'Not for an age, but for all time'.[6]

It is the idea of Shakespeare's playhouse as the site of 'the world we have lost',
an organic community where writing was still inspired by talk, and a more representative arena than Parliament itself, which gives the plays their quasi-legislative
force. A popular Globe legitimises the sleight-of-hand by which Shakespeare's
historically determined, middle-class drama becomes the modern Magna Carta; an
elision further authorised by Derrideans with their anti-historicist mystification
of Elizabethan language as a deconstructive feast. And nowhere is this illusion more
binding than with respect to the Shakespearean representation of the poor. Of
course, it is a well-known embarrassment that the Bard did not love the people as
a proper modern democrat should, but it is those commentators who attend to this,
such as Shaw and Tolstoy, who have been dismissed as cranks. Academic criticism
has responded to their objections that Shakespeare demonised the mob for reasons
of social antagonism, by insisting that, on the contrary, what he recorded was
merely the eternal empirical facts about lower-class existence. As Philip Brockbank
authoritatively reported, the dramatist's depiction of commoners proves that 'he
had an eye for the outrages of the London streets, a nose for the sour breath of
the plebeians, and an ear for riotous chop-logic; but at no point in any play do they
pervert Shakespeare's objectivity of judgement or his rich human sympathies'. For
such critics, there is no inconsistency in Shakespeare's reputation as a popular
entertainer and his denigration of the people themselves as (in the words of
Coriolanus) 'the rank-scented meinie', and a 'beast with many heads' (III, i, 65; IV,
i, 1–2), because 'He is indulgent to the mob as individuals', and besides, 'He has
done his duty by the poor when he has reminded us that they are human'.[7]

It is the paternalist dread of popular solidarity that this criticism perpetuates,
in a form as offensive as it is unexamined. So, just as Shakespeare's 'rich human
sympathies' are evinced in his 'admirable studies of simple people', his 'objectivity'
is shown in his 'understanding of the tragic rhythm of political history' whereby
'the populace is transformed into the mob'. As Bradley argued, Shakespeare's 'poor
and humble are, almost without exception, sound and sweet at heart, faithful and

pitiful', until incited by rabble-rousers: 'He has no respect for the plainer and sim-
pler kind of people as politicians.' Such critics agree that 'Shakespeare hated and
despised' popular leaders 'with a bitterness he rarely felt towards any creatures', but
maintain that this was because 'He was saying what happens when power falls into
the hands of those whose innocence delivers them to any adventurer with enough
wit to make the right promises.' Almost unanimously, they endorse as self-evident
Shakespeare's analysis – the analysis of the 1571 'Homily of Obedience' – that it is
through 'restless ambitious' agitators that the 'ignorant multitude' is converted into
an anarchic rabble which is 'beyond all possible defence', because it stands for 'the
repudiation of law, learning, society, and natural order'. 'We can only marvel', they
concur, 'at the timeliness of Shakespeare's imagination and the certainty of his
political judgements. "Big Brother" has thrown a dark enough shadow on our own
century for us to be able to acknowledge the accuracy of the diagnosis.' To Shakespeareans like this, organised labour has only one possible purpose, which is to
undermine 'the national interest'. Always and everywhere, it is 'the enemy within'
the state.[8]

The critics are not, of course, blindly wrong about Shakespeare and the common people; but, influenced themselves by the modernist disgust of the 'unreal
city' and its crowd, they universalise a paternalism that belongs to a specific social
formation. As they intuit, Shakespeare dramatises the crucial moment when a deferential 'populace degenerates into the uncontrolled and predatory mob'.[9] Put less
rhetorically, therefore, his crowd scenes relate to the historical phase that has been
documented by historians such as Eric Hobsbawm and George Rudé, when the
rulers of the Old Regime were thrown off balance by the mass of urban poor that
coalesced into the early modern 'city mob'. This occurred at different times between
the sixteenth and eighteenth centuries in the cities of Western Europe, but as Brian
Manning has shown, it was London craftsmen and apprentices who first joined
together in a mass movement with a coherent set of political demands, and in
December 1641 it was this metropolitan mob of 'the lower sort of people' which
proved decisive in driving Charles I out of his palace and capital. Later, it was the
same corps of 'the common people of London who made up the rank and file of the
Parliamentary army', so the mob's ultimate revolutionary role was far from futile.
Its origins can be traced back to the gangs and customs of the city's medieval artisanal culture; but the emergent identity of the London mob actually dates from the
crisis years at the end of the sixteenth century, when a spate of calamitous harvests
and exorbitant wars accelerated the collapse of social consensus in the transition
to market capitalism, provoking a rash of urban revolts across Europe which were
a forecast of the great revolutionary civil wars to come.[10] Though critics speak of
Shakespeare's mutinous crowds, then, as if they represented perennial human
traits, it was only around 1590 that conjunctural circumstances produced the point
of critical mass that precipitated the popular disorders in London reflected in plays
like *Sir Thomas More* and *Julius Caesar*. Until then, urban rioting was extremely rare
in England; so much so that a crowd which dared to heckle Mary in 1554 was
viewed as an outrage; and when riots began to break out in the capital in the 1590s,
memories had to reach back to Evil May Day 1517 – when weavers attacked immig-
rant competitors – to find a parallel. And it was for this reason that, apart from

academic plays like *Gorboduc*, drama of civil discord did not feature on the London stage until after the Armada.[11]

Once welded in economic necessity, the London mob soon displayed the characteristics that made it so different from either the modern crowd observed by Poe, Benjamin and Canetti, or the old-style peasant rout caricatured by Chaucer as a barnyard in *The Nun's Priest's Tale*. What distinguished the mob from either was precisely its sense of purpose, for as Hobsbawm reminds us, the classical mob did not simply riot to order or as a protest, but because it expected to achieve something. So although the new social formation was anathematised by officials as a monstrous Hydra without shape or purpose, it had objectives and organisation which contradicted this governmental canard. It took its leadership from the semi-legal 'yeoman' craft fraternities and its programme from the set of values that E. P. Thompson calls 'the moral economy of the poor': 'a popular consensus as to what were legitimate practices and what were illegitimate' in the community. Thus, according to Hobsbawm, far from being motiveless, the mob had four clearly defined and driving ideas: it believed in cheap, tax-free food; it despised ostentatious wealth and harked back to a 'merry world' of social harmony; it resented entrepreneurs, especially foreign ones; and, most importantly, it assumed that once alerted, the authorities would remedy its grievances. Together, these assumptions made the city mob a formidable corrective both to local profiteering and royal despotism; but the mob possessed one other feature that made it particularly inimical to the nation-state. It legitimated its protests and resistance 'by rite', that is to say, by linking them to the 'wild justice' of traditional folk festivities and calendar games. Thus, as Emmanuel Le Roy Ladurie has recounted in his collective 'psychohistory' of the Carnival uprising in Romans in 1580, the millennialist dream of the Land of Cockaigne could curdle into a cannibal fantasy aimed at the rich, and finally turn to action to 'modify society in the direction of social change'.[12] The mob unwittingly carried the heresy of social justice as a more powerful weapon than its clubs and staves.

Shakespeare's crowd-scenes belong, then, to the period of the emergence of the city mob as a force to be reckoned with in English politics. Though interpreted by modernist critics as if they demonstrated universal imperatives of law and order, no part of Shakespeare's writing is more entangled with the exigencies of his own time and place. That much is clear from his first reaction to the London mob itself, the venomous fourth act of *Henry VI, Part Two*, written during July 1592,[13] when he was suddenly diverted from the palace intrigue that comprises the remainder of the play to fire off an incandescent version of Jack Cade's 1450 rising. A blueprint for all his later and more famous crowd-scenes, this travesty of evidence is itself a revealing example of Tudor historiography, an instance of the brazen manipulation of documentary records practised to buttress the regime. Its source was Edward Hall's 1548 Chronicle, itself a glorification of the ruling dynasty, but to blacken Cade and his followers still further Shakespeare conflated this account with reports of the Peasants' Revolt of 1381, and Cade with Wat Tyler, producing by this synthesis what critics loftily imagine as a more 'timeless impression of the chaos that occurs whenever the irrational phantoms of desire walk unchecked'. Shakespeare, as Brockbank explained, dispenses with the vulgar 'Positivist view that truth is co-extensive with the facts', to 'emphasise a more significant movement of cause and effect'. So Cade, whom Hall respects as 'a young man of goodly stature and pregnant wit', 'a subtle captain', 'sober in communication' and 'wise in disputing', whose advisers were 'schoolmasters and teachers', is metamorphosed into a cruel, barbaric lout, whose slogan is 'kill and knock down', and whose story as 'the archetype of disorder' is one long orgy of scatological clowning, arson and homicide fuelled by an infantile hatred of literacy and law.

Even the critics are unsettled by the stridency of this cartoon, though they defend it, of course, by maintaining that to libel the workers' leader as a boorish thug is actually to cut 'through the immediate situation' to highlight the 'basic human pattern . . . when any demagogue is successful in persuading the people to act as an uncritical collective'. It does not matter, therefore, that the tax reforms of the Chronicle Cade are described as 'profitable for the commonwealth', for what counts in the eyes of the academy is 'the impious spectacle of the proper order reversed' when workers are driven 'by their leader's vulgar energy and simplifications' into 'taking the law into their own hands'. Hall has Cade 'prohibiting men murder, rape or robbery'; whilst Shakespeare has him inflaming the people's blood lust. In Hall Cade co-operates with 'the king's justices'; whereas in Shakespeare he executes lynch-law. Hall's Cade is 'seen [to be] indifferent' in punishing friend and foe alike; Shakespeare's hangs the gentry for the cut of their clothes. Hall's Cade believes his protest is 'honourable to God and the king'; to seize the throne for himself, Shakespeare's calls the king a usurper. Faced with such systematic misrepresentation of sources, the critics have been in no doubt which of these versions of history is closer to what they see as the essential truth about all social protest. It is Shakespeare, 'with the authority of his moral and artistic insight', who has explored through Cade 'what happens when authority passes to the uninstructed multitude'.[14]

Authority and authorship, this slippage makes clear, are synonymous in Shakespearean politics. In *Julius Caesar,* the worst atrocity by the mob is when they 'tear' the poet Cinna 'for his bad verses' (III, iii, 30); and Cade's most vainglorious crime is when he orders his men to 'burn all the records of the realm' in the flames as the city blazes. To the writer of these scenes, rebellion is the rage of the illiterate against the written word, and the rioters' first act is therefore to lynch the aptly named Clerk of Chartham, 'with his pen and ink-horn about his neck', in fury 'that parchment, being scribbled o'er, should undo a man'. The civil war in this play is between an educated elite who 'write courthand' and sign their names and the illiterate mass who make their mark and communicate only in plain, rude English. So Cade's kangaroo court condemns anyone who 'can write and read', or speak French or Latin, accusing the well-to-do of 'erecting a grammar school', causing 'printing to be used', or having 'built a paper-mill'. Christopher Hill remarks that there is some poetic justice in this hatred of education, since a third of those sentenced to death in Shakespearean London 'escaped by pleading benefit of clergy' (including the murderer, Ben Jonson).[15] But here the rebels' grievance that 'because they could not read' the law 'hast hang'd them', is turned by them against 'All scholars, lawyers, courtiers [and] gentlemen' in an indiscriminate bloodbath. And the height of Cade's impudence is when he abolishes all statutes and decrees that henceforth 'the laws shall come out of my mouth . . . my mouth shall be the parliament of England'. There is an animus in these episodes, and in those satirising the people's garbled testimony or laboured puns, which gives the lie to those, like Leavis, who see Shakespeare as rooted firmly in an oral culture. On the contrary, what is advertised here, in a text that was to be one of his earliest publications, is the sneering impatience with the language of peasants and artisans of the literate parvenu. Both in subject matter and in their cavalier distortions, these scenes are a triumph of text over orality. Shakespeare's Cade is a Gargantuan Big Mouth, but nothing could be more unlike the demotic laughter of Rabelais than the young playwright's revulsion from the *vox populi* and the stinking breath he insists goes with it.

Cade's supporters hate 'men that talk of a noun, and a verb'. They are mirror opposites, therefore, of the writer himself, who established a favourite comic practice here of ridiculing all who had not benefited from grammar school. His debunking of bookmen came later; in this very early work he laid bare the cultural prejudices he brought to writing. So, when he parodies popular religion in Cade's sermon lamenting that 'the skin of an innocent lamb should be made parchment', it is an entire rival system of oral authority which the learned writer's script has 'scribbled o'er' to deface it. The writer portrays the poor as philistine vandals, but there is in fact a more subtle vandalism at work when history is rewritten to flatter lawyers and common speech is degraded into crass literalism. Clearly, Shakespeare was wearily familiar with the way in which (as Coriolanus mimics it) the commons 'sighed forth proverbs – / That hunger broke stone walls; that dogs must eat; / That meat was made for mouths, that the gods sent not / Corn for the rich men only' (I, i, 204–7); and Charles Hobday has itemised his knowledge of the egalitarian tradition that descended by word of mouth in peasant and artisanal communities.[16] But when he gave Cade 'the old seditious argument', as it was known, that 'Adam was a gardener', or had the rioters complain that 'it was never merry world since gentlemen came up', he exploited this familiarity with derision. His stage mobs flaunt the peasants' 'clouted shoon' and craftsmen's 'leather aprons', but these radical emblems are staged to look farcical. Son of a provincial glover whose only testimony is the mark he scratched beside his name in borough records, Shakespeare, who seems to have discriminated between even his own daughters, educating his favourite to write and leaving the other illiterate, used his professional debut to signal scorn for popular culture and identification with an urban elite in whose eyes authority would henceforth belong exclusively to writers.

'There is no document of civilisation which is not at the same time a document of barbarism': Benjamin's sage aphorism was never truer than when the written text held power over life and death in Shakespeare's England.[17] Yet when the stage Cade is butchered by Alexander Iden, a Kentish squire and prototype of the Adamic Kent in *King Lear*, modernist critics applauded what they saw as the victory of 'immaculate authority' over 'the intrusive presence of "Big Brother"', a restoration of 'national sanity' by 'an ornament of the professional classes, perhaps a civil servant or local government officer, a family man with fixed habits and no ideas above his station'. As Benjamin warns, it is through such 'cultural treasures' as the Shakespearean text that 'Whoever has emerged victorious participates to this day in the triumphal procession in which the present rulers step over those they have defeated':[18] but what criticism quaintly salutes in this way as symbolic of the repulse of the labour unions by the commuters of the Home Counties, is, of course, nothing but the obliteration of popular history by Tudor propaganda. Far from securing 'the stability of society', the death of Cade in Shakespeare's play marks an irreparable split in English life, with what Peter Burke has termed 'The Withdrawal of the Upper Classes' from popular culture, a rift that led to the eclipse of folk tradition by the literate world-view.[19] After Cade, there is no commoner who speaks so much in Shakespearean drama, and 'The Triumph of Lent' is the title Burke gives to this silencing of the people's voice in the writers' culture of print and profit. Looked at from this perspective, the playhouses erected in London from 1576 can no longer be idealised as organic developments from the medieval inn-yard or street-theatre, the foci of 'a national culture rooted in the soil', as Leavis taught. In the context of the taming and suppression of customary culture – the culture, as Burke describes it, of Carnival – Shakespeare's commercial playhouse, with its joint-stock ownership, must be viewed as part of the apparatus of the English nation-state: as an institution, in fact, of separation and enclosure, where bourgeois 'order' was legitimated by the exclusion of the 'anarchy' and 'sedition' of the mob. In practice, the ideological function of the 'wooden O' was less to give voice to the alien, outcast and dispossessed, than to allow their representatives the rope to hang. Rather than perpetuating a true liberty of the Bankside, the Globe was an institution where Carnival was disciplined by Lent.

'The Triumph of Lent' is a phrase with particular relevance to the Cade interlude, which is often called a saturnalia. A Lord of Misrule, who capers when wounded 'like a wild Morisco' (or morris dancer), and whose name connotes a barrel of herrings and an upstart caddie, Cade personifies the topsy-turvydom of Carnival, with his proclamation of a Land of Cockaigne, where gutters run wine, bread is dirt cheap, and 'all the realm shall be in common'. And in his energy and appetite this Kentish Green Man is the type of 'lusty guts' alleged to lead the 'wildheads of the parish' in the folk games reviled by Puritans like Stubbes. Shakespeare's researches into the history of Jack Cade's incursion into London led him to the inglorious story of Sir John Falstaff's cowardice before the peasants when he fled his Southwark property, and there is an affinity between the two anti-heroes, since Cade is a draft for the carnivalesque grotesque body to be comprehensively repudiated in the fat knight. But here Silenus has a precise artisanal habitat. Rampaging through Southwark, over London Bridge, and 'Up Fish Street! Down Saint Magnus' Corner!' Cade and his 'rabblement' follow the exact route into the heart of civilisation as so many Elizabethan apprentices in their Shrovetide and May Day tumults, when they forayed out of the festering suburb into the financial quarter of the City. Their pillaging then was targeted on the brothels frequented by their employers, but Shakespeare recycles the old smear that the workers need only an excuse to fornicate, as the rebels run to the Cheapside prostitutes or rape the aldermen's daughters and wives as Cade urges. Similarly, he reproduces one of the' deepest establishment myths about the populace when its festive images of meat and gluttony are literalised as cannibalism. For like Gargantua, Cade starts his career with a cattle-slaughtering feast, but in this dystopia the carcasses he hews belong to the rich, hacked down 'like sheep and oxen', their 'throats cut like calves' and skin 'flayed to make dog's leather'. 'Thou hast behav'st thyself as if thou had'st been in thine own slaughter-house', he tells his henchman, Dick, the Butcher of Ashford, rewarding him with a 'licence to kill' in Lent. Butchers, Michael Bristol notes, fought fishmongers in the rite of spring that schematised the medieval economy; but that key Shakespearean metaphor of 'appetite' as a 'universal wolf' (*Troilus and Cressida*, I, iii, 121) has its origin in a class nightmare of Carnival as carnage. So, though Bakhtinians correctly detect the carnivalesque elements in Shakespeare, they underestimate the extent to which these are contained and contradicted.[20] For when the writer has Cade's head impaled, his text arrogates to itself Lent's finality, bringing down the curtain on both comedy and communism.

Cade's bleeding head might be taken as symbolic of the silenced 'World of Carnival' – traditional popular culture – doomed from Shakespeare's time to speak only through the 'distorting viewpoints and intermediaries' of the dominant written culture.[21] Instead, these scenes have been interpreted as a permanently topical warning against the dangers of 'excessive concern for social justice'. Reinforcing the bourgeois myth that workers have no history of their own, but are for ever exploited by troublemakers, critics regularly treat Cade as the 'timeless embodiment of lawlessness', and ignore the signs that the motive for this character assassination stem from Shakespeare's own involvement in social process.[22] In fact, his defamation of Jack Cade was prompted by a crisis in London's culture which, perhaps more than other incidents, explodes the legend of a democratic Bankside. The clue to this local motivation lies in the characterisation of the rebels. The 1450 rising had been an agrarian *jacquerie*, like that of 1381, but Shakespeare changed the occupations of the rioters, who appear not as medieval peasants but Renaissance artisans. Specifically, he made Cade a shearman – a clothing worker involved in the garment-finishing process – and his lieutenants mostly weavers or other 'handicraftsmen' in allied clothing industries. Hill relates how, when the Civil War began, it was reckoned that 'the clothiers through the whole kingdom were rebels by their trade', because of the long-standing radicalism of the textile industry – technically and economically the most advanced sector of artisanal capitalism – and how it was from the clothing workers that the Levellers and other revolutionary groups drew their strength.[23] So, when 'Jack Cade the clothier' erupts into Shakespeare's play, unaccountably railing against the 'silken-coated' army, and condemning the 'serge' and 'buck'ram' lords for clothing their horses in velvet, 'when honester men go in hose and doublet', it is the militant clothing industry of London in the 1590s, rather than, as critics maintain, the 'prejudices of the workers of any age', which forms the context.[24]

'Jack Cade the clothier means to dress the commonwealth, and turn it, and set a new nap on it': the first words of Shakespeare's caricature are a sarcastic résumé of the fiercest Elizabethan industrial dispute, coupled with a gibe at the skills of the shearmen. In 1592 the London clothing workers were fighting a rear-guard action against long-term structural changes in their industry. Their problems arose from the capitalisation of the textile business by dealers determined to break the monopolies and regulations of the gilds and to force open a free market in goods and labour, and their struggle centred on the defence of the city's finishing crafts, undermined by the export of unfinished fabric or cloth dressed in the provinces. Clothing workers were on the sharp end, that is to say, of developments in urban capitalism known to Weber as 'non-legitimate domination', whereby control of production was wrested from producers by free-trading wholesalers or trading companies, in a shift 'from gild-based production to a putting-out or domestic system'.[25] The stresses of this deregulation were most acute in London's suburban parishes, notably St Olave's, Southwark, adjoining the theatre district, where the local shearmen, weavers and feltmakers were unprotected by the City by-laws that held north of the river, and entrepreneurs could breach their apprenticeship walls with impunity. There too the tension was aggravated in the 1570s and 1580s by the influx of war-refugees from Europe, whose competition revived the racism that had long been a virulent factor in London's industrial relations. Yet if these French and Dutch artisans were resented, the middlemen were detested, since their dealing in undressed broadcloth or Midlands hosiery threatened the very survival of the London industries and drove a wedge within the gilds themselves between the craftsmen and the merchants who traded with them. As it happens, Shakespeare would have a financial stake in these capitalist developments, and documents reveal him in the hated role of middleman. They record how in 1598 he invested £30 in a consignment of 'knitted stockings' at Evesham, the main depot for Cotswold woollens, helping to make a shrewd killing in a market where he was assured that 'you may do good, if you can have money'. With his background in the leather industry, Stratford contacts (who tipped him off on this occasion), and London lodging in St Helen's, Bishopsgate, beside Leaden Hall, the largest wool warehouse in Europe, Shakespeare was ideally placed to profit from speculation in Midlands textiles, and his part in this enterprise perfectly illustrates the activities that were driving London craftsmen out of business by diverting trading capital.[26]

Shakespeare's text makes crude humour out of the business of taking 'up commodities', such as 'a kirtle, a petticoat, and a smock'; but historians of the Tudor wool trade describe such broking by letter as a revolutionary technique that would erode the public market by spreading a network of invisible transactions, which an investor such as Shakespeare could manipulate from a distance. By the end of the seventeenth century the new system had destroyed the London industry and funded cheaper manufacture in West Yorkshire;[27] but Cade's plan to 'dress the whole commonwealth' is Shakespeare's mockery of the Elizabethan finishing workers' utopian solution to the conflict, which was to rig an export monopoly, a scheme that would eventually see its day in Alderman Cockayne's well-named but ill-fated project of 1614 to export only finished material. Similarly, when Cade proposes to the rebels to 'apparel all in one livery', Shakespeare is not anticipating Orwell, as critics like to believe, but sniping satirically at the cloth workers' dream of extending the jurisdiction of the Livery Companies to the unarticled labour in London's extra-mural parishes. These scenes are peppered with slighting allusions to the clothing industries which make Shakespeare's partisanship explicit. It is even sharper in the episode he interpolated earlier in his play, when an armourer's apprentice, Peter Thump, strikes his master dead for disloyalty to the Crown (II, iii, 60–102). In 1592 there were rich pickings for profiteers (such as the Eastlands Company) supplying Essex's 'silken-coated' troops in France,[28] and Shakespeare, who took care to depict his villain as a disaffected veteran returned from Ireland, aligned himself squarely with the empire and the free market in timely opposition to London's small masters.

If it was mercantile money that talked on Shakespeare's earliest stage, however, the industrial metropolis had at least one spokesman in the *petit-bourgeois* press. There, in adventure stories that heroised the 'famous Cloth Workers of England', such as *Jack of Newbury* (1597) – the life of the historical John Winchcomb, a 'poor broad cloth Weaver' who rose to fortune by sticking with his workers – Thomas Deloney voiced the artisanal point of view which Shakespeare attributes to Cade. Nostalgically evoking a world of good fellowship and social mobility that was, in fact, fast coming to an end with the exclusion of journeymen from mastership in the gilds, Deloney canvassed among the literate the creed (which he attributed to an idealised Henry VIII) that 'the trade of Clothing brought benefit to the whole Common Wealth', and that just as the country needed clergy, 'So is the skilful Clothier necessary'. Himself a Norwich weaver, he wrote, he said, for the 'poor people who laboured to get their own bread', so his hero, Jack, embodies a collective fantasy that is not without malice towards those, like the jester Will Summers or foreign merchants, who deserve to be duped. Deloney's Land of Cockaigne is an artisanal paradise where 'city slickers are outwitted by unsophisticated and innocent labourers'; but when the London weavers distributed a bare twenty copies of a pamphlet in 1595, protesting that they were 'greatly decayed and injured' by immigrants and speculators, it was Deloney who was gaoled for it.[29] The fate of the workers' writer differed from that of the dramatist who spoke for his patrons at court and the merchant oligarchy.

The clothing workers' fight was doomed to fail. Their nostalgic corporatism was bound to be swept aside by the market forces Shakespeare heralded. Nor was there a place in the new capitalism for the representation that had united men and masters in the gild, as Shakespeare himself recognised, when he had the commons' petitions against enclosure and abuses spurned in his play by government. Disenfranchised as the merchants rewrote the rules to suit the profit motive, London artisans turned increasingly during the sixteenth century towards unofficial forms of solidarity and action. Typical was the story of the Southwark felt-cap makers whose workshops abutted the playhouses, swindled in the trade by the retail Haberdashers Company and undercut by provincial competition. Their plight was a chronic scandal in the Borough, but when they elected two 'Orators' and appealed for relief in 1579 they were discredited by the classic ploy: they had been duped, the merchants said, by agitators: 'Bradford and Caunton, two of the worst sort of feltmakers, haunters of taverns where they plot devices to live by other men's goods. The best and honestest feltmakers make no such petition.' Throughout Elizabeth's reign the feltmakers were denied an organisation and charter of their own to set them free from such domination by the haberdashers; yet in 1585 they were lectured that if they had only put their complaints about sweatshops and untrimmed goods formally in writing, 'they might have been better considered'.[30] It was at this point, therefore, with the breakdown of social consensus and the blocking of redress, that 'mechanic men' such as these began to organise in the illegal combinations that evolved into the city mob.

The district into which the players intruded with their Rose Theatre in 1587 was home to a complex community whose centre, known as the Maze, was a warren of tenements off the High Street, where 'strangers and other poor people' worked unprotected by legal safeguards in the Liberty of the former Bermondsey Abbey. Like every garment industry, Southwark's production line involved each stage of 'hat manufacture and its branches of hat-block makers, hat-dyers, hat-lining- and leather-cutters, hat shag-makers, hat-tip makers, bonnet-string makers, furriers and trimming-makers'.[31] With such an extended structure, it is not surprising that garment workers have been the advance guard of industrial action, and the flash-point in Southwark came in the sweltering summer of 1592, when conjunctural circumstances similar to those that ignited the explosion in 1517 recurred to exacerbate the long-term confrontation. The price of wool, which had doubled in five years, now stood at its highest level, and the consequence was that the poorest feltmakers were squeezed out of the market. In 1577 a government inquiry had found that soaring prices were hiked by middlemen, but in the manufacturing parishes it was inevitably the neighbouring foreigners who were blamed for outbidding locals. As on Evil May Day, the economic crisis inflamed anti-alien sentiment and the problems of unemployment and immigration became enmeshed. So in May 1592 the Lord Mayor petitioned on behalf of 'the natural born subjects and freemen of the city' who were 'being supplanted by the strangers and their living taken from them', while Dutch manufacturers from Southwark complained in turn to the Privy Council about harassment. Alarmed ministers responded by ordering an urgent census of the extent of the aliens' operations, hoping not to exacerbate hostilities. Evidently their investigators failed in this, because on 6 June officers of the local Marshalsea Prison arrested a feltmaker and his apprentices for offences against aliens, bursting into his house in Bermondsey Street 'with daggers drawn' and 'a most rough and violent manner', in a raid that would spark one of London's worst disorders of the century and end seventy-five years of civic peace.[32]

In their study of England's 'last rising', the 'Captain Swing' riots of 1830 in the South, Hobsbawm and Rudé outline the actions available to workers resisting the onslaught of capitalism in the early modern period, and emphasise that these 'essentially modified traditional collective practices' such as 'annual feasts, processions and waits'. Victims of the decay of customary culture, the poor fell back during times of crisis on the 'World of Carnival' which once defined and guaranteed their roles. So, in 1830 the Sussex 'Bonfire Boys' exploited 5 November by burning farmers' ricks, just as the Yorkshire Luddites went the season's round of 'Ned Ludd's Mummers' at Christmas in 1812, yelling for alms and satisfaction outside the mill-owners' doors with the ludic licence of blackened faces and women's clothes. Those who broke the rules were thereby shamed to 'play the game', as the new machinery which was breaking up the old communities was confronted by the hallowed rituals of dependence and obligation. And in 1592 the Southwark clothing workers similarly turned, for want of an ideology, to a time-honoured cultural script. For as Paul Slack confirms, in the crisis of the 1590s Londoners clung to fragments of what traditions they could, 'whether in streets, in alehouses or in church'.[33] They marched, therefore, as they always had, through the Borough on 11 June, 'Old Midsummer', the Feast of St Barnabas and the longest day, to light a bonfire and perform a play . . .

. . . But on Midsummer evening in 1592 the rite of solstice came to a premature and unexpected end. For at 'about eight' the celebrations were suddenly stopped when 'the Knight Marshal's men issued forth with their daggers drawn and basti-nadoes in their hands, beating the people' indiscriminately and killing 'several innocent persons' among the spectators in the street. In the ensuing 'tumult' the officers lost control and, despite laying about with swords, were only saved from lynching by the arrival on the scene of a hasty posse with the Sheriff and Lord Mayor. As the bodies were laid out in Maypole Lane, and the officers ignominiously withdrew, some 'principal offenders' were picked from the apprentices and carted to Newgate gaol. Midsummer madness had brought the London cloth workers a real carnival of blood.[34]

From revelry to rebellion was a short semantic step in the symbolism of Renaissance culture, and reading between the Carnival signs the Knight Marshal's men had evidently decided that the cloth workers' riotous play had taken it, and that their raucous mêlée was a danger to the prison. But the question for the author-ities in getting to what Burghley called 'the bottom of that outrageous fact', was the one that vexes historians in pursuit of the 'elusive quarry' of popular culture, whether, as Burke puts it, 'one is considering songs or rituals: who is saying what, to whom, for what purpose and to what effect?'[35] Interpreting the signs is always problematic in the case of riots and risings, he explains, because what we know about them is filtered through officials who are 'unreliable mediators', interested in interpreting 'as a "blind fury" a movement which the participants saw as a planned defence of specific traditional rights'.[36] What seems to have happened outside the Marshalsea was an instance not of spontaneous combustion but of the early modern sequence depicted by Burke as a 'switching of codes', when festival erupted into political action;[37] but the dilemma for the state was how to determine the point when the ritualised theatre of protest ignited into a political 'theatre of rebel-lion', in Buchanan Sharp's phrase, especially when the rituals consisted, as they did at Midsummer, of such violent actions as lighting fires, burning effigies and leaping through flames 'with frantic mirth'.[38] 'Actions speak louder than words, and riots may be seen not only as "blind fury", but dramatic expressions of popu-lar attitudes and values';[39] yet deafness to rough music had a long history, and the instinct of magistrates must have been to hear the 'confused noise' of the bonfire boys with the same bewilderment as Chaucer had listened to the 'shrill shouts' of 'Jack Straw and his men' when they attacked the Flemish weavers in 1381 on this same ground:

> Of bras thay broghten bemes[1], and of box[2], [[1] trumpets / [2] wood]
> Of horn, of boon[3], in whiche they blewe and pouped [[3] bone]
> And therwithal thay shryked and houped:
> It semed as that heven sholde falle.[40]

When he reported to the government next morning the Lord Mayor was equally convinced that the whole blame lay with the cloth workers, and that 'the principal actors' were 'certain of the feltmakers out of Bermondsey Street', who had 'assembled by occasion of a play' only as a 'pretense' to spring their workmates from the gaol . . .

. . . The revival of the Midsummer watch was a symptom of the fragmentation of London's consensus, rather than, as critics still believe, a celebration of social harmony.[41] Until 1539 the Midsummer Corpus Christi procession had indeed expressed corporate solidarity, but after that year the civic festival was postponed from the volatile summer months, to evolve into the November Lord Mayor's Show. Now the restoration of the tattoo for purposes of social control coincided with the refinement of the mayoral feast as propaganda, with the commission for the 1591 inauguration of a masque, *Descensus Astraea* by George Peele. There the incoming Mayor, William Webbe, was flattered with a conceit of England's textile manufacture as a seamless 'web' spun effortlessly by the shepherdess Elizabeth/Astraea from the fleece of her contented flock. London's public was splitting into separate audiences with radically opposing visions of the city's industry and wealth. Even the days on which Londoners enjoyed their pleasures had diverged. Thus, 11 June 1592 had been a Sunday, and ever since the opening of his playhouse in Southwark, Philip Henslowe had obeyed the prohibition on all 'interludes and plays on the Sabbath', barring city workers therefore (as James I complained) on the only afternoon of the week when they did not officially 'apply their labour'. In the Sabbatarian debate dividing England before the Civil War, London's commercial theatre sided with the wealthy masters who saw a strict observance as the means to police their workforce. So, while the poor of Southwark marked the ancient day of the sun, Shakespeare's playhouse had been locked on them, as always, to mark the modern Sunday. As the crowd gathered around 'the Bull Ring' and the maypole in the Borough Street to honour 'Barnaby the bright', the Rose stood silent as the site and symbol of a new phase of metropolitan culture: partitioned, disciplined and hierarchic.[42]

The modernist nostalgia for Elizabethan England as a model of some classless, pre-industrial *Gemeinschaft* cannot withstand the picture that is emerging of London's crystallising class consciousness in the acute social and economic crisis of the 1590s. And with it has also been discredited the unitary conception of power implicit in the received version of 'The Elizabethan World Picture'. As critics such as Jonathan Dollimore and Alan Sinfield remind us, far from constituting a mono-lithic centralised power system, early modern England was rent by a competitive interplay between numerous blocs and factions, who contested hegemony through a multiplicity of economic, political and cultural practices. Power was splintered and dispersed in this polity, and just as the English state knew a mosaic of distinct and contradictory traditions of law, so authority was legitimated through not one but a plurality of Elizabethan cultures.[43] Nowhere was this fragmentation better demonstrated than in Southwark, with its patchwork of inconsistent jurisdictions, rival courts and capricious liberties. And the events of 1592 exposed the intricacy of the mechanism, for as a Commission of Inquiry sat through the smouldering summer, all parties issued conflicting interpretations of the 'tumult'. Even the rioters were defended when Webbe scandalised the Privy Council and wrecked his credit at court by reversing his opinion after sounding out 'men of best reputation' in the Borough, protesting to Burghley about the habitual violence of the officers, attest-ing that the victims 'were no meddlers but passers by' who 'came to gaze' at the show, and warning that if 'exemplary punishment' were inflicted on the 'sundry apprentices' accused of riot, 'it were best the same were done with an even hand upon the Knight Marshal's men who incited these multitudes by their violent behaviour'. After 'deeper consideration', Webbe now concurred with 'the popular sort', moreover, that the roots of the crisis lay in 'discontentment against strangers such as hinder the trades and occupations of this City', and predicted 'seditions to kindle the coals of further disorder' unless the grievances of the cloth workers were addressed. The feltmakers charivari had at last been heard . . .[44]

. . . It was in the interests of the City Fathers to back their apprentices against the Surrey magistrates and the shocktroops of the royal prison. But Shakespeare's company had no such common cause. With their Sabbatarian alibi, they had every reason instead to seize the opportunity to dissociate themselves from the folk drama of the streets, with its 'whores and zanies' and subversive taint, and to broadcast, as Thomas Nashe now did in *Pierce Penniless*, how their patrons were 'men that are their own masters, as gentlemen of the Court', who crossed to Southwark by river, and that they 'heartily wish they might be troubled with none' of the local 'youth or prentices'. Nashe insulted the City when he defined an upstart as a 'greasy son of a clothier', whose 'weaver's loom framed the web of his honour'; but it was in the plays the actors commissioned that their campaign for respectability was waged fiercest. As the Queen went on progress through the Midlands, to be saluted with masques by John Lyly idealising the wool trade as a country sport of 'shepherds and simplicity, in which nothing is esteemed by whiteness', the professional theatre prepared to impress the censors with a darker product. In the luridly anti-populist *Jack Straw*, Marlowe's frenzied urban horror story, *Massacre at Paris*, and above all the scarifying mêlée appended to *Henry VI*, Shakespeare's company earned exemption from their ban by protesting that, as Nashe swore, far from inciting 'the ruder handicraft servants' to their 'undoing . . . no play they have encourageth any man to tumults or rebellion, but lays before such the halter and the gallows'. Registered with the Stationers on 8 August, when the lives of the clothiers' leaders hung by a thread, this manifesto affiliated the players bluntly with the Crown and its officers against 'any club-fisted usurer, sprung-up by base brokery' who imagined that 'burgomasters might share government and be quarter-masters of our monarchy'. Printed beside a patriotic puff for *1 Henry VI*, which 'ten thousand' had paid to see, Nashe's interference was a reminder not only of the actors' powerful friends, but of the profit lost by the termination of their run. Renaissance drama-clubs were always class-based, Le Roy Ladurie deduces, and festivities frequently ended with the elite raining Lenten blows on the craftsmen's rival league.[45] In 1592 the sweetness of the Rose was likewise to hang before its neighbours the shadow of a noose.

Five years after the Southwark riot, Nashe was still complaining that the 'persecution' of the players by the Lord Mayor and aldermen was like the barbarism of Jack Cade's rebels when 'they hanged up the Lord Chief Justice'.[46] Skilled at hiding behind the Surrey judges from the Recorder of London, the actors knew exactly where they stood in law: outside the old 'moral economy' and in the 'Liberties' of the new market. Their representation of Cade should be interpreted, therefore, within the context of its 'micro-history', as a self-interested aggravation by the Rose managers of an opportune crisis, designed to play off 'the national interest' against the City council. For with his gruesome 'slaughter-house' of victims and plot to rape the burghers' wives, Shakespeare's Cade is a projection of the atavistic terrors of the Renaissance rich. His creator would come to revise his response to popular protest when dearth hit Warwickshire; but it is to his juvenile nightmare of worker revolution that Shakespeareans, with their Freudian sociology and Orwellian imagery, are heirs. If they notice the plebs at all, it is as violators of high culture: like the apprentices who sacked the Cockpit Theatre in Drury Lane on Shrove Tuesday 1617, or the weavers from Ludlow Fair in 1627 who broke into the private performance being given by actors from the Globe and drove them out with flaming brands.[47] The world of Carnival which gave these gestures meaning was suppressed by Puritanism and print, while the literate promoted the writer *The Financial Times* declares to be 'the archetypal bourgeois West Midlander', as the voice of 'the people of Southwark, the people of England of all walks of life, and people of all ages and all countries'. Thus, supporting plans to rebuild the Globe on site in 1985, Southwark's Liberal MP argued that Shakespeare's playhouse 'hadn't been a stuffy theatre putting on plays that none of the locals wanted to see. It was a people's theatre'; and the Labour council of Britain's third most deprived Borough was told that 'The shape of the Globe had united everyone' and would do so again if the 'radical middle' held sway. So, in the fractured inner city the site of Shakespeare's playhouse was treasured as the birthplace of that consensus which was demonstrated by Prince Philip, Lord Olivier, Derno Property Developers and Professor Brockbank, when they joined as patrons to raise the Globe and preserve for ever the foundations of the Rose.[48]

'The British have always enjoyed a little ritual violence', lectured *The Independent*, when poll-tax riots erupted in London in 1990, but though 'the *mobile vulgus*, the fickle crowd, the "mob" of eighteenth century London, was a fearsome sight when it rioted, overturning carriages, setting buildings alight and roaring with drunken pleasure at its own power', no one ever doubted the futility of such 'street theatre', since the 'lusty anarchy' of this 'national game' led inevitably to restoration, and 'the epic of law and order in danger' always ended with rescue from 'the boys in blue'. Thus, the 'dark stereotypes of insurrectionary lawlessness', which the playhouse had staged in Cade's revolt, lived on in the London of the 1990s, along with the belief of Britain's rulers that the scenario of Carnival is one that must proceed, like Shakespeare's, from subversion to containment.[49] It was because of the tenacity of this belief that no one marked the place outside the Marshalsea where the feltmakers had staged their parade. Misdated by editors and then relocated as a 'theatre riot' inside the 'wooden O' itself, even their protest was taken from them to prove that Shakespeare had always spoken for 'the common man'. Yet the illegal combination they began in 1592 would outlast the culture of consensus, for it would be the London weavers, dressed in their uniform green aprons, whose rioting in 1675 carried the mob over the threshold of modern political consciousness (according to Burke); and the feltmakers of 'radical Southwark' whose carnivalesque strike in 1696 was the turning-point from which (the Webbs believed) British Trade Unionism descends.[50] The Midsummer revels of 1592 saw the separation of London's elite theatre from the customs of its neighbourhood; but, patronised by the writer in the antics of Bottom the Weaver, or pilloried in the buffoonery of the Clothier Cade, the cloth worker's festival would have a history of its own.

NOTES

1. Reprinted from RICHARD WILSON, *Will Power: Essays on Shakespearean Authority* (New York and London: Harvester, 1993).

2. Reviews of *Othello* in *The Financial Times* and *The Times*, 12 May 1984, and *The Stage and Television Today*, 24 May 1984; of *Macbeth* in *The Guardian*, 20 October 1984, *The Sunday Times*, 28 October 1984, *The Evening Standard*, 23 October 1984, *The Field*, 10 November 1984; and of *Hamlet* in *The Financial Times*, 6 February 1985.

3. Reviews of *Coriolanus* in *The Guardian*, *The Daily Telegraph*, *The Times* and *The Financial Times* for 17 December 1984.

4. In C. WOOLF AND J. M. WILSON (eds), *Authors Take Sides on the Falklands* (London, 1982), p. 67.

5. F. R. LEAVIS, 'Joyce and the revolution of the word', *Scrutiny*, 2, 2 (September, 1933), p. 200: 'A national culture rooted in the soil'; A. HARBAGE, *Shakespeare and the Rival Traditions* (New York, 1952), p. 25; see also *Shakespeare's Audience* (New York, 1941), *passim*.

6. A. GURR, *The Shakespearean Stage, 1574–1642* (Cambridge, 1980), p. 196; A. J. COOK, *The Privileged Playgoers of Shakespeare's London* (Cambridge, 1983), *passim*.

7. J. P. BROCKBANK, 'The frame of disorder: *Henry VI*', in J. R. Brown and B. Harris (eds), *Stratford-upon-Avon Studies*, Vol. 3: *Early Shakespeare* (London, 1961), p. 87; M. M. REESE, *The Cease of Majesty: A study of Shakespeare's history plays* (London, 1961), p. 126. For the Renaissance background to this prejudice, see C. HILL, 'The many-headed monster in late Tudor and early Stuart political thinking', in C. H. Carter (ed.), *From the Renaissance to the Counter-Reformation: Essays in honour of Garret Mattingley* (London, 1968), pp. 296–324.

8. Brockbank, *op. cit.*, p. 88; A. C. BRADLEY, *Shakespearean Tragedy* (London, 1904), p. 326; R. W. CHAMBERS, 'The expression of the ideas – particularly the political ideas – in the three pages of *Sir Thomas More*', in A. W. Pollard (ed.), *Shakespeare's Hand in the Play of Sir Thomas More* (London, 1920), p. 168; Reese, *op. cit.*, p. 126; D. TRAVERSI, *An Approach to Shakespeare: 'Henry VI' to 'Twelfth Night'* (London, 1968), p. 33. 'The homily on obedience' is quoted from *Certain Sermons Appointed by the Queen's Majesty* (London, 1587).

9. Traversi, *op. cit.*, p. 33.

10. E. HOBSBAWM, *Primitive Rebels* (Manchester, 1971), p. 111; G. RUDÉ, *Ideology and Popular Protest* (London, 1980), pp. 87–8, 138–9; B. MANNING, *The English People and and the English Revolution* (London, 1976); J. F. C. HARRISON, *The Common People: A history from the Norman Conquest to the present* (London, 1984), pp. 193–4. For the European context, see T. ASTON (ed.), *Crisis in Europe, 1560–1660* (London, 1965); and D. R. KELLY, *The Beginning of Ideology: Consciousness and society in the French Reformation* (Cambridge, 1981), p. 340.

11. See D. BEVINGTON, *Tudor Drama and Politics* (Cambridge, Mass., 1968), pp. 233–4. For the minor 1554 disturbance, in which the heckling was led by a Protestant clothier, see J. PROCTOR, *The History of Wyatt's Rebellion* (London, 1554), pp. 54–5. For the passivity of urban society in Tudor England, see P. ZAGORIN, *Rebels and Rulers, 1500–1660*, Vol. I: *Society, States and Early Modern Revolution* (Cambridge, 1982), p. 235; and P. CLARK AND P. SLACK (eds), *Crisis and Order in English Towns, 1500–1700* (London, 1972), p. 19. The crisis in London in the 1590s is discussed in P. CLARK (ed.), *The European Crisis of the 1590s: Essays in comparative history* (London, 1985), Chap. 1; in M. J. POWER, 'London and the control of the crisis of the 1590s', *History*, 70 (October, 1985): pp. 371–85; and S. RAPPAPORT, 'Social structure and mobility in sixteenth-century London: part I', *London Journal*, 9 (1983), pp. 128–31.

12. E. P. THOMPSON, 'The moral economy of the English crowd in the eighteenth century', *Past and Present*, 50 (February, 1971), pp. 76–136; Hobsbawm, *op. cit.*, pp. 110–13; E. LE ROY LADURIE, *Carnival at Romans: A people's uprising at Romans, 1579–1580* (Harmondsworth, 1981), p. 292. For the topos of the mob as a Hydra without aims, leadership or collective consciousness, see the definitive survey, C. A. PATRIDES, 'The beast with many heads: Renaissance views on the multitude', *Shakespeare Quarterly*, 16 (1965), pp. 241–6.

13. The date of *2 Henry VI* was conclusively established by H. R. BORN in 'The date of *2 Henry VI*', *Shakespeare Quarterly*, 25 (1974), pp. 323–34. Born's conclusion that 'Shakespeare finished the two sequels [to *Henry VI, Part 1*] by late July or early August [1592]' has since been accepted by N. SANDERS, *The New Penguin Shakespeare of 2 Henry VI* (Harmondsworth, 1981), p. 42. Though rival theories are sifted by M. Hattaway in the *New Cambridge* edition (Cambridge, 1991), pp. 60–8, Born's dating remains unchallenged.

14. Reese, *op. cit.*, pp. 122–3, 126; Brockbank, *op. cit.*, pp. 87–8; Sanders, *op. cit.*, pp. 35–6; E. M. W. TILLYARD, *Shakespeare's History Plays* (London, 1944), pp. 183–5. All quotations from Hall's Chronicle are from G. BULLOUGH, *Narrative and Dramatic Sources of Shakespeare: Earlier English history plays* (London, 1960), pp. 113–18.

15. C. Hill, *op. cit.*, p. 303.

16. C. HOBDAY, 'Clouted shoon and leather aprons: Shakespeare and the egalitarian tradition', *Renaissance and Modern Studies*, 23 (1979), pp. 63–78.

17. W. BENJAMIN, 'Theses on the philosophy of history, VII', in *Illuminations*, ed. H. Arendt, trans. H. Zohn (London, 1970), p. 258.

18. Ibld.; Reese, *op. cit.*, p. 125; Sanders, *op. cit.*, p. 37.

19. P. BURKE, *Popular Culture in Early Modern Europe* (London, 1978), pp. 270–81.

20. M. BRISTOL, 'Lenten butchery: Legitimation crisis in *Coriolanus*', in J. Howard and M. O'Connor (eds), *Shakespeare Reproduced: The text in history and Ideology* (London and New York, 1987), p. 215; M. BAKHTIN, *Rabelais and his World*, trans. I. Iswolsky (Bloomington, Ind., 1984), p. 275.

21. C. GINZBURG, *The Cheese and the Worms: The cosmos of a sixteenth-century miller*, trans. J. Tedeschi and A. Tedeschi (London, 1980), p. xv.

22. Reese, *op. cit.*, pp. 125–6.

23. C. HILL, *The World Turned Upside Down: Radical ideas during the English Revolution* (Harmondsworth, 1975), pp. 23, 97 and 112.

24. Reese, *op. cit.*, p. 125.

25. See A. L. BEIER, 'Engine of manufacture: The trades of London', in A. L. BEIER AND R. FINLAY (eds), *The Making of the Metropolis, London, 1500–1700* (London, 1986), pp. 160–1.

26. The documents are reproduced in E. CHAMBERS, *William Shakespeare* (London, 1930), pp. 101–3. For the economic background, see G. UNWIN, *Industrial Organisation in the Sixteenth and Seventeenth Centuries* (Oxford, 1904), pp. 112–25. Cloth amounted to 80 per cent of England's exports by the mid-sixteenth century and had increased on even this proportion by the mid-seventeenth: see A. G. R. SMITH, *The Emergence of a Nation State: The commonwealth of England* (London, 1984), p. 177.

27. P. J. BOWDEN, *The Wool Trade in Tudor and Stuart England* (London, 1962), pp. 70 and 93. For the importance of Evesham in the distribution of Cotswold wool, see p. 30.

28. See BL, Lansdowne MS, 70, fos 13–16, 20–2, for the controversy over the irregular sale of ordnance and matériel to the expeditionary force.

29. T. DELONEY, *The Novels of Thomas Deloney*, ed. M. E. Lawlis (Bloomington, Ind., 1961), 'Jack of Newbury', pp. 3 and 58; 'Thomas of Reading', p. 267; F. O. MANN (ed.), *The Works of Thomas*

Deloney (Oxford, 1912), pp. xxvi–xxx. For the economic background, see F. Consett, *The London Weaver's Company*, Vol. 1 (London, 1933), pp. 146–52.

30. Unwin, *op. cit.*, pp. 130–5.

31. J. Stow, *Survey of the Cities of London and Westminster*, ed. J. Strype (London, 1720), Vol. 2, iv, pp. 74–5; E. Walford, *Old and New London* (London, 1873), pp. 108–9.

32. BL, Lansdowne MS, 71, fo. 15. The minutes from the City records are printed in W. H. Overall (ed.), *Remembrancia: Analytical index to the series of records known as the Remembrancia, preserved among the archives of the City of London, 1579–1664* (London, 1878), p. 474; where, however, they are wrongly dated 30 May, a mistake subsequently followed by Shakespeare scholars. For the feltmakers' petition and the government response, see J. R. Dasent (ed.), *Acts of the Privy Council [APC]*, Vol. 22, p. 506, 2 June 1592. See also P. Williams, *The Tudor Regime* (London, 1979), pp. 329–30.

33. E. Hobsbawm and G. Rudé, *Captain Swing* (London, 1969), p. 18; P. Slack, 'Metropolitan government in crisis', in Beier and Finlay, *op. cit.*, p. 75.

34. Details of the riot are in BL, Lansdowne MS, 71, fos 15 and 17, and the minutes of the Privy Council in *APC*, Vol. 22, pp. 549 and 592; Vol. 23, pp. 19, 24, 28, 220, 232 and 242. For Southwark see D. J. Johnson, *Southwark and the City* (Oxford, 1969), pp. 67–72 and 227–29.

35. *APC*, Vol. 23, p. 20, 9 July 1592; P. Burke, 'Popular culture in seventeenth-century London', in B. Reay (ed.), *Popular Culture in Seventeenth-Century England* (London, 1988), p. 32.

36. Burke, *op. cit.* (1978), p. 76.

37. Ibid., p. 203.

38. B. Sharp, 'Popular protest in seventeenth-century England', in Reay, *op. cit.*, pp. 284–5; R. Chambers, *The Book of Days: A miscellany of popular antiquities* (London, 1869), Vol. 1, p. 815. See R. Darnton, *The Great Cat Massacre and Other Episodes in French Cultural History* (Harmondsworth, 1984), p. 83, for continental analogues.

39. Burke, *op. cit.* (1978), p. 75.

40. G. Chaucer, *The Canterbury Tales*, ed. V. A. Kolve and G. Olson (New York, 1989), pp. 229–30, 'The Nun's Priest's Tale', lines 628–35. See N. Simms, 'Nero and Jack Straw in Chaucer's *Nun's Priest's Tale*', *Parergon*, 8 (April, 1978), pp. 2–12.

41. M. Bristol, *Carnival and Theatre* (London, 1985), pp. 4–5, 201.

42. D. H. Horne (ed.), *The Life and Minor Works of George Peele* (New Haven, Conn., 1952), 'Descensus Astraea', pp. 214–19. *APC*, Vol. 21, p. 324, minute of 25 July 1591. The Rose Theatre reopened in February 1592, and Chambers concludes that by that time the controversy over Sunday playing had been won by the Sabbatarians as far as the commercial theatres were concerned (E. Chambers, *The Elizabethan Stage* (Oxford, 1923), Vol. 1, p. 315; Vol. 4, p. 307). See also Burke, *op. cit.* (1988), p. 39; W. B. Whittaker, *Sunday in Tudor and Stuart Times* (London, 1933), pp. 45–6. For King James's comments, see L. A. Govett (ed.), *The King's Book of Sports* (London, 1890), p. 30. See also C. Hill, 'The uses of Sabbatarianism', *Society and Puritanism in Pre-Revolutionary England* (London, 1964), pp. 145–218. For the increasing segregation of metropolitan culture as the traditional festivals made way for 'professionalised entertainment' with its 'passive audience', see Burke, *op. cit.* (1988), pp. 38–41; and R. Ashton, 'Popular culture in seventeenth-century London', *London Journal* 9 (1983), pp. 3–19.

43. See especially, A. Sinfield, 'Power and ideology: An outline theory and Sidney's "Arcadia" ', *English Literary History*, 52 (1985), pp. 261–5.

44. BL, Lansdowne MS, 71, fo. 17. The cloth workers delivered a further petition against the foreign weavers on 2 July: *HMC* (Historical Manuscripts Commission), 9(d), Salisbury MSS, 4, p. 216. For

the longstanding tug-of-war over jurisdiction in Southwark between the Surrey magistrates and Knight Marshal on one side, and the City of London and the Recorder of London on the other, see Johnson, *op. cit.*, pp. 226–9 and 286–7. Technically the Marshalsea also had its own Court with jurisdiction within the 'verge': a radius of twelve miles of wherever the Queen happened to be.

45. T. NASHE, *The Unfortunate Traveller and Other Works,* ed. J. B. Steane (Harmondsworth, 1972), 'The defence of plays', in 'Pierce Penniless', pp. 64 and 112–15 (and see *Lenten Stuff,* pp. 405–6, for mockery of Deloney's claim that the cloth workers were indispensable to the English economy); R. WARWICK BOND (ed.), *The Complete Works of John Lyly* (Oxford, 1902), Vol. 1, p. 477, 'Speeches delivered to Her Majesty this last progress' (Oxford, 1592); Le Roy Ladurie, *op. cit.*, p. 279. The documents submitted to persuade the Privy Council to exempt the Rose from the ban on assemblies, together with the warrant for the reopening of the theatre dated 13 August 1592 (subsequently rescinded due to plague) are printed in Chambers, *The Elizabethan Stage* (Oxford, 1923), Vol. 1, pp. 311–12.

46. Ibid., Vol. 4, p. 319. Nashe was protesting about the arrest of Ben Jonson and the actors after the performance of *The Isle of Dogs.*

47. See Chambers, ibid., Vol. 1, p. 265 for the Shrove Tuesday apprentice riots, and M. C. BRADBROOK, *The Rise of the Common Player* (London, 1963), p. 115 for the Ludlow episode. Bradbrook assumes that the rioters arrived at the private performance, which was in Shrewsbury, drunk; but for the actual motives and economic background – a bitter struggle to protect local finishing crafts from the entrepreneurial operations of the Midland dealers – see Unwin, *op. cit.*, pp. 186–90.

48. *The Financial Times,* 12 May 1984, review of Young Vic *Othello*; D. DEVLIN, 'Drama behind the scenes', *Southwark Globe,* publicity brochure of the International Shakespeare Globe Centre distributed throughout south London in March 1985; S. HUGHES, 'Simon Hughes MP writes . . .', ibid.

49. *The Independent,* editorial, 10 March 1990.

50. Burke, 'Popular culture in seventeenth-century London', in Reay, *op. cit.*, pp. 46–7; see also R. M. DUNN, 'The London weavers' riot of 1675', *Guildhall Studies in London History,* 1 (1974). For the 'factious people' of 'radical Southwark', see C. Hill, *The World Turned Upside Down: Radical ideas during the English Revolution* (Harmondsworth, 1975), pp. 112 and 354; and for the feltmakers' strike of 1696, see S. WEBB AND B. WEBB, *A History of Trade Unionism* (London, 1894), p. 46; and Unwin, *op. cit.*, pp. 213–27. The riot was misdated by Overall (see note 32); and the account offered in B. MANNING, *Village Revolts: Social protest and popular disturbances in England, 1509–1640* (Oxford, 1988), muddies the waters still more by displacing the events by a year and a month and by echoing the account In *APC* without reference to BL Lansdowne MSS, which provide the City and cloth workers' sides of the conflict. The upshot of these mistakes and the reliance on Chambers by literary critics is that the context of *2 Henry VI* continues to be buried beneath the anachronistic myth of Shakespeare as a 'democrat'. Thus, M. C. Bradbrook automatically assumed that the feltmakers' protest was a 'theatre riot' inside the Rose and evidence of Shakespeare's 'common audience': *op. cit.*, p. 114; and by perpetuating this error C. RUTTER suppresses any connection with popular festivity (*Documents of the Rose Playhouse* (Manchester, 1984), p. 62). Meanwhile, as Penry Williams writes, 'The true tensions and dissatisfactions underlying these disturbances have yet to be revealed' (*op. cit.*, p. 330).

CHAPTER THREE

Descanting on Deformity: Richard III and the Shape of History[1]

MARJORIE GARBER

Marjorie Garber's book *Shakespeare's Ghost Writers* has the subtitle 'Literature as Uncanny Causality'. Her psychoanalytical approach draws on Freud's idea of the uncanny, taking particular interest in phenomena such as doubling, the compulsion to repetition, and the uncanny replication of textual effects. Studying Richard III, Garber adopts Freud's insight into the character which goes some way to account for his strange fascination: 'Richard is an enormously magnified representation of something we can all discover in ourselves. We all think we have reason to reproach nature and our destiny for congenital and infantile disadvantages; we all demand reparation for early wounds to our narcissism, our self-love. . . . Why were we born in a middle-class dwelling instead of a royal palace?'

For Garber, Richard's deformity is 'a catachresis masquerading as a metaphor'. Her own pursuit of the metaphor of deformity verges on deliberate catachresis (the application of a term to a thing it does not properly denote), so that the distortions of the body can stand for the distortions of writing and history. This enables her to enlarge her enquiry to embrace the inevitable deformation that is history, as well as its pre-formation, its textual, scripted qualities. She traces the way in which Richard displaces deformity on to the world and other people, shouldering his way out of the text, carrying images of lameness and unshapeliness even into the language of his modern editors. She interprets not only Richard in the light of Freud but Freud in the light of his account of Richard – specifically, his analogy between deformities of character and the behaviour of nations. As for bodily deformity, 'His twisted and misshapen body' (which, as Garber reminds us, is largely if not wholly the invention of later portraitists and historians) 'encodes the whole strategy of history as a necessary deforming and *un*forming – with the object of *re*forming – the past'.

And thus having resolued all the doubts, so farre as I can imagine, may be moued against this Treatise; it onely rests to pray thee (charitable Reader) to interprete fauorably this birth of mine, according to the integritie of the author, and not looking for perfection in the worke it selfe. As for my part, I onely glory thereof in this point, that I trust no sort of vertue is condemned, nor any degree of vice allowed in it: and that (though it not be perhaps so gorgeously decked, and richly attired as it ought to be) it is at the least rightly proportioned in all the members, without any monstrous deformitie in any of them.

James I, Basilikon Doron

Upon a time when Burbidge played Richard III there was a citizen grew so far in liking with him that, before she went from the play, she appointed him to come that night unto her by the name of Richard the Third. Shakespeare, overhearing their conclusion, went before, was entertained and at his game ere Burbidge came. Then, message being brought that Richard the Third was at the door, Shakespeare caused return to be made that William the Conqueror was before Richard the Third.

John Manningham's Diary, 13 March 1601

How does the logic of ghostly authorship inform – or deform – not only the writing of literature but also the writing of history? As a way of approaching this question, I begin with a passage from *The Comedy of Errors*:

O! grief hath chang'd me since you saw me last,
And careful hours with time's deformed hand
Have written strange defeatures in my face:
But tell me yet, dost thou not know my voice?

(5.1.298–301)[2]

A complex interrelationship between time and deformation is clearly outlined in Egeon's plea for recognition. For time's hand is already deformed as well as deforming, and it is, explicitly, a writing hand. Between the 'deformed hand' and the still recognizable speaking voice comes, as always, the shadow. Hand/voice; written/ spoken. Here, though, that which is *written is* deformed, twisted out of shape, imbued with 'strange defeatures'. The wonderful word *defeature* means both 'undoing, ruin' and 'disfigurement; defacement; marring of features' (*OED*). In *The Comedy of Errors* it is twice used to describe the change of appearance wrought by age upon the face, both in Egeon's speech given above, and in Adriana's lament for her lost beauty, its loss hastened, she thinks, by her husband's neglect: 'Then is he the ground/Of my defeatures' (2.1.97–8). It is unfortunate that 'defeature' has become, as the *OED* points out, 'obsolete', 'archaic', 'now chiefly an echo of the Shakespearean use' because it offers a superbly concrete picture of the *effects* of ruin, the visible, readable consequences of being – or coming – undone.

I would like to arrive, in this chapter, at a consideration of the way in which 'time's deformed hand' writes, and thus defaces, history. The concept of 'defeature' is a useful place to start from, since the visible marks of political defeat are often written, or characterized, in what one age will call history-writing and another, propaganda. My subject, the 'defeatured' player in this exemplum, will be Richard III, an especially interesting case not only because of the fascination that history has exercised on both admirers and detractors, but also because, like Oxford and Bacon in the Shakespeare authorship controversy, Richard III has been the occasion for more amateur detective work, and for the foundation of both English and American societies to clear his name. The Richard III Society, originally known as the Fellowship of the White Boar, was founded in England in 1924; the Friends of Richard III Incorporated, the Society's American counterpart, included among its founding members the actresses Helen Hayes and Tallulah Bankhead.

The most recent full-length study of Richard, by Charles Ross,[3] while in most ways apparently an extremely careful and balanced account, shows the usual pique at this 'amateur' espousal of Richard's cause, which has led in turn to the un-welcome development of amateurs writing history: 'an Oxford professor of English law, a headmaster at Eton, several peers of the realm and a number of historical novelists and writers of detective stories', prominent among them women. Ross cites Josephine Tey, Rosemary Hawley Jarman, and 'a number of others, nearly all women writers, for whom the rehabilitation of the reputation of a long-dead king holds a strange and unexplained fascination'.[4] By implication these women are fol-lowing the self-deluded path of the Lady Anne, whose 'strange and unexplained' capitulation to Richard's suit in Shakespeare's play demonstrates female folly and a slightly sentimental belief that a bad man can be reformed or redeemed by the love of a good woman.

Ross's view of Richard is fact-oriented, balanced but binary. He concludes that Richard 'does not appear to have been a complex man', and that 'any contrarity of "character" of Richard III stems not from what we know about him but from what we do not know about him'.[5] It is the historian's job to discover the facts, and thus to dispel mystery, fantasy, undecidability. With this decidedly 'professional',[6] male, and hegemonic view of the use and abuse of history-writing, set forth in an intro-ductory chapter that is designed to articulate 'The Historical Reputation of Richard III: Fact and Fiction', we may begin our consideration of a dramatic character who is self-described as both deformed and defeatured, himself compact of fact *and* fiction: 'Cheated of feature . . . Deformed, unfinished . . . scarce half made up' (*Richard III* 1.1.19–21).

Shakespeare's use and abuse of history in the *Henry VI* plays, and particularly in *Richard III*, is often viewed as a consequence, deliberate or adventitious, of the move by Tudor historians to classify Richard III as self-evidently a villain, his deformed body a readable text. Shakespeare, in such interpretations, emerges as either an unwitting dupe of More, Hall, and Holinshed, or as a co-conspirator, complicit in their design, seizing the opportunity to present the Plantagenet king defeated by Elizabeth's grandfather as unworthy of the throne, as unhandsome in person as in personality. Either the dramatist was himself shaping the facts for political pur-poses, or he was taken in by the Tudor revisionist desire to inscribe a Richard 'shap'd' and 'stamp'd' for villainy.

In either case, the persuasive power of the portrait has endured. As recently as 1984, for example, René Girard could assert confidently that 'When Shakespeare wrote the play, the king's identity as a "villain" was well-established. The dramatist goes along with the popular view, especially at the beginning. Richard's deformed body is a mirror for the self-confessed ugliness in his soul.'[7]

It is clear, however, that no account of Shakespeare's literary or political motiva-tions in foregrounding his protagonist's deformity is adequate to explain the power and seductiveness of Richard's presence in the plays. Indeed, the very fascination exerted by the historical Richard III seems to grow in direct proportion to an increase in emphasis on his deformity.

It may be useful here to document briefly the ways in which the vagaries of transmission, like a game of historical telephone, succeeded in instating Richard's deformity as the party line. The story of Richard's prolonged gestation, 'held for two years in his mother's womb, emerging with teeth, and with hair down to his shoulders', like the picture of the hunchback, 'small of stature, having a short figure, uneven shoulders, the right being higher than the left', is first told in the *Historia Regium Angliae* of Warwickshire antiquary John Rous, who died in 1491.[8] Polydore Vergil, Henry VII's Italian humanist historian, situated Richard in the scheme of providential history as the antagonist of Tudor ascendancy. Thomas More's *History of Richard III* established the enduring popular image of the villainous king as monster, in an account that artfully ascribes some of the more lurid details to rumor while passing them on:

Richarde the third sonne, of whom we nowe entreate, was in witte and courage egall with either of them, in bodye and prowesse farre vnder them bothe, little of stature, ill fetured of limmes, croke backed, his left shoulder much higher then his right, hard fauoured of visage, and suche as in states called warlye, in other menne other wise. He was malicious, wrathfull, enuious, and from afore his birth, euer frowarde. It is for trouth reported, that the Duches his mother had so muche a doe in her trauaile, that shee coulde not bee deliuered of hym uncutte: and that hee came into the worlde with the feete forwarde, as menne bee borne outwarde, and (as the fame runneth) also not vntothed, whither menne of hatred reporte aboue the trouthe, or elles that nature chaunged her course in hys beginninge, whiche in the course of his lyfe many thinges vnnaturallye committed.[9]

More's account was borrowed by both Hall and Holinshed, and survives substantially unchanged in Shakespeare's *Richard III*. We might note that there is already a disparity between Ross's 'history' and More's. Ross describes Richard's right shoulder as being higher than his left. More, with equal particularity, asserts that 'his left shoulder [was] much higher than his right'. The augmentation *much* puts a spin on the reversal; More grounds his own authority in rhetorical emphasis, and in doing so further distorts the figure of Richard – and the rhetorical figure for which he will come to stand. Both the change of shoulder – toward the sinister – and the emphasis implied by *much* suggest the pattern of amplification and embellishment characteristic of the Richard story throughout its own history.[10]

In the first tetralogy, unusual stress is placed on Richard's physical deformity, which is repeatedly anatomized and catalogued. King Henry calls him 'an indigested and deformed lump' (*3 Henry VI* 5.6.51), Clifford a 'foul indigested lump, / As crooked in thy manners as thy shape!' (*2 Henry VI* 5.1.157–8), and the Lady Anne a 'lump of foul deformity' (*Richard III* 1.2.57). Significantly, he is at once 'misshap'd', unshaped, and preshaped. Born in a sense prematurely ('sent before my time'), feet first, and with teeth already in his mouth, to the wonderment of the midwife and waiting women (*3 Henry VI* 5.6.52; 75–6), he is disproportioned and deformed, but also at the same time unfinished, incomplete, as his own testimony makes plain. Nature, he says in *3 Henry VI*, conspired with love

To shrink mine arm up like a wither'd shrub,
To make an envious mountain on my back
Where sits deformity to mock my body;
To shape my legs of an unequal size,
To disproportion me in every part,
Like to a chaos, or an unlick'd bear-whelp
That carries no impression like the dam.

(3.2.156–62)

In the opening soliloquy of *Richard III*, he recurs to this description, again placing the blame on nature and love:

I, that am rudely stamp'd, and want love's majesty
To strut before a wanton ambling nymph;
I, that am curtail'd of this fair proportion,
Cheated of feature by dissembling nature,
Deformed, unfinished, sent before my time
Into the breathing world scarce half made up,
And that so lamely and unfashionable
That dogs bark at me as I halt by them –
Why I, in this weak piping time of peace,
Have no delight to pass away the time,
Unless to spy my shadow in the sun,
And descant on mine own deformity.

(1.1.16–27)

Generations of readers have been strongly affected by this relation between the deformity and the moral or psychological character of Richard. One such reader was Sigmund Freud, who turned to the example of Richard's deformity to characterize patients who think of themselves as 'exceptions' to normal rules. Such patients, Freud says, claim that 'they have renounced enough and suffered enough, and have a claim to be spared any further exactions; they will submit no longer to disagreeable necessity, for they are *exceptions* and intend to remain so too'.[11] This claim seems apt enough for Richard's opening soliloquy, which Freud goes on to quote: 'that figure in the creative work of the greatest of poets in whose character the claim to be an exception is closely bound up with and motivated by the circumstance of congenital injury'.[12] But when Freud comes to discuss the passage, he finds it to signify not Richard's desire to deflect his energies from love (for which his deformity renders him unsuitable) to intrigue and murder, but rather a more sympathetic message for which the resolution to 'prove a villain' acts as a 'screen'. The 'something much more serious'[13] that Freud describes behind the screen is, essentially, a variation on the theme of the family romance. His Richard declares

Nature has done me a grievous wrong in denying me that beauty of form which wins human love . . . I have a right to be an exception, to overstep those bounds by which others let themselves be circumscribed. I may do wrong myself, since wrong has been done to me – and now [says Freud] we feel that we ourselves could be like Richard, nay, that we are already a little like him. Richard is an enormously magnified representation of something we can all discover in ourselves. We all think we have reason to reproach nature and our destiny for congenital and infantile disadvantages; we all demand reparation for early wounds to our narcissism, our self-love. . . . Why were we born in a middle-class dwelling instead of a royal palace?[14]

For Freud, then, Shakespeare's Richard III represents not so much a particular aberrant personality warped by the accident of congenital deformation, as (or, but rather) the general psychological fact of deformation at birth and by birth, the congenital deformation that results 'in ourselves', in 'all' of us, by the fact that we are born to certain parents, and in certain circumstances, incurring, inevitably, certain narcissistic wounds. Thus for Freud the character of Shakespeare's Richard marks the fact of deformation in the register of the psychological, just as we shall see the same character mark the inevitability of deformation in the registers of the political and the historiographical.

Moreover, in Freud's narrative the political is also explicitly present, though it is signified by a lacuna, a lapse in the progress of his exposition:

For reasons which will be easily understood, I cannot communicate very much about these . . . case-histories. Nor do I propose to go into the obvious analogy between deformities of character resulting from protracted sickliness in childhood and the behaviour of whole nations whose past history has been full of suffering. Instead, however, I will take the opportunity of pointing to that figure . . .'[15]

and so on to Shakespeare and Richard III. What is the 'obvious analogy' he resists? It seems reasonable to associate the 'deformities of character resulting from protracted sickliness in childhood', and, indeed, the 'behavior of whole nations whose past history has been full of suffering' with some specific rather than merely general referent. And if we consider the year in which this essay was first published, in *Imago* 1915–1916, we may be reminded of the circumstances of Germany in the First World War, and, most directly, of the personal circumstances of Kaiser Wilhelm. For Wilhelm II of Prussia was born with a withered arm, a congenital defect that made him the target of gibes from his childhood playmates, including his cousin, who would become Czar Nicholas of Russia. As a recent historical study describes him, Wilhelm II

was a complicated man of painful insecurity – his left arm was withered and useless – who sought in pomp and bluster, in vulgar displays of virility, to mask his handicap and to assert what he devoutly believed in: his divine right to rule. But he craved confirmation of that right and yearned to be loved and idolized. Beyond the flawed character was a man of intelligence and vision.[16]

Wilhelm II, then, is also considered – or considered to have considered himself – an 'exception' to normal rules. Freud takes exception to mentioning him – or even, perhaps, to consciously identifying him – and instead displaces his analysis onto the safely 'literary' character of Shakespeare's Richard. And Richard's opening soliloquy, descanting on deformity, provides a revealing narrative of the ways in which the line between the 'psychological' and the 'historical' is blurred.

'Unlick'd', 'unfinished', 'Indigested' – 'not shaped' for sportive tricks, 'scarce half made up'. The natal circumstances and intrapsychic discourse of Shakespeare's Richard, who ironically resolves, despite his initial disclaimers, to 'court an amorous looking-glass' (1.1.15; 1.2.255; 1.2.262), uncannily anticipate the language of Jacques Lacan's description of the 'mirror stage'. Lacan writes of

the view I have formulated as the fact of a real specific prematurity of birth in man . . . This development is experienced as a temporal dialect that decisively projects the formation of the individual into history. The *mirror stage* is a drama whose internal thrust is precipitated from insufficiency to anticipation – and which manufactures for the subject, caught up in the lure of spatial identification, *the succession of phantasies that extends from a fragmented body-image to a form of its totality that I shall call orthopaedic* – and, lastly, to the assumption of the armour of an alienating identity, which will mark with its rigid stricture the subject's entire mental development.[17]

Characteristically, Richard turns his chaotic physical condition into a rhetorical benefit, suggesting that he can 'change shapes with Proteus for advantages' (*3 Henry VI* 3.2.192); be his own parent and his own author, lick himself into shape – whatever shape the occasion requires. Queen Elizabeth tells him that he cannot win her daughter 'Unless thou couldst put on some other shape' (*Richard III* 4.4.286). But the shape in which we encounter him is already a deformed one – the natural deformity of historical record.

Peter Saccio gives a highly useful account of the evolution of Richard the monster in his study of Shakespeare's English kings:

This lurid king, hunchbacked, clad in blood-spattered black velvet, forever gnawing his nether lip or grasping for his dagger, has an enduring place in English mythology. He owes something to the facts about the historical Richard III. He owes far more to rumor and to the political bias, credulity and especially the literary talent of Tudor writers . . .

As myth, the Tudor Richard is indestructible . . . As history, however, the Tudor Richard is unacceptable. Some of the legend is incredible, some is known to be false, and much is uncertain or unproved. The physical deformity, for example, is quite unlikely. No contemporary portrait or document attests to it and the fact that he permitted himself to be stripped to the waist for anointing at his own coronation suggests that his torso could bear public inspection.[18]

In fact, when we come to examine the portrait evidence, we find that it is of considerable interest for evaluating Richard's alleged deformity. A portrait now in the Society of Antiquaries of London, painted about 1505, shows a Richard with straight shoulders. But a second portrait, possibly of earlier date, in the Royal Collection, seems to emblematize the whole controversy, for in it, X-ray examination reveals an original straight shoulder line, which was subsequently painted over to present the raised right shoulder silhouette so often copied by later portraitists.[19]

Richard is not only deformed, his deformity is itself a deformation. His twisted and misshapen body encodes the whole strategy of history as a necessary deforming and *un*forming – with the object of *re*forming – the past. Shakespeare exemplifies this strategy with precision in a remarkable moment in *Much Ado About Nothing*, when the vigilant and well-intentioned Watch overhears a comment by Borachio. 'Seest thou not what a deformed thief this fashion is?' 'I know that Deformed', remarks the Second Watch wisely to himself, "a has been a vile thief this seven year; 'a goes up and down like a gentleman. I remember his name' (3.3.125–7). Like Falstaff's eleven buckram men grown out of two, this personified concretion takes on an uncanny life of its own in the scene. When Borachio and Conrade are confronted with their perfidy, Deformed is identified as a co-conspirator: 'And one Deformed is one of them; I know him, 'a wears a lock' (169–70), and again, 'You'll be made bring Deformed forth, I warrant you' (172–3). This is precisely what happens to the reinvented historical figure of Richard III.

Created by a similar process of ideological and polemical distortion, Richard's deformity is a figment of rhetoric, a figure of abuse, a catachresis masquerading as a metaphor. In a viciously circular manifestation of neo-Platonic determinism, Richard is made villainous in appearance to match the desired villainy of his reputation, and then is given a personality warped and bent to compensate for his physical shape. For Shakespeare's play, in fact, encodes what we might call a supposititious presupposition. Richard's deformity is not claimed, but rather presupposed, given as fact in service of the question, 'was his villainy the result of his deformity?' – a question not unlike 'have you stopped beating your wife?' Jonathan Culler has shown that the presuppositions that govern literary discourse are mistakenly designed as givens, as 'moments of authority and points of origin', when in fact they are only 'retrospectively designated as origins and . . . therefore, can be shown to derive from the series for which they are constituted as origin'. As with literary conventions, so also with historical presuppositions that constitute the ground of a discursive continuum – here the 'History' of Richard III. To adapt Culler's argument about speech acts, 'None of these [claims of historical veracity] is a point of origin or moment of authority. They are simply the constituents of a discursive space from which one tries to derive conventions.'[20]

Richard's deformity, itself transmitted not genetically but generically through both historiography and dramaturgy, becomes the psychological and dramatic focus of the play's dynamic. Shakespeare has written history backward, taking Hall's and More's objective correlative (he looked the way he was; he should have looked this way because he was in fact this way; he should have been this way, so he must have looked this way) and then presupposed it. Richard's own claim that he can 'change shapes with Proteus for advantages' is a metahistorical comment on his Lamarckian evolution as villainous prototype, every misshaped part an overdetermined text to be interpreted and moralized, descanting on his own deformity. Shakespeare's play brings 'Deformed forth' as an embodiment of the historical process that it both charts and epitomizes.

History is indeed shown by the play to be a story that is deformed from the outset, by its very nature. The figure of Hastings, for instance, seems predestined to bring out particularly uncanny modes of deformation through the ghostly doublings of the Scrivener and the Pursuivant. The Pursuivant (an official empowered to serve warrants) who accosts Lord Hastings in *Richard III* Act 3 scene 2 is also named Hastings, and appears by that name not only in the Quarto text but also in Hall's *Union of the Two Illustre Families of Lancaster and York*. The absence of his name from the Folio has caused some editorial speculation, and the Arden editor's long discussion of this absent name emphasizes the strangeness of the figure:

The entire episode as it appears in F seems pointless: it merely repeats what has already been said by Hastings, adds a superfluous character, and would probably be cut by an economy-minded producer. The fact that it was not cut in Q suggests that someone felt strongly enough about it to retain it, and that the identity of the pursuivant served to make an ironical point.[21]

According to both Hall and Shakespeare, Hastings receives a number of warnings of the fate that is to befall him. His horse stumbles, Stanley dreams that the boar will rase their helms and sends a cautionary word to Hastings, and still Hastings remains adamantly blind to his danger.

At this point, in a remarkable scene reported by Hall and dramatized by Shakespeare, Hastings encounters the Pursuivant who bears his own name. He greets him warmly, reminiscing about the last time they met, when Hastings was fearful for his life. Now, ironically feeling more secure, he rejoices to note that his former enemies, the Queen's allies, have been put to death, and he himself is 'in better state than ere I was' (3.2.104). Hall moralizes with some satisfaction on this latest ironic twist: 'O lorde God, the blyndnesse of our mortal nature, when he most feared, he was in moste surety, and when he reconed him selfe most surest, he lost his lyfe, and that within two houres after.'[22] Shakespeare makes the same point more subtly and forcefully by prefacing this encounter with Richard's decision to 'chop off his head' if Hastings will not agree to their 'complots' (3.1.192–3) and then following it with a knowing aside from Buckingham to the audience. The encounter with the Pursuivant (literally, a 'follower') named Hastings is an example of the uncanny in one of its most direct forms, recognizable and strange at once. The action itself is doubled, as Hastings meets 'Hastings' coming and going, and does not understand what he sees. Hastings's own name functions in a subdued allegorical way throughout this scene, which could be emblematized as *festina lente*, making Hastings slowly.[23]

Another example of doubling and displacement within a historical event is provided by the odd little scene with the Scrivener (3.6). Borrowed by the playwright from his chronicle sources, this scene becomes in its dramatic embodiment a model of history as a kind of ghost writing, since it encodes and 'engross[es]' the fashioning of a rival text. The Scrivener complains that he has spent eleven hours copying the indictment of Hastings 'in a set hand', or legal script. The first draft, or 'precedent' (7), 'was full as long a-doing, / And yet within these five hours Hastings liv'd / Untainted, unexamin'd, free, at liberty' (7–9). The Scrivener laments the duplicity of the times – 'Who is so gross / That cannot see this palpable device' (10–11) 'engross'd' by his own set hand (2) – and yet who dares to say he sees it?

This packed little scene demonstrates at once the play's preoccupation with writing and the preemptive – indeed pre*script*ive – nature of its political design. The Scrivener's indignation is both moral and professional, for his task of scriptwriting had begun before the incident that was to occasion it, and ended too late to authorize – although it will retrospectively 'legitimitize' – the death of Hastings. Since the previous scene has already presented the spectacle of Hastings's decapitated head, displayed by Lovell and Ratcliffe to the London populace and an apparently grief-stricken Richard, the existence, belatedly revealed, of a meticulously crafted indictment undercuts the idea of historical accident or spontaneous action. History is not only deformed but also preformed. Hall recounts the story with particular attention to the length of time the drawing of the indictment would take:

Nowe was thys proclamacion made within two houres after he was beheaded, and it was so curiously endyted and so fayre writen in Parchement in a fayre hande, and therewith of it selfe so long a processe, that every chyld might perceyve that it was prepared and studyed before (and as some men thought, by Catesby) for all the tyme betwene hys death and the proclamacion proclaimyng, coulde skant have suffyced unto the bare wrytyng alone, albeit that it had bene in paper and scribeled furthe in haste at adventure.[24]

Like the disparity between the 'truth' of Shakespeare's play and the historical figure it encodes, the 'palpable device' of the long-prepared indictment and the apparent hasting of Hastings's demise opens the question of authority. Which comes first, the event or the ghost writer?

So far is Richard from being merely the passive psychological victim of his deformity, he early on becomes deformity's theorist and manipulator, not only 'descanting' upon it, but projecting and displacing its characteristics onto others. The death of Clarence is a good example of how this works in the play. Clarence is imprisoned at Edward's order, but at the instigation of Richard. The two murderers who go to the Tower to carry out the execution bear Richard's warrant for entry. And Edward is nonplussed when, at the worst possible time from a political standpoint, Clarence's death is announced. 'Is Clarence dead?' he asks, 'The order was reversed.' 'But he, poor man, by your first order died', says Richard. 'And that a winged Mercury did bear; / Some tardy cripple bare the countermand, / That came too lag to see him buried' (2.1.87–91).

The phrase 'tardy cripple' spoken by the crippled Richard is doubly ironic. He himself is represented in this account not by the cripple, but by 'winged Mercury', fleet of foot, who bears the message of execution – here, in fact, made possible by Richard's forged warrant. The 'tardy cripple', coming 'too lag' to save Clarence, is Richard's displacement of deformity onto the foiled intentions of his well-formed brother the King.

An even more striking instance of this crippling or deforming of the world outside Richard occurs in the scene at Baynard's Castle (3.7) in which Richard enters aloft between two bishops, 'divinely bent to meditation' (62), and Buckingham stages a public entreaty to persuade him to accept the throne. Buckingham describes Richard as the rightful heir, with 'due of birth' and 'lineal glory,' (120–1), able to prevent the resigning of the crown 'to the corruption of a blemish'd stock' (122). But his description of the present state of governance is oddly pertinent (and impertinent) to the man he is apparently addressing:

The noble isle doth want her proper limbs;
Her face defac'd with scars of infamy,
Her royal stock graft with ignoble plants,
And almost should'red in the swallowing gulf
Of dark forgetfulness and deep oblivion. (125–9)

Here the cripple is England, wanting 'proper limbs' (compare Richard's own ironic description of 'me that halts and am misshapen thus' as 'a marv'llous proper man' in the eyes of the Lady Anne [1.2.250–4]). 'Defac'd' and especially 'should'red' make the transferred anatomical references unmistakable.

In the final scene of *3 Henry VI* an ambitious and disgruntled Richard had murmured aside, 'yet I am not look'd on in the world. / This shoulder was ordain'd so thick to heave, / And heave it shall some weight, or break my back' (5.7.22–4). In the scene of the wooing of Anne, Richard protests that Queen Margaret's slanderous tongue 'laid their guilt upon my guiltless shoulders' (*Richard III* 1.2.98), again mischievously calling attention to his own physical deformity; later he is twitted by young York to the same effect ('Because that I am little like an ape / He thinks that you should bear me on your shoulders' [3.1.130–1]). Richard's deformed shoulder is what 'shoulders' the noble isle of England into near oblivion, but in Buckingham's anatomy of the deformed state the 'proper man' is the well derived Richard, who will restore the kingdom to its wonted shape. In both of these cases a condition of deformity is transferred, to the hypothetical messenger or the diseased polity.

Deformity as a self-augmenting textual effect, contaminating the telling of Richard's story as well as Richard's story itself, has been associated with his literary presence almost from the first. More's account of the notorious sermon of Dr Shaa is a good example. Dr Shaa had been persuaded to preach a sermon in which he would impute the bastardy of Edward's sons and point out Richard's physical resemblance to his father the Duke of York. He was to have intoned these sentiments, comparing Richard's visage and behavior to those of the admired Duke, at the point when Richard himself appeared in the congregation. Richard, however, was late, and the key passage already past when he did turn up. Seeing him enter, Dr Shaa, in a flurry of discomfiture, began to repeat his point for point comparison, but 'out of al order, and out of al frame'[25] to the consternation of the audience. The 'shamefull sermon' having backfired, Shaa fled to his house and was forced to 'kepe him out of sight lyke an owl', and soon 'withered away' of shame.

In this little story Dr Shaa sees himself as a writer of predictive history, predicating the future on a repetition of the past (the second Richard an image of the first). But his narrative, out of all order and out of all frame, like Richard's own misshapen body, becomes in More's retelling the perversion and distortion of its intended form and design. Moreover, Dr Shaa himself is contaminated by the rhetorical force of the prevailing mythology about Richard. In the course of More's account Shaa himself becomes deformed, or 'withered', as if by the disseminated agency of his ignoble association with Richard, whose own arm is 'like a with'red shrub' (*3 Henry VI* 3.2.156), 'like a blasted sapling, with'red up' (*Richard III* 3.4.69). The figure of Richard keeps escaping its own boundaries, to appear uncannily replicative in the authors of his twisted history.

Other putative sources for Shakespeare's play have suffered the same suggestive narrative contamination. Francis Seager's complaint, *Richard Plantagenet, Duke of Gloucester*, one of the tragedies published in the 1563 *Mirror for Magistrates*, is described by a prose commentator in the volume as appropriate to its subject. The roughness of the meter was suitable, since 'kyng Rychard never kept measure in any of his doings . . . it were agaynst the *decorum* of his personage, to use eyther good

Meter or order'.[26] The 'decorum of his personage' seems also to have affected the Arden editor, Antony Hammond, who describes this same poem as 'a dull, lame piece of verse'.[27]

Such observations reflect the powerful ghostly presence of the lame and halting Richard. E. M. W. Tillyard, writing of the first tetralogy, remarks upon 'the *special shape* in which the age of Elizabeth saw its own immediate past and its present political problems', and again of 'the *shape* in which the War of the Roses appeared to Shakespeare's contemporaries'.[28]

That 'special shape' is Richard's. Images of 'the beauty of virtue and the deformity of vice' were commonplace in Tudor writings (this particular phrase comes from the second preface to Grafton's *Chronicle at Large* [1569], probably written by Thomas Norton, the author of *Gorboduc*); but when the subject turned explicitly to Richard, the correspondence of physical, moral, and poetic or stylistic deformity seems particularly overdetermined.

Bacon's essay 'Of Deformity', reads like a description of Richard III, though it may have been provoked more directly by Robert Cecil:

Deformed persons are commonly even with nature; for as nature hath done ill by them, so do they by nature; being for the most part, as the Scripture saith, 'Void of natural affection,' and so they have their revenge of nature. Certain there is a consent between the body and the mind, and where nature erreth in the one, she ventureth in the other. . . . Whosoever has anything fixed in his person that doth induce contempt, hath also a perpetual spur in himself, to rescue and deliver himself from scorn; therefore all deformed persons are extreme bold. . . . Also it stireth in them industry . . . to watch and observe the weakness of others that they may have somewhat to repay. Again, in their superiors it quencheth jealousy and it layeth their competitors and emulators asleep; as never believing they should be in possibility of advancement, till they see them in possession. So that, upon the matter, in a great wit deformity is an advantage to rising . . . they will, if they be of spirit, seek to free themselves from scorn, which must be either by virtue or malice.[29]

Samuel Johnson cites these sentiments with approbation in his notes on *3 Henry VI*, making explicit their relevance to Richard ('Bacon remarks that the deformed are commonly daring, and it is almost proverbially observed that they are ill-natured. The truth is, that the deformed, like all other men, are displeased with inferiority, and endeavour to gain ground by good or bad means, as they are virtuous or corrupt').[30] And, indeed, this too may be an instance of overdetermined contamination. Dr Johnson's stress on 'deformities' reflects his own self-consciousness of deformation. Suffering from scrofula as an infant, Johnson was marked throughout life by 'scars on the lower part of the face and on the neck'[31] which he sought to conceal in his portraits by presenting the better side of his face to the painter's view. Until the age of six he bore on his arm an open, running sore, or 'issue', cut and left open with the idea of draining infection. This, and the partial blindness also induced by tuberculosis in infancy, produced in him a 'situation so appalling', writes Walter Jackson Bate, that 'we are naturally tempted to speculate on the psychological results'.[32]

But Johnson's most striking observations about deformity in Shakespeare occur in another connection. 'We fix our eyes upon his graces, and turn them from his deformities, and endure in him what we should in another loathe or despise.' The subject of these comments, astonishingly, is not Richard III, but Shakespeare himself – and the 'deformities' are those of literary and dramatic creation. 'I have seen,' he continues, 'in the book of some modern critic, a collection of anomalies, which shew that he has corrupted language by every model of depravation, but which his admirer had accumulated as a monument of honour.'[33] 'Anomalies', 'corrupted language', 'model of depravation' – all this sounds very like Richard III as he is received by a reluctantly admiring audience. Not only does Richard theorize his own deformity, he generates and theorizes deformity as a form of power.

NOTES

1. Reprinted from MARJORIE GARBER, *Shakespeare's Ghost Writers: Literature as Uncanny Causality* (New York and London: Methuen, 1987).
2. See *The Riverside Shakespeare*, ed. G. BLAKEMORE EVANS (Boston: Houghton Mifflin, 1974). All citations from the plays are to this edition unless noted in the text.
3. CHARLES ROSS, *Richard III* (Berkeley: University of California Press, 1981).
4. Ibid., p. li.
5. Ibid., p. 229.
6. Ibid., p. li.
7 RENÉ GIRARD, 'Hamlet's Dull Revenge', *Stanford Literary Review*, 1 (Fall 1984): 159.
8. GEOFFREY BULLOUGH, ed., *Narrative and Dramatic Sources of Shakespeare* (London: Routledge & Kegan Paul, 1975), 3, p. 223.
9. [SIR THOMAS MORE] *The Yale Edition of the Complete Works of Sir Thomas More*, Vol. 2, *The History of King Richard III*, ed. Richard Sylvester (New Haven and London: Yale University Press, 1963), p. 7. SIR HORACE WALPOLE, one of the earliest defenders of Richard's reputation, characterized More as 'an historian who is capable of employing truth only as cement in a fabric of fiction' (Walpole, *Historic Doubts on the Life and Reign of Richard III* (London: J. Dodsley, 1768; [1965 ed.]), p. 116 and recent scholars have explicitly identified the kind of 'fiction' More is writing as *drama*. Thus A. R. MYERS asserts that 'his history is much more like a drama, unfolded in magnificent prose, for which fidelity to historical fact is scarcely relevant' (Myers, 'The Character of Richard III', originally published in *History Today*, 4 (1954), reprinted in *English Society and Government in the Fifteenth Century*, ed. C. M. D. Crowder (Edinburgh and London: 1967), p. 119; cited in Ross, *Richard III*; and ALISON HANHAM argues that the *History* is really a 'satirical drama' meant to display More's own cleverness rather than his command of fact. (Hanham, *Richard III and His Early Historians* [Oxford: Clarendon Press 1975], pp. 152–90.)
10. I am indebted to Richard Strier for this observation.
11. SIGMUND FREUD, 'Some Character-Types Met With in Psychoanalytic Work', in *Character and Culture*, ed. Philip Rieff (New York: Collier Books, 1961), p. 159.
12. Ibid., p. 160.
13. Ibid., p. 161.
14. Ibid.
15. Ibid., p. 160.
16. FRITZ STERN, *Gold and Iron* (New York: Vintage Books, 1979), p. 437.

17. JACQUES LACAN, 'The Mirror Stage as Formative of the Function of the I', in *Écrits*, trans. Alan Sheridan (New York: W.W. Norton 1977), p. 4.

18. PETER SACCIO, *Shakespeare's English Kings* (New York: Oxford University Press, rpt 1978), pp. 158–9. In a recent study of biography and fiction in Tudor–Stuart history writing (*Biographical Truth: The Representation of Historical Persons in Tudor–Stuart Writing* [New Haven: Yale University Press, 1984]), JUDITH H. ANDERSON notes that historians regularly impeach Shakespeare's play for its lack of fidelity to historical fact, and points out accurately that the play would lose its power if it did not convince the audience that it was 'somehow real history' (p. 111) – 'Despite ourselves, we believe it' (p. 123). Yet Anderson's view of Richard's deformity is a relatively conventional one. Citing Freud, and reasserting the humanistic commonplace that suffering creates art, she describes Richard as 'the misshapen product of his nature and time and also, as we watch him in the play, the product of his own making' (p. 117). Whether self-fashioned or twisted by his own deformity, Richard is seen as compensating for a disability, rather than seizing that disability as the occasion for a theoretical exploration of the nature of deformation.

19. PAMELA TUDOR-CRAIG, *Richard III* (1973); cited in Ross, *Richard III*, pp. 80, 92–3.

20. JONATHAN CULLER, 'Presupposition and Intertextuality', in *The Pursuit of Signs* (Ithaca: Cornell University Press, 1981), p. 177.

21. ANTONY HAMMOND, ed., *King Richard III*, The Arden Shakespeare (London and New York: Methuen, 1981), p. 338.

22. EDWARD HALL, *The Union of the Two Noble . . . Families of Lancaster and York* (1548) cited in Hammond, ed., p. 353.

23. See SIGMUND FREUD, 'The Uncanny' (1919), in *Studies in Parapsychology*, ed. Philip Rieff (New York: Macmillan, 1963), pp. 19–60, especially pp. 38–42 on 'the double' and the repetition-compulsion.

24. Hall, cited in Hammond, ed. p. 354.

25. More, p. 68.

26. Bullough, ed., p. 232.

27. Hammond, ed., p. 87.

28. E. M. W. TILLYARD, *Shakespeare's History Plays* (New York: Collier Books, 1962), p. 72. Emphasis added.

29. FRANCIS BACON, *Essays Civil and Moral* (London: Ward, Lock, 1910), pp. 69–70.

30. ARTHUR SHERBO, ed., *Johnson on Shakespeare* (New Haven and London: Yale University Press, 1968), 7, p. 605.

31. WALTER JACKSON BATE, *Samuel Johnson* (New York: Harcourt Brace Jovanovich, 1979), p. 7. See Bate's sensitive treatment of these physical deformities and Johnson's apparent repression of their origins, esp. p. 9. My thanks to Joseph Bartolomeo for reminding me of the relevance of Johnson's own physical disabilities.

32. Bate, p. 7.

33. SAMUEL JOHNSON, 'Preface to Shakespeare', in Sherbo, ed., 7, p. 91.

CHAPTER FOUR

Stages of History: Ideological Conflict, Alternative Plots[1]

PHYLLIS RACKIN

Phyllis Rackin is one critic who has argued that Shakespeare is to be taken seriously as a historiographer, interested in ways of writing about the past. She argues in this extract from her book *Stages of History* for Shakespeare's awareness of 'the abyss at the center of the historiographic project: the impossibility of recovering the past or of getting behind the historiographic text (whether that text be a written record or a dramatic representation) to discover the always postulated and never graspable fiction called historical truth'.

Rackin tackles directly the question as to where the authority resides which makes history. Is history a Machiavellian spectacle, driven by *Realpolitik* and a human lust for power; or is it a providential one where events are ordained by God? She sees both forces at work in the plays in complex interaction. So, for example, *Richard III* imposes a retrospective providential interpretation on the Machiavellian world of the *Henry VI* plays and clears the way for the Tudor settlement. She argues that the later plays become more, not less, providential, the very opposite of the general trend of Renaissance historiography; but that as the plays become more providential, they also become more self-consciously theatrical, and their exposing of their own 'compromised status as theatrical performances' becomes a way of interrogating the very 'process of historical representation that produces images of authority and the myths that authorize them'. In noting how the language of chivalry gives way to 'gross terms taken from the new commercial economy', Rackin suggests that the change from a providential to a Machiavellian view of history was related to the transition to a capitalist social organisation. Thus Hal, like an entrepreneur or meritocrat, becomes one forced to struggle for his achievement rather than inherit it.

Rackin sees a contradiction between the subject-matter and the medium of the plays, the former being the 'patriotic piety of historical mythmaking' and the latter the 'Machiavellian subversion of theatrical performance'. Without succumbing to the temptation to make the plays into an uncontradictorily unified sequence or smoothly epic sweep, Rackin succeeds in covering the whole run of the plays. Her survey argues for the circular nature of Shakespeare's entire historiographic project, with the recursive lines at the end of *Henry V* taking us back to the beginning of *Henry VI Part 1* and Joan of Arc's image of the circle in the water – the image with which the first essay in this volume also began.

History is always constructed in retrospect. Thus, the criticism of the 1940s and 1950s found in the medieval world, and in Shakespeare's representations of it, a story of national union and English patriotism that answered to their own desires and needs, just as the radical criticism of the present finds a story of conflict and subversion. In both cases, present desire is projected in the form of a historical plot: alternative political agendas construct alternative plots. In Shakespeare's own time, the Tudors, like the conservative critics of the mid-twentieth century, projected the authoritarian world they wished to build into an imagined medieval past.[2] The story that begins with Richard II and ends with Henry VII shows the passage from an idealized medieval England through the crime against God and the state that destroyed it and the long process of suffering and penance that led to its redemption in the divinely ordained accession of the Tudor dynasty. Following the structure of the providential historical plot of the Bible and the medieval cycles that dramatized biblical history, it begins with a myth of the Fall in the deposition and murder of Richard II and ends with a story of redemption in the accession of Henry VII.

The traditional view of Shakespeare's history plays reproduces the teleological providential narrative of Tudor propaganda, focusing on the second tetralogy and *Richard III* to construct a plot that traces the passage from the medieval world to Shakespeare's own. It starts with *Richard II*, which represents the beginning of the providential narrative Shakespeare found in Hall and depicts a ceremonial, medieval world that looks back to an even more perfect union of authority and power in John of Gaunt's idealized vision of the time of Edward III.[3] It proceeds, in the Henry IV plays, to depict an abrupt plunge into a contemporary, fallen world,[4] where the future Henry V must engage in a long struggle to reconstruct the uncontested union of authority and power that obtained in the older, Edenic world ruled by kings whose power was rooted in unambiguous hereditary authority and validated by divine right. Henry V cannot inherit the Edenic England described by John of Gaunt because it is already lost, but what he can do to reproduce it, he does; when he conquers France, he 'achieves' 'the world's best garden' (Epilogue.7), as close a postlapsarian approximation to Eden as human endeavor can produce. The final redemption will have to wait for the end of *Richard III* and the advent of Henry Tudor.

An ideological construction, designed in retrospect to ratify the Tudor claim to the throne, this is the story that Shakespeare found in his historiographic sources and twentieth-century conservative critics found in Shakespeare's history plays. It is also implicit in the First Folio arrangement of the plays in a sequence that begins with *King John* and *Richard II* and ends with *Henry VIII*. But it is not the only story Shakespeare could have learned from Tudor historiography, and it is certainly not the only story that modern critics have found in his plays. The plot of Tudor historiography constructs a myth of original order followed by a fall in the deposition of Richard II and leading finally to a glorious redemption in the person of Henry VII, but the order in which Shakespeare composed his English history plays constructs a much more complicated story, whose plot is embedded in the cultural history of his own time. The series of plays that begins with *Henry VI* and ends with *Henry V* replaces the teleological, providential narrative of Tudor propaganda with a self-referential cycle that ends by interrogating the entire project of historical mythmaking. The first tetralogy Shakespeare wrote ends in providential redemption; but although the second recapitulates that process, it does so in much more problematic terms. The deposition of Richard II, like the death of Henry V, initiates a period of civil strife, penance, and purgation and ends with the advent of a savior-king, but the redemption depicted in *Henry V* is severely qualified. The order in which Shakespeare produced his two tetralogies follows the progress of Renaissance historiography, towards an increasingly self-conscious and skeptical attitude, not only toward its subjects but also toward the very process of historical production. Increasingly opposing historical fact to literary artifact, Shakespeare exposes the processes of historical mythmaking even as he engages in them.

*

From the beginning, the plays seem guided by this double agenda: the historical story they tell is also a story of historiographic production. Shakespeare's historical protagonists, in fact, repeatedly conceive their actions as versions of history-writing. In *I Henry VI*, English heroes identify their struggle to retain Henry V's French conquests as an effort to preserve the historical record of English glory, an identification that recurs in *King John* in the French king's effort to defend Arthur's hereditary right to the English throne, and in *Henry V* with Henry's effort to win his place in history by defeating the French in battle.

In structure as in subject, the plays signal their discursive origins. The retrospective process of historical construction informs the structure of *King John* and *Henry VIII* as well as the entire first tetralogy. The disorderly and disturbing plot of *King John* ends with the assurance that Prince Henry will 'set a form upon that indigest / Which [John] hath left so shapeless and so rude' (V.vii.26–27) and the Bastard's ringing declaration that England will never be conquered so long as it 'to itself do rest but true' (V.vii.118), denying the subversive implications of its chaotic plot with assurances of future stability and the imposition of a conventional moral lesson.[5] In Henry VIII, the birth of the princess Elizabeth ends a similarly disjointed and painful narrative with similar assurances. The rush of coincidences that resolves the plot in *King John* undermines the concluding rationalizations, making the play increasingly popular with recent critics, who have discovered in it anticipations of their own project of historical demystification.[6] In *Henry VIII* the birth of Elizabeth redeems the preceding action without rationalizing it: like Shakespeare's emphasis on Katherine's virtue even as he depicts her fall, the entire plot seems calculated to demonstrate that the ways of providence are inscrutable. In the first tetralogy, by contrast, the process of retroactive reconstruction is fully realized.

The first three plays are set in a Machiavellian universe. Linked together by open-ended conclusions that conclude nothing but initiate actions to be pursued in the subsequent play, their episodic plots depict an increasingly chaotic and mean-ingless world and an action that seems devoid of ethical significance or providen-tial purpose until it is explained in retrospect in *Richard III*. At the beginning of *1 Henry VI*, Henry V, the mirror of all Christian kings, has just died; as the *Henry VI* trilogy progresses, the chivalric, civic, patriotic, and ethical virtues associated with Henry V also die, often in the persons of human exemplars like Talbot and the dead king's brothers, Bedford and Gloucester, who retain and exemplify the virtues of an older world. Finally, in *3 Henry VI*, the kingdom is reduced to a Machiavellian jungle where Yorkists and Lancastrians vie with each other in treachery and atrocity, and even the loyalties that bind parent and child are violated in senseless battles in which fathers kill sons and sons kill fathers. Authority is effaced, power becomes an end in itself, and the crown becomes a commodity, tossed back and forth from one head to another at the whim of blind fortune and the Earl of Warwick. Even the pretense of hereditary legitimacy and divine right is left behind.[7]

In *3 Henry VI*, a Machiavellian figure erupts from this maelstrom of history turned savage: Richard of Gloucester, who promises to 'set the murtherous Machevil to school' (III.ii.193), defining in advance the role he will play in the final play in this tetralogy. In *Richard III*, however, the ideological tables are turned. Richard believes (as well he might, given his background in the *Henry VI* plays) that the world runs on Machiavellian principles, but almost from the first the audience is given reason to believe that he may be mistaken. Prophecies, prophetic dreams, curses that take effect – all suggest that supernatural forces are involved in the events that Richard believes and claims are completely under his control. For instance, we have Richard's clever manipulations and self-congratulatory solilo-quies as he arranges his brother Clarence's death, but we also have Clarence's prophetic dream and death's-door recognition that his impending doom is, in fact, a recompense for the crimes he committed in the time of Henry VI.

Richard thinks he is living in a world governed by Machiavellian *Realpolitik*, but Shakespeare places him in a world governed by providence, a dissonance that pro-duces heavy dramatic irony in the scenes when Richard gloats happily about the success of his machinations while the audience, informed not only by their fore-knowledge of Richard's historically appointed doom but also by the intimations of a providential agenda provided by the women's prophecies, know better. At the end of the play, Richmond, the agent of providence, heralded by prophetic dreams and heavenly imagery, kills the tyrant and takes over, but not before Richard has been forced to suffer the horrified recognition that he does indeed live in a providential universe, one where he will be punished now and forever for the crimes he com-mitted in the past.

Richard III offers a neat, conventional resolution to the problem of historical causation. All the cards have been stacked in advance, and the entire play reads like a lesson in providential history. In the first English treatise on historiography, *The true order and Methode of wryting and reading Hystories . . .* (1574), Thomas Blundeville advised,

As touching the providence of God . . . though things many times doe succeede accord-ing to the discourse of man's reason: yet mans wisedome is oftentymes greatlye deceyved.

And with those accidents which mans wisedome reiecteth and little regardeth: God by his providence useth, when he thinketh good, to worke marveylous effects. And though he suffreth the wicked for the most part to live in prosperitie, and the good in adversitie: yet we may see by many notable examples, declaring aswell his wrath, and revenge towards the wicked, as also his pittie and clemencie towards the good, that nothing is done by chaunce, but all things by his foresight, counsell, and divine providence.[8]

A 'notable example' of providential justice, the entire action of *Richard III* is subsumed in the ideological scheme that Blundeville recites. Richard 'greatlye deceyves' himself and the other characters, but Shakespeare's audience knows from the beginning that this is a providential universe and that Richard will fall. The audience came into the theater knowing Richard's history and they came to see a play called 'The Tragedy of Richard III'. That knowledge offers the audience a privileged vantage point, removing them from the flux of human temporality and placing them in the omniscient position of providence itself.

The only threat to that position is Richard himself, who reaches out to seduce the audience by the sheer energy and dramatic force of his characterization. By the end, however, even Richard has been subsumed in the providential scheme, first as the diabolical figure defined, as John Blanpied suggests, 'as an antitype of the providentialism it opposes',[9] and then, like the devil himself, as an unwitting instrument for the fulfillment of a providential plan. Killing off all the characters stained by the lingering guilt of the Wars of the Roses, Richard purges the kingdom to make it ready for Richmond's accession. Counting over Richard's victims and recalling the past crimes which justify their deaths, Margaret concludes,

> Richard yet lives, hell's black intelligencer,
> Only reserv'd their factor to buy souls
> And send them thither. But at hand, at hand
> Ensues his piteous and unpitied end.
> Earth gapes, hell burns, fiends roar, saints pray,
> To have him suddenly convey'd from hence.
> Cancel his bond of life, dear God I pray,
> That I may live and say 'The dog is dead.'

(IV.iv.71–78)

Richard is a 'factor',[10] a purchasing agent acting for a superior power, even though he denies the authority of that power and supposes he acts on his own behalf.

In *Richard III* Shakespeare reconstructs the history he has already written, retroactively imposing a providential order that makes sense of the Machiavellian chaos he depicted in the Henry VI plays. The women's litanies of old wrongs and the repeated pattern of Richard's victims recalling just before they die the past crimes for which they are now about to pay subsume the events they recall into a teleological providential plot. Shakespeare brings all the chickens home to roost in *Richard III*, framing and containing the wild melee of human treachery, bloodshed, and injustice he depicted in the Henry VI plays in a totalizing explanatory scheme that purges moral ambiguity and eradicates ideological conflict.

Richard III has remained a popular play on the stage, although it is frequently revised for performance, but its neat structure probably did not satisfy Shakespeare;[11] for all the issues so comfortably resolved in the end of that play are opened up again in *King John*, a 'problem history' where the audience has no sure guide through the ideological ambiguities but instead finds itself lost, like the Bastard, 'among the thorns and dangers of this world' (IV.iii.141). Historical events take on meaning and coherence only after they have passed into history. Experienced in the present tense, as they happen, 'actions outstrip comprehension'; the 'truth' a historical narrative constructs is, as Marshall Brown points out, 'a reification that only exists outside of time' or after the fact.[12] Of all Shakespeare's English histories, *King John* is set farthest back in the past, and yet of all of them it depicts a world that is least medieval and most insistently present. Caught up in the whirl of events, the audience shares the characters' uncertainties as they find themselves lost together in a 'thorny wood' of ideological confusion and confused plot. In *King John* Shakespeare abandons the Tudor historians' anachronistic ascriptions of divine right and providential theory to their medieval ancestors in order to depict a world without faith or ceremony,[13] where failure and success ride on the shifting winds of chance. Late in the play, beset by political and military attack, King John gives 'the ordering of this present time' to the Bastard (V.i.77); but it is tempting to speculate that Shakespeare gave it to him from the beginning. The Bastard is a fictitious character; that is, not historically legitimate, and his cynicism and illegitimate birth epitomize the lawless forces that substitute for providential order to motivate the action and move the plot in the confused 'present time' of *King John*.

In many ways, *King John* offers a Machiavellian antithesis to the providential thesis so insistently laid down and retroactively imposed upon the entire first tetralogy in *Richard III*. But the second tetralogy would be difficult to read as a synthesis. Moving further into the past and retreating from the providential resolution he imposed in *Richard III*, Shakespeare reopens the question of historical causation and complicates the conflicts it involves with an increasingly intense interrogation of his own historiographic project. Instead of reconciling the binary oppositions between past and present, providence and Machiavelli, theater and history, the second tetralogy destabilizes them in a whirling dialectic that increasingly calls into question both the adequacy of its own dramatic representations and the possibility of historical knowledge.

At the beginning of the second tetralogy, Shakespeare seems to be replaying the conflicts he staged in the first tetralogy, ringing new changes on the same chimes. *Richard II* begins with a situation exactly opposite to the one in *Richard III*. This time, the king who is the play's protagonist sits on an inherited throne to which he is entitled by divine right. If Richard III thinks he lives in a Machiavellian universe where authority is only another name for power, Richard II thinks he lives in a providential world where authority alone is sufficient to maintain him in office. He imagines that the king's very name can be armed against a would-be usurper – 'Is not the king's name twenty thousand names? / Arm, arm, my name! a puny subject strikes / At thy great glory' (III.ii.85–87) – and that angels will fight to defend his title to the crown:

The breath of worldly men cannot depose
The deputy elected by the Lord;
For every man that Bullingbrook hath press'd
To lift shrewd steel against our golden crown,
God for his Richard hath in heavenly pay
A glorious angel: then if angels fight,
Weak men must fall, for heaven still guards the right.

(III.ii.56–62)

Shakespeare gives Richard glorious poetry, but he also supplies him with a Machiavellian antagonist, a character who speaks few words but raises large armies and rejects the comforts of imagination and philosophy with the materialistic protest,

O, who can hold a fire in his hand
By thinking on the frosty Caucasus?
Or cloy the hungry edge of appetite
By bare imagination of a feast?
Or wallow naked in December snow
By thinking on fantastic summer's heat?

(I.iii.294–99)

In this play, unlike *Richard III*, it is the Machiavel who wins.

Despite their opposite outcomes, both plays project the ideological conflict into the opposition between a protagonist king and the antagonist who deposes him. In *Richard II*, however, Shakespeare does not simply reverse the terms of the opposition; he also complicates and compromises them. In *Richard III* the principle of historical causation is unambiguous: providentialism and divine right are clearly privileged. The dangerous theatrical power of the Machiavel is contained by his unequivocal definition as a villain. Richmond, the providential figure, is clearly a paragon of royal virtue, his victory the fulfillment of God's plan. No such simple assignment of virtue, vice, or agency can be made in *Richard II*. Richard, the hereditary king who believes heaven will protect his divine right to the throne, is still depicted as being largely at fault in his deposition. Bullingbrook, the usurper, is an enigmatic figure, clearly at fault in taking a throne that he has not inherited, but otherwise not obviously reprehensible, and certainly endorsed with the warrant of success. Moreover, the obscurity of Bullingbrook's motives makes it impossible to determine whether his victory represents the will of God or the triumph of his own Machiavellian strategy.

In the *Henry IV* plays, this duplicity intensifies. All the actions can be explained on two levels, the mystical and the political. As Matthew Wikander points out, 'traditional patterns and images refuse to stay put as they do in the earlier history plays. . . . The clear rhetorical lesson that each scene seems to offer is undercut and questioned even as it is taught.'[14] The duplicity is probably most obvious in the king's plans to make a pilgrimage to Jerusalem, which are explained both as a political stratagem ('to busy giddy minds with foreign quarrels' 'lest rest and lying still might make them look too near unto my state'; *2 Henry IV*: IV.v.211–214) and as a religious obligation ('to wash this blood off from my guilty hand'; *Richard II*:

V.vi.50; cf. *I Henry IV*: I.i.19–27), but it characterizes every component of the king's action. Hal's wildness is both a political problem (How will civic order be maintained in the future if the king is a riotous wastrel?) and a supernatural affliction.[15] The rebellions that beset the king throughout his reign have a similar duplicity, sometimes rationalized as retributions for Bullingbrook's crime against Richard, sometimes explained as the ambitious strivings of power-hungry nobles. Thus, *Henry IV* is a play that can be understood on either or both of two levels, like the Tudor histories that, acknowledging that all things have their first causes in the will of God, still found it profitable and useful to explore their second causes in the deeds of men.

In *Henry V*, the last play in the second tetralogy, the two views are deliberately clashed against each other. We get not only two interpretations of the action but two accounts of the action, one in the discourse of the chorus and one in the dramatic representation staged before us; and the two accounts not only differ from each other but also insist upon each other's inadequacies. Moreover, instead of reconciling the two views at the end of the play or discarding one for the other, Shakespeare lets both of them stand, directing our attention to the abyss at the center of the historiographic project: the impossibility of recovering the past or of getting behind the historiographic text (whether that text be a written record or a dramatic representation) to discover the always postulated and never graspable fiction called historical truth.

The two emblems of royal perfection, English triumph, peace, and prosperity that frame the first tetralogy – Henry V at the beginning, Henry VII at the end – are never problematized. Indeed, Henry V never even appears on stage, and Henry VII appears only at the very end of *Richard III* and only as Richmond, not as the ideal king he will become. Both, therefore, exemplify an authority that is never really seen or subjected to the tests and strains of theatrical representation. In the second tetralogy, by contrast, Shakespeare subjects his icon of royal authority to those tests and strains, exploring the theatricality of royal authority and the fictiveness of historical truth even as he creates their dramatic embodiments. Henry VII, briefly introduced at the end of *Richard III* as England's savior, is never anything but God's soldier, the destined king who will unite the red rose and the white to found the Tudor dynasty. Henry V and his England, recalled with nostalgic longing as the world of his son sinks into chaos, is projected in the *Henry VI* plays in unproblematic terms as an image of lost perfection. In the second tetralogy, however, Shakespeare complicates that image by showing the process of its creation.

The second tetralogy depicts a world where 'miracles are ceas'd; / And therefore we must needs admit the means / How things are perfected' (*Henry V*: I.i.67–69). The Henry we see on stage in the second tetralogy anticipates the Tudors in using the resources of theatrical role-playing to produce the perfect image of royal authority that he could not inherit from the ambiguous genealogy that left him the throne. Producing himself as 'the mirror of all Christian kings', Henry appropriates the legitimating emblems of an older world to authorize himself.[16] Just as Henry VII looked to the dim mists of legendary Welsh history to ratify his claim to the English throne, Henry V invokes a tortuous, distant genealogy to ratify his claim to France. Just as Elizabeth's aspiring courtiers engaged in mock tournaments and her newly rich merchants purchased genealogical titles to authorize their newly acquired gentility, Henry appropriates Hotspur's chivalric honor to reproduce the anachronistic ideals of the world his father destroyed when he usurped the English throne.[17]

*

There is a sense in which Shakespeare's progress as a writer of English history seems to run against the current of Renaissance historiography, which moved from providential to Machiavellian explanations of historical causation. In the Machiavellian world of the Henry VI plays, Shakespeare celebrates the pagan virtues of heroic warriors like Talbot and good citizens like Alexander Iden. Moreover, these plays, like *King John*, highlight the forces that subvert the project of patriarchal history. The characters who dominate the worlds of these plays act on the Machiavellian principle of self-interest, and they prevail because they live in a Machiavellian universe governed by force and fortune rather than the providential hand of God. Moving in *Richard III* and the second tetralogy to a providential universe, Shakespeare depicts history in mythic, Christian terms, thus, it would seem, inverting the progress of Renaissance historiography, which developed in the direction of rational analysis and demystification. But there is another way to see this progress; for at the same time that Shakespeare's historical representations became more providential, they also became more self-consciously theatrical, increasingly complicated by metadramatic allusions that emphasize their status as theatrical representations. Even as he celebrates the glamor of Richard II and the perfect royalty of Henry V and depicts the working out of God's holy purpose in English history, Shakespeare emphasizes the theatricality of his own representations. The metadramatic self-consciousness of the plays of the second tetralogy invokes the growing rift between historical fact and fictional artifact to emphasize the constructed character of all historical representation.

Moving backward to the mystified medieval past of Richard II, Shakespeare's second tetralogy self-consciously reconstructs the providential order that was deconstructed in the Henry VI plays, but it also moves forward into Shakespeare's own theatrical future. Reconstituting a providential universe in explicitly theatrical terms, the plays of the second tetralogy expose their own compromised status as theatrical performances to interrogate the process of historical representation that produces images of authority and the myths that authorize them. Henry V, the great image of royal authority in the second tetralogy, is depicted from the first as a player of roles. Conquering France, unifying the English nation, submitting himself first to the legal counsel of churchmen and finally to the verdict of God in heaven, Henry V frames his story in providential terms; but his continual recourse to theatrical strategies to achieve those ends also identifies Henry as a Machiavel. As Kenneth Burke points out, Machiavelli's *Prince* 'can be treated as a rhetoric insofar as it deals with the *producing of effects upon an audience*'.[18] Separating moral virtue from political efficacy and private character from public mask, Machiavelli conceived politics in theatrical terms, as, in Wylie Sypher's words, 'a form of role-playing'.[19]

In Shakespeare's history plays there is a persistent association between Machiavellianism and theatricality. Richard III, the only one of Shakespeare's English kings explicitly associated with Machiavelli, is also the most theatrical. Images of the theater hover around Richard from the beginning. Contemplating his impending death at Richard's hands, Henry VI asks, 'What scene of death hath Roscius now to act?' (*3 Henry VI*: V.vi.10). Plotting with Buckingham to seize the English throne, Richard prepares him for a theatrical performance where he will 'counterfeit the deep tragedian' (*Richard III*: III.v.1–9). It is significant, moreover, that Richard announces himself as a Machiavel in the same speech wherein he announces himself as an actor:

Why, I can smile, and murther whiles I smile,
And cry 'Content' to that which grieves my heart,
And wet my cheeks with artificial tears,
And frame my face to all occasions.
I'll drown more sailors than the mermaid shall,
I'll slay more gazers than the basilisk,
I'll play the orator as well as Nestor,
Deceive more slily than Ulysses could,
And like a Sinon, take another Troy.
I can add colors to the chameleon,
Change shapes with Proteus for advantages,
And set the murtherous Machevil to school.

(III.ii.182–93)

Richard describes his diabolical theatrical power in the same terms that Renaissance writers typically used to describe actors. Both Edward Alleyn and Richard Burbage, the actor who first played Richard's role, were compared by admiring contemporaries to Proteus the shape-shifter;[20] but in Richard's self-description, the reference to Proteus slides inexorably into the reference to Machiavelli, a far more sinister symbol of perfect hypocrisy, who was also associated with Proteus in contemporary thought.

Although Richard represents the apotheosis of the Machiavellian forces in the first tetralogy, he has numerous and varied antecedents. Subverters of history, opponents of true royalty and the English state, characters like Joan, Margaret, and Jack Cade deceive their fellow characters and seduce the audience with a dangerous theatrical energy. They pursue a power to which they have no legitimate claim with the ruthless, amoral ambition that associated the image of Machiavelli in Elizabethan thought with the new commercial forces that threatened the status quo. Deceitful, ambitious, scornful of traditional restraints and traditional notions of honor, the Machiavel represented the threats to traditional order posed by emergent capitalism.

The associations between actor, merchant, and Machiavel are explicit in Thomas Heywood's satiric pamphlet, *Machiavel as He lately appeared to his deare Sons, the Moderne Projectors* (1641). Of one group of projectors, Heywood writes, 'Their scene was the whole Kingdome. In every part of which, they stoutly acted their well seasoned interlude, which now at last is proved the Tragedie of the Actors themselves.'[21] In fact, Heywood's description of the Machiavellian deceptions of 'A Projector in generall' employs the same images that Richard uses in his self-characterization as a Machiavel. Just as Richard can 'frame [his] face to all occasions' and 'add colors to the chameleon', Heywood's projector can 'change himself into as many shapes as Painters can doe colours'. Like Richard, the projector has 'more wit than honestie', and like him, he uses his Machiavellian devices to rise in the world and acquire titles that bespeak a nobility he does not possess.[22] The Protean, shape-shifting actor, the ruthless image of the Florentine and the new commercial adventurer merge in a single figure that combines subversive threat with theatrical power. Cut loose from the traditional bonds that unite feudal society and define the place of individuals in terms of hereditary rights and obligations, no longer subsumed under the old generic categories that reduced individuals to representations of their classes, these strikingly individualized characters represent the emergence of individual subjectivity in a changing world.[23]

Like the 'new men' of emergent capitalism that Heywood satirizes, the Machiavellian subverters of established order provide the subjects for sharply individualized characterizations. Intensely theatrical, they represent not only a new kind of dramatic characterization that substitutes individual for generic attributes but a new conception of personal identity. No longer imposed by an inherited social position, the new man's identity is constructed in action: the theatrical principle of present performance replaces the historical principle of hereditary status as its defining ground.

The most compelling dramatic presences in the first tetralogy, these characters speak with distinctive dramatic voices that emerge from the undifferentiated blank verse that constitutes most of the dialogue. Nonetheless, despite the lively dramatic particularity of their voices and personalities, they are all contained ideologically within the binary opposition that defines them as enemies to royal authority and established order. The French peasant Joan and the English queen Margaret, the great Cardinal Beauford and the knavish priest John Hume, the noble lady Eleanor Cobham and the poverty-stricken Simpcox, the bricklayer's son Jack Cade and the Plantagenet pretender to the throne range in characterization from the heights of aristocratic pride to the depths of poverty and humiliation. Their languages range from learned eloquence to inarticulate illiteracy, but they all share the Machiavellian attributes of treachery and selfish, amoral ambition that define them as demonic Others. Peasant rebels, aristocratic traitors, and noble usurpers are all contained within the binary opposition between legitimate authority and Machiavellian subversion.

In *King John* and the second tetralogy, these characters become increasingly prominent, and their theatrical power becomes increasingly dangerous, reaching out to the audience with a seductive, amoral appeal and influencing the course of the action by the sheer force of their personalities. Character, in fact, emerges along with Machiavellianism as a motive force in Shakespeare's historical universe. In the providential universe of the morality play, as in the paradigmatic expressions of universal rules of causality that Aristotle found in tragedy,[24] character is subordinated to plot. As Catherine Belsey points out, the protagonist of a morality play is 'a fragmented and fragmentary figure', the battlefield for a struggle between Christ and Satan 'which exists before he is born and continues after his death'.[25] Character, however, becomes increasingly important in the increasingly secularized worlds of Elizabethan drama (and in the increasingly secularized world of

Elizabethan England), as human agency rather than transcendental teleology comes to motivate the action. This opposition between providential plot and Machiavellian character can be seen in the first tetralogy, where the emblematic flatness of the characters who act in the name of God and country and the uniformity of their language contrast with the vivid particularity of the characters who oppose providential order to pursue their own agendas. In the later plays, however, although characters like the Bastard in *King John* and Falstaff in the Henry IV plays exhibit many of the traits that marked their dramatic antecedents as Machiavels, they are no longer contained within the simple binary scheme that opposes character to plot and Machiavellian subversion to legitimate authority.

With the deposition of Richard II, royal authority is dispersed, and so is the subversive force that opposes it. In the second tetralogy, Machiavellianism is no longer contained by association with characters who threaten to destroy or usurp royal authority. In *1 Henry IV* the rebels Worcester and Northumberland are marked as Machiavels by their calculation and duplicity, but so is the king, the man Hotspur calls 'this vile politician, Bullingbrook' (I.iii.241). The most ruthless act of Machiavellian cunning in the Henry IV plays is used, significantly, to *subdue* rebel forces. Prince John deceives the rebels at Gaultree Forest when he swears 'by the honor of my blood' and gives his 'princely word' (IV.ii.55–66), corrupting and compromising the very authority he invokes to win an ignoble victory. The characterization of the royal prince as a cold-blooded Machiavellian deceiver shows how far royal authority has been compromised in the second tetralogy, for the same historical personage, grown old, was depicted in *1 Henry VI* as a paragon of the old chivalric virtues, the 'valiant Duke of Bedford' (III.ii.87), the subject of Talbot's eulogy, 'A braver soldier never couched lance, / A gentler heart did never sway in court' (III.ii.134–35). It is Bedford who leads the chorus of praise and mourning for Henry V in the opening scene and Bedford whose gallant courage inspires the English victory at Rouen. Old and sick, Bedford refuses to leave the battlefield,

> for once I read
> That stout Pendragon in his litter sick
> Came to the field and vanquished his foes.
> Methinks I should revive the soldiers' hearts,
> Because I ever found them as myself.

> (III.ii.94–98)

Bedford's emblematic characterization is completely subsumed within the binary scheme that associates noble English valor with a heroic, historic past.

In the world of Henry IV, by contrast, the only character who is thoroughly animated by the old feudal values is Hotspur, and it is in the name of those values, of personal honor and Mortimer's hereditary right to the throne, that Hotspur rebels against the king. Hotspur's honor is never questioned in the play, but the very absoluteness of his commitment to honor serves to compromise honor itself. To Douglas, Hotspur is the very 'king of honor' (IV.i.10); and even the king he opposes calls him 'the theme of honor's tongue' (I.i.81). Personified in Hotspur, the old knightly honor is doubly compromised, not only by the slightly comical enthusiasm with which he embraces it but also by the fact that it inspires him to rebel against the king.

Royal authority is compromised too. Not only opposed by Hotspur in the plot, but also characterized as the calculating, political antithesis to the impetuous, idealistic young rebel, the king has none of the honor that should belong to royalty. Prince Henry is perfectly aware that he must appropriate the honor he needs from Hotspur. He tells Hotspur before their battle, 'all the budding honors on thy crest / I'll crop to make a garland for my head' (V.iv.72–73). Earlier, he used the same chivalric language, even the same metaphor, when he promised his father that he would 'redeem' his shame 'on Percy's head':

> And stain my favors in a bloody mask,
> Which wash'd away shall scour my shame with it.
> And that shall be the day, when e'er it lights,
> That this same child of honor and renown,
> This gallant Hotspur, this all-praised knight,
> And your unthought-of Harry chance to meet,
> For every honor sitting on his helm,
> Would they were multitudes, and on my head
> My shames redoubled!
>
> (III.ii.136–44)

Hal's promise is a heroic vaunt in the old chivalric tradition. He promises to 'die a hundred thousand deaths / Ere break the smallest parcel of this vow' (III.ii.158–59). But even in the course of making that promise, he slips into another idiom, contaminating the language of chivalry with gross terms taken from the new commercial economy. When he swears to 'make this northren youth exchange / His glorious deeds for my indignities' (III.ii.145–46), the prince transforms glorious deeds and indignities into objects of commercial exchange:

> Percy is but my factor, good my lord,
> To engross up glorious deeds on my behalf;
> And I will call him to so strict account
> That he shall render every glory up,
> Yea, even the slightest worship of his time,
> Or I will tear the reckoning from his heart.
>
> (III.ii.147–52)

The 'factor' image defines in advance Hal's victory over Hotspur in knightly combat as a repossession of the honor that rightly belongs to royalty, but it also compromises that honor by terms – 'factor', 'render up', 'engross', 'strict account' and 'reckoning' – that reduce the chivalric battle to a closely calculated financial transaction.[26]

Like the aspiring commercial men of Shakespeare's time, the future Henry V must struggle to achieve a status he did not inherit. Unlike Richard II, who had a clear, hereditary claim to the throne, Henry V must *earn* his legitimacy. The honor he could not inherit from the 'vile politician Bullingbrook', he must acquire from

Hotspur in battle. The 'cold blood he did naturally inherit of his father' he warms by drinking 'good and good store of fertile sherris', in Falstaff's company (*2 Henry IV*: IV.iii.118–21).[27] Like the son of a rich tradesman sent to university to acquire the education that will make him a gentleman, Hal revels and carouses, but he also 'studies his companions' (*2 Henry IV*: IV.iv.68) and acquires new languages. Learning the names of his humble subjects and mastering the terms in which they speak, he wins their recognition as the 'king of courtesy' (*1 Henry IV*: II.iv.5–11). The two parts of *Henry IV*, in fact, depict a long educational process in which Prince Hal learns the skills and assumes the attributes that constitute the 'mirror of all Christian kings' he will become in *Henry V* (II.Chorus,6). Like the new gentility that successful commoners were acquiring by their own efforts, the royal authority that Henry V finally represents is an achievement, not an inheritance.

What Henry V does inherit is a taint – his father's guilt for usurping Richard II's crown. The hereditary taint of his father's low origins and dishonorable ascent threatens Henry's own aspirations for worldly power and success: 'Not to-day, O Lord!', he prays before his climactic battle of Agincourt, 'O not to-day, think not upon the fault my father made in compassing the crown' (IV.i.292–94). Henry's struggle for France represents an effort to wipe out that taint and legitimate his status as King of England. 'No king of England, if not king of France' (II.ii.193), Henry uses Agincourt as an enormous trial by combat to establish the legitimacy of his rule and earn his place in providential history. The providential legitimation, in fact, is the sole purpose of the battle. Refusing to accept any credit for the victory, he insists, 'Take it, God, / For it is none but thine!' and he threatens his soldiers, 'be it death proclaimed through our host / To boast of this, or take that praise from God / Which is his only' (IV.viii.111–16). The stridency of the threat exposes the anxiety that produced it, the keen sense of the absence of divine right that Henry attempts to fill by the exercise and mystification of earthly power.

It takes three plays for Henry to reconstruct the royal authority that was lost when Bullingbrook usurped the English throne, and although he finally succeeds in producing the perfect icon of royal authority in Henry V, the authority he reconstructs is deeply compromised by his recourse to Machiavellian strategies of political manipulation and theatrical display.[28] His constant role-playing celebrates the power of theater to produce the perfect image of royalty, but it also compromises the authority it produces by associating it with the ambiguous figures of actor, Machiavel, and merchant.

The authority of the playwright is also compromised. The playwright of *Richard III* conceived his authorial role in the same exalted terms that Sidney used to describe the poet. Contriving his plot to show 'virtue exalted and vice punished'[29] he distributed rewards and punishments with a poetic justice that bespoke the providential order it imitated. Like God, he created and ruled a providential universe, and he ended his play with a prayer, designed to inspire his audience to piety and patriotism. In the second tetralogy, the authorial role is divided against itself by the social and ethical differences that separated Sidney's gentleman poet writing to inspire his readers from a commercial playwright manufacturing public entertainments for financial gain.[30] As a poet, the dramatist works in imitation of divine providence to teach the ways of righteousness and draw his audience 'to as high a perfection as our degenerate souls, made worse by their clay lodgings, can be capable of'.[31] As a commercial playwright, he deceives and manipulates for his own profit like a Machiavel.

A deep contradiction, therefore, divides the subject of Shakespeare's English history plays from their medium, opposing the patriotic piety of historical myth-making to the Machiavellian subversion of theatrical performance. The theater, in fact, was associated with every sort of transgression of the social and religious order that the historical myths were designed to support.[32] Common players acting the parts and wearing the clothes of kings and noblemen transgressed the hierarchical status system; providential order and genealogical history supported it. The rhetoric of antitheatrical polemic, denouncing the theater as a seat of dangerous allure 'whereunto more people resort than to sermons or prayers', set the playhouse in diametrical opposition to the house of God: 'More have recourse to Playing houses, then to Praying houses.'[33] Sidney's poet inspired his readers to virtuous action, but the playwright of the antitheatrical tracts provided the 'springs of many vices, and the stumbling blocks of godliness and virtue', seducing his audience to 'adulterie and uncleannesse', and every sort of 'ungodly desires', crimes, and treason:[34]

if you will learne to . . . blaspheme both Heaven and Earth: . . . If you will learn to rebel against Princes, to commit treasons . . . if you will learne to contemne GOD and all his lawes, to care nither for heaven nor hel, and to commit al kinde of sinne and mischeef, you need to goe to no other schoole, for all these good Examples may you see painted before your eyes in enterludes and playes.[35]

This final statement, taken from Phillip Stubbes' *Anatomie of Abuses*, represents an extreme example of antitheatrical invective, and the theater had its defenders as well.[36] The statement is significant, however, because it reveals the extent to which the subversive power of the theater was associated with rebellion against the authority of God and the king, the same authority that providential history was designed to justify.

*

Henry V ends the two tetralogies in a play of unresolved contradictions. The action Shakespeare dramatizes contradicts the story the chorus tells. The king's recourse to Machiavellian plotting contradicts his representations of his achievements as manifestations of providential purpose, and his role-playing contradicts his characterization as a true embodiment of royal authority. The chorus constantly urges the audience to suppose that the historical persons and events the play depicts are actually present, and just as constantly reminds them that they are only watching a theatrical representation that falls far short of the historical reality it attempts to imitate.

The final chorus echoes these contradictions even as it attempts to deny them. Cast in the form of a sonnet, the chorus employs the familiar sonnet strategy of translating existential contradiction into verbal antithesis and paradox[37] and resorting to rhetorical appeal to escape from logical impasse:

Thus far, with rough and all-unable pen,
Our bending author hath pursu'd the story,
In little room confining mighty men,
Mangling by starts the full course of their glory.
Small time; but in that small most greatly lived
This star of England. Fortune made his sword;
By which the world's best garden he achieved,
And of it left his son Imperial lord.
Henry the Sixt, in infant bands crown'd King
Of France and England, did this king succeed;
Whose state so many had the managing,
That they lost France, and made his England bleed;
Which oft our stage hath shown; and for their sake,
In your fair minds let this acceptance take.

The chorus's description of Henry's French conquest ('Fortune made his sword: / By which the world's best garden he achieved') redeems the Machiavellian and commercial implications of 'fortune' and 'achieved' with the providential warrant implied by the allusion to Eden. And the sestet erases the distinction the chorus has emphasized throughout the play – the intractable difference between the historic past and Shakespeare's dramatic representations. The sestet moves imperceptibly from England's historical future in the troubled reign of Henry VI to Shakespeare's theatrical past in the successful plays he had written about that reign, from the painful history of bleeding and loss to the pleasing theatrical spectacles that represented that history.

Refusing to distinguish between historical event and theatrical performance, the sestet of the final sonnet also denies the irreconcilable opposition between past pain and present pleasure. Conflating bloody battles with theatrical pleasure, the chorus now elides the social and ethical differences that separate participation in heroic history from attendance in a commercial theater. At the end of the first tetralogy, Richmond invited Shakespeare's audience to join him in a patriotic prayer for a common future of 'smooth-fac'd peace', 'smiling plenty' and 'fair prosperous days'. At the end of *Henry V* the chorus asks the audience to approve a theatrical performance. The playwright of the second tetralogy takes on a divided role, compromising the notable image of virtue he produces in Henry V and the providential plot that depicts Henry's triumph with the Machiavellian taint of his own theatrical, commercial contrivance.

When the Bastard in *King John* compared the citizens of Angiers to the members of a theater audience who 'gape . . . at . . . industrious scenes and acts of death' (II.i.375–76), he exposed the debasement and commodification of the heroic past in the hands of professional actors working for the pleasure of a low-born audience and their own profit. At the beginning of *Henry V*, the Prologue addressed the same problem when he complained about the inadequacy of 'this wooden O' to contain the heroic past and wished for 'princes to act, and monarchs to behold the swelling scene'; only then, he said, would 'warlike Harry' be 'like himself'. He wished, as David Kastan points out, 'that the contradictions of playing would disappear'.

Purified of the social contamination of bourgeois actors and a socially heterogeneous audience, the representation of the heroic past 'would be simply presentation and history plays would be history itself'.[38] In the final sonnet, he papers over all these deficiencies and contradictions – the social deficiencies of actors and audience and the inadequacy of the theatrical representation – when he submits himself and the play to the public theater audience he actually has. The sonnet ends with a rhetorical appeal to the audience that is also a commercial appeal – if the audience does not accept the play, the play will not make money. The appeal rests on an ambiguous pronoun – the 'their' in 'for their sake' – that conflates the authority of history with the popularity of the Henry VI plays.

The final chorus's reference to the Henry VI plays defines the place of *Henry V* in Shakespeare's historical plot. Not only the last play in the two tetralogies, it is also their center; for the plot of Shakespeare's historical reconstruction bends the teleological, chronological line of his historiographic sources into a circle, beginning and ending with the death of Henry V. The circle is joined at the point that represents the moment of loss, and, like the 'wooden O' of Shakespeare's theater, it circumscribes an absence – the heroic past and royal authority that the name of Henry V denotes. It replaces the purposeful, linear progress of history with the endless work of historiography and the endless repetition of theatrical performance, obsessively moving about a lost center they can never recover. Enacting the obsessive movement it describes, the image of the circle itself circles back to the first act of *1 Henry VI* to recall Joan's resonant lines:

Glory is like a circle in the water,
Which never ceaseth to enlarge itself,
Till by broad spreading it disperse to nought.
With Henry's death the English circle ends,
Dispersed are the glories it included.

(I.ii.133–37)

Here too the circle encloses an absence, and here too it is associated with Henry's death and the erasure of English heroic history.

The desired object of theatrical recuperation, the king who presided over the transcendent moment when the English star 'most greatly lived' is finally revealed as the product of his own theatrical recuperation, his providential authority the product of Machiavellian manipulation. The unresolved contradictions of *Henry V* are those of Shakespeare's entire historiographic project. Infused by nostalgic yearning, the plays begin in a heroic effort to recuperate a lost, heroic past, but they end by calling attention to the ineluctable absence of that past and their own compromised status as commercial, theatrical representations.

NOTES

1. Reprinted from PHYLLIS RACKIN, *Stages of History: Shakespeare's English Chronicles* (London: Routledge, 1991).

2. They also recognized that history was a field of ideological contention and that alternative accounts of the past threatened their present political hegemony. See LILY B. CAMPBELL,

Shakespeare's 'Histories' (London: Methuen, 1964), pp. 182–92, for an account of the use of Sir John Hayward's history of Henry IV as evidence at the Essex conspiracy trial.

3. For an especially perceptive version of this reading, see JAMES L. CALDERWOOD, '*Richard II*: The Fall of Speech', in *Shakespearean Metadrama* (Minneapolis: University of Minnesota Press, 1971), pp. 149–86.

4. LEONARD BARKAN, 'The Theatrical Consistency of *Richard II*', *Shakespeare Quarterly* 29 (1978), 5–19.

5. For especially perceptive discussions of the way this structure interrogates the process of historiographic mythmaking, see JOHN R. ELLIOTT, 'Shakespeare and the Double Image of King John', *Shakespeare Studies* 1 (1965), 64–84; and VIRGINIA M. VAUGHAN, '*King John*: A Study in Subversion and Containment', in *King John: New Perspectives*, ed. DEBORAH T. CURREN-AQUINO (Newark: University of Delaware Press, 1989), pp. 62–75.

6. See the two essays cited in the preceding note and the entire Aquino anthology, especially LARRY S. CHAMPION, 'The "Un-end" of *King John*: Shakespeare's Demystification of Closure', pp. 173–85.

7. For an excellent account of the shape of the first tetralogy, to which I am much indebted, see EDWARD I. BERRY, *Patterns of Decay: Shakespeare's Early Histories* (Charlottesville: University Press of Virginia, 1975).

8. F3. Hugh G. Dick points out (Huntingdon Library Quarterly 3 (1940) p. 149) that Blundeville's was 'the first separately printed treatise in English on the art of history'.

9. JOHN W. BLANPIED, *Time and the Artist in Shakespeare's English Histories* (Newark: University of Delaware Press, 1983), p. 100.

10. On the Machiavellian, commercial implications of the 'factor' image, see my discussion in section VI of this chapter of Hal's statement in *1 Henry IV*, III.ii.147–50: 'Percy is but my factor, good my lord, / To engross up glorious deeds on my behalf; / And I will call him to so strict account / That he shall render every glory up.'

11. Cf. Blanpied, p. 100, where he too sees *King John* as an expression of Shakespeare's dissatisfaction with *Richard III*, although he defines that dissatisfaction in terms somewhat different from mine: 'What he finds he needs, the morning after the *Richard III* blowout, is a strongly centered play that, paradoxically, does not refuse to relinquish control.'

12. MARSHALL BROWN, ' "Errours Endlesse Traine": On Turning Points and the Dialectical Imagination', *PMLA* 99 (1984), 11, 21.

13. SIGURD BURCKHARDT (in '*King John*: The Ordering of This Present Time', *Shakespearean Meanings*, pp. 116–43) sees *King John* as Shakespeare's critique of the Tudor myth, pointing out that Shakespeare greatly reduces the Protestant propaganda in his source, where John was depicted as a martyr to Roman Catholic wickedness.

14. MATTHEW H. WIKANDER, *The Play of Truth and State* (Baltimore: Johns Hopkins University Press, 1986), p. 27.

15. Henry IV is characteristically skeptical: 'I know not whether God will have it so / For some displeasing service I have done / That in his secret doom, out of my blood / He'll breed revengement and a scourge for me; / But thou dost in thy passages of life / Make me believe that thou art only mark'd / For the hot vengeance, and the rod of heaven, / To punish my mistreadings' (*1 Henry IV*: III.ii.4–11).

16. Like a playwright or actor, Henry is characterized from the very beginning as an 'imitator'. Note, for instance, his first soliloquy in *I Henry IV* (I.ii.197), where he announces that he will 'imitate the sun'. As ALEXANDER LEGGATT points out, the 'promise to imitate the sun takes us back to *Richard II*; but while Richard, as rightful king, was naturally identified with the sun, Hal can only promise to

imitate it – to produce, as his father did, a good performance in the role of king'. *Shakespeare's Political Drama: The History Plays and the Roman Plays* (London: Routledge, 1988), p. 89.

17. DAVID NORBROOK, *Poetry and Politics in the English Renaissance* (London: Routledge & Kegan Paul, 1984), p. 99, points out that 'despite the archaising feudal costumes they wore at court entertainments', many of the 'members of Leicester's circle were essentially nouveaux riches' and that no less a person than the Queen's Champion at the Accession Day tilts, Sir Henry Lee, 'owed much of his wealth to enclosures'.

18. KENNETH BURKE, *A Grammar of Motives and a Rhetoric of Motives* (Cleveland: Meridian Books, 1962), p. 682.

19. WYLIE SYPHER, *The Ethic of Time: Structures of Experience in Shakespeare* (New York: Seabury Press, 1976), p. 28. Cf. JONAS BARISH, *The Antitheatrical Prejudice* (Berkeley: University of California Press, 1981), p. 97: 'Machiavelli rarely asks whether the prince should practice such and such a vice . . . or should possess such and such a virtue . . . but rather whether he should be *thought* to practice it. . . . The image is all, the reality nothing.' Recent critics, especially American new historicists and especially during the Reagan presidency, have been fascinated with the Renaissance theatricalization of power. For an influential early exploration, see STEPHEN ORGEL, *The Illusion of Power: Political Theater in the English Renaissance* (Berkeley: University of California Press, 1975); for an especially committed later one, see LEONARD TENNENHOUSE, *Power on Display: The Politics of Shakespeare's Genres* (New York: Methuen, 1986).

20. For a good summary of Elizabethan descriptions of actors, including those of Alleyn and Burbage, see LOUIS ADRIAN MONTROSE, 'The Purpose of Playing: Reflections on a Shakespearean Anthropology', *Helios* n.s. 7.2 (1980), 56–57. On the image of Proteus, see Barish, pp. 99–107.

21. (London, 1641), D2^r.

22. Sigs. B3–B4. For a perceptive discussion of Renaissance associations between theatrical deception and commercial trickery, see JEAN-CHRISTOPHE AGNEW, *Worlds Apart: The Market and the Theater in Anglo-American Thought, 1550–1750* (Cambridge: Cambridge University Press, 1986), pp. 1–148. On pp. 76–77 Agnew cites Heywood's pamphlet to illustrate the way 'English dramatists forced on Machiavelli's principles an association with commercial trickery that would have horrified the Florentine'.

23. On the intellectual roots of the conjunction between Machiavellianism and this new sense of personality, see HUGH M. RICHMOND, 'Personal Identity and Literary Personae: A Study in Historical Psychology', *PMLA* 90 (1975), 209–21, especially pp. 215–18. On the roles of social change and theatrical representation in the Renaissance production of a new concept of subjectivity, see CATHERINE BELSEY, *The Subject of Tragedy: Identity and Difference in Renaissance Drama* (London: Methuen, 1985).

24. *Poetics*, VI. 9–11, in *Aristotle's Theory of Poetry and Fine Art*, ed. S. H. BUTCHER, 4th ed. (New York: Dover, 1951), pp. 24–27.

25. Belsey, *The Subject of Tragedy*, p. 15.

26. Cf. Leggatt, *Shakespeare's Political Drama*, p. 94: 'The thinking is that of a chivalric hero, but the words belong to the counting-house.'

27. This speech is placed, significantly, at the end of the Gaultree Forest episode. Celebrating the virtues of sherris-sack to explain the difference between the heat and valor of Prince Henry and the cold-blooded calculation of Prince John, Falstaff emphasizes that Henry's virtues are achievements and not inheritances.

28. For an extended discussion of Hal's Machiavellianism, see Blanpied, chap. 9, especially pp. 160–66. On the ways the mere fact of theatrical representation threatened to compromise royal authority,

see Franco Moretti, '"A Huge Eclipse": Tragic Form and the Deconsecration of Sovereignty', *Genre* 15 (1982), 7–40, reprinted in *The Power of Forms in the English Renaissance*; and David Scott Kastan, 'Proud Majesty Made a Subject: Shakespeare and the Spectacle of Rule', *Shakespeare Quarterly* 37 (Winter 1986), 459–75.

29. Lewis Soens (ed.) *Sir Phillip Sidney's Defense of Poetry* (Lincoln: University of Nebraska Press, 1970), p. 21.

30. On Sidney's association of social rank with poetic quality, see Norbrook, *Poetry and Politics in the English Renaissance*, p. 92. See also Stephen Greenblatt, 'Murdering Peasants: Status, Genre, and the Representation of Rebellion', in *Representing the English Renaissance* (Berkeley: University of California Press, 1988; originally published in *Representations* 1 [1983]), pp. 17–18 for a perceptive discussion of Sidney's anxious efforts to mark the status boundaries between himself as a gentleman amateur and the commoner who practices art as a profession.

31. Sidney, *Defense*, p. 13 *et passim*.

32. Many writers have explored the ways the Elizabethan theater constituted a site of transgression, but see especially Montrose, 'The Purpose of Playing'; Peter Stallybrass and Allon White, *The Politics and Poetics of Transgression* (Ithaca: Cornell University Press, 1986), chap. 1; and Steven Mullaney, *The Place of the Stage: License, Play, and Power in Renaissance England* (Chicago: University of Chicago Press, 1988).

33. Samuel Cox, letter of January 15, 1591, and I. H., *This World's Folly. Or a Warning-Peece discharged upon the Wickednesse thereof* (1615), both reprinted in E. K. Chambers, *The Elizabethan Stage* (Oxford: Clarendon Press, 1923), 4: 237, 254.

34. George Whetstone, *A Touchstone for the Time*, printed as an 'Addition' to *A Mirour for Magestrates of Cytles* (1584), and Gervase Babington, *A very Fruitful Exposition of the Commandements* (1583), reprinted in Chambers, 4:227, 225.

35. Phillip Stubbes, *The Anatomie of Abuses: Contayning a Discoverie, or briefe Summarie of such Notable Vices and Imperfections, as now raigne in many Christian Countreyes of the Worlde: but (especiallie) in a verie famous Ilande called Ailgna* (London, 1583), in Chambers, 4:224.

36. For an account of these defenses, and of the deep instability of contemporary conceptions of the theater, see Chapter 3, section III.

37. I am indebted to an unpublished paper of Myra Jehlen's for the distinction between paradox and unresolved contradiction.

38. Kastan, 'Proud Majesty Made a Subject', pp. 473–74.

CHAPTER FIVE

Engendering a Nation: *Richard II*[1]

JEAN E. HOWARD AND PHYLLIS RACKIN

Although Phyllis Rackin's book *Stages of History*, from which the previous extract is taken, devotes one of its chapters to patriarchal history and subversive women, it is her more recent book, *Engendering a Nation*, written with Jean E. Howard, which examines the entire body of the history plays from a feminist perspective. Such an enterprise goes well beyond looking at women's roles. The book is an ambitious attempt to make connections between gender roles, the formation of national identity, and the emergence of the modern. Howard and Rackin detect in the plays an idealised heroic masculine past in contrast to a degraded effeminate present, plus an emergent conception of masculinity based on performance and represented by Henry Bullingbrook. Thus even the contrast between past and present – and such accompanying responses as nostalgia – are shown to be connected with gender. They note how a performative masculinity, which in the early plays is demonic, becomes normal and legitimate in the later.

In earlier chapters of the book they examine the transgressive, strong warrior women of the early plays. They argue that a change sets in with *Richard III*, which, although it has more lines spoken by women than any other history play, reduces them to passive roles. In *Richard II*, the subject of this extract, they see the continuation of the process of defining women as 'feminine': women are driven back into emotional and domestic roles as part of the movement into modernity. This definition of 'public' and 'private' in gendered terms is a fine retort to those critics of the third quarter of the twentieth century for whom 'the public versus the private man' (not woman) became a stock theme or cliché in their analysis of the history plays.

From a feminist standpoint, one of the most striking features of the second tetralogy is the restriction of women's roles. We have already seen how the formidable power of the women warriors in the Henry VI plays and *King John* was replaced in _Richard III_ by the pathetic laments of mourning widows and bereaved mothers. In the second tetralogy, women's roles are further constricted. There are fewer female characters; they have less time on stage and less to say when they get there. Moreover, virtually all the women we see in these plays are enclosed in domestic settings and confined to domestic roles. The only exceptions to the wholesale domestication of female characters are the disreputable, comic women at the Eastcheap Tavern: Mistress Quickly, the hostess; and Doll Tearsheet, the prostitute.

Even foreign women are domesticated. The dangerous, demonic otherness and vivid, subversive speech of Joan La Pucelle are replaced by the appealing, feminine helplessness and the broken English of the French princess in _Henry V_. The women warriors of the earlier plays are no longer seen on stage. Their only vestige is the fleeting reference at the beginning of _Henry IV, Part I_ to the 'beastly shameless trans-formation' performed by Welsh women upon the bodies of the English soldiers killed in the Battle of Holmedon (I.i.44). The atrocity is performed offstage and never explicitly described (the only Welsh woman who appears on stage is a weep-ing wife). Even the terms in which the women's savagery is reported at the English court – as an act 'as may not be / Without much shame retold or spoken of' (I.i.45–6) – mark its erasure from the scene of English history.

In the plays of the second tetralogy, as in _Richard III_, female sexuality no longer threatens to disrupt legitimate authority. When Bullingbrook charges in _Richard II_ that Bushy and Green 'have in manner with [their] sinful hours / Made a divorce betwixt his queen and him, / Broke the possession of a royal bed' (III.i.11–13), the sexual culprits are the king and his male favorites: It is not even clear that any women are involved.[2] The only reference to the queen's sexuality is purely metaphorical – the 'unborn sorrow, ripe in fortune's womb' her feminine intuition detects (II.ii.10). The sorrow, moreover, is a fully legitimate conception: caused by a premonition of her husband's impending fall, it is implicitly designated as the offspring of her lawful marriage. The other women in the play – the Duchess of Gloucester and the Duchess of York – are too old to pose a sexual threat. The Duke and Duchess of York, in fact, make this point explicit. In V.ii the duchess reminds her husband that her 'teeming date' is 'drunk up with time' (91); and in V.iii, York opposes her attempt to plead for her son's life by reminding her how preposterous it would be if her 'old dugs' should 'once more a traitor rear' (90).

Barbara Hodgdon's observation about _Henry IV, Part I_ – that the play is 'unlike Shakespeare's earlier histories, where conflict centers on genealogical descent in a struggle for the crown's rightful ownership' (1991: 155) – is applicable to the entire second tetralogy and to _Henry VIII_ as well. In _Richard II_ York gives his allegiance to Bullingbrook despite his knowledge that Richard is the legitimate heir of Edward III. Because patrilineal inheritance is no longer sufficient to guarantee patriarchal authority, female sexual transgression no longer threatens to subvert it. The issues of bastardy and adultery arise only briefly and only in Act V, when the action degenerates from the historical tragedy of Richard's fall to the farcical domestic quarrel between the Duke and Duchess of York about their son. Terrified by her hus-band's threat to report Aumerle's treason to the new king, the duchess assumes, wrongly, that he is motivated by doubts about his son's paternity:

But now I know thy mind, thou dost suspect
That I have been disloyal to thy bed,
And that he is a bastard, not thy son.
Sweet York, sweet husband, be not of that mind,
He is as like thee as a man may be
Not like to me, or any of my kin.

(V.ii.104–9)

Neither York nor the audience has any reason to doubt what the duchess says. In fact, her anxious suspicion that York doubts his son's paternity is expressed in terms that render it ludicrous. Instead of empowering the duchess as a sexual threat to the authority of her husband and the legitimacy of her son, her reference to the possibility of her adultery is designed to elicit dismissive laughter.

Here, as in *Richard III*, the constriction of women's roles represents a movement into modernity, the division of labor and the cultural restrictions that accompanied the production of the household as a private place, separated from the public arenas of economic and political endeavor.[3] To move from the first tetralogy to the second is to move backward to the time of Richard II, but it is also to move forward from a story of warring feudal families to one of the consolidation of the English nation under the power of a great king. In the first tetralogy, virtue and military power like Talbot's are inherited along with the patrilineal titles of nobility; in the second, they are the personal assets that enable the son of an enterprising upstart like Henry Bullingbrook to achieve the status of the mirror of all Christian kings and the aspiring men in the theater audience to earn their places in the commonwealth.

In *Richard II* the contradictions between those two models of personal and royal legitimacy are personalized in the opposition between Richard and Bullingbrook; but they are also framed as abstract issues, the subjects for repeated debate by male characters in the play, the motives and rationalizations for their acts and decisions. The dynastic loyalties that motivate much of the action in the first tetralogy typically make political action the product of filial devotion, but in *Richard II* the private affective bonds that unite fathers and sons are opposed to and superseded by the demands of political principle and civic duty. Gaunt agrees to the banishment of his own son because, as he tells King Richard, 'You urg'd me as a judge' and not 'like a father' (I.iii.237–8). The Duke of York, discovering that his son has joined a conspiracy to kill the new king, Henry IV, pleads that his son *not* be pardoned because, he explains, 'If thou do pardon, whosoever pray, / More sins for this forgiveness prosper may. / This fest'red joint cut off, the rest rest sound, / This let alone will all the rest confound' (V.iii.83–6). Even the instructions the gardener gives his helpers take the form of a lesson in political theory:

Go thou, and like an executioner
Cut off the heads of [too] fast growing sprays,
That look too lofty in our commonwealth:
All must be even in our government.

(III.iv.33–36)

The concern for the commonwealth that unites the lowly gardeners with their betters at court also separates men from women. All of the female characters in *Richard II* come from the top of the social and political hierarchy, but their interests are delimited by the private affective bonds of family loyalty, and the women are entirely preoccupied by concerns for their male relations. These concerns differ significantly from the strong genealogical ties that bind fathers to sons in the Henry VI plays. Those ties, while they often include an affective dimension, as in Talbot's concern for his son, also have a public political and economic dimension: the defense and consolidation of dynastic power and its transmission from one generation to the next. Gaunt shares the Duchess of Gloucester's grief for her murdered husband, who was his own brother, but when the duchess tries to persuade him to avenge Gloucester's death, Gaunt refuses because his loyalty to the principle of divine right takes precedence over his personal loyalty to his brother: Richard, he explains, is God's 'deputy', and 'I may never lift / An angry arm against His minister' (I.ii.38–41). The same gendered difference distinguishes the gardener and his helper from the queen. The common men lament Richard's bad government and its effects upon the commonwealth as well as his downfall; the royal woman responds to the news as a personal catastrophe for herself and her husband. Intensified to the point of caricature, the opposition between masculine political considerations and feminine affective loyalty is reiterated in Act V when the Duke and Duchess of York wrangle over whether their son should be punished or pardoned for his part in the conspiracy to assassinate the new king.

Like the bereaved and grieving women in *Richard III*, the Duchess of Gloucester and the queen in *Richard II* dramatize the private emotional costs of the men's public, political conflicts; and, like the women in *Richard III*, they are powerless to affect the outcome of those conflicts. When Gaunt refuses to avenge her husband's murder, the Duchess of Gloucester leaves the stage to die of grief. The queen does not even learn that Richard is to be deposed until she eavesdrops on the gardeners' conversation. When Bullingbrook pardons Aumerle, the Duchess of York becomes the only woman in the play who manages to influence the action, but her farcical wrangling with her husband also reinforces the separation between the public, political concerns of men and the private, affective loyalties of women. The bickering between the duke and duchess – and with it the lowering of the dramatic register – begins in V.ii when York struggles frantically to get his boots so he can ride off to warn the king about Aumerle's participation in a conspiracy to assassinate him, while the duchess, equally frantic, struggles to prevent him. In the following scene the domestic quarrel resumes in the royal presence, and this time the humor is explicitly identified with the inappropriateness of the duchess's intervention. Her demand to be admitted to the royal presence initiates a telling remark from the new king: 'Speak with me, pity me, open the door!', she cries, 'A beggar begs that never begg'd before', In a comment probably meant to be addressed to the audience, the king responds, 'Our scene is alt'red from a serious thing, / And now changed to "The Beggar and the King"' (V.iii.77–80), signalling that the historical 'Tragedy of Richard II' is being interrupted by the low comic farce of 'The Beggar and the King'. Significantly, it is the woman who is blamed for initiating both the generic lowering of the drama and the social lowering of the action (Hodgdon 1991: 139). The solemn dignity of the court (and of the history play) has no place for domestic quar-rels or the shrill-voiced supplications of an anxious mother.

The gendering of excessive emotion as feminine has unsettling effects on the gender position – and the authority – of Richard II, perhaps the most emotive of all Shakespeare's kings. While masculinity and femininity are never the exclusive prop-erties of male and female persons, aspects of English culture in the late sixteenth and early seventeenth centuries made the performative and constructed nature of gender difference disturbingly visible. In the theaters, boys played women's roles and many kinds of social distinctions were indicated by a semiotics of dress and ges-ture. On the throne, there was a female monarch who claimed masculine authority by referring to herself as a 'prince' (Marcus 1988: 60). In the streets of London, women paraded in masculine dress (Harrison 1587: 147). An increasingly urbanized and performative culture destabilized traditional status distinctions, including the distinctions between men and women (Newman 1991: 123), and produced a wide variety of anxious attempts to reestablish them. For the literate, increasing con-cern with the need to observe masculine and feminine roles was expressed in satiric writing that made the 'womanish' man and the 'mannish' woman stock objects of invective. In villages, failure to abide by the codes of gendered behavior was pun-ished by court prosecutions of scolds and witches and community shaming rituals such as charivaris (Underdown 1985: 127).

All these efforts to enforce gender difference can be seen as responses to an emergent culture of personal achievement. If a man's place in the social hierarchy had to be achieved and secured by his own efforts, any claims to authority required that both social status and gender status had to be sustained in performance. In *Richard II*, the king's patrilineal authority is vitiated by his womanish tears and his effeminate behavior: he has no taste for foreign wars, he talks when he should act, and he wastes his kingdom's treasure by indulging in excessive luxuries. Bullingbrook, who has no hereditary right to the crown, acquires it by the success-ful performance of masculine virtues.

Many critics have remarked that the conflict between Richard and Bullingbrook is framed as a conflict between two models of royal authority, Richard associated with a nostalgic image of medieval royalty, grounded in heredity and expressed in ceremonial ritual, Bullingbrook with the emergence of an authority achieved by personal performance and expressed in the politically motivated theatrical self-presentation of a modern ruler. What is less frequently noted is how thoroughly the binary opposition personalized in the conflict between Bullingbrook and Richard is implicated in an early modern ideology of 'masculine' and 'feminine'. Deborah Warner's 1995 production of the play, which starred Fiona Shaw as Richard, exploited this gendered opposition to brilliant dramatic effect. Shaw, in the words of one reviewer, 'simply played Richard as a woman' (Berkowitz 1996: 9). Although Shakespeare does not literalize the gendered opposition between the two antagon-ists, his Bullingbrook, like Warner's, plays the 'man' to Richard's 'woman'. A mas-ter of military and political strategy, Bullingbrook is shown in company with a noble father, and he alludes to the existence of an 'unthrifty' son (V.iii.l); but we hear nothing of his wife or mother, and he is never represented in association with women. Richard, by contrast, has a wife but no son. Although our own gender ideology privileges male heterosexual passion as an expression of virility, this was not yet the case in Shakespeare's time. Richard is characterized as 'effeminate', but this does not mean that he is 'homosexual': indeed, the terms 'homosexual' and 'heterosexual', along with the conceptions of gendered personal identity they denote, are post-Shakespearean inventions (Bray 1988: 13–32; Bredbeck 1991: 3–30; Goldberg 1992: 1–26; Rackin 1992: 37–52). Richard is effeminate because he prefers words to deeds, has no taste for battle, and is addicted to luxurious pleasures. His rapid fluctuations from overweening confidence to the depth of despair (III.ii) recall early modern misogynist denunciations of feminine instability (Ferris 1981), but even his virtues are represented in feminine terms: York's sympathetic description of Richard's behavior in adversity – his 'gentle sorrow' and 'His face still combating with tears and smiles, / The badges of his grief and patience' (V.ii.31–3) – draws on the same discourse of suffering feminine virtue as the description of Lear's Cordelia smiling and crying at once as 'patience and sorrow [strove] / Who should express her goodliest' (IV.iii.16–17). Bullingbrook speaks few words but raises a large army. Richard is a master of poetic eloquence, unsurpassed in what Mowbray calls 'a woman's war . . . of . . . tongues' (I.i.48–9), but he surrenders to Bullingbrook without waging a single battle. His viceroy is the superannuated York, who appears 'weak with age', 'with signs of war about his aged neck' (II.ii.83, 74); confronted by Bullingbrook's military challenge, York immediately capitulates, declaring that he will 'remain as neuter' (II.iii.159).

The gendered opposition between Richard and Bullingbrook takes much of its force from the predicament of the English aristocracy at the time the play was produced. The noblemen who support Bullingbrook's rebellion are motivated by what they perceive as monarchial threats to their traditional power and authority, threats which are explicitly identified as emasculation when Ross charges that Richard's appropriation of Bullingbrook's inheritance has left him 'bereft and gelded of his patrimony' (II.i.237). As Richard Halpern points out, 'the aristocracy felt emasculated by conversion from a militarized to a consuming class'. This anxiety was heightened during Elizabeth's reign by the presence of a female monarch and by the queen's transformation of the medieval culture of aristocratic honor from martial service to courtly display (Halpern 1991: 245). Richard's possession of the throne, like Elizabeth's, is authorized by the old warrant of patrilineal inheritance, but his loss of it is defined in terms of the new anxieties that Halpern describes.

Richard's father, York recalls, 'Did win what he did spend, and spent not that / Which his triumphant father's hand had won' (II.i.180–1). Richard, by contrast, has 'basely yielded upon compromise / That which his noble ancestors achiev'd with blows' (II.i.253–4) and wasted the land's wealth in luxurious pleasures and courtly extravagance. Holinshed's *Chronicles*, Shakespeare's main historical source for the play, also represents Richard as indulging in unprecedented personal extravagance at the expense of the commonwealth:

He kept the greatest port, and mainteined the most plentifull house that ever any king in England did either before his time or since. . . . In his kitchen there were three hundred servitors, and everie other office was furnished after the like rate. Of ladies, chamberers, and landerers, there were above three hundred at the least. And in gorgious and costlie apparell they exceeded all measure, not one of them that kept within the bounds of his degree. Yeomen and groomes were clothed in silkes, with cloth of graine and skarlet, over sumptuous ye may be sure for their estates. And this vanitie was not onelie used in the court in those daies, but also other people abroad in the towns and countries, had their garments cut far otherwise than had beene accustomed before his daies, with imbroderies, rich furres, and goldsmiths worke, and everie daie there was devising of new fashions, to the great hinderance and decaie of the common-welth.

(Holinshed 1587:2:868)

In Holinshed's account, as in Shakespeare's, Richard's extravagance is both a fabulous image of lost splendor and a socially disruptive innovation. Like Elizabethan pageantry, it appeals to nostalgia and to an appetite for gorgeous display, but the newfangled 'vanities' Holinshed describes also evoke the anxieties that were associated with an increasingly unstable social hierarchy. Shakespeare makes those anxieties explicit when he associates Richard's appetite for the vanity of luxurious new fashions with the figure of the 'Italianated Englishman' who was a familiar object of satire in the sixteenth, but not the fourteenth, century (Ure 1961: 48–9n). York explains that Richard cannot hear his venerable uncles' good advice because his ear is stopped by

Report of fashions in proud Italy,
Whose manners still our tardy, apish nation
Limps after in base imitation.
Where doth the world thrust forth a vanity –
So it be new, there's no respect how vile –
That is not quickly buzz'd into his ears?

(II.i.21–6)

Like the absentee landlords of Shakespeare's own time who betrayed the old feudal traditions of obligation to enclose their property and exploit it for money to spend on lavish displays at court, Richard's taste for effeminate luxury forces him to degrade his office from king to 'landlord' (II.i.113).

Confronted by rapid cultural change, Shakespeare's contemporaries often idealized the past as a time of stable values and national glory, when social status was firmly rooted in patrilineal inheritance and expressed in chivalric virtue. In Shakespeare's representation of Richard II, however, the schematic oppositions between an idealized masculine past and a degraded effeminate present give way to expose the cultural contradictions that lay at the heart of Elizabethan nostalgia for the medieval past. In Richard's characterization – as in the case of Elizabeth herself – the polluting forces of effeminate modernity are embodied in the same person who represents the patrilineal royal authority they threaten to subvert.

Despite (or perhaps because of) its association with the cult of Elizabeth, the nostalgic ideal of a glorious English past was overwhelmingly masculine. Just as Elizabeth's male courtiers paid tribute to their queen with elaborate reconstructions of medieval tournaments, Edmund Spenser used archaic language and the conventions of chivalric romance to celebrate Elizabeth, but the form of Spenser's narrative minimizes her power. Although the Faerie Queene is the nominal center of

Spenser's poem, she is actually confined to its margins. As Richard Helgerson points out, she 'never appears in the poem and exercises only the loosest and most intermittent control over its action' (1992: 48). A similar paradox informs John of Gaunt's nostalgic projection of the England that Richard has betrayed. For although Gaunt's ideal England is a 'nurse', a 'teeming womb of royal kings' (II.i.51), none of its inhabitants are women. A 'fortress' surrounded by a sea which serves it as a 'moat', a 'royal throne of kings' who are 'renowned . . . for Christian service and true chivalry', the object of Gaunt's nostalgic longing is inhabited exclusively by a 'happy breed of men' (11140–54), and the deeds that prove its worth are their heroic battles.

Gaunt invokes an ideal past in order to rebuke a degenerate present – the degraded world of an effeminate king who wastes the land's wealth and honor on luxurious pleasures rather than augmenting them in manly wars against the French. The antithesis he constructs between a warlike, masculine historical world and a degenerate, effeminate present employs exactly the strategy that Thomas Nashe described as the virtue of the history play – the representation of a 'valiant' world of English 'forefathers' as a 'rebuke' to 'these degenerate effeminate dayes of ours'. Written in the time of Elizabeth – a queen frequently compared to Richard II – Shakespeare's English histories appealed to a similar nostalgia for a masculine, historical world projected in idealized opposition to the present realities of female power and authority.[4] In the second tetralogy, however, this gendered opposition between past and present is increasingly disrupted and deconstructed.

In the earlier plays, performative masculinity is demonic. Richard III, in fact, is its prime exemplar. By the end of the second tetralogy, however, performance will provide the basis for the legitimate royal authority that Henry V achieves despite what he explicitly acknowledges as 'the fault / My father made in compassing the crown' (*Henry V*: IV.i.293–4). In *Richard II*, as in *King John*, both forms of authority are compromised. The older model of royal authority based on patrilineal succession (which had produced a female monarch in Elizabeth I) is represented in the person of an effeminate, theatrical king, who is nonetheless the legitimate heir to the throne. The emergent masculine ideals of personal merit and performance are associated with the usurper, who is empowered by the support of the overwhelming majority of his countrymen.

Although Bullingbrook explains his unauthorized return from banishment in terms of the feudal logic of hereditary entitlement, claiming that he does so only to secure his patrilineal legacy as Duke of Lancaster, he quickly redefines it as service to the 'commonwealth' (II.iii.166–7). In Shakespeare's account, as in Holinshed, Bullingbrook has the overwhelming support of the people. Describing Bullingbrook's departure for exile, Holinshed reports, 'A woonder it was to see what number of people ran after him in everie towne and street where he came, before he took the sea, lamenting and bewailing his departure, as who would saie, that when he departed, the onelie shield, defense and comfort of the commonwealth was vaded and gone' (1587: 2: 848). Shakespeare's Richard reports the same event with anxious contempt: we 'Observ'd his courtship to the common people', he says, 'what reverence he did throw away on slaves, / Wooing poor craftsmen with the craft of smiles . . . Off goes his bonnet to an oyster-wench / A brace of draymen bid God speed him well, / And had the tribute of his supple knee' (I.iv.24–33). Holinshed notes that Bullingbrook's rebellion had 'the helpe and assistance (almost) of all the whole realme' (1587: 2: 855), and Shakespeare repeatedly alludes to the universal dissatisfaction with Richard's government and support for Bullingbrook (II.i. 246–88; III.ii.112–19).

In the context of a public theater, these allusions work to empower Bullingbrook and discredit Richard. Shakespeare's descriptions of Richard's offenses against both 'the commons' and 'the nobles' (II.i.246–8) and of the crowds that take up arms in support of the rebellion ('white-beards', 'boys, with women's voices', 'distaff-women', 'both young and old' [III.ii.112–19]) emphasize their inclusiveness, and they could stand equally well for a description of the heterogeneous audience in the playhouse. The theatrical milieu tended to support the emergent form of authority, in which a king, like a player, had to depend on the favorable responses of the people for whom he performed. Moreover, Richard's contempt for his humble subjects is not likely to have endeared him to their counterparts in Shakespeare's audience.

Hereditary legitimacy, projected in the first tetralogy as a lost ideal represented by the name of Henry V, is now compromised in the person of its leading representative. When the play begins, Richard is already guilty of a crime against the royal blood, the murder of the Duke of Gloucester, his uncle. Contrasting Richard and his father, York defines that crime as a separation from the patrilineal line: 'His hands were guilty of no kindred blood, / But bloody with the enemies of his kin' (II.i.182–3), a recurrent charge in the first two acts of the play. The Duchess of Gloucester recalls Richard's murder of her husband in the same terms, as the spilling of a 'vial full of Edward's sacred blood' (I.ii.17). Richard continues to undermine the patrilineal principle upon which his own authority depends when he disinherits Bullingbrook. As York explains,

Is not Gaunt dead? and doth not Herford live?
Was not Gaunt just? and is not Harry true?
Did not the one deserve to have an heir?
Is not his heir a well-deserving son?
Take Herford's rights away, and take from Time
His charters and his customary rights;
Let not to-morrow then ensue to-day;
Be not thyself; for how art thou a king
But by fair sequence and succession?

(II.i.191–9)

Bullingbrook makes the same argument: 'If that my cousin king be King in England, / It must be granted I am Duke of Lancaster' (II.iii.123–4).

In Gaunt's nostalgic projection of medieval England as a 'royal throne of kings', there is a seamless union between English patriotism and loyalty to the king, but Richard's offenses set them in opposition to each other. The wars between York and Lancaster in the Henry VI plays are motivated by competing claims to genealogical authority, but the conflict in *Richard II* is framed in terms that recall the ideological conflicts in early modern England between an emergent national consciousness and the Tudor and Stuart monarchs' efforts to rationalize, defend, and extend royal authority. To Bullingbrook, as to the gardeners, England is a 'commonwealth' (II.iii.166). To Richard it is simply his personal property, to be used as he desires for his own benefit. The dialogue in the early scenes is laced with patriotic sentiment, which is mobilized in opposition to Richard. Gaunt charges that the 'blessed plot' England 'Is now leas'd out . . . / Like to a tenement [i.e. land held by a tenant] or pelting [i.e. paltry] farm' (II.i.59–60). The banishment of Mowbray and Bulling-brook elicits moving affirmations of national identity, but always with the implica-tion that Richard is to blame for violating the bond between faithful subjects and mother England. Mowbray protests that he has deserved better at Richard's hands than to be exiled for life: 'The language I have learnt these forty years, / My native English, now I must forgo. . . . What is thy sentence [then] but speechless death, / Which robs my tongue from breathing native breath?' (I.iii.159–73). As Richard Helgerson has observed, 'a kingdom whose boundaries are determined by the language of its inhabitants is no longer a kingdom in the purely dynastic sense' (1992: 2). The ringing couplets with which Bullingbrook departs for his own exile also invoke an emergent sense of national identity grounded in the place of his nativity:

> Then England's ground, farewell, sweet soil, adieu:
> My mother, and my nurse, that bears me yet!
> Where e'er I wander, boast of this I can,
> Though banish'd, yet a true-born Englishman.

> (I.iii.306–9)

Bullingbrook defines his relationship to the land in the same terms that John of Gaunt uses when he describes 'This blessed plot, this earth, this realm, this England' as 'This nurse, this teeming womb of royal kings' (II.i.50–1); but for Bullingbrook the 'sweet soil' is the 'mother' and 'nurse' of every 'true-born English-man'. To the Richard of the first two acts, it is his personal property and a source of ready cash: 'We are enforc'd to farm our royal realm [i.e. sell the profits from future taxes], / The revenue whereof shall furnish us / For our affairs in hand' (I.iv.45–7). Moreover, even when Richard speaks lovingly of the English land, the terms he uses construct a gendered contrast that favors Bullingbrook. When Richard returns from Ireland, he 'weep[s] for joy' and salutes the 'dear earth . . . as a long-parted mother with her child' (III.ii.4–8). The rhyme words in Bullingbrook's final couplet – 'boast of this I can' and 'a true-born Englishman' emphasize his masculinity as well as his Englishness. Richard's language effeminizes him as a mother and infantilizes the land as his child. And unlike Bullingbrook, he does not identify the earth as English; in fact, although Richard has by far the greatest number of lines in the play, he speaks the words 'England' or 'English' only five times in the entire script (I.iv.35; II.i..220; III.iii.97, 100; IV.i.264) and almost always perfunctorily.

Richard II destabilizes the schematic oppositions between past and present, male and female, patrilineal authority and its subversion, English patriotism and foreign threat that defined the meaning of the dramatic conflicts in the first tetralogy. It also destabilizes the binary opposition between theatrical power and historical authority, and in so doing begins the renegotiation of their relationship that will be a major project in the succeeding plays. The rhetorical impact of Richard's theatricality, like that of Richard III, is ambivalent. On the one hand, both characters are associated by their theatricality with the feminine and with the loss of integrity in an increasingly complicated contemporary world. On the other hand, both are empowered by their theatricality, because of its inevitable attraction for a theater audience. What is new in *Richard II* is the association of theatrical power with legitimate royal authority.

The contest between Richard and Bullingbrook, in fact, is specifically framed as a contention between rival actors. As early as Act I, Richard anxiously describes the success of Bullingbrook's theatrical self-presentation to the London citizens:

> How he did seem to dive into their hearts
> With humble and familiar courtesy,
> What reverence he did throw away on slaves,
> Wooing poor craftsmen with the craft of smiles
> And patient underbearing of his fortune,
> As 'twere to banish their affects with him.
> Off goes his bonnet to an oyster-wench,
> A brace of draymen bid God speed him well,
> And had the tribute of his supple knee,
> With 'Thanks, my countrymen, my loving friends,'
> As were our England in reversion his,
> And he our subjects' next degree in hope.

(I.iv.25–36)

Publicly acting like a king, Bullingbrook finally becomes one, and in Act V York explicitly compares the Londoners' enthusiastic reception of the newly crowned Henry IV to the response of a theater audience to a 'well-graced actor', their contempt for Richard to the indifference of playgoers to an inferior performer:

> As in a theatre the eyes of men,
> After a well-graced actor leaves the stage,
> Are idly bent on him that enters next,
> Thinking his prattle to be tedious,
> Even so, or with much more contempt, men's eyes
> Did scowl on gentle Richard.

(V.ii.23–8)

It is significant, however, that although Bullingbrook's theatrical power is described, it is never shown. Instead of seeing these scenes, the audience in Shakespeare's playhouse is told about them – and told, moreover, by characters who do not share the London crowds' enthusiasm for Bullingbrook's performance.

The reports of Bullingbrook's spectacular success in staging himself in the streets of London anticipate the politically motivated theatricality of Tudor and Stuart monarchs, but Richard's self-dramatization on Shakespeare's stage anticipates the theatrical appeal of Shakespeare's later tragic heroes. The quarto title page of *Richard II*, like that of *Richard III*, identifies the play as a tragedy, and Richard II, even more than his dramatic predecessor, prefigures the heroes of Shakespeare's later tragedies. Like a true tragic hero, he gives long and eloquent expression to his feelings and motivations. Unlike Bullingbrook's theatricality, which is described as an effective political strategy, Richard's is presented as a powerful expression of personal subjectivity.

Bullingbrook has very little to say on stage beyond what is required to advance the plot, and his motives are notoriously inscrutable, provoking many fruitless critical debates as to when or whether he decided to seize the crown. Richard's personality is a major issue in the play; but not Bullingbrook's. There is only one place, in fact, where the dramatic action seems designed to portray Bullingbrook's character – the dialogue in Act I when John of Gaunt advises his son to sweeten his exile by imagining himself at court: 'Suppose the singing birds musicians', Gaunt says, 'The grass whereon thou tread'st the presence strow'd, / The flowers fair ladies, and thy steps no more / Than a delightful measure or a dance' (I.iii.288–91). Discounting both the effeminate pleasures of the court and the feminine pleasures of the imagination, Bullingbrook replies,

> O, who can hold a fire in his hand
> By thinking on the frosty Caucasus?
> Or cloy the hungry edge of appetite
> By bare imagination of a feast?
> Or wallow naked in December snow
> By thinking on fantastic summer's heat?
>
> (I.iii.294–9)

Bullingbrook's 'bare imagination' provides a striking, gendered contrast to the fertility of Richard's. Confined, in Act V, to a solitary prison cell, Richard launches into a sixty-six-line soliloquy. 'My brain I'll prove the female to my soul', he says, 'My soul the father, and these two beget / A generation of still-breeding thoughts' to 'people this little world, / In humors like the people of this world. . . . Thus play I in one person many people' (V.v.6–10, 31). The androgynous fertility of Richard's imagination and his ability to play multiple roles associate him with playwright and actor (McMillin 1984: 46). Although Bullingbrook knows how to stage himself to the people for political advantage, his manly rejection of 'fantasy' associates him with the anti-theatrical writers who decried the deceptive fictions of the stage. It also reiterates his association with the forces of modernity, for as James Calderwood has observed, the opposition between Richard and Bullingbrook is also an opposition between two ideals of language, one 'medieval, sacramental, and poetic' and the other 'modern, utilitarian, and scientific' (Calderwood 1971: 162).

Richard imagines himself as a figure in a medieval tableau, his mortal life as 'a little scene, / To monarchize . . . and kill with looks', abruptly ended when the personified figure of Death pierces 'his castle wall' with 'a little pin' (III.ii.164–70). In the deposition scene, he compares himself to the crucified Christ, and he turns on the assembled audience with an indictment that recalls speeches delivered by actors who portrayed Christ in medieval mystery plays, reminding the spectators that 'all of you that stand and look upon me / . . . Though some of you, with Pilate, wash your hands, / Showing an outward pity, yet you Pilates / Have here deliver'd me to my sour cross, / And water cannot wash away your sin' (IV.i.237–42). Once Bullingbrook takes the throne, theatrical display assumes the modern forms of royal procession and commercial performance. York alludes to both when he describes the new king's triumphant entry into London with Richard at his heels.

Associating royal authority with theatrical display, York's simile signals the modernity of the world of Henry IV. Paradoxically, however, the performance in Shakespeare's own commercial playhouse seems designed to elicit a response opposite to the one York describes, for although Bullingbrook wins in the represented action, the play that depicts his triumph came to Shakespeare's audience, not as the celebration of the accession of Henry IV, but as 'The Tragedy of Richard II'. Although Richard's feminine self-indulgence and histrionic narcissism disqualify him for political action, Richard and not Bullingbrook was the 'well-graced actor' in Shakespeare's theater: no acting company would give the smaller and less demanding role of Bullingbrook to its best actor and deny him the chance to play the leading role of Richard.

Even in the deposition scene, where the represented action depicts Bullingbrook's acquisition of Richard's power, Richard dominates the stage. He deposes himself and makes long and eloquent speeches about his complicated emotional responses to the action. The other actors are restricted for the most part to single lines or even half-lines. Richard calls for a looking-glass, and it instantly appears (IV.i.275). Taking the glass and contemplating his own image, he meditates aloud for sixteen lines about his face. The instrument of feminine vanity becomes the means of theatrical empowerment, for it demands that all eyes in the playhouse, including Richard's own, will be fixed on Richard's face. Then, in a remarkable *coup de théâtre*, he dashes the glass against the floor and turns to Bullingbrook with his conclusion: 'Mark, silent king, the moral of this sport, / How soon my sorrow hath destroy'd my face' (IV.i.290–1). The silent, practical new king attempts to arrest the theatrical display with a terse rebuttal that draws on the familiar Elizabethan association between shadows and actors: 'The shadow of your sorrow hath destroy'd / The shadow of your face.' But Richard is much too quick-witted and voluble to be silenced by this literal-minded reply. He takes off for another twelve lines, making metaphors about shadows and ironically thanking Bullingbrook for 'not only [giving him] cause to wail but [teaching him] the way / How to lament the cause' (IV.i.300–2). In the represented historical action, Bullingbrook has taken the crown of England from Richard, but he is still compelled to play straight man to Richard's agile wit on Shakespeare's stage.

The new king plays straight man again in Act V, when the Duke and Duchess of York force him to participate in their domestic quarrel over the fate of their son. Replacing the gorgeous pageantry of Richard's late medieval court with the vulgar domestic farce of a suddenly modern world, this episode reproduces in a lower register the loss of patriarchal authority that has already taken place in the main action of the play. The entire scene, in fact, seems calculated to exhibit the new king's lack of inherent authority and to degrade him by association with the low concerns of ordinary subjects. To do so, it turns from the political to the domestic realm, naturalizing Henry's lack of patriarchal authority in the image of the troubled family that will be a *leitmotif* in both parts of *Henry IV*. At the very beginning of the scene, before York enters, the king complains about his 'unthrifty' son – absent from the court for three months and rumored to be consorting with dissolute companions in London. Both the king's inability to control his son and his use of the term 'unthrifty' associate him with York, who uses the same monetary language when he refuses the king's offer to pardon Aumerle. If he accepts it, he says, Aumerle 'shall spend mine honor with his shame, / As thriftless sons their scraping fathers' gold' (V.iii.68–9). Refiguring the offer of royal largesse as a degrading commercial transaction in which aristocratic honor is transformed into money to be spent, York's amplification of the image of the thriftless son degrades both himself and the new king by association with the money-grubbing, miserly father of a spendthrift son, a stock character with a disquieting resemblance to an ambitious Elizabethan merchant.

The most explicit marks of the men's debasement, however, are the work of the duchess. Both York and Henry are diminished by their inability to silence the woman and their ultimate capitulation to her demands, and degraded by their participation in the indecorous scene she stages. When York first enters, the king speaks to him in blank verse and the language of royal decorum, but once the duchess enters, she inducts him into the debased idiom of domestic wrangling. He answers her unceremonious demand for admission to the royal presence – 'What ho, my liege! for God's sake let me in' – without rhyming. 'What shrill-[voic'd] suppliant makes this eager cry?', he asks. But the duchess's response – 'A woman, and thy aunt, great King, 'tis I' – signals his incorporation in the domestic farce; identifying, herself as the king's aunt, she also rhymes her answer to his question. The king's next speech – four lines that consist of two self-contained couplets – signals his entry into the low discourse of domestic comedy (V.iii.74–82).

Richard also has a domestic scene in Act V, but his is anything but comic. Apparently designed to contrast with the farcical wrangling between the Duke and Duchess of York, the elegiac parting between Richard and his queen is steeped in nostalgic pathos. Like the other scenes in Act V, its purpose is retrospectively to ratify Richard's authority and discredit that of Henry IV. Despite this nostalgic purpose, however, the means are modern, for the difference between legitimate and illegitimate kings is no longer defined by differences in patrilineal authority, but instead by their personal character and performance, by the allegiance of humble subjects, and by their roles as husbands. Richard has always surpassed his rival in the extravagance of his theatricality, but in Act V, he is also shown as the recipient of a humble subject's heartfelt devotion when the groom visits his prison (V.v.67–97). Most important, however, is the contrast between the Duchess of York's comic victory over her husband and the new king and the noble pathos of the parting between Richard and his loving queen.

The importance of the women's roles in Act V is attested by the fact that both are unhistorical. York's first wife, Isabel of Castille, had died in 1393, six years earlier; but although the Duchess of York at the time of Richard's deposition and Aumerle's treachery was actually Aumerle's stepmother, Shakespeare insists on the biological connection. His duchess reproaches her husband, 'Hadst thou groan'd for him / As I have done, thou wouldst be more pitiful' (V.ii.102–3). York, in turn, rejects her desperate efforts to save her son by asking, 'Thou frantic woman, what dost thou make here? / Shall thy old dugs once more a traitor rear?' (V.iii.89–90). Richard's wife at the time of his deposition, also named Isabel, was a ten-year-old child, the daughter of the King of France, whom Richard had married when she was seven in order to secure a truce with her father (Saccio 1977: 22). Shakespeare transforms the child into a mature woman and the dynastic marriage into a loving affective union in order to provide a retrospective ratification for Richard's patriarchal authority, now grounded in the matrimonial authority of a husband rather than the royal patrimony that Richard lost when he betrayed the legacy of his forefathers (see II.i.163–85). Neither the usurpers' insistence on sending the queen back to France nor the tearful parting between husband and wife has any basis in Holinshed, who reported that after Richard's death Henry attempted, against the will of the French, to keep the child and her dowry in England and marry her to the Prince of Wales (Holinshed 1587: 3: 16–18).

Shakespeare's mature queen is nameless to the end and powerless to affect the historical action, but she provides the mystical warrant for Richard's legitimacy. Her grief, like that of the women in *Richard III*, endows her with a prophetic power that is specifically identified as feminine. She has premonitions of disaster, which she describes as an 'unborn sorrow, ripe in fortune's womb' (II.ii.10), and when Green brings her the news that Bullingbrook has returned to England, she calls him 'the midwife to my woe' (II.ii.62). At the end of the play, Richard entrusts the queen with the task of telling his story:

> In winter's tedious nights sit by the fire
> With good old folks and let them tell [thee] tales
> Of woeful ages long ago betid:
> And ere thou bid good night, to quite their griefs,
> Tell thou the lamentable tale of me,
> And send the hearers weeping to their beds.
> For why, the senseless brands will sympathize
> The heavy accent of thy moving tongue,
> And in compassion weep the fire out,
> And some will mourn in ashes, some coal-black,
> For the deposing of a rightful king.

(V.i.40–50)

Imagining his story as a nostalgic tale 'of woeful ages long ago betid' told by a fire on a winter night, Richard consigns his history to the female genre of domestic oral narrative.[5] Enjoining the queen to tell it, he depends on the 'moving tongue' of a woman and the compassionate responses of her auditors to provide the posthumous ratification of his legitimacy as 'a rightful king'.

Like the women in *Richard III*, the queen has been a focus for pathetic sentiment from the beginning. As Scott McMillin points out, she 'speaks at length in only three scenes' and 'in each of them she weeps – tears are her leading characteristic'

(McMillin 1984: 42). It is not until the moment of their parting, however, that the sympathy she evokes is extended to Richard. In the earlier scenes where she appeared, she grieved for her husband, but always in isolation from him, and there was nothing to counter Bullingbrook's accusation that the nameless sins of Richard's courtiers had somehow 'Made a divorce betwixt his queen and him, / Broke the possession of a royal bed, / And stain'd the beauty of a fair queen's cheeks / With tears drawn from her eyes by your foul wrongs' (III.i.12–15). In Act V, by contrast, the queen's tears come from the prospect of separation from the husband who is now identified as her 'true-love', and the 'divorce' between them is the work of the usurpers.

In both cases, the accusation of royal divorce is a political charge, empowered by the mystification of patriarchal marriage as a paradigm of political order. Hall used it to authorize the Tudor dynasty when he entitled his history of all the kings from Henry IV to Henry VIII 'The Union of the Two Noble and Illustre Famelies of Lancastre & Yorke' and explained that 'the union of man and woman in the holy sacrament of matrimony' symbolized political peace and unity.[6] Naturalizing royal authority in the image of a patriarchal family, both Elizabeth and James repeatedly likened their relationships to England to that of a husband to his wife. But the husband–sovereign analogy also worked in the opposite direction, to justify the authority of every husband by reference to the mystified image of sovereignty. At the end of *The Taming of the Shrew*, for instance, Kate rationalizes her submission by declaring that a husband is his wife's 'sovereign' and comparing her duty to him to 'Such duty as the subject owes the prince' (V.ii.147, 155). The troubled families in Act V of *Richard II*, like the imagery of troubled families that appears in both parts of *Henry IV*, imply an analogy between the failure of royal authority in Bullingbrook's kingdom and the failure of patriarchal authority in the families of ordinary subjects. Richard II makes the same connection when he accuses Bullingbrook's men: 'Doubly divorc'd! Bad men, you violate / A twofold marriage – 'twixt my crown and me, / And then betwixt me and my married wife' (V.i.71–3). The accusation, like the queen's wifely devotion, displaces an emergent basis for masculine authority backward in time to the Middle Ages and upward in status to the royal family when it naturalizes Richard's status as king by equating it with his status as husband. Although Richard has a clear, hereditary right to the English throne, he loses it by squandering his patrimony. He regains it in retrospect by his possession of a devoted, domesticated wife.

NOTES

1. Reprinted from JEAN E. HOWARD AND PHYLLIS RACKIN, *Engendering a Nation: A Feminist Account of Shakespeare's English Histories* (London and New York: Routledge, 1997).

2. The indeterminacy often worries modern readers, but it may have been less important to Shakespeare's original audience because sexual lust was regarded as effeminating to men, regardless of the gender of the sexual partner. In this case, it is not clear whether the dissolute courtiers introduced other women into the king's bed or were themselves involved in sexual dalliance with him.

3. As Carole Pateman argues, the erosion of classical patriarchal ideology based on father right did not mean that patriarchy disappeared from political thought: it simply took a new form. Fraternal patriarchy and the emergent ideology of the civil subject required that 'women must be subject to men because they are naturally subversive of men's political order' (Pateman 1988: 96).

4. Many critics have discussed Elizabethan anxieties and ambivalence about the queen's authority, but see especially Montrose (1983) and Ferris (1981). Ferris also provides an excellent analysis of the many ways in which Richard is gendered feminine.

5. Cf. the allusion in *Macbeth*, III.iv.64–5 to 'a woman's story at a winter's fire, / Authoriz'd by her grandam.'

6. Both the Duchess of Gloucester's description of Edward's seven sons as 'seven fair branches springing from one root' (I.i.13) and the queen's description of Richard as 'my fair rose' (V.i.8) seem to recall the title page of Hall's *Union*, with its representation of Henry VIII and his dynastic forebears as roses growing on a bush. The image of the rose associates Richard with a stereotypical emblem of feminine beauty (Ferris 1981: 13), but it also naturalizes his patrilineal authority as a true branch of the royal tree.

CHAPTER SIX

Prince Hal's Falstaff: Positioning Psychoanalysis and the Female Reproductive Body[1]

VALERIE TRAUB

Valerie Traub's psychoanalytical study of the *Henry IV* plays and *Henry V* places ideas of the maternal at the centre of things. She sees Prince Hal's progress from companionship with Falstaff in the *Henry IV* plays to marriage with Katharine at the end of *Henry V* as a parallel to the process of rejecting the maternal reproductive body which psychoanalysis identifies as an essential stage in 'normal' male development. Like Howard and Rackin, Traub is concerned with aspects of an emergent modernity and its connections with gender; like them, she sees this as a politicised, not a 'natural', territory. She argues that the plays 'do not merely exclude women; they *stage* the elimination of women from the historical process (an exclusion that *is* the historical process), thus exhibiting the kinds of repressions a phallocentric culture requires to maintain and reproduce itself. By means of this staged repudiation, the *Henriad* embodies a marginal, subversive discourse, if only to demonstrate the fantasized expulsion of that discourse.' To trace this, Traub focuses specifically on sexuality. For her, sexuality is socially constructed, as is the unconscious. 'Sexuality in Shakespearean drama anonymously traverses the text.' Her case is that Shakespeare's plays present a contradiction: 'on one side, an elevated, naturalized, transcendent "sexuality" coincident to and synonymous with a historically incipient ideology of romantic love; on the other side, a politicized "sexuality" simultaneously physical and psychological, often bawdy, and constituted as much by anxiety as by desire'. These latter terms are key, for anxiety is seen as the corollary of desire. She employs psychoanalysis and feminism, but also uses a model of cultural negotiation and the circulation of social energy which owes something to the New Historicists.

Despite the specific meanings we may ascribe to the female reproductive body historically, whether they derive from an Aristotelian, Galenic, or modern gynecological paradigm, the bare fact of biological reproduction remains irrefutable, ineffable. In our own cultural tradition the figure of the maternal is simultaneously an object of terror (fears of maternal engulfment) and idealization (the Virgin Mother). That 'dark continent' traversed by every infant, where we are conceived and from which we are delivered, the maternal figure exists in our pre-natal memories – before culture, language, law, before knowledge of the father, before the Law of the Father.

Psychoanalysis offers a brilliant reading of the enculturation of the infant who is expelled from this body into the social order, of the simultaneous development of its subjectivity, gender, and sexuality. But, as feminist critics have made abund-antly clear, the psychoanalytic narrative of psychic development is predicated upon a male subject. Not only is the trajectory of the male posited as normative, but that subject is constituted in relation to a fantasized other – an other that is at once engendered as 'woman' and eroticized in reference to female reproductive functions.

The reflexivity and redundancy of the psychoanalytic narrative of psychic development also characterize its analysis of literary texts: it generally tells the same tale, a story of 'real' or fantasized loss, with all psychic conflict organized around the threat of castration. Despite the variety of literary plot, image, and metaphor, psychoanalytic criticism tends to rehearse a drama of the same, seeing only its own image in the face of the other.

In an attempt to break out of this circle, I pose the female reproductive body as the repressed figure upon which two paradigmatic narratives of male subjectivity depend: Lacan's revision of the Freudian oedipal drama as the subject's entrance into the symbolic order, and Shakespeare's drama of the development of a 'proto-typical' male subject in the *Henriad*. In a recursive reading of drama through psy-choanalysis, and psychoanalysis through drama, I argue that despite significant differences in family and social structure between late-sixteenth-century England and twentieth-century Vienna and Paris, Shakespearean drama and psychoanalytic theory share in a cultural estimation of the female reproductive body as a Bakhtinian 'grotesque body', and that they repress this figure in their narratives of psychic development.[2]

I am interested not so much in posing the *Henriad* as case history, applying psychoanalytic terminology to individual characters, but in the interrogation of persistent repetitions of psychoanalytic and dramatic narratives, repetitions that demonstrate their cohabitation within a dominant structure of gender. The *Henriad* and psychoanalysis are parallel narratives, similarly positioning male subjectivity and the female reproductive body, staging a conflict between 'paternal authority and maternal priority'.[3] By using the terms 'drama' and 'narrative' in reference to both, I mean to stress that psychoanalytic theory is as shaped by the politics of narrative convention and the constraints of a historically constructed cultural unconscious as is early modern drama.

In asserting such a connection between Shakespearean and psychoanalytic texts, I acknowledge the risk of effacing historical differences in ideology and rep-resentation. However, early modern texts in fact demonstrate indigenous cultural rationales that, as today, construct the maternal as a locus of profound ambivalence. If, as Thomas Laqueur argues, the Galenic paradigm which dominated sixteenth- and seventeenth-century medicine understood men to originate as female, then the fear of a reverse teleology – of being turned back into a woman – may have been a common masculine fantasy.[4] And if 'lust' was seen as effeminizing in its power to subordinate men to women by making men more 'like' women, then anxiety about desire itself obviously infused and structured heterosexual relations.[5] Finally, if the practice of wet-nursing caused not only early separation of the infant from the biological mother, but competition for maternal nurturance and subsequent ambivalence in object-relations (and perhaps in class identifications as well),[6] then 'getting back to the mother' was not only massively prohibited, but enormously problematical.[7] For aristocratic children especially, mothering itself was so much a field of dispersal that one hardly knows who the 'mother' is. In addition, insofar as children of most classes and both genders were kept in an almost exclusively female world, wearing skirt-like dress until the age of seven,[8] the moment of boys' 'breeching' instances not only a delayed physical separation, but an enforced conceptual dichotomization, of male from female. Indeed, that men were perceived to originate as female, and that infant and toddler boys were dressed as 'girls' does not obviate the centrality of the cultural opposition of male and female; on the contrary, these practices suggest a psychic rationale for the dualism defensively and reactively enforced by the adult system of gender evidenced in Shakespeare's plays. Material practices and their psychological corollaries converge to render women generally, and mothers specifically, as objects to be desired, resented, and most importantly, feared.

In noting the similarities that exist despite historical differences in family and social structure, I do not propose that the line between Shakespeare and Freud is direct or continuous. Clearly, as the Victorian idealization of the maternal attests, the female reproductive body has been variously constructed and valued within different periods. Rather, I mean to suggest that in respect to the female reproductive body and its influence on male subjectivity, Shakespearean drama and psychoanalytic theory share in a cultural moment, in much the same way as we can say that the narrative strategies of *Tristram Shandy* or *Don Quixote* share in those of a 'postmodern moment'. History is neither smooth teleology nor total disruption. It may repeat itself – but always with a difference. The salient difference between the *Henriad* and psychoanalysis is, I would argue, less ideological than stylistic, less political than performative.

The relationship of feminist critics to Shakespeare's history plays has until recently been one of not-so-benign neglect. For many feminists, the lack of powerful female characters in the histories forecloses the critical questions they bring to Shakespearean drama. 'Women don't figure' seems to sum up the stance of many critics who turn their analyses of gender and power to the greater presence of women, and the themes of chastity, courtship, marriage, and adultery in the comedies, tragedies, and romances.[9] In a recent article, Carol Thomas Neely takes this argument even further: she maintains that the focus of new historical critics on the histories is in part evidence of their antipathy to feminism.[10]

In arguing against this trend of dismissing the histories, I mean to suggest that the *Henriad* is a 'seminal' point for an examination of the construction and maintenance of phallocentric ideology, particularly in regard to male subjectivity and sexuality. Although the histories depend on a resolutely hierarchical representation of gender difference, they do not merely exclude women; they *stage* the elimination of women from the historical process (an exclusion that *is* the historical process), thus exhibiting the kinds of repressions a phallocentric culture requires to maintain and reproduce itself. By means of this staged repudiation, the *Henriad* embodies a marginal, subversive discourse, if only to demonstrate the fantasized expulsion of that discourse. This expulsion, however, is neither final nor total; we thus see in the *Henriad* not only the 'rehearsal' of power stressed by new historical critics, but also the possibility of the deconstruction of dominant sixteenth-century ideologies of gender, sexuality, and power.[11] In short, male dominated as it is, the *Henriad* contains within itself the means for its own meta-critique.

Access to this meta-critique is possible through a reading of the *Henriad* as paradigmatic of the gendered and erotic repressions upon which sixteenth-century male subjectivity depends. In psycho-dramatic terms, Prince Hal's subjectivity is constituted, first, in his relation to Falstaff, whose somatic iconography metonymically positions him as the fantasized pre-oedipal maternal, against whom Hal must differentiate; and, second, in relation to the French princess, Katharine, whose material and linguistic subjugation demonstrates the extent to which the male subject's (hetero) sexuality depends upon the repression and control of a female other.

My reading of the *Henriad* draws an explicit parallel with the Lacanian description of the development of subjectivity within phallocentric culture. In Lacanian psychoanalysis the individual is constituted simultaneously as a subject, a gender, and a sexuality through entrance into the symbolic order of language. With the insertion of the third term, the phallus, into the imaginary pre-oedipal relation of mother and child, the child loses its fantasized symbiosis with the mother, falling into a pre-existing order of culture that, through its endlessly substitutive chain of signification, enforces an always-divided subjectivity or 'lack-in-being'.[12] The signifier of this lack-in-being is the phallus: first, because by breaking the imaginary dyad, it inaugurates all subsequent desire as substitutive; and second, because all subjects, male and female, are psychically castrated, learning the meaning of separation and difference through their alienation into language.

The symbolic order governed by the Law of the Father is implicitly phallocentric, in part because of the resolutely hierarchical binaries by which it structures all categories of being and thought, beginning with gender: 'The Father's Law enjoins the subject to line up according to an opposition, man/woman, to assume its place as "he" or "she" in a preexisting order of language and culture.'[13] From this binarism of gender, all subsequent difference is defined as oppositional and hierarchical, leading to the ascription of a host of related oppositions: rational/irrational, strength/weakness, civilized/primitive.

Like Freud, Lacan describes a sequence of psychic events – the movement from the pre-oedipal through the oedipal – that is both constituted by and constitutive of patriarchal culture. For feminists, the value of Lacanian analysis is precisely in this description of how phallocentrism reproduces itself within and through a family structure that is inscribed by larger cultural codes. Despite its embeddedness in patriarchal ideology, Lacanian psychoanalysis provides the means for a critique of the pretensions of phallocentrism. As the signifier of the *fiction* of unmediated presence and integrated identity, as the metaphor for a fragmented and precarious subjectivity, the phallus exposes even as it upholds the artificiality of the division upon which gender and sexual identity are based. As Jane Gallop remarks, 'The penis is what men have and women do not; the phallus is the attribute of power which neither men nor women have.'[14]

As Gallop is well aware, however, the danger in this formulation is that historically the phallus has stood for precisely the kind of power men have had – as metaphor for their male identity and as figuration of their sexual, political, and economic power over women. A feminist psychoanalysis must therefore conscientiously resist subsuming gender hierarchies under the aegis of the radical instability of all speaking subjects.[15] While retaining the Lacanian description of the way gendered subjects are constituted by and through phallocentric culture, language, and logic, feminists will continue to intervene strategically in this course of events.

Psychoanalytic criticism of the *Henriad* has tended to perceive Prince Hal's developmental problem as a choice between two fathers: a biological father, King Henry IV, standing for conviction, duty, and control, yet burdened by his guilty acquisition of the crown; and a father substitute, Falstaff, whose hedonism, lawlessness, and wit provide an attractive, if temporary, alternative. In his classic 1952 formulation, Ernst Kris argued that Prince Hal dissociates himself from the court both as protest against his father's regicide, and to escape his own unconscious temptation to parricide.[16] Upon his father's death, Hal ascends the throne, displacing his parricidal impulses onto his father substitute; his harsh rejection of Falstaff thus acts as a symbolic killing of the father.

Kris's normalizing account of psychosexuality celebrates the successful reintegration of the wayward, unruly child into the patrilineal order of kingship. The tetralogy ends as a comedy, with the marriage of the newly crowned and martially victorious King Henry V to the French princess Katharine ensuring the continued generation of patriarchal power through the expectation of male progeny.

More recently, Murray Schwartz and Peter Erickson also posit Falstaff as a paternal figure, but they view with ambivalence the tetralogy's close. In stressing that Falstaff represents in non-legitimate, infantile ways adult male fantasies of omnipotence, avarice, orality, and egotism, Schwartz argues that as low-life 'sport' is channeled into high-minded military exploits, the drama expresses the cultural legitimation of infantile egotism.[17] And Erickson's examination of male bonding suggests that the guilt Hal feels toward both Henry IV and Falstaff prevents the *Henriad* from reaching a clear resolution. Both father figures are 'scapegoats who refuse to stay away'.[18]

I see Schwartz and Erickson as beginning a movement to problematize psychoanalytically the *Henriad* from the perspective of a troubled masculinity, based in a flawed father–son dynamic that replicates the larger problems of patriarchy. I want to take their analyses of patriarchal relations one step further by arguing that Falstaff represents to Hal not an alternative paternal image but rather a projected fantasy of the pre-oedipal *maternal*, whose rejection is the basis upon which patriarchal subjectivity is predicated. I see in this process of the oedipal rejection of the maternal and identification with the paternal not merely the individual psychosexuality of one character, but a paradigm for the cultural construction of early modern masculine subjectivity. Furthermore, through his militaristic courtship of Katharine, Hal's subjectivity is established as thoroughly phallocentric, depending upon the repression of the object of his erotic desire.

That Falstaff is figured in female terms is suggested first by his body, which is associated with the metaphors of women's bodies and carnality that Shakespeare elsewhere exploits in his denunciation of female eroticism. Physically, Falstaff is most like *The Comedy of Errors'* spherical, oily kitchen maid (variously referred to as Luce and Nell, who mistakenly attempts to seduce the Syracusian Dromio) and the bawdy Nurse of *Romeo and Juliet*, who, like Falstaff, huffs and puffs as she waddles on fat legs.[19] In contrast to the disembodied voices of Shakespeare's other fools, Falstaff's being is exceedingly corporeal; indeed, his corpulence is referred to constantly, invoking, in the emphasis on a swollen and distended belly, associations of pregnancy.[20] In the space of three scenes, Hal calls Falstaff 'fat rogue' twice, 'damn'd brawn' (pig or fatted swine), 'fat-kidney'd rascal', 'fat-guts', 'whoreson round man', 'clay-brain'd guts', 'emboss'd [swollen] rascal', and 'my sweet beef'.[21] Not only fat Jack's gut, but also what goes in and comes out of his body is the object of constant discussion – especially sweat and oil: Falstaff is an 'oily rascal', a 'greasy tallow-catch' who 'sweats to death, / And lards the lean earth as he walks along'.[22]

Such a focus on the bulging and the protuberant, the openings, permeabilities, and effusions of Falstaff's body situate him as a 'grotesque body'. According to Peter Stallybrass and Allon White, who reformulate Bakhtin's paradigm, early modern somatic concepts were organized into mutually exclusive iconographies of the low and high, the open and closed, the grotesque and the classical, with the grotesque body being

an image of impure corporeal bulk with its orifices (mouth, flared nostrils, anus) yawning wide and its lower regions (belly, legs, feet, buttocks and genitals) given priority over its upper regions (head, 'spirit', reason) . . . a subject of pleasure in processes of exchange . . . it is never closed off from either its social or ecosystemic context.[23]

When Hal calls Falstaff 'gross as a mountain, open, palpable' (*H.IV, pt 1*, II.iv.224), or 'this bed-presser, this horse-back-breaker, this huge hill of flesh' (*H.IV, pt 1*, II.iv.240–1), or a 'tun of man', a 'bolting-hutch of beastliness', a 'swoll'n parcel of dropsies', a 'huge bombard of sack', a 'stuff'd cloak-bag of guts', a 'Manningtree ox with the pudding in his belly' (*H.IV, pt 1*, II.iv.443–8), he instantiates Falstaff as a grotesque body.

The many references to Falstaff as a pig, including his self-identification as 'a sow that hath overwhelm'd all her litter but one' (*H.IV, pt 2*, I.ii.11–12), not only further locate him as a grotesque body, but also create a web of associations that direct our attention to Falstaff's belly, which becomes increasingly feminized.[24] When, after he has had a scuffle with Pistol, Hostess Quickly asks Falstaff, 'Are you not hurt i' th' groin? Methought 'a made a shrewd thrust at your belly' (*H.IV, pt 2*, II.iv.207–8), she shifts the linguistic emphasis from the masculine 'groin' (in danger of castration) to the more feminine 'belly', the 'already castrated', vulnerable recipient and receptacle of a 'shrewd thrust'. False-staff becomes precisely a false phallus, in inverse relation to the Freudian declaration that, upon entry into the 'phallic phase' of sexual development, 'the little girl is a little man'.[25] Falstaff himself makes the link between his belly, its 'effeminacy', and his identity when, in response to the Knight Colevile's question, 'Are you not Sir John Falstaff?' he replies, 'I have a whole school of tongues in this belly of mine, and not a tongue of them all speaks any other word but my name. . . . My womb, my womb, my womb undoes me' (*H.IV, pt 2*, IV.iii.18–22).[26]

I will argue soon that his womb does indeed undo him. For now, I merely mean to suggest that the associational chain from pig, sow, groin, belly, to womb effects a transposition from the grotesque body to the female reproductive body. As Bakhtin has argued, sexual as well as excremental functions form the core of the category of the 'grotesque' that was operative throughout early modern culture. Although Bakhtin elides gender specificity in his work, the symbolic functioning of the bodily processes of menstruation, pregnancy, childbearing, and lactation – which render women, particularly in respect to their genitals and breasts, open, protuberant, and never-quite-sealed-off – all metonymically instantiate the maternal body as 'grotesque'.[27]

Obviously, Falstaff could be analyzed as a 'grotesque body' without specific reference to his maternal functions: many resonances echo between the Rabelaisian carnivalesque and Falstaff's gluttony and drunkenness, between the early modern marketplace and the Eastcheap tavern.[28] However, precisely because gender is repressed in Bakhtin's account, the demonstration of its salience is all the more pressing.

That the maternal was linked to the 'grotesque body' in early modern societies is evidenced in part by the performance of certain pollution behaviors. The practice of 'churching' women after menstruation and childbirth suggests that the products of women's sexual and reproductive bodies posed enough of a psychic threat to the social order to call for ritual purification.[29] I would argue, further, that the fantasy represented by the non-sexualized maternity of a Virgin Mary further manages anxieties about female reproductive corporeality. With the Reformation's institutionalized occlusion of Mariolatry, the social and psychic functions the Virgin performed were left with little institutional accommodation.[30] The symbolic complex of the 'grotesque body' was one intervention in this social field, performing the psycho-social function of containing psychic phenomena perceived as threatening. The danger posed by the grotesque-body-as-maternal is the physical contamination which, by virtue of the birth process – '*inter urinas et faeces nascimur*', to quote Freud, who was himself quoting St Augustine – the maternal body represents to early modern psyches, socially constructed as they were through a dualistic logic of mind over matter, spirit over body, or, to invoke Simone de Beauvoir, transcendence over immanence.[31] Hal's development as a male subject depends not only upon separation and differentiation from a state of physical dependency and a fantasized state of psychic symbiosis, but also on the exorcism of the figure responsible for and associated with that state: mother, *mater*, matter.[32] Hal's public disavowal and humiliation of Falstaff in *Henry IV, part 2* – 'I know thee not, old man' (*H.IV, pt 2*, V.v.47) – suggest his need to externalize just such an inter-psychic threat.

The rejection of Falstaff, like the signification of his body, is overdetermined; within the absolutist paradigm of early modern rule and kingship, his transgressions are obviously dangerous. Yet, interestingly enough, Hal's statement of rejection likens his previous relationship with Falstaff to a dream, a pre-oedipal fantasy of nondifferentiation of boundaries: 'I have long dreamt of such a kind of man, / So surfeit-swell'd, so old, and so profane, / But, being awak'd, I do despise my dream' (*H.IV, pt 2*, V.v.49–51). As C. L. Barber notes, 'Elsewhere in Shakespeare, to dismiss dreams categorically is foolhardy.'[33] Part of Hal's 'dream' has included role playing such as that indicated by his statement, 'I'll play Percy, and that damn'd brawn shall play Dame Mortimer his wife' (*H.IV, pt 1*, II.iv.109–10). Whereas the homo-erotics of the *Henriad* deserve fuller treatment than I can render here, it is apparent that homoerotic desire infuses the relationship of Falstaff and Hal, signaled both by Falstaff's 'feminine' qualities and Hal's predominant lack of interest in women. Although Falstaff portrays himself as a womanizer, his relations with neither Mistress Quickly nor Doll Tearsheet carry the erotic impress and tenderness of his bond to Hal. Indeed, the connection between Falstaff and Hal seems to invert the power relations we so often assume structure male homoerotic relations: rather than involving a powerful older man who protects and mentors his young lover, the Falstaff/Hal relation concerns an older, less attractive, socially marginalized man who is emotionally and financially dependent on a younger, more attractive, increasingly independent and powerful aristocrat – the same asymmetry explored in greater detail in Shakespeare's sonnets.

Hal's rejection of Falstaff thus seems temporarily to assuage anxieties, first, about the intimacy of their homoerotic bond and, second, about the equation of woman and maternity. The repudiation simultaneously exorcises both possible threats to Hal's development of adult heterosexuality. Indeed, the threat of mater-nal power is mapped onto anxieties about homoerotic desire, insofar as Falstaff's eroticization is based precisely on the 'grotesque body' (damn'd brawn) of the mature woman – 'Dame Mortimer [my] wife'. When Hal charges Falstaff to 'Make less thy body hence, and more thy grace; / Leave gormandizing. Know the grave doth gape / For thee thrice wider than for other men' (*H.IV, pt 2*, V.v.52–4), he not only pointedly situates Falstaff's grotesque body as the problem, but metaphorically hurries this body off to its material end, Mother Earth's hungry maw.

Death holds specifically maternal associations for both Hal and his father. When a nobleman enters the tavern in quest of the prince, Hal retorts, 'Send him back again to my mother' (*H.IV, pt 1*, II.iv.288). Insofar as the queen, Mary de Bohun, had long been laid to rest, the editor of the *Riverside Shakespeare* percept-ively glosses this line as 'get rid of him permanently'.[34] *Henry IV, part 1* begins with the king imagining his country's recent period of war and destruction in maternal terms: 'No more the thirsty entrance of this soil / Shall daub her lips with her own children's blood' (*H.IV, pt 1*, I.i.5–6) – a projection of maternal destructiveness later repeated in Falstaff's description of himself as a sow that has devoured her litter (*H.IV, pt 2*, I.ii.11–12).[35]

That Hal is disturbed by precisely such associations between the 'grotesque' maternal body and potential death is made evident by the language in which he voices his aspirations. He envisions his redemption in the eyes of men as a separa-tion from 'the base contagious clouds' that 'smother up his beauty from the world'. His maturity, identity, and freedom will be achieved by 'breaking through the foul and ugly mists / Of vapors that did seem to strangle him' (*H.IV, pt 1*, I.ii.192–7). Such suffocation anxiety takes on the configuration of a bloody birth fantasy during his later repetition of this vow. He tells his father:

> I will redeem all this on Percy's head,
> And in the closing of some glorious day
> Be bold to tell you that I am your son,
> When I will wear a garment all of blood
> And stain my favors in a bloody mask,
> Which, wash'd away, shall scour my shame with it.
>
> (*H.IV, pt 1*, III.ii.132–7)

The vapors that threatened to strangle him in the enclosure of the womb become the blood of birth that, when washed away, will scour off the filth of his maternal associations. Cleansed in a battle both martial and natal, the newborn babe will become simultaneously his father's son and his nation's hero.

Hal's escape from maternal suffocation, from threatened retention in the world of the mother – and thus his re-enactment of early modern boys' 'breeching' – is predicated upon his assumption of martial arms and engagement in fraternal rivalry with a brother surrogate, Hotspur.[36] Hotspur early provides both the opposition between femininity and militarism, and the equation of sexuality with violence, that will later designate Hal's assumption of the masculine role. As Hotspur says upon leaving his wife for battle: 'This is no world / To play with mammets and to tilt with lips. / We must have bloody noses and crack'd crowns' (*H.IV, pt 1*, II.iii.90–2). Heterosexuality not only gives way to male homosocial bonding and warfare, but is reconstituted through a military paradigm: that 'this' is not a time to 'tilt with lips' implies that there is a time for heterosexuality, but it is imaged in specifically militaristic terms.[37]

As if to underscore this relation between militarism and male maturity, *Henry IV, part 2* begins with the official separation of Falstaff from Hal on martial orders of the king; Falstaff is to join Hal's younger brother, John of Lancaster, while the Prince of Wales asserts himself independently in battle. When the Lord Chief Justice comments to Falstaff, 'the King hath sever'd you' (*H.IV, pt 2*, I.ii.201), he incisively indicates the necessity for the newly minted soldier-prince to renounce the maternal in favor of the Name-of-the-Father. That the motivation for such identification is based precisely on a connection between aggression and masculinity is clarified by Nancy Chodorow: 'A boy gives up his mother in order to avoid punishment, but identifies with his father because he can then gain the benefits of being the one who gives punishment, of being masculine and superior.'[38] Ironically, it is Falstaff's repeated use of the term 'prick' to denote the selection of commoners for battle that enforces a chain of signification between military conscription, sharp weaponry, and the penis (*H.IV, pt 2*, III.ii).[39] By the beginning of *Henry V*, the violence of war has thoroughly permeated male subjectivity and sexuality. Both on the military front and in the French court, Henry V's language demonstrates the extent to which the phallus and military might are mutually constitutive. Henry V threatens the citizens of Harfleur with phallic violence: 'What is't to me . . . ,' he says, 'If your pure maidens fall into the hand / Of hot and forcing violation?' (*H.V*, III.iii.19–21) Invading a city is imagined as rape (*H.V*, III.iii.7–35), just as the object of Henry V's desire, Katharine, is figured by her father as virginal property, a city 'all girdled with maiden walls that war hath never ent'red' (*H.V*, V.ii.321–2).

With the conquest of France, the time is right for Henry, if not Hotspur, to 'play with mammets and to tilt with lips'. The achieved heterosexualization of Henry is a 'triumph' which is perversely fulfilled by his inability to woo Katharine except through military metaphors. Henry himself is aware of his inadequacies as a lover; he remarks,

If I could win a lady at leap-frog, or by vaulting into my saddle with my armour on my back . . . I should quickly leap into a wife. Or if I might buffet [box] for my love, or bound my horse for her favors, I could lay on like a butcher and sit like a jack an apes, never off.

(*H.V*, V. ii.138–43)

As Erickson notes, Henry's

'speaking plain soldier' (V.ii.149) causes him to portray sexuality as a form of military aggression and conquest. Phrases like 'I love thee cruelly' and 'I get thee with scamblin' [fighting] (202–3, 204–5) contain ironies the king cannot control.[40]

Henry is, even in courtship, 'a soldier / A name that in my thoughts becomes me best' (*H.V*, III.iii.5–6).

The military dimension of Henry's sexuality is paralleled by his linguistic domination of Katharine. When he asks her to 'teach a soldier terms / Such as will enter at a lady's ear' (*H.V*, V.ii.99–100), his subsequent behavior attests that the linguistic emphasis is more on penetration than the acquisition of a new language. As Henry says, 'It is as easy for me, Kate, to conquer the kingdom as to speak so much more French' (*H.V*, V.ii.185–7). Like Lady Mortimer, who speaks only Welsh and thus relies on her father, Glendower, to translate even marital endearments, Katharine's linguistic status positions woman as a foreign language. It is she who must give up her native tongue – a French language and nationality that throughout the play are associated with the despised 'effeminacy' of French nobles – for the 'plain soldier' language and nationality of manly 'Harry of England' (*H.V*, V.ii.248).

Thus far my analysis has suggested that insofar as Katharine is the object of Henry's discourse, *Henry's* subjectivity and sexuality are predicated upon his repression of Katharine's linguistic power. But what of Katharine as the subject of her own discourse? In the scene between Katharine and her lady-in-waiting (*H.V*, III.iv), in which Katharine not only learns English but metaphorically dismembers it – 'd'hand, de fingres, de nails, de arm, d'elbow, de nick, de sin, de foot, le count' – we encounter a Katharine who skillfully engages in linguistic play.[41] Indeed, in this private scene between two women, Katharine takes control of the specifically erotic aspects of language; while asserting that 'O Seigneur Dieu! Ils sont les mots de son mauvais, corruptible, gros, et impudique, et non pour les dames d'honneur d'user' (50–2), Katharine nonetheless continues to recite 'une autre fois' her 'leçon ensemble', including the offending 'de foot and le count' (54–7). Insofar as this female appropriation of the sexual body directly follows Henry's threats of rape to the virgins of Harfleur, we are, I think, encouraged to see Katharine as temporarily subverting the play's overwhelmingly male representation of the proper role of female sexuality.

Despite her appropriation of linguistic and sexual power, however, Katharine fails to maintain such control once in the presence of Henry V. During the 'wooing scene', her language is reduced to 24 short lines of maidenly embarrassment and deference compared to Henry's 150 lines of vigorous self-presentation. Listen to the tenor of her response to Henry's kissing of her hand, her longest speech (I follow the *Bevington* translation of her French): 'don't, my lord, don't, don't; by my faith, I do not wish [you] to lower your greatness by kissing the hand of an – Our dear Lord! – unworthy servant; excuse me, I beg you, my most powerful lord' (*H.V*, V.ii.254–8n). Although, as Helen Ostovich points out, Katharine attempts to evade Henry's 'battery of questions' and thus deflect his desire by answering him mainly through the negative ('I cannot tell what is dat', 'I do not know dat'),[42] Katharine's predicament is structural; whatever her individual power, it is subsumed by her ideological, political, and economic function in the systematic exchange of women between men.[43] As Katharine says when Henry asks if she will have him: 'Dat is as it sall please de roi mon pere' (*H.V*, V.ii.248).

That nationality in *Henry V* is gender marked is often noted. Less obvious is that women's bodies are figured as territory: when Henry describes Katharine as 'our capital demand, compris'd / Within the fore-rank of our articles' (*H.V*, V.ii.96–7), not only does the giving of her body symbolize the capitulation of French territory; her body *becomes* that territory. Once married to the masculine kingdom of England, the subservient state of France embodied by Katharine will be partially enclosed, its watery borders policed by British soldiers. At the same time, Falstaff's body, that unruly 'globe of sinful continents' (*H.IV, pt 2*, II.iv.284), is tamed and appropriated through its transfiguration into a more manageable 'state'.[44]

The symbolic substitution of Falstaff by Katharine effects a strategic displacement and containment, as the debased maternal is replaced with an idealized woman, the 'classical body', which, as Stallybrass and White note, is 'elevated, static and monumental' with 'no openings or orifices'.[45] Katharine's virginal body, while presumably to be used for reproductive purposes, is yet in Henry V's fantasies free of implication in maternal bodily processes. As 'fair Katharine', 'dear Kate', 'gentle Princess', 'queen of all', 'an angel', 'my fair flower-de-luce', Katharine is positioned, in the space of a hundred lines, as far as possible from the 'grotesque' maternal body (*H.V*, V.ii.104, 154, 203, 246, 110, 210–11).

Such a replacement of the 'grotesque body' by the idealized 'classical body' is an ambivalent and troubling resolution; for although Hal's psychic anxiety is transcoded into erotic desire, the 'classical' and the 'grotesque' are two sides of the same coin, arising from the same cultural /psychic complex. Because of our dualistic system of thought, all women, regardless of their individual maternal status, are implicated in male fantasies of maternal omnipotence, nurturance, seduction, engulfment, and betrayal. To the extent that they are gendered, both the 'grotesque' and the 'classical' body are masculine projections – one, an anxious debasement, the other, a defensive idealization of the physical body from which we are born and to which, in the Shakespearean (and Freudian) equation of womb and tomb, we return.[46]

NOTES

1. Reprinted from VALERIE TRAUB, *Desire and Anxiety: Circulations of Sexuality in Shakespearean Drama* (London and New York: Routledge, 1992).

2. MIKHAIL BAKHTIN, *Rabelais and His World*, trans. Helene Iswolsky (Bloomington: Indiana University Press, 1984).

3. MADELON SPRENGNETHER, *The Spectral Mother: Freud, Feminism, and Psychoanalysis* (Ithaca: Cornell University Press, 1990), p. xi.

4. According to THOMAS LAQUEUR, *Making Sex: Body and Gender from the Greeks to Freud* (Cambridge: Harvard University Press, 1990), the contemporary medical literature conceived of males and females as structurally inverted: both genders originate as female, with the greater presence of 'heat' in the male forcing outward that which lies hidden in the interior folds of the female – hence, male genitalia. The male fantasy of reversion is explored by [STEPHEN] GREENBLATT in 'Fiction and Friction', *Shakespearean Negotiations: The Circulation of Social Energy in Renaissance England* (Oxford: Clarendon Press, 1988).

5. PHYLLIS RACKIN, 'Historical Difference/Sexual Difference', forthcoming, in *Privileging Gender in Early Modern England,* ed. Jean R. Brink (Kirksville: 16th Century Journal Publishers, 1992).

6. See LAWRENCE STONE, *The Family, Sex and Marriage in England 1500–1800* (New York: Harper and Row, 1977). Infants of the upper and to some extent the middle classes were farmed out to working-class households for the first twelve to eighteen months of life.

7. I am indebted to Peter Stallybrass for this particular turn of phrase.

8. STEPHEN ORGEL, 'Nobody's Perfect: Or Why Did the English Stage Take Boys for Women?', *South Atlantic Quarterly* 88 (1989), pp. 7–29.

9. Important exceptions to this trend are PHYLLIS RACKIN, 'Anti-Historians: Women's Roles in Shakespeare's Histories', *Theatre Journal* 37 (1985), pp. 329–44, and 'Patriarchal History and Female Subversion', in *Stages of History: Shakespeare's English Chronicles* (Ithaca: Cornell University Press, 1990), pp. 146–200, as well as LINDA BAMBER, *Comic Women, Tragic Men: A Study of Gender and Genre in Shakespeare* (Stanford: Stanford University Press, 1982), pp. 135–68. MARILYN FRENCH, *Shakespeare's Division of Experience* (New York: Ballantine Books, 1981) and IRENE G. DASH, *Wooing, Wedding, and Power: Women in Shakespeare's Plays* (New York: Columbia University Press 1981) examine the Henry VI tetralogy, but not the *Henriad.* COPPÉLIA KAHN, *Man's Estate: Masculine Identity in Shakespeare* (Berkeley: University of California Press, 1981), PETER ERICKSON, *Patriarchal Structures in Shakespeare's Drama* (Berkeley: University of California Press, 1985), and DAVID SUNDELSON, *Shakespeare's Restorations of the Father* (New Brunswick: Rutgers University Press, 1983) all include chapters on the development of male subjectivity through the reproduction of male bonds in the histories, but they do not focus specifically on the role of women. Although MARILYN WILLIAMSON's *The Patriarchy of Shakespeare's Comedies* (Detroit: Wayne State University Press, 1986) includes a chapter on the romances, it excludes the histories. MARIANNE L. NOVY, *Love's Argument: Gender Relations in Shakespeare* (Chapel Hill: University of North Carolina Press, 1984), CAROL THOMAS NEELY, *Broken Nuptials in Shakespeare's Plays* (New Haven: Yale University Press, 1985), KAY STOCKHOLDER, *Dream Works: Lovers and Families in Shakespeare's Plays* (Toronto: University of Toronto Press, 1987), THOMAS W. MACCARY, *Friends and Lovers: The Phenomenology of Desire in Shakespearean Comedy* (New York: Columbia University Press, 1985), and the essays in *Representing Shakespeare: New Psychoanalytic Essays,* ed. MURRAY M. SCHWARTZ and COPPÉLIA KAHN (Baltimore: Johns Hopkins University Press, 1980) all focus on plays other than the histories.

10. CAROL THOMAS NEELY, 'Constructing the Subject: Feminist Practice and the New Renaissance Discourses', *ELR* 18:1 (Winter 1988), pp. 5–18.

11. For the 'rehearsal' of culture, see STEVEN MULLANEY, *The Place of the Stage: License, Play, and Power in Renaissance England* (Chicago: Chicago University Press, 1988).

12. JACQUES LACAN, 'The Signification of the Phallus', *Ecrits: A Selection*, trans. Alan Sheridan (New York: W. W. Norton, 1977), pp. 281–91, and *Feminine Sexuality: Jacques Lacan and the école freudienne*, ed. Juliet Mitchell and Jacqueline Rose, trans. Jacqueline Rose (New York: Norton, 1982).

13. SHIRLEY NELSON GARNER, CLAIRE KAHANE, AND MADELON SPRENGNETHER, *The (M)Other Tongue: Essays in Feminist Psychoanalytic Interpretation* (Ithaca: Cornell University Press, 1985), p. 21.

14. JANE GALLOP, *The Daughter's Seduction* (Ithaca: Cornell University Press, 1982), p. 97.

15. Such a subjugation of gender categories under the rubrics of 'identity' and 'power' seems to occur in the recent Shakespearean criticism of JONATHAN GOLDBERG, 'Shakespearean Inscriptions: the Voicing of Power', and JOEL FINEMAN, 'The Turn of the Shrew', both in *Shakespeare & the Question of Theory*, ed. Patricia Parker and Geoffrey Hartman (New York: Methuen, 1985), pp. 116–37 and 138–59, as well as in Stephen Greenblatt's 'Fiction and Friction', *Shakespearean Negotiations*, pp. 66–93. For a critique of this subjugation, see Neely, 'Constructing the Subject', LYNDA E. BOOSE, 'The Family in Shakespeare Studies; or – Studies in the Family of Shakespeareans; or – The Politics of Politics', *Renaissance Quarterly* 40 (Winter 1987), pp. 707–42; PETER ERICKSON, 'Rewriting the Renaissance, Rewriting Ourselves', *Shakespeare Quarterly* 38:3 (1987), pp. 327–37; MARGUERITE WALLER, 'Academic Tootsie: The Denial of Difference and the Difference it Makes', *Diacritics* 17:1 (1987), pp. 2–20; and JUDITH NEWTON, 'History as Usual? Feminism and the "New Historicism"', *Cultural Critique* (1988), pp. 87–121.

16. ERNST KRIS, 'Prince Hal's Conflict', *Psychoanalytic Explorations in Art* (New York: International University Press, 1952), pp. 273–88.

17. Schwartz, discussion at the University of Massachusetts, Amherst, 1986.

18. Erickson, *Patriarchal Structures in Shakespeare's Drama*, p. 46.

19. *The Comedy of Errors* (III.ii.81–154) and *Romeo and Juliet* (II.v.29–52).

20. At least four other critics have noted Falstaff's 'femininity', In 'The Prince's Dog', W. H. AUDEN notes that a fat man 'looks like a cross between a very young child and a pregnant mother . . . fatness in the male is the physical expression of a psychological wish to withdraw from sexual competition and, by combining mother and child in his own person, to become emotionally self-sufficient', *The Dyer's Hand and Other Essays* (New York: Random House, 1962), pp. 195–6. In *Man's Estate*, [COPPELIA] KAHN credits Falstaff with a 'curiously feminine sensual abundance' and goes on to remark that 'a fat man can look like a pregnant woman, and Falstaff's fatness is fecund; it spawns symbols'. However, Kahn sees in Falstaff mainly an 'avoidance of sexual maturity', a 'wish to bypass women' (pp. 72–3). Kahn refers to a talk by SHERMAN HAWKINS, 'Falstaff as Mom', given at the 1977 MLA Annual Meeting, but Hawkins' article has not, as far as I know, appeared in print. More recently, PATRICIA PARKER includes Falstaff as one of her 'literary fat ladies' in her book *Literary Fat Ladies: Rhetoric, Gender, Property* (London: Methuen, 1987). In a brilliantly 'dilated' argument about the link between gender and the denial of textual closure, she sees Falstaff's corpulence as embodying Prince Hal's delay in 'reformation' (pp. 20–2).

21. *Henry IV, part 1*, II.ii.110, II.iv.540, II.iv.109, II.ii.5, II.ii.30, II.iv.138, II.iv.224–5, III.iii.158, III.iii.177.

22. *Henry IV, part 1*, II.iv.52l, II.iv.226, II.ii.197–8. According to J. DOVER WILSON, in Renaissance usage the word 'tallow' referred to 'liquid fat, as well as dripping or suet or animal fat rendered down . . . [H]uman sweat, partly owing perhaps to the similarity of the word to "suet", was likewise thought

of as fat, melted by the heat of the body', *The Fortunes of Falstaff* (New York: Macmillan, 1944), p. 28.

23. Peter Stallybrass and Allon White, *The Politics and Poetics of Transgression* (Ithaca: Cornell University Press, 1986), pp. 9 and 22. In 'Patriarchal Territories: The Body Enclosed', Stallybrass suggests that the dominant Renaissance ideology constructed 'woman's body' as *'naturally grotesque'* (*Rewriting the Renaissance*, ed. Margaret Ferguson *et al.*, Chicago: University of Chicago Press, 1986), p. 126; he ends his essay with a 'validation of the female grotesque' (p. 142). In 'Female Grotesques: Carnival and Theory', *Feminist Studies/Critical Studies*, ed. Teresa de Lauretis (Bloomington: Indiana University Press, 1986), pp. 213–29, Mary Russo delineates the difficulties involved in such a validation. And, in an essay that complements mine, Gail Kern Paster deciphers blood as a trope of gender in a reformulation of the Bakhtinian 'grotesque'; see ' "In the spirit of men there is no blood": Blood as Trope of Gender in *Julius Caesar*', *Shakespeare Quarterly* 40:3 (1989), pp. 284–98.

24. Falstaff is also referred to as 'blown Jack' (*H.IV, pt 1*, IV.ii.48), 'brawn' [fatted swine] (*H.IV, pt 1*, II.iv.109; (*H.IV, pt 2*, I.i.19), 'martlemas' [fatted ox killed at Martinmas] (*H.IV, pt 2*, II.ii.96), 'old boar' (*H.IV, pt 2*, II.ii.138) and 'Bartholomew boar-pig' [roast succulent pig] (*H.IV, pt 2*, II.iv.228–9).

25. Sigmund Freud, 'Femininity', *New Introductory Lectures on Psychoanalysis*, ed. James Strachey (New York: W.W. Norton, 1965), p. 104.

26. In 'Language, Linguistics and the Study of Literature', *Tracking the Signifier: Theoretical Essays: Film, Linguistics, Literature* (Minnesota University Press, 1985), pp. 113–30, Colin MacCabe informs us that 'The verb *to womb*, meaning *to enclose an empty space*, gave rise to a series of nominal derivations which included both the sexually unspecific *stomach* as well as the meaning of *uterus* that is current today. It is crucial to a reading of the role of Falstaff to recognise that both meanings were available at the end of the sixteenth century, and we should not be surprised at Falstaff's consequent sexual ambiguity, particularly in the context of a claim about the disruption of the normal order of language. . . . [S]uch a figure should undermine even the possibility of representing sexual difference. Falstaff's body constitutes a polymorphously perverse threat to the possibility of representation. It even claims to undo the arbitrary and social nature of the sign and to speak its own name independently of any social order of language' (116–17). Ivy Schweitzer also suggested to me that Falstaff's linguistic style exhibits the 'semiotic' as described by Julia Kristeva.

27. Two references which specifically link mothers with the excretions of tears are *H.IV, pt 1*, II.iv.391–4 and *H.V*, IV.iv.29–32. For an analysis of early modern body fluids, see Gail Kern Paster, 'Leaky Vessels: The Incontinent Women of City Comedy', *Renaissance Drama* 18 (1987), pp. 43–65.

28. Falstaff's genealogical forebears in stage devils, vice figures, and iniquity further position him as 'grotesque'.

29. I am indebted to Stephen Greenblatt for bringing my attention to 'churching' in 'Martial Law and the Land of Cockaigne', *Shakespearean Negotiations,* pp. 129–63.

30. See C. L. Barber, 'The Family in Shakespeare's Development: Tragedy and Sacredness', *Representing Shakespeare*, ed. Schwartz and Kahn, pp. 188–202.

31. Sigmund Freud, *Dora: An Analysis of a Case of Hysteria*, ed. Philip Rieff (New York: Collier Books, 1963), p. 47, and 'The Most Prevalent Form of Degradation in Erotic Life', *Sexuality and the Psychology of Love*, ed. Philip Rieff (New York: Collier Books, 1963), p. 69. See also Simone de Beauvoir, *The Second Sex* (New York: Vintage Books, 1952).

32. I have learned much from Janet Adelman's analyses of fantasies of the maternal in Shakespearean drama; see especially ' "Born of Woman": Fantasies of Maternal Power in *Macbeth*', *Cannibals,*

Witches, and Divorce: Estranging the Renaissance, ed. Marjorie Garber (Baltimore: Johns Hopkins University Press, 1987), pp. 90–121, and ' "This Is and Is Not Cressid": The Characterization of Cressida', in Garner *et al.*, *The (M)Other Tongue*, pp. 119–41. In addition to (Gohlke) Sprengnether, Dinnerstein, and Chodorow, I am indebted to the work of ADRIENNE RICH, *Of Woman Born: Motherhood as Experience and Institution* (New York: Norton, 1976), and SUSAN BORDO, 'The Cartesian Masculinization of Thought', *Signs* 11:3 (1986), pp. 439–56.

33. C. L. BARBER, *Shakespeare's Festive Comedy: A Study of Dramatic Form and its Relation to Social Custom* (New York: Princeton University Press, 1963), p. 219.

34. *The Riverside Shakespeare*, ed. G. BLAKEMORE EVANS (Boston: Houghton Mifflin, 1974).

35. Compare these and the following images of maternal destruction to those concerning Richard III in *Henry VI, part 3* (III.iii.168–81), and Macduff, Malcolm, and Macbeth in *Macbeth*. See Adelman, ' "Born of Woman" ', pp. 92–3, 100, and 107.

36. See JOEL FINEMAN, 'Fratricide and Cuckoldry: Shakespeare's Doubles' in *Representing Shakespeare*, ed. Schwartz and Kahn, pp. 70–109.

37. The *Oxford English Dictionary* [*OED*] defines 'tilt' (1511) as 'A combat or encounter (for exercise or sport) between two armed men on horseback, with lances or similar weapons, the aim of each being to throw his opponent from the saddle'. David Bevington glosses 'mammets' as 'dolls, or else, breasts'.

38. NANCY CHODOROW, *The Reproduction of Mothering: Psychoanalysis and the Sociology of Gender* (Berkeley: University of California Press, 1978) p. 113.

39. The *OED* defines 'prick' as 'the penis' (1592). Its earlier definition are 'A pointed weapon or implement. Applied to a dagger or pointed sword' (1552); and 'to select (persons) . . . to appoint, choose, or pick *out*' (1557).

40. Erickson, *Patriarchal Structures*, p. 60.

41. I am indebted to Linda Boose for insisting on viewing Katharine as a subject in her own right. However, I am aware that one can both laugh *with* Katharine and *at* her at the same time, depending on inflection and how the scene is played. Thus, as Peter Erickson pointed out to me, Shakespeare seems to have it both ways through the juxtaposition of Henry's Harfleur speech (III.iii) and Katharine's tutorial (III.iv): he detaches himself from Henry without going over unequivocally to Katharine's side.

42. HELEN OSTOVICH, ' "Teach you our princess English?" Equivocal Translation of the French in *Henry V*', unpublished manuscript, pp. 8–9.

43. For an analysis of the homosocial exchange of women in Shakespearean drama, see KAREN NEWMAN, 'Portia's Ring: Unruly Women and Structures of Exchange in *The Merchant of Venice*', *Shakespeare Quarterly* 38:1 (1987), pp. 19–33.

44. Women's bodies figure territory in other Shakespearean plays; notably, Falstaff's counterpart in *The Comedy of Errors*, Nell, is imagined as a monstrous globe. 'She is spherical, like a globe. I could find out countries in her', Dromio says, proceeding to enumerate the Western European nations embodied in her abundant flesh and foul breath (III.ii.114–15). Comic though this treatment is (supposed to be), it was given a more serious precedent in the Ditchley portrait of Queen Elizabeth as conquering ruler standing firm atop a map of England. See ROY STRONG, *Portraits of Queen Elizabeth* (Oxford: Clarendon Press, 1963), pp. 75–76 and plate XV.

45. Stallybrass and White, *Politics and Poetics*, pp. 21–2.

46. See *Romeo and Juliet* (II.iii.9–14), and [SIGMUND] FREUD, 'The Theme of the Three Caskets' (1913), *The Standard Edition of the Complete Psychological Works of Sigmund Freud*, ed. James Strachey (London: Hogarth Press, 1958) Vol. 12, pp. 291–301.

CHAPTER SEVEN

Carnival and History: *Henry IV*[1]

GRAHAM HOLDERNESS

Graham Holderness is the author or editor of many books and articles on Shakespeare's history plays, and has also written extensively on the 'Shakespeare myth'. In the following extract from a chapter of his 1992 study of the history plays *Shakespeare Recycled* he examines Falstaff in the light of well-known work on popular custom and carnival by writers such as C. L. Barber and Mikhail Bakhtin. Festivals which temporarily inverted the social order (so that, for example, masters would wait on servants or a 'fool' would become 'king' for a day) are analysed in terms of a conflict: for the people, they are subversive, an expression of a fantasy of freedom and equality; for the authorities, they are permissive, a means of controlling those impulses on the part of the people.

Holderness argues that for most critics Falstaff's misrule operates to consolidate rule. For him this is to take 'the "official", permissive view of saturnalian comedy rather than its popular subversive view'. What exactly would be different if we incline more to the popular view is not entirely clear: certainly not the fate of Falstaff or the outcome of the plays, in which, as Holderness says, 'there is much to support the reductive strictures of the moralists' – though Holderness exposes the crudity of their arguments that Falstaff's rejection and the monarch's triumphant transition to respectability reveal Shakespeare's 'balance' and 'wisdom'.

Holderness argues that Falstaff is a kind of collective figure, standing for the people, larger than any individual both in his body and in his language(s) and his dramatic roles: 'Falstaff is not a coherent individual subject but a polyphonic clamour of discourses, a fluid counterfeiter of dramatic impersonations.' Holderness also shows that the tendency to see Falstaff as a rampant egotist is another way of reducing him to the mere individual, a bundle of appetites, neutralising his subversive political implications. His essay marks a significant trend: the dismantling of Falstaff as 'Shakespeare's greatest comic creation'. No longer is he seen as a character portrait of a loveable rogue whose threat to the King is easily dismissed and neutralised.

It is a commonplace that the figure of Falstaff, or the 'world' that figure inhabits or creates, constitutes some kind of internal *opposition* to the ethical conventions, political priorities and structures of authority and power embodied in the sovereign hegemony of king, prince and court: the state. Falstaff is at the centre of a popular comic history, located within the deterministic framework of the chronicle-history play, which challenges and subverts the imperatives of necessitarian historiography. The chronicle-history frame is qualified and criticized by a confrontation of different dramatic discourses within the drama, a confrontation which brings into play genuinely historical tensions and contradictions, drawn both from Shakespeare's own time and from the reconstructed time of the historical past.

The kind of 'opposition' represented by Falstaff is often compared with the other oppositional tendencies which challenge the state in these plays: Falstaff's moral rebelliousness and illegality are seen as analogous to those forces of political subversion – the rebellion of the Percies and the Archbishop of York's conspiracy – which shake the stability of the Lancastrian dynasty. But though moral riotousness and political opposition are often arbitrarily connected by hostile propaganda, a state which ruthlessly suppresses the latter often finds space for the former – regarded perhaps as the legitimate exercise of freedom guaranteed to a despotic ruling class by the 'stability' of its government (e.g. the court of the Stuarts). It has been recognized that the revelry and satire of Falstaff constitute kinds of social practice which were afforded a legitimate space in medieval culture. Medieval European hierarchies, secular and ecclesiastical, sought to preserve the rigidity of their social relations, to control and incorporate internal tensions and oppositions, by allowing, at fixed times, temporary suspensions of rule, order and precedence: festive holidays in which moral freedom and opposition to political authority, the flouting of moral conventions and the inversion of ordinary social structures, were allowed to flourish. These periods of temporary suspension were closely analogous to, possibly related back to, religious practices of antiquity:

Many peoples have been used to observe an annual period of licence, when the customary restraints of law and morality are thrown aside, when the whole population give themselves up to extravagant mirth and jollity, and when the darker passions find a vent which would never be allowed them in the more staid and sober course of ordinary life. Such outbursts of the pent-up forces of human nature, too often degenerating into wild orgies of lust and crime, occur most commonly at the end of the year, and are frequently associated . . . with one or other of the agricultural seasons, especially with the time of sowing or of harvest.[2]

Dance, song, feasting, moral freedom, were a natural element of most pre-Christian European religions, and were sternly condemned as unchristian, immoral licence by zealous and reforming Christian clerics, from the early Church fathers (who attacked the Roman Saturnalia) to the sixteenth-century Puritans. More generally they were modified, and incorporated into Christian observance (in the same way as the more prudent and discerning Christian missionaries tried to *adapt* rather than supplant the beliefs of those they wished to convert), so that the pagan fertility myths of the Mummers' Play became a Christmas or Springtime celebration.[3] Such social practices were far from being simply a period of release, with bouts of drinking and lust and frenzied dancing: they were often characterized by a specific ritual shape, involving the suspension of ordinary structures of authority. The Roman Saturnalia reveals a clear ritual structure within the general surrender to appetite and passion: within it social relationships were not merely suspended but *inverted*:

Now of all these periods of license the one which is best known and which in modern languages has given its name to the rest, is the Saturnalia . . . no feature of the festival is more remarkable, nothing in it seems to have struck the ancients themselves more than the license granted to slaves at this time. The distinction between the free and servile classes was temporarily abolished. The slave might rail at his master, intoxicate himself like his betters, sit down at table with them, and not even a word of reproof would be administered to him for conduct which at any other season might have been punished with stripes, imprisonment, or death. Nay, more, masters actually changed places with their slaves and waited on them at table; and not till the serf had done eating and drinking was the board cleared and dinner set for his master.[4]

The custom was called saturnalian because it purported to be a temporary imitation of the 'Golden Age' society of peace, fertility, freedom and common wealth, without private property or slavery, presided over by the God Saturn: 'The Saturnalia passed for nothing more or less than a temporary revival or restoration of the reign of that merry monarch.'[5] The nostalgic sentimentalism of Roman patricians and the utopian longings of their slaves met on the common ground of saturnalian revelry and ritual: a clear acknowledgment that such a society must have been preferable to the present order, co-existed with a more pragmatic sense of the essentially limited nature of human ideals and aspirations, a sad recognition that 'order' (i.e. the contemporary state) can be suspended, but never, in practice, abolished or transformed. So the Saturnalia, and the associated rituals of medieval Europe, were:

. . . an interregnum during which the customary restraints of law and morality are suspended and the ordinary rulers abdicate their authority in favour of a temporary regent, a sort of puppet king, who bears a more or less indefinite, capricious and precarious sway over a community given up for a time to riot, turbulence and disorder.[6]

Similar customs are visible in later English folk-ceremonies by which the rural people celebrated spring or summer: festivities in praise of fertility would involve the election of a mock ruler – a 'May King', a 'Summer Lord', a 'Mock Mayor' – or a King and Queen whose mock marriage would seem to symbolize some ancient myth of fertility. Such festivities, it is suspected, would probably include the exercise of practical fertility among the celebrants: 'It may be taken for granted that the summer festivals knew from the beginning that element of sexual licence which fourteen centuries of Christianity have not wholly been able to banish.'[7]

Those ancient cults and practices can be linked to Shakespeare's time by a famous passage from the Puritan Phillip Stubbes' *Anatomy of Abuses* (1583):

Against May, Whitsunday, or other time, all the young men and maids, old men and wives, run gadding overnight to the woods, groves, hills and mountains, where they spend all night in pleasant pastimes; and in the morning they return, bringing with them birch and branches of trees, to deck their assemblies withall. And no marvel, for there is a great Lord present amongst them, as Superintendent and Lord over their pastimes and sports, namely, Sathan, prince of hell. But the chiefest jewel they bring from thence is their May-pole, which they bring home with great veneration. . . . And then they fall to dance about it, like as the heathen people did at the dedication of the Idols, whereof this is a perfect pattern, or rather the thing itself.[8]

Stubbes also inveighs against the custom of electing a 'Lord of Misrule' to preside over ritual celebrations. Those May celebrations persisted in folk-culture and continued to be the target of Puritan attack: various legislative attempts to control or suppress them seemed to have little success before 1644. On the basis of this folk culture saturnalian customs developed throughout medieval society: in cathedral and collegiate schools the Church permitted festivities such as the Feast of Fools, a revelry presided over by a member of the lower clergy reigning as temporary sovereign; and where such customs were suppressed by reforming clerics, the local bourgeoisie would often revive them as civic festivities. In Universities, Inns of Court and in the Royal Court itself, such revels flourished under a 'Lord of Misrule' or king of fools: Henry VIII often participated personally in such celebrations.

The relation to these popular traditions of the Elizabethan drama has been well enough understood and documented – E. K. Chambers's pioneering work built upon the findings of Frazer and the early anthropologists to produce a new perspective on the relation between drama and social custom; and the field still remains dominated by the fine studies of C. L. Barber and Robert Weimann.[9] There is still room, however, for further theoretical work on this relation, especially on the specific *social* significance of saturnalian custom and its passage into drama: and this work is made infinitely more feasible by the fairly recent 'discovery' of Mikhail Bakhtin's theories on 'carnivalization' in medieval and Renaissance literature, developed in his study of Rabelais (1940).[10]

In the Middle Ages, Bakhtin writes: 'a boundless world of humorous forms and manifestations opposed the official and serious tone of medieval ecclesiastical and feudal culture . . . the culture of folk carnival humour'. These forms were, according to Bakhtin's most illuminating emphasis, basically *popular* expressions of folk culture: though they were built into the formal structure of medieval culture, they contained and signified (like the Roman Saturnalia) a completely different conception of human society:

All those forms of protocol and ritual based on laughter and consecrated by tradition existed in all the countries of medieval Europe; they were sharply distinct from the serious, official, ecclesiastical, feudal and political cult forms and ceremonials. They offered a completely different, non-official, extra-ecclesiastical and extra-political aspect of the world, of man, and of human relations; they built a second world in which all medieval people participated more or less, in which they lived during a given time of the year.[11]

Clearly the 'carnival' (Bakhtin's generic title for all saturnalian customs and practices) was a contradictory social institution: its whole *raison d'être* was that of opposition to established authority; it rejected all official norms and conventions; inverted established hierarchies; flouted, satirized and parodied the rituals, institutions and personalities of power. And yet it was countenanced, permitted, even fostered by those very authorities.

The medieval feast had, as it were, the two faces of Janus. Its official, ecclesiastical face was turned to the past and sanctioned the existing order, but the face of the people of the market place looked into the future and laughed, attending the funeral of the past and present.[12]

Only a very rigid, hierarchical and static society needs such organized release and limited, temporary liberation; only a very stable, confident society can afford to permit them. By the late sixteenth century matters were different; the continuities of pagan ritual and belief were being harshly attacked by the Puritans; the precarious religious settlement made any mockery of religious authority (even, later in Elizabeth's reign, of Catholicism)[13] impossible; and the various attempts to stabilize a rapidly changing social and class structure, continued under the Stuarts, made the image of the world turned upside down particularly distasteful to established authority. The potency of these ideas can be measured by the fact that later, in the Civil War period, such comic inversions became the basis of serious, revolutionary social criticism. From the medieval rituals in which the text 'He hath put down the mighty from their seats, and exalted them of low degree' inaugurated a temporary inversion of social hierarchy, to the radical social theories of Winstanley and the Fifth Monarchy men, there is a definite though complex and contradictory historical continuity.[14]

Bakhtin argues that such carnival customs expressed and embodied an oppositional ideology: and that in such events the people themselves could temporarily live out an ideology of alternative values: 'The carnival and similar marketplace festivals . . . were the second life of the people, who for a time entered into the utopian realm of community, freedom, equality and abundance.' In carnival all were equal: all everyday order and hierarchy dissolved, leaving people reborn to new and more truly human relations. These relations required a new philosophy, a new language, which Bakhtin calls 'dynamic expression': a new kind of logic in which the real world is criticized by living out a fantasy of its dissolution – the world turned upside down, the logic of parody and travesty, comic humiliation of power and greatness, comic uncrowning of authority and the crowning of the low.

It should then be possible to analyze any example of carnival festivity or saturnalian custom, and any literary production flowing from these social forms, in terms of this contradiction: from the point of view of the people, carnival is an expression of the independent values, the humanism of popular culture, a fantasy of equality, freedom and abundance which challenges the social order; from the point of view of authority, carnival is a means of incorporating and controlling the energies and anti-authoritarian emotions aroused by carnival licence. This cultural contradiction, this confrontation of popular and authoritarian discourses, will prove a sound basis for defining the function of Falstaff. It will first be necessary to provide a detailed account of Bakhtin's theory of carnival.

Bakhtin finds that the central *image* of the carnival attitude is that of the *body*: the 'material bodily principle' which is always regarded as 'deeply positive'. It is a symbol for (or rather a direct imaginative expression of) 'the people, constantly growing and renewed'. As a conception of human nature this image of the people as a giant (gargantuan) collective body pre-dates the formation of a strictly-defined and differentiated atomized individual which, in Bakhtin's terms, is a development of the Renaissance (in Rabelais, for example, the individual body has not yet been completely severed from the general body of the people):

In grotesque realism the bodily element is deeply positive . . . something universal, representing all the people. . . . The complex nature of Renaissance realism has not as yet been sufficiently disclosed. Two types of imagery reflecting the conception of the world have met at crossroads; one of them ascends to the folk culture of humour, while the other is the bourgeois conception of the complete atomised being. The conflict of these two contradictory trends is typical of Renaissance realism. The ever-growing, inexhaustible, ever-laughing principle which uncrowns and renews is combined with its opposite: the petty, inert, 'material principle' of class society.[15]

The dominant *style* of carnival discourse is the *grotesque*: '. . . all that is bodily becomes grandiose, exaggerated, immeasurable'.[16] The carnivalizing imagination creates gargantuan images of huge bodies, enormous appetites, surrealistic fantasies of absurdly inflated physical properties.

Carnival is humorous and satirical, and its laughter always *materializes*: concretizes the spiritual in the physical, the ideal in the material, the 'upper' strata of life and society into the 'lower'. Ideals, pretensions, elevated conceptions of human nature cannot survive the enormous assertions of human sensuality: the pride of physical life mocks and degrades everything which seeks to transcend or escape it. Hence this grotesque humour of the body provides a firm basis for satire (a word often historically confused with the half-human, half-bestial figure of the satyr).

While the 'bourgeois ego' limits human life to the birth and death of a differentiated individual, the grotesque bodily image of carnival is that of a perpetually unfinished process of change and renewal: 'The grotesque image reflects a phenomenon in transformation, an as yet unfinished metamorphosis, of death and birth, growth and becoming.'[17] The grotesque body is therefore deeply ambivalent, since it contains both processes of creation and destruction, vitality and dissolution – a simultaneity of the antitheses of life glimpsed in one dimension: 'In this image we find both poles of transformation, the old and the new, the dying and the pro-creating, the beginning and the end of the metamorphosis.'[18]

The grotesque image is not sealed off from the outer world: it merges into its environment as if symbolizing some unity of man and nature. Hence in carnival and carnivalesque literature there is a recurrent emphasis on the physical points of entry and exit (mouth, nose, genitals, anus) and on processes of reproduction and defecation – processes which guarantee the perpetuity of 'the ever unfinished, ever creating body'. Where classicism in art later represented the body as complete, self-sufficient, enclosed and perfect, with its relation to the outer world sealed off, the grotesque insisted on that relation by displaying and caricaturing the body in its external relations.

Subsequent to the Middle Ages the grotesque became generally subject to a moralistic perspective which severely limited its power and significance:

During the domination of the classical man in all the areas of art and literature of the seventeenth and early eighteenth centuries, the grotesque related to the culture of folk humour was excluded from great literature; it descended to the low comic level or was subject to the epithet 'gross naturalism'. . . . During this period (actually starting in the seventeenth century) we observe a process of gradual narrowing down of the ritual, spectacle and carnival forms of folk culture . . .

Having lost its living tie with folk culture and having become a literary genre, the grotesque underwent certain changes. There was a formalisation of carnival-grotesque images, which permitted them to be used in many different ways and for various purposes. This formalisation was not only exterior; the contents of the carnival-grotesque element, its artistic, heuristic, and unifying forces were preserved in all essential manifestations during the seventeenth and eighteenth centuries: in the *commedia dell'arte* (which kept a close link with its carnival origin), in Molière's comedies . . . in the comic novel and travesty of the seventeenth century, in the tales of Voltaire and Diderot, in the work of Swift . . . in all these writings, despite their differences in character and tendency, the carnival-grotesque form exercises the same function: to consecrate inventive freedom, to permit the combination of a variety of different elements and their rapprochement, to liberate from the prevailing point of view of the world, from conventions and established truths, from clichés, from all that is humdrum and universally accepted. This carnival spirit offers the chance to have a new outlook on the world, to realise the relative nature of all that exists, and to enter a completely new order of things.[19]

Falstaff clearly performs the function, in *Henry IV Parts One* and *Two*, of carnival. He constitutes a constant focus of opposition to the official and serious tone of authority and power: his discourse confronts and challenges those of king and state. His attitude to authority is always parodic and satirical: he mocks authority, flouts power, responds to the pressures of social duty and civic obligation by retreating into Bacchanalian revelry. His world is a world of ease, moral licence, appetite and desire; of humour and ridicule, theatricals and satire, of community, freedom and abundance; a world created by inverting the abstract society, the oppression and the hierarchy of the official world. In the tavern the fool reigns as sovereign; on the high road the thief is an honest man; while in the royal court the cares and duties of state frown on the frivolity and absurdity of saturnalian revelry. To this extent Falstaff can be located in that *popular* tradition of carnival and utopian comedy defined by Bakhtin.

Bakhtin's most innovatory and useful emphasis lies on the *oppositional* character of popular traditions. Falstaff's relation to 'folk culture' may seem remote, though he bears vestigial (or perhaps simply parallel) traces of ancient fertility gods, mythical figures like the Silenus, refers to popular culture and the figures of popular ritual dance and drama (ballads, morality-plays, the May-game and morris-dance figure, Maid Marian), and undergoes at the end of *Henry IV Part One* a comic resurrection probably imitated from the popular drama. But he certainly bears a strong relation to popular traditions of the sixteenth century, some elements of which were isolated by Dover Wilson[20] (the morality-play relation for example); and his various languages all derive from popular culture – the cant of criminals, the accents of anti-Puritan parody and satire, the language of tavern and high-road. His flexible command of different popular discourses goes with another factor, to be discussed at length below: variety of dramatic roles, which bear no coherent relation to what we call 'character', but operate only as part of a specific relation between actor and audience.

Falstaff *is* Bakhtin's 'material bodily principle' writ large: his enormous size and uncontrolled appetite characterize him as a collective rather than an individual being. His self-descriptions employ a grotesque style of caricature and exaggeration to create the monstrous image of a figure larger than life, bigger than any conceivable individual:

Have you any levers to lift me up again, being down?

(*IHIV*, II, ii, 34)

I do here walk before thee like a sow that hath overwhelmed all her litter but one.

(*2HIV*, I, ii, 10–11)

– and he frequently discourses in his own brand of grotesque fantasy, which works by inflating the small into the enormous: his subsequent narrative of the robbery (*IHIV*, II, iv, 160–212) or his disquisition on Bardolph's nose (*IHIV*, III, iii, 23–49). The collective being is created by foregrounding this concrete image of the material body, but also by means linguistic and dramatic: Falstaff is not a coherent individual subject but a polyphonic clamour of discourses, a fluid counterfeiter of dramatic impersonations.

Falstaff's satirical humour 'degrades' – that is, translates the abstract into the concrete, the spiritual into the physical: 'A plague of sighing and grief! It blows a man up like a bladder!' (*IHIV*, II, iv, 327–8). The conventional physical effects of grief are inverted, producing fatness rather than emaciation: the breath exhaled in sighs becomes the gaseous inflation of an unsettled stomach. The Prince observes that Falstaff's enormous sensual concreteness contains no space for non-material entities: 'There's no room for faith, truth nor honesty in this bosom of thine: it is all filled up with guts and midriff' (*IHIV*, III, iii, 152–3).

For Bakhtin the grotesque bodily image 'reflects a phenomenon in transformation', contains the processes of both creation and dissolution. This deep ambivalence is utterly characteristic of Falstaff, who seems to constitute a medium in which these antithetical processes generate simultaneously. Physical sloth and inertia coexist with vivid vitality of imagination; age and youth are interchangeable. During the Gad's Hill robbery Falstaff poses, under cover of darkness, as a lithe young gallant mugging the elderly and obese bourgeoisie:

Ah, whoreson caterpillars, bacon-fed knaves, they hate us youth! . . . No, ye fat chuffs, I would your store were here! On, bacons, on! What, ye knaves! young men must live!

(*IHIV*, II, ii, 81–2; 84–6)

and later to the Lord Chief Justice:

You that are old consider not the capacities of us that are young; you do measure the heat of our livers with the bitterness of your galls; and we that are in the vaward of our youth, I must confess, are wags too!

(*2HIV*, I, ii, 172–6)

To moralize these passages would give us a pitiable image of age masquerading as youth. In fact, they present the audacious paradoxes of carnival, in which death and life, age and youth co-exist in the same figure, held together in impossible simultaneity by the force, zest and gaiety of carnival humour, balanced but unillusioned, poised but explosively liberating. The Prince again acknowledges this as Falstaff's essential nature in seasonal metaphors: 'Farewell, the latter spring! Farewell, All-Hallow summer!'; which anticipates Bakhtin's: 'in this image we find both poles of transformation, the old and the new, the dying and the procreating, the beginning and the end of the metamorphosis'.[21]

Bakhtin's account of the demise of the carnival and the grotesque in literature as neo-classicism advanced, coincides precisely with the fate of Falstaff in criticism. The modern critical traditions derive from John Dover Wilson's *The Fortunes of Falstaff* (1943), a monument of ideological consolidation dating from that amazingly fertile period of Shakespeare reproduction (discussed below), the Second World War. Dover Wilson argues that the later eighteenth century inaugurated a diversionary tendency of Falstaff criticism: where Dr Johnson had been able to hold, with neo-classical centrality, a 'balanced' view (which Dover Wilson attempts to reconstitute), romanticism, *via* the sentimentalism of Maurice Morgann and the republicanism of Hazlitt, introduced an 'imbalance' into the poised edifice of criticism, establishing as norms certain radical attitudes: disloyalty and distaste towards the prince, unqualified admiration for Falstaff, a preference for comic opposition over conservative royalism, for instinct and desire over reason and self-control, for moral and political subversion over the preservation of 'order' in the state.[22] Dr Johnson, apparently, 'still lived in Shakespeare's world, a world which was held together, and could only be held together by authority based on and working through a carefully preserved gradation of rank. He was never tired of proclaiming 'the virtues of the Principle of Subordination . . .'[23] According to Dover Wilson, Johnson 'shared Shakespeare's political assumptions', which are embodied in Ulysses' speech on 'degree' in *Troilus and Cressida*; and was therefore able to understand Shakespeare where the romantics could not. Dover Wilson does not, however, claim to derive his critical authority from the same ground of sympathetic – because partisan – comprehension. In fact his position is identical to that of Tillyard, whose *Shakespeare's History Plays* (already referred to, and discussed at length below) belongs to the same historical moment, the same cultural intervention, as Dover Wilson's book on Falstaff: both share the apparently scholarly (but implicitly polemical) privileging of 'order', defined as a hierarchical state ruled by the 'Principle of Subordination'. Dover Wilson's cultural/ideological strategy is clear: to re-establish a pristine but disrupted 'order' in the criticism of *Henry IV*, in Shakespeare studies, and thence in the problematical society of war-time Britain. The political intention is obvious, but naturally unacknowledged; it is articulated instead as a *moral* reconstituting of the proper context for appreciating Falstaff:

Shakespeare's audience enjoyed the fascination of Prince Hal's 'white-bearded Satan' for two whole plays, as perhaps no character on the world's stage had ever been enjoyed before. But they knew, from the beginning, that the reign of this marvellous Lord of Misrule must have an end, that Falstaff must be rejected by the Prodigal Prince, when the time for reformation came. And they no more thought of questioning or disapproving of that finale, than their ancestors would have thought of protesting against the vice being carried off to Hell at the end of the interlude.[24]

'Shakespeare's audience' here is a fictional construction invented merely to confirm the critic's own views. Yet Dover Wilson can confidently ascribe to that phantom a definitive moral perspective in which Falstaff plays a strictly temporary and limited role: an isolated space of pleasure circumscribed by the unshakeable certainties of moral truth. With even greater confidence Dover Wilson asserts his definition of the moral judgment Shakespeare's audience would have passed on Prince Hal's riotous youth:

Vanity . . . was a cardinal iniquity in a young prince or nobleman of the sixteenth and seventeenth century; . . . this is the view that his father and his own conscience take of his mistreadings; and as the spectator would take it as well, we must regard it as the thesis to which Shakespeare addressed himself.[25]

In short, the play is being located within a moralistic framework developed by critics like Tillyard and Dover Wilson during the Second World War, a moralistic perspective entirely out of sympathy with the popular traditions of carnival comedy from which Falstaff developed. Once this structure was erected and consolidated and the threat posed by Falstaff to bourgeois criticism deflected, it became possible to affirm a nostalgic and sentimental pleasure in what Falstaff had to offer. This balancing act, a strategic counterpointing of constraint and canonization, is skilfully engineered in Dover Wilson's conclusion:

Falstaff, for all his descent from a medieval devil, has become a kind of god in the mythology of modern man, a god who does for our imaginations very much what Bacchus or Silenus did for those of the ancients; and this because we find it extraordinarily exhilarating to contemplate a being free of all the conventions, codes and moral ties that control us as members of a human society, . . .

Yet the English spirit has ever needed two wings for its flight, Order as well as Liberty . . . this balance which the play keeps between the bliss of freedom and the claims of the common weal has been disturbed by modern critics . . . I have endeavoured to do something to readjust the balance. In effect, it has meant trying to put Falstaff in his place . . . I offer no apologies for constraining the old boar to feed in the old frank . . .[26]

Dover Wilson, scholar, critic and public servant, has evidently inherited the world and the ideology of Prince Henry: there is an unbroken continuity of the 'English spirit' between himself and

. . . English Harry, in whose person Shakespeare crowns *noblesse oblige*, generosity and magnanimity, respect for law, and the selfless devotion to duty which comprise the traditional ideals of our public service.[27]

Falstaff can be afforded only a severely limited space in this scheme of things, which is evidently Dover Wilson's bizarre conception of an actual world, his view of the point where the play's ideology merges into a reality outside itself: but once his influence within it has been securely controlled by 'balanced' criticism, he can be safely distanced into myth, given the freedom of an unreal realm of 'imagination', and canonized as a quaint, lovable but innocuous minor divinity.

A measure of the powerfully influential character of this view on subsequent criticism of the *Henry IV* plays, is the extent to which C. L. Barber's study of saturnalian comedy depends upon it. Barber adopts the same image of the Prince as Tillyard and Dover Wilson:

. . . the play is centered on Prince Hal, developing in such a way as to exhibit in the prince an inclusive, sovereign nature fitted for kingship.[28]

Barber, like Tillyard and Dover Wilson, considers the play's central issue to be that of the Prince's position relative to 'misrule': will he prove noble or degenerate? will he learn to exercise strict control over saturnalian licence, or will his 'holiday' become his 'everyday'?

The interregnum of a Lord of Misrule, delightful in its moment, might develop into the anarchic reign of a favorite dominating a dissolute King. Hal's secret, which he confides early to the audience, is that for him Falstaff is merely a pastime, to be dismissed in due course . . .[29]

Even within Barber's extremely subtle and perceptive account can be discerned a gravitation towards the 'official', permissive view of saturnalian comedy rather than its popular, subversive view: misrule operates only in relation to rule, disorder cannot exist without order, a mock king derives his meaning from the real king and can have no independent status or validity – 'the dynamic relation of comedy to serious action is saturnalian rather than satiric . . . the misrule works, through the whole dramatic rhythm, to consolidate rule'.[30] Barber acknowledges in a very interesting passage[31] that Falstaff represented some force potentially subversive: not the 'dependent holiday scepticism' which could be comfortably accommodated within a monolithic medieval society, but, in the much more diverse and rapidly changing society of Elizabethan England, a 'dangerously self-sufficient everyday scepticism' threatening to fracture the imposed perimeters, expand the allotted space of licensed saturnalian revelry. He argues further that the rejection of Falstaff can only be accomplished by the employment of primitive magic in the hands of a king whose 'inclusive, sovereign nature' has been drastically reduced and narrowed. Yet Barber will not admit that Falstaff represents a power which the play can barely contain because the historical contradiction it brings into play by confronting popular and establishment discourses are so sharp and insoluble: to do so would break down the sustained effort to achieve and maintain 'balance'. Instead Barber sees the rejection as the inevitable, the only possible outcome of the play's interrogation or 'trial' of Falstaff: 'The result of the trial is to make us see perfectly the necessity for the rejection of Falstaff as a man, as a favorite of the king, as the leader of an interest at court.'[32]

The editor of the Arden Shakespeare texts of *Henry IV* is able to quote approvingly from both Dover Wilson and Barber, and to support the idea of the plays as a 'unified vision' with the names of New Critics Cleanth Brooks and Robert B. Heilman.[33] He writes, in the Tillyard tradition, of 'the great idea of England', quotes (with qualification but with overall approval) Dover Wilson's '*Henry IV* is Shakespeare's vision of the "happy breed of men" that was his England', and endorses

C. L. Barber's view that in saturnalian comedy misrule operates to consolidate rule.[34] There is a gestural recognition of Falstaff's comic opposition, but a correspondingly firm insistence that Shakespeare was not 'amoral' or 'infinitely tolerant':

There is history here, as well as comedy – history which requires responsible action . . . [Shakespeare] upholds good government, in the macrocosm of the state, and the microcosm of man . . . his vision is of men living, however conflictingly, in a nation, a political-moral family.[35]

The rejection of Falstaff is 'necessary, well-prepared, and executed without undue severity'; 'Shakespeare has here achieved a balanced complexity of wisdom'.[36]

It would be possible then to locate Falstaff within that popular tradition of carnival and utopian fantasy defined by Bakhtin, and to argue that the moralistic defamation of Falstaff is analogous to the demise of carnival humour as it lost its living tie with folk culture and became subject to the moral and aesthetic dominance of neoclassicism. Yet there is clearly much in Falstaff's dramatic contribution to contradict the categorization here employed: much to support the reductive strictures of the moralists. By the end of *Henry IV Part Two*, Falstaff has become something much more akin to Bakhtin's concept of the 'isolated bourgeois ego': 'I have a whole school of tongues in this belly of mine, and not a tongue of them all speaks any other word but my name.' The inflated egoism displayed here is not carnival: the clamorous popular voices of the collective being have been reduced to monotone: the 'isolated bourgeois ego' has secured complete totalitarian rule over the complex multifarious variety of carnivalized humanity. This dramatic tendency evidently has such power that it induces criticism emanating from various positions on the left to collaborate with conventional criticism in isolating egoistic individualism as Falstaff's sole or primary dramatic role. The passages on the *Henry IV* plays in John F. Danby's *Shakespeare's Doctrine of Nature* (1961) recognize no fundamental contradiction between dominant and subordinate worlds in the plays: though mutually exclusive, the separate spheres share a general condition of moral and political malaise, '. . . with no common term except the disease of each'. In 'an England pervaded throughout court tavern and country retreat by pitiless fraud', Falstaff, far from constituting any serious opposition, 'is himself the most pitiless creature in the play'. The related energies of 'Appetite' and 'Power' are the universal motivations driving this corrupt and diseased political body.[37] More recently, Elliot Krieger's marxist analysis of Shakespearean comedy reaffirms Danby's emphasis, defining Falstaff as a predatory, competitive self, dedicated entirely to appetite and exploitative consumption:

Falstaff opposes only the forces of authority that place limits on his own autonomy, whereas he works to maintain and uphold his authority – the autonomy of the ego.[38]

Evidently then we are confronted here either with a process of degeneration or a site of contradictions: or possibly with a combination of the two. Does Falstaff begin as the 'ever-growing, inexhaustible, ever-laughing principle' and end as 'the isolated bourgeois ego'? Is the 'character' actually a site of perpetual conflict between these antithetical principles: a literary figure offering to an audience *alternative* positions of intelligibility? Do those opposing forces, if present from the outset, shift their positions of relative power? Conventional criticism, when it does not seek to invalidate Falstaff *ab ovo*, opts for the first of these possibilities: *Henry IV Part Two is* usually regarded as the history of Falstaff's degeneration towards deserved dismissal. I will argue that Falstaff is in fact a site of contradictions: that the relation between the contradictory forces is unstable and changing; that under the pressure of external determinations built into the play's historical vision, its fundamental aesthetic form, and its location in the originating moment of its production, the balance of forces develops in tension until it reaches an ultimate breakdown at the end of *Henry IV Part Two*.

> Fal.   Now, Hal, what time of day is it, lad?
>
> Prince   Thou art so fat-witted with drinking of old sack, and unbuttoning thee after supper, and sleeping upon benches after noon, that thou hast forgotten to demand that truly which thou wouldst truly know. What a devil has thou to do with the time of the day? Unless hours were cups of sack, and minutes capons, and clocks the tongues of bawds, and dials the signs of leaping-houses, and the blessed sun himself a fair hot wench in flame-coloured taffeta, I see no reason why thou shouldst be so superfluous to demand the time of the day.

> (*IHIV*, I, ii, 1–12)

The specific context of the Prince's fantasy is provided by the material principle of the physical body, which is here seen in a characteristically relaxed condition ('unbuttoning', 'sleeping'). The emphases are on physical appetites, of eating, drinking and sex ('old sack', 'capons', 'a fair hot wench'); on the carnival device of *degrading* the intellectual or spiritual into the physical ('fatwitted'); and on the kind of *inversion* of the established world-order (signified here by the language and imagery of time) which is the constitutive activity of the carnivalistic imagination. Falstaff's existence, alleges the Prince, rejects the discipline of the hour: and this apparent privileging of time as the structure of social order could be (and has been) taken as a moralistic condemnation of Falstaff's essential *raison d'être*. But this is to ignore the mode of the Prince's speech, which is precisely that discourse of fantasy in which the inversion of the existing world-order produces an exhilarating sense of liberation: those ideologies implied by the concept of time (moral seriousness, civic duty, work) are interrogated by this practice of inversion. The signs of time – hours, minutes, clocks, dials, the blessed sun – are all liberated from the fixity of their common social meanings, wrenched from their legitimate place in the hierarchy of language, and degraded to the dimension of physical pleasure. The Prince may seem to be castigating Falstaff's freedom from accepted limitation, routine, system and convention: but his playful manipulation of those signs which act as guarantees of social order shows him equally excited by the liberty of carnival discourse. Fantasy, Rosemary Jackson has argued, is based on 'an obdurate refusal of prevailing definitions of the "real" or "possible" ',[39] it subverts rules and conventions taken to be normative. It is the inverse side of reason's orthodoxy; and therefore can reveal 'reason' and 'reality' to be arbitrary, shifting constructs rather than the solid foundations of human existence and social order. In terms of this definition the Prince's imagination is characteristically fantastic: he participates in a discourse which calls into question the very rules and conventions on which he is to base his ultimate power as king.

Falstaff's response is to reaffirm and develop this freedom of language: he also turns the world upside down in fantasy:

> Indeed, you come near me now, Hal, for we that take purses by the moon and the seven stars, and not 'by Phoebus, he, that wand'ring knight so fair' . . . when thou art king let not us that are squires of the night's body be called thieves of the day's beauty: let us be Diana's foresters, gentlemen of the shade, minions of the moon; and let men say we be men of good government, being governed as the sea is, by our noble and chaste mistress the moon, under whose countenance we steal.
>
> (*IHIV*, I, ii, 13–15; 23–29)

Falstaff identifies himself and the Prince with a culture of inversion: in which the reality of the world is to be sought in darkness rather than in light, ruled by the moon rather than the sun; and in which 'good government' is reversed from its normal moral and political associations (firm political rule of the state, strenuous personal discipline of the self) to signify a universal surrender to natural appetite ('being governed as the sea is . . .') in a kingdom of thieves. This discourse of criminality affords a context in which moral criticism can be positively rejected from the alternative ground of a counter-culture: the law calls them thieves, morality condemns them for wasting time and besmirching the day's brightness; but they can confidently invoke their own values, the professional ethics of their own occupation; they have their own 'brightness' in the shadowy glamour of romance ('knights', 'squires', 'minions'); they serve another god. The world is turned upside down in both these fantasies: the Prince's vision of a world in which those objects regarded as securities of reality are carnivalized, transformed into images of appetite and vice, is no different from Falstaff's imaginative ability to invert the world of positive reality in his fantasy of criminal romance.

The stock critical problem concerning the Prince's 'real attitude' to Falstaff, invariably discussed with reference to the soliloquy which ends the scene ('I know you all, and will awhile uphold The unyok'd humour of your idleness') is then misplaced. The real question is not: how does the Prince really regard Falstaff? But rather: what kind of dramatic relationship is constituted by this sharing of a fantastic discourse? Carnival does not merely 'rub off' onto the Prince when he is in Falstaff's company: he can command its language in his own right:

> . . . What a disgrace is it to me to remember thy name! or to know thy face tomorrow! or to take note how many pairs of silk stockings thou hast – viz. these, and those that were thy peach-coloured ones! or to bear the inventory of thy shirts – as, one for superfluity, and another for use! But that the tennis-court keeper knows better than I, for it is a low ebb of linen with thee when thou keepest not racket there; as thou has not done a great while, because the rest of thy low countries have made a shift to eat up thy holland. And God knows whether those that bawl out the ruins of thy linen shall inherit his kingdom: but the midwives say the children are not in the fault; whereupon the world increases, and kindreds are mightily strengthened.
>
> (*2HIV*, II, ii, 12–26)

The Prince's diatribe against Poins is usually understood as an expression of his increasing disgust with his low companions, customarily regarded as a symptom of his growing remorse and imminent reformation. In fact, the speech is an exercise in exactly the mode of satirical fantasy the Prince shares with Falstaff. In the course of apparently criticizing Poins, the Prince's wit constructs a fantasy world in which games, vices, topical allusions, religious parody, all interact in an inverted image of received reality: where the lower regions of the body devour the higher; where a race of illegitimate children are envisaged as the inheritors of a 'kingdom'; and where the Prince's own problematic relation with the royal family ('kindreds') is projected as a fantasy of family strength confirmed, not dissipated, by the prodigality of vice, the abundant proliferation of bastards. The Prince's subsequent attempt (58–60) to dissociate himself from Falstaff appears, in the light of his speech, to be the denial of a constitutive element of himself or of his dramatic role: when he later rejects Falstaff as a figure of his own 'dream', he also renounces, from himself and from his theatrical potentialities, the liberating power of fantasy.

It is true, as conventional wisdom would be swift to point out, that the Prince signals this intention as early as the soliloquy which closes *Henry IV Part One*, I, ii:

> I know you all, and will awhile uphold
> The unyoked humour of your idleness.
> Yet herein will I imitate the sun,
> Who doth permit the base contagious clouds
> To smother up his beauty from the world,
> That, when he please again to be himself,
> Being wanted, he may be more wondered at
> By breaking through the foul and ugly mists
> Of vapours that did seem to strangle him.
> If all the year were playing holidays,
> To sport would be as tedious as to work . . .
>
> *(1HIV*, I, ii, 190–200)

The relation between 'work' and 'holiday' articulated here is very much a dominant/subordinate antithesis: 'holiday' is a temporary release from the permanent responsibilities of 'work', a transient suspension of quotidian duties and obligations. The Prince expresses the 'official' attitude towards saturnalian licence: its strictly limited function is that of confirming, by a liberation as temporary as it is violent, as impermanent as it is affirmative, statutory authority and constituted order. The image of the sun is rehabilitating: what Falstaff has inverted, the Prince sets upright again; light and the sun are re-established in their dominant relation to darkness and clouds. Authority places a limit on carnival freedom, re-establishes what carnival overturns.

The mode of soliloquy should also be recognized as determining the dramatic effect of the Prince's confession. By soliloquizing, a character expresses a clearly defined individuality, an isolated singleness expressing a formidable self-consciousness. Falstaff is often associated with the individualism of soliloquy, since some of his most memorable utterances belong to the mode. It is worth pointing out that in *Henry IV Part One* he hardly uses it at all. In this particular scene, for the first sixty lines he does not even use the pronoun 'I': but speaks of 'we' and 'us', invoking his identity as member of a collective. The Prince consistently employs the first person singular, and with the departure of Falstaff and Poins he is able to turn aside from the action and address the audience directly, displaying his capacity for detachment and egoistic self-assertion. The device also allows for the possibility of an 'alienation-effect', since soliloquy was actually (in Shakespeare's theatre) colloquy, an exchange between actor and audience, which partly suspends the dramatic illusion, making the audience aware of the character as an individual separable from the action in which he is participating, his identity not wholly absorbed into the dramatic interaction with other characters. The Prince is briefly prised away from the illusionistic narrative, offering himself for inspection to the audience's curiosity. The device can have many different effects: here it shows the Prince uniquely capable of individuation, a singling-out from the collective enterprise of the drama into solitary self-assertion and self-justification. This differs strikingly from Falstaff's habit of overt self-dramatizing, since unlike Falstaff, the Prince lays claim to an authentic individual identity independent of his dramatic roles: whatever role he plays, he assures the audience, he will implicitly remain, and at some future point will become in reality, 'himself'.[40] Falstaff never lays claim to such an authentic self: he exists only as a series of dramatic roles, a succession of self-conscious *rapprochements* between actor and audience. His discourse is certainly self-reflexive, but never invokes a distinct personality; rather it alludes to the self as a gargantuan collective creature of myth, a grotesque and hugely inflated caricature. Whether Falstaff is addressing the audience, as in his reaction to the Page's cheek:

> The brain of this foolish-compounded clay, man, is not able to invent anything that intends to laughter more than I invent, or is invented on me . . .
>
> (*2HIV*, I, ii, 5–8)

– or for another character, as in his parodic boasting to the Lord Chief Justice:

> I would to God my name were not so terrible to the enemy as it is . . .
>
> (*2HIV*, I, ii, 217–19)

– he never claims the possession of a distinct centre of self: in the first instance he is openly revealing himself to the audience as a theatrical figure, a dramatic conceit; in the second he manipulates the audience's awareness that this 'name' is an empty title, cheated from the Prince by a comic act of deceit and expropriation. Falstaff's much discussed and much maligned egoism can scarcely be equated with moral categories: there is no self to centre on.[41]

The Prince's life, unlike Falstaff's, is obviously a part of history: its significant episodes are constrained within the fixed, predetermined process of historical event viewed retrospectively as a *fait accompli*. However long he tarries in Eastcheap, Shrewsbury and Agincourt are his fixed destinations. With Falstaff he can experience a relative autonomy which is strictly limited and temporary: he can play roles other than that determined for him by the course of historical necessity, the freer roles established for him by popular romance-history as distinct from Protestant chronicle. But at some point his identity will inevitably be subsumed into the intransigent fixity of fact, the 'known' of history. The Prince anticipates this point as the recovery or realization of 'himself': an undertaking offered in the form of a promise to his father in the scene already discussed:

> I shall hereafter, my thrice gracious lord,
> Be more myself.

> (*IHIV*, III, ii, 93–4)

The 'self' he offers to become sounds suspiciously like the chivalric public image required by the king:

> I will redeem all this on Percy's head . . .
> And that shall be the day, whene'er it lights,
> That this same child of honour and renown,
> This gallant Hotspur, this all-praised knight,
> And your unthought-of Harry chance to meet.
> For every honour sitting on his helm,
> Would they were multitudes . . . !

> (*IHIV*, III, ii, 132; 139–43)

When the moment of self-realization arrives, it becomes evident that in the process the Prince loses all independent individual being and submits to the tyranny of historical determinism: the famous passage describing his battle array dissolves the person into the derealization of chivalric romance, beautiful but banal, eloquent but empty:

> I saw young Harry with his beaver on,
> His cushes on his thighs, gallantly armed,
> Rise from the ground like feather'd Mercury,
> And vaulted with such ease into his seat
> And if an angel dropp'd down from the clouds
> To turn and wind a fiery Pegasus,
> And witch the world with noble horsemanship.

> (*IHIV*, IV, i, 104–10)

The glamour of this poetry has proved universally captivating. In fact its abstract romanticism represents a final absorption of the free individual into history. The Prince appears transformed into a figure of heroic myth; an illustration from Froissart, the mythical protagonist of an Elizabethan romance epic or a Stuart court masque, our Sidney and our perfect man. This, it could be argued, is role-playing with a vengeance, and that is true, but the role is a pre-determined one, fitted to the individual by historical destiny: the 'self' is a mere dissolution into the current of a deterministic process. Falstaff is not a part of history in the same sense, although he had a historical genesis. His origins are by contrast obscure and contradictory, bestowing on him a much greater potentiality for change. He continues to do the opposite of what is required of him: here he plays the coward, in *Henry IV Part Two* the mock-hero. The Prince has ultimately only one role, one destiny: a splendid figure of chivalric myth, the apotheosis of an antiquated culture already rendered archaic and ridiculous by Hotspur's suicidal violence and Falstaff's destructive satire.

NOTES

1. Reprinted from GRAHAM HOLDERNESS, *Shakespeare Recycled. The Making of Historical Drama* (New York and London: Harvester Wheatsheaf, 1992).
2. J. G. FRAZER, *The Golden Bough*, Part VI: *The Scapegoat* (London: Macmillan, 1925), p. 306.
3. See E. K. CHAMBERS, *The Mediaeval Stage* (Oxford: Oxford University Press, 1903), pp. 95–6.
4. Frazer, *Scapegoat*, pp. 306–8.
5. Ibid., p. 308.
6. Ibid., p. 329.
7. Chambers, *Mediaeval Stage*, p. 145.
8. PHILLIP STUBBES, *Anatomy of Abuses in England* (1583), edited by Frederick J. Furnivall (London: New Shakespeare Society, 1877), p. 149.
9. See C. L. BARBER, *Shakespeare's Festive Comedy* (Princeton, N.J.: Princeton University Press, 1959), and ROBERT WEIMANN, *Shakespeare and the Popular Tradition in the Theatre*, edited by Robert Schwarz (Baltimore: Johns Hopkins University Press, 1978), pp. 15ff.
10. MIKHAIL BAKHTIN, *Rabelais and His World*, translated by Helen Iswolsky (Cambridge, MA: CIT Press, 1968). This work was first published in the USSR in 1965, though written in 1940.
11. Bakhtin, *Rabelais*, pp. 5–6.
12. Ibid., p. 81.
13. See Barber, *Festive Comedy*, pp. 50–1.
14. See A. L. MORTON, *The English Utopia* (London: Lawrence and Wishart, 1978).
15. Bakhtin, *Rabelais*, pp. 9; 24.
16. Ibid., p. 19.
17. Ibid., p. 24.
18. Ibid.
19. Ibid., pp. 33–4.
20. J. DOVER WILSON, *The Fortunes of Falstaff* (Cambridge: Cambridge University Press, 1964), pp. 5ff.
21. Bakhtin, *Rabelais*, p. 24.
22. Dover Wilson, *Fortunes of Falstaff*, pp. 5ff.
23. Ibid., p. 7.
24. Ibid., p. 22.
25. Ibid., p. 25.
26. Ibid., p. 128.
27. Ibid.
28. Barber, *Festive Comedy*, p. 195. See Holderness, *Shakespeare Recycled*, pp. 7–8 for Tillyard on the Prince.
29. Ibid., p. 195.
30. Ibid., p. 226.
31. Ibid., pp. 213–14.
32. Ibid., p. 216.

33. A. R. Humphreys (ed.), *The Arden Shakespeare: Henry IV Part One* (London: Methuen, 1960), p. lvi.

34. Ibid.

35. Ibid., p. lvii.

36. A. R. Humphreys (ed.), *The Arden Shakespeare: Henry IV Part Two* (London: Methuen, 1960), pp. lx–lxi.

37. J. F. Danby, *Shakespeare's Doctrine of Nature* (London: Methuen, 1961), pp. 83–4.

38. Elliot Krieger, *A Marxist Study of Shakespeare's Comedies* (London: Macmillan, 1979), p. 133.

39. Rosemary Jackson, *Fantasy: the Literature of Subversion* (London: Methuen, 1981), p. 14.

40. Cf. Daniel Seltzer, 'Prince Hal and Tragic Style', *Shakespeare Survey*, vol. 30 (1977), p. 24.

41. Cf. A. C. Bradley, 'The Rejection of Falstaff', *Oxford Lectures on Poetry* (London: Macmillan, 1959).

CHAPTER EIGHT

The Future of History: *1* and *2 Henry IV*[1]

KIERNAN RYAN

Kiernan Ryan, in his book *Shakespeare*, is more sceptical of some recent critical theory than most other writers in this volume. For him, Shakespeare's plays show a 'superior imaginative grasp' of the issues of historical interpretation to that of modern critics. The literature of the past is 'an imaginative historiography in its own right', and Ryan condemns the 'hermeneutics of suspicion routinely practised by more disenchanted political critics'. Yet like several other writers here, he is profoundly concerned not just with promulgating an interpretation of the plays but with reflecting upon the conditions, modes, and possibilities of interpretation of historical drama. Drawing on the work of Fredric Jameson, Ryan seeks to avoid both the move to bury the work in its own past context to the exclusion of present concerns, and on the other hand the absorption of the work into modern categories from which historicity has been emptied. This requires a dialogue between past and present, but the key element for Ryan is keeping alive a utopian idea of a future. It is this that enables the literature to offer a critique of the present 'from a utopian standpoint irreducible to ideology of any sort'.

Ryan argues that through dramatic structure, language, and incident, via irony and careful dramaturgy, the *Henry IV* plays 'forge a prospect of egalitarian community which exposes the national and royal principles of union as frauds'. He notes all kinds of devices which are used to disrupt the flow of history, to create 'the flickering supposition that all might have been otherwise, that the chronicles could quite plausibly have been obliged to tell another tale'. These are the devices which bring chronicle history to life, 'flushing act and incident with the indeterminacy denied them by the Medusan gaze of providential narrative'. Where other critics wish to show how the plays are reflections or embodiments of ideology, Ryan shows them wriggling out of 'their supposed contract with the presiding ideology'. For Ryan, it is only in discursive representations that long-gone realities become intelligible; they are 'active transfigurations of vanished realities, capable of vexing modern preconceptions and signposting the end of oppressive institutions'. Hence his belief that Shakespeare's plays are drawn to 'a future beyond our own apprehension'. It is a boldly conjectural vision but an eloquent one.

THE POLITICS OF INTERPRETATION

As dramatisations of the fate of Crown and nation two centuries before the time of Shakespeare and his audience, the *Henry IV* plays pose explicitly the key questions facing radical criticism today. What is the relationship between the reality of history and its creative representation, between the world of the past and the work's account of it? What is the political role of the work in its own world: to shore up or shake the foundations of power? Can the literature of the past speak only of the past, or has it secrets to reveal to the present and appointments to keep with the future?

No attempt to answer these questions in recent years has been more ambitious or compelling than Fredric Jameson's *The Political Unconscious* (1981), which seeks to construct nothing short of a new Marxist hermeneutics, a comprehensive political theory of interpretation.[2] My own proposals in Chapter 1 for a fresh approach to the interpretive task find much in that theory with which to concur. Part of my purpose in this chapter, therefore, is to show how Jameson's sharpest initiatives can help carve out a more searching account of the *Henry IV* plays than the most influential criticism to date has delivered. Jameson's basic view of literature, however, is fatally flawed by the tunnel vision to which so much radical criticism seems congenitally predisposed. So by reappraising these plays I also want to establish the power of Shakespeare's drama to confound such misconceptions through its superior imaginative grasp of the problems Jameson addresses.

But let me begin by underscoring those ideas of Jameson's, developed both in *The Political Unconscious* and in his essay 'Marxism and Historicism' (1979), which point towards a more plausible way of engaging with literary texts, and which consolidate some of the arguments I have advanced so far. The first concerns the claims of the literature of the past on the critical practice of the present. As we have already observed, contemporary criticism offers two main strategies for dealing with a work that confronts us from the temporally remote and culturally estranged past which first housed it. One is the retrospective route followed by both the traditional and the newer kinds of historicist response: the restoration of the work to some apposite original context, in which its meaning may be more authentically and so more securely moored. The other path leads in the opposite direction, towards the colonisation of the past by modernity: the collapsing of historical distance, and hence the erasure of difference, by an act of appropriation which makes the author of the text our contemporary. At the extremes, the work is either embedded in a past world which excludes modern consequence, or absorbed into current categories from which historicity has been drained.

Jameson's response to 'the question of the claims of monuments from distant and even archaic moments of the cultural past on a culturally different present' is to reject 'this unacceptable option, or ideological double bind, between antiquarianism and modernising "relevance" or projection'. Interpretation can be released from this disabling impasse only by implementing a view of history 'capable of respecting the specificity and radical difference of the social and cultural past while disclosing the solidarity of its polemics and passions, its forms, structures, experiences, and struggles, with those of the present day'.[3] But this should not mean merely a revamped, politicised historicism, which continues to submit texts to the superior gaze of belated comprehension. The ideal relationship is one of genuine dialogue rather than the simulated exchange contrived between a dummy version of the past and the modern critical ventriloquist. If we can achieve such a dialogue,

We will no longer tend to see the past as some inert and dead object which we are called upon to resurrect, or to preserve, or to sustain, in our own living freedom; rather, the past will itself become an active agent in this process and will begin to come before us as a radically different form of life which rises up to call our own form of life into question and to pass judgement on us and through us on the social formation in which we exist. At that point the very dynamics of the historical tribunal are unexpectedly and dialectically reversed: it is not we who sit in judgement on the past, but rather the past . . . which judges us, imposing the painful knowledge of what we are not, what we are no longer, what we are not yet.[4]

It is in the sense implied in that last phrase that Jameson believes the past 'speaks to us about our own virtual and unrealised "human potentialities"'. The attempt to initiate an authentic dialogue between history and modernity through literature is indivisible from the quest to restore to the process of interpretation the dimension of futurity: 'the hermeneutic contact between past and present . . . cannot fully be described without the articulation within it of what Ernst Bloch has called the Utopian impulse'. The mode of literary interpretation Jameson envisages should involve 'a hermeneutic relationship to the past which is able to grasp its own present as history only on condition it manages to keep the idea of the future, and of radical and utopian transformation, alive'.[5]

Jameson proposes an equally valuable revision of the ways in which the relationship between the world and the work, between literature and history, is commonly perceived. His reappraisal of this relationship makes it easier to break another basic critical deadlock I have already touched upon, a deadlock wrought once again by the antagonism of two powerful but lopsided positions. To take the line toed by old-fashioned practical critic and daredevil deconstructionist alike, and treat the literary work as a largely autonomous textual event, whose meaning owes few debts to biographical and social fact, is plainly unsatisfactory. But to espouse an approach that reduces the work to no more than a symptom or suffix of its age, which alone can illuminate its significance and value, is scarcely less problematic. Jameson's thesis endeavours to do justice both to the text's aesthetic integrity, its seeming independence of history, and to its power to animate through language and form a version of that lived world in which it is rooted, but to which it cannot be reduced. Far from being a mere echo or imprint of history, the literary text in Jameson's view 'always entertains some active relationship with the Real'. It comes equipped to 'draw the Real into its own texture', to select and incorporate its own indispensable contexts, and thus 'carry the Real within itself as its own intrinsic or immanent subtext'.[6] On this point Jameson is at one with Greenblatt, whose remarks about 'the presence within the work of its social being' allowing it 'to survive the disappearance of its enabling social conditions' I quoted earlier.[7]

If it is true that significant literature absorbs and transports through time whatever circumstances it requires to make sense to its readers or spectators, then the kind of criticism which labours to 'restore' text to context by exhuming the world to which it refers is labouring to little purpose. For those who still regard literature as a distinct, privileged enterprise, not to be confused with or subordinated to history, there is no point turning the text into a pretext for unpacking backgrounds and expanding contexts which the work itself has already looted, or which it has ruled out as redundant from the outset. Indeed the current drive to dissolve literary into cultural and historical studies might strike the cynic as the fashionable resort of those who have failed to recognise the literature of the past as an imaginative historiography in its own right. Whatever the truth of that, this part of Jameson's argument can be recruited to tighten the focus on 'the transformations of form'[8] to which the work submits whatever materials it has chosen to translate from the discourse of history into the language of literature.

The trouble is that Jameson's lack of faith in literature's powers of vision and resistance scuppers the positive potential of his argument from the start. No sooner has the work been sprung from its incarceration in mere subsequence than it is flung back in the airless slammer of ideology with slim prospects of reprieve. What might have blossomed into a hermeneutics of hope withers into the hermeneutics of suspicion routinely practised by more disenchanted political critics. Thus Jameson allows literature the agency to submit reality to the transformations of form, but purely in the interests of the ruling account of that reality: 'the aesthetic act is itself ideological, and the production of aesthetic or narrative form is to be seen as an ideological act in its own right, with the function of inventing imaginary or formal "solutions" to unresolvable social contradictions'.[9] Jameson shares with most devotees of new historicism and cultural materialism 'a manipulatory theory of culture'[10] – a kind of cultural conspiracy theory, which compels them to treat the work of literature as a seductive technique of containment, historically programmed to prop up the status quo and delay or disguise the advent of liberating change.

But how can such a craven tool of reaction speak so trenchantly of its time as to rattle the complacency of the present and unfold premonitions of an expansive future? The answer for Jameson is that it can be made to do so only in spite of itself. Once the text has been lured onto the psychiatrist's couch to deliver an account of its intent, the critical analyst's role is to tease from that account involuntary clues to the undeluded understanding the text has distorted and repressed, to coax its political unconscious to the surface. The best the radical modern critic can do with a past masterwork is to read it with hindsight against its conservative grain, forcing its symptomatic slips and silences to betray the secret truths of history it has connived so ingeniously to efface. The utopian aspect of the work can likewise be wrested from its reactionary grasp only by an act of hermeneutic violence determined to construe the ideology of the text as a travesty of that ideal condition which it unwittingly predicts. For inasmuch as they thrive on creating illusions of unanimity, on feeding us intimations of a true, classless community, 'even hegemonic or ruling-class culture and ideology are Utopian, not in spite of their instrumental function to secure and perpetuate class privilege and power, but rather precisely because that function is also in and of itself the affirmation of collective solidarity'.[11]

In other words, even the most powerful feats of the poetic mind are doomed to conceal the conflicts of their world behind facades of formal harmony and structural unity; but these fantasies of reconciliation and closure cannot help symbolising the very dispensation whose arrival in reality they were expressly designed to forestall. This might well prove a fruitful way of tackling works plainly transfixed by the legitimating myths of their day. What is questionable is the need to stifle at birth the possibility that literature may not always be so completely beguiled by ideology as Jameson presumes, but may prove intent on exposing the current map of experience to critique from a utopian standpoint irreducible to ideology of any sort.

The strengths and the drawbacks of Jameson's theory emerge clearly when it is brought to bear on the *Henry IV* plays and put to the test of textual analysis. Both works are directly engaged with history, politics and ideology. They are as preoccupied as Jameson with the relationship of the past to the present, with the implications of converting historical realities into verbal fictions, and with the role of language and representation in preserving and contesting power. To what extent do these history plays not only speak to us of what our world once was, but challenge us to confront what it remains and what it has yet to become? If the relation of Shakespeare's writing to reality is indeed one of active formation rather than supplementary expression, then to answer that question we need to examine how the plays' formal resources and dramatic effects organise our perception of their version of history. This in turn will enable us to determine to what degree both parts of *Henry IV* seek to ratify the power-structures they portray, and in what ways they foreshadow the extinction of hierarchy itself.

'FROM A PRINCE TO A PRENTICE'

On the face of it, it might seem hard to imagine drama more eager to comply with Jameson's expectations than *1* and *2 Henry IV*. Here, surely, is a perfect instance of art in the frank service of the reigning ideology, dramatising the central contradictions of society in order to forge their imaginary resolution in a final vision of personal and political unity. Why else devote two plays to the triumphant defeat of rebel forces by the incumbent monarch, and the inseparable victory of Prince Hal over the mutinous impulses destroying his credibility as heir to the throne of England? The divisions in the kingdom parallel the divisions in its future king, and their reciprocal suppression allows *Part 2* to culminate in the prospect of a renewed nation unified by a transfigured sovereign, poised to divert the collective aggression of his people upon the French. Jameson's notion of literature imposing a spurious harmony on intractable social conflicts, but projecting through that illusion the true reconciliation anticipated from a classless community, appears to fit *Henry IV* like a gauntlet. Even without Hal's subsequent consecration as glorious warrior-king in *Henry V*, *1* and *2 Henry IV* arguably achieve a sense of closure strong enough to invest their history of bloodshed and guilt with the retrospective sanction of providential design.

What binds both plays into this reading is, of course, the myth of the Prodigal Son. The opening scene of *Part 1* reveals Hal's sire so ashamed of the 'riot and dishonour' visited upon the House of Lancaster by his offspring that he wishes himself the father of Northumberland's boy, Hotspur, instead: 'a son who is the theme of honour's tongue' (*1 Henry IV*, I.i.85, 81). Hal has betrayed his identity as Prince of Wales and heir to the realm by preferring the idle fellowship of thieves, drunkards and whores to the resolute pursuit of his royal vocation. As his father puts it in their taut confrontation in Act III, Hal has, like 'the skipping King' Richard, 'mingled his royalty with cap'ring fools'; he has diluted his latent sovereignty in wanton familiarity with his inferiors, whose vision of him is consequently 'sick and blunted with community', when it should be awestruck: 'For thou hast lost thy princely privilege / With vile participation' (*1 Henry IV*, III.ii.60, 63, 77, 86–7). The most scandalous effect of Prince Hal's delinquency is this erasure of the line dividing the ruler from the ruled, the ultimately metaphysical distinction on which not only his own right to rule, but the whole social hierarchy depends.

The conflict between 'vile participation' and the enforcing of regal distance is central to Hal's story and the shaping of both plays. It is vitally entwined with the concern to preserve the fragile difference between the regicidal usurper Henry IV and the rebellious lords who helped him seize the throne they now seek to hijack in their turn. It is to defend this discrimination, upon which the legitimacy of the Lancastrian line relies, that the climactic battle at Shrewsbury is fought in *Part 1* and Prince John dupes the rebels at Gaultree at the end of *Part 2*. The twin peaks of Hal's personal battle with his own wayward drives coincide dramatically with these victories over insurgence on the national plane. That the prodigal prince will return to the royal fold seems, however, a cast-iron bet from the start. The soliloquy with which he concludes his first scene with Falstaff notoriously charts the exact course his life will follow over both parts of *Henry IV*. The agile ease with which he divorces himself from the alehouse intimates of a moment before, reduces them to terms of unequivocal contempt, and swaps spontaneous banter for the calculated scripting of his public image, proves his father's anxieties unfounded:

> Yet herein will I imitate the sun,
> Who doth permit the base contagious clouds
> To smother up his beauty from the world,
> That, when he please again to be himself,
> Being wanted, he may be more wonder'd at
> By breaking through the foul and ugly mists
> Of vapours that did seem to strangle him . . .
> So when this loose behaviour I throw off
> And pay the debt I never promised,
> By how much better than my word I am,
> By so much shall I falsify men's hopes,
> And like bright metal on a sullen ground,
> My reformation, glitt'ring o'er my fault,

Shall show more goodly and attract more eyes
Than that which hath no foil to set it off.

(*1 Henry IV*, I.ii.197–203; 208–215)

This prince needs no lessons from the king in impressing the singularity and exclusiveness of his identity upon his people.

The dramatic interest is created, therefore, not by a genuine, unpredictable conflict in the 'sword-and-buckler Prince of Wales' (*1 Henry IV*, I.iii.230), but by the suspense of his deferral of the inevitable. We are constantly reminded that we are dealing with a strategic postponement rather than a purely feckless refusal of his appointment with history. Hal's sobering assurance at the end of the 'play extempore' that one day he will indeed 'banish plump Jack, and banish all the world' (*1 Henry IV*, II.iv.280, 479–80) already foretells the chilling dismissal of Falstaff for real in the final scene of *2 Henry IV*: 'I know thee not, old man, fall to thy prayers' (V.v.47). Sharply upbraided by the father Hotspur calls 'this king of smiles' (*1 Henry IV*, I.iii.246), Hal responds by reiterating the pledge framed in his earlier monologue and thus reinstating between himself and his future subjects the crucial disparity which he has allowed to evaporate:

I will redeem all this on Percy's head,
And in the closing of some glorious day
Be bold to tell you that I am your son,
When I will wear a garment all of blood,
And stain my favours in a bloody mask,
Which wash'd away shall scour my shame with it.

(*1 Henry IV*, III.ii.132–7)

At the Battle of Shrewsbury with which *Part 1* concludes, where he saves his father's life and defeats his extravagant rival Hotspur, Hal heroically proves himself a man of his word and a monarch in the making. His affectionate indulgence of Falstaff on the battlefield confirms, nevertheless, that the narrative of redemption is still incomplete when the curtain falls on Act V. The story can therefore be picked up in *Part 2*, which recycles the pattern of disaffection and delay finally expiated by the promise fulfilled, only this time with a resounding sense of sublime culmination:

My father is gone wild into his grave;
For in his tomb lie my affections,
And with his spirits sadly I survive,
To mock the expectation of the world,
To frustrate prophecies, and to rase out
Rotten opinion, who hath writ me down
After my seeming. The tide of blood in me
Hath proudly flow'd in vanity till now;
Now doth it turn and ebb back to the sea,
Where it shall mingle with the state of floods,
And flow henceforth in formal majesty.

(V.ii.123–33)

This elegant tailoring of history to fit the moral myth of the Prodigal Son, of the sinner's salvation, works powerfully in *Henry IV* to rationalise hierarchy, glorify royalty, and disguise contingency as destiny, eventuality as providence. From Jameson's point of view, the radical critic's job would be to expose the plays' obfuscation of political reality by reading them against the drift of their orthodox import, by deciphering the undoctored version of the situation secreted between their lines. Their conformity could then be turned inside out to disclose the prophecy of collective emancipation and true unity concealed in the very instrument of divisive misprision. But to return to the texts of *Henry IV* with this dual objective in mind is to recognise its redundancy in the light of a closer reading. The conventional account of the plays I have given so far can survive only through the systematic neglect of formal techniques, structural implications and dramatic parentheses, whose realised import changes the meaning of the narrative they articulate. By abstracting the double tale of Hal's redemption and the royal victory over rebellion from the syntax of its dramatisation, and thus from the way we are induced to understand it, *1* and *2 Henry IV* are reduced to the ideology they are intent on unravelling. A refusal to sunder what the plays say from how they say it restores to us more fascinating texts, which do not need to be read against the grain in order to be saved from themselves.

Consider two of the many scenes and passages in *Henry IV* commonly skipped over or marginalised in critical accounts, but whose function is to punctuate and inflect what is said and done in ways which not only complicate but transmute the meaning of the drama.

In the first scene of Act II of *1 Henry IV* there is an intriguing exchange between Gadshill and the chamberlain of the inn near which the robbery involving Hal is to proceed. It is ushered in by the complaints of the two carriers preparing their day's labours. One observes: 'This house is turn'd upside down since Robin ostler died' (II.i.10–11). The line suggests, perhaps, a plebeian parallel with the state of the kingdom following the death of Richard: the previous scene has witnessed the conspiracy of the rebels. The other echoes his abuse of the flea-pit they have just slept in: 'there is ne'er a king christen could be better bit than I have been since the first cock' (II.i.16–18). Fleas observe no distinctions of rank. Gadshill's badinage with the crooked chamberlain accentuates the scene's awareness of the play's key concerns. Chamberlain and pickpurse are interchangeable titles, quips Gadshill, 'for thou variest no more from picking of purses than giving direction doth from labouring: thou layest the plot how' (II.i.50–2). The collapsing of distinctions between those who give the orders and those who obey them supplies the logic governing Gadshill's assurance that the participation of the powerful makes their criminal enterprise impregnable:

> *Gadshill.* . . . I am join'd with no foot land-rakers, no long-staff sixpenny strikers, none of these mad mustachio purple-hu'd malt-worms, but with nobility and tranquillity, burgomasters and great oney'rs, such as can hold in, such as will strike sooner than speak, and speak sooner than drink, and drink sooner than pray; and yet, 'zounds, I lie, for they pray continually to their saint, the commonwealth, or rather, not pray to her, but

	prey on her, for they ride up and down on her, and make her their boots.
Chamberlain.	What, the commonwealth their boots? Will she hold out water in foul way?
Gadshill.	She will, she will, justice hath liquor'd her. We steal as in a castle, cock-sure; we have the receipt of fern-seed, we walk invisible.

(II.i.73–87)

The passage conflates the common thieves with their more elevated brethren, whose ransacking of the commonwealth differs only in the legitimacy which renders its criminality 'invisible'. The prince's role in the robbery creates the occasion for this illuminating identification, which pivots in turn on the more fundamental reflection with which Gadshill bows out of the scene: '*homo* is a common name to all men' (II.i.95).

Comparable implications can be quarried from otherwise pointless remarks made by Falstaff in *Part 2*. During his evasive encounter with the Lord Chief Justice in the second scene of the play, Falstaff pleads the malady of deafness as his reason for not responding to the Justice's admonitions, and he attempts to distract the latter by snatching up the topic of the king's ill-health: 'And I hear, moreover, his Highness is fall'n into this same whoreson apoplexy.' This apoplexy is 'a kind of lethargy', Falstaff informs the exasperated magistrate, 'a kind of sleeping in the blood'; in short, according to Galen, 'it is a kind of deafness'. 'I think you are fallen into the disease,' retorts the Lord Chief justice, 'for you hear not what I say to you' (I.ii.107–8, 111–13, 117). The full value of these lines, in which the lord of the land and the lord of misrule are subject to the same affliction, becomes apparent if we turn to Falstaff's meditation on the peculiar affinity between Shallow and his servants:

It is a wonderful thing to see the semblable coherence of his men's spirits and his. They, by observing him, do bear themselves like foolish justices; he, by conversing with them, is turn'd into a justice-like servingman. Their spirits are so married in conjunction with the participation of society that they flock together in consent, like so many wild geese. If I had a suit to Master Shallow, I would humour his men with the imputation of being near their master; if to his men, I would curry with Master Shallow that no man could better command his servants. It is certain that either wise bearing or ignorant carriage is caught, as men take diseases, one of another . . .

(V.i.64–77)

The revelation of consanguinity running beneath the threshold of social difference is conveyed this time by an appeal to the democratic impartiality of infection, which holds the privileges of birth and blood in contempt. But here there is a further glimpse of the utopian potential of such benign confoundings of rank through 'the participation of society' (what Henry IV in *Part 1* denounced in Hal as 'vile participation'): an idyllic condition in which spirits normally segregated by the antagonistic principle of subordination become 'so married in conjunction . . . that they flock together in consent, like so many wild geese'.

Such passages supply the keys to decode more sustained enactments of improvised irrelevance, whose liberty from the burden of advancing the historical plot permits them to explore the cost and consequences of that history, to reinstate the exclusions and suppressions that made it possible. In Act II of *Part 1* Hal confesses wryly to Poins: 'I have sounded the very base-string of humility. Sirrah, I am sworn brother to a leash of drawers, and can call them all by their christen names, as Tom, Dick, and Francis' (II.iv.5–8). The witty substitution of the tapster's name for the expected 'Harry' invites the equation of the former's plight with the prince's in the practical joke which follows. Francis is torn between the temptation 'to play the coward with [his] indenture and show it a fair pair of heels' (II.iv.47–8) and the immediate obligation to answer the call of a customer, which he postpones with 'Anon, anon, sir', the parroted watchword of his trade. Simultaneously hailed by vocation and desire, *'the Drawer stands amazed, not knowing which way to go'* (II.iv.79: s.d.), the plebeian epitome of the future king's suspension in a limbo of delay. Hal's jest fleetingly lifts the barrier between the destinies of both men, and dissolves Hal's aristocratic identity in the broad stream of diverse humanity through the ages: asked by Poins for the upshot of the gulling of Francis, he replies, 'I am now of all humours that have show'd themselves humours since the old days of goodman Adam to the pupil age of this present twelve a' clock at midnight' (II.iv.92–5).

The intensity of this compulsion to lose himself in the soul of a subordinate by projection or displacement is confirmed by *Part 2*'s obsessive return to the theme. The price of the prince's elision of difference by deferment is anxiety, guilt and melancholy. 'Before God, I am exceeding weary' (II.ii.1), he laments to Poins at the opening of Act II, at once disenchanted with his royalty and ashamed of his abandonment of eminence: 'But indeed these humble considerations make me out of love with my greatness. What a disgrace is it to me to remember thy name, or to know thy face to-morrow' (II.ii.11–14). The sense of a character caged in his own myth, stranded in a trance of procrastination until the cue to pace the stage of history breaks the spell, is insistent. But the whole point of forcing open such lacunae, in which history is put on hold, is to create the space to demolish the foundations on which that reading of history is built.

The Prince of Wales strives stoutly to drive the wedge back between his heritage and the 'vile company' he blushes to acknowledge, appealing to his script for ultimate vindication: 'Let the end try the man' (II.ii.49, 47). It requires, however, rather less than 'A crown's-worth of good interpretation' (II.ii.92) to see that separatist urge vanquished by the need for communion in the hoax that springs from this scene. The path to the jape is paved by quips haunted by more of the same demarcation disputes. Poins glances at those who 'never prick their finger but they say: "There's some of the King's blood spilt"' as a prelude to claiming themselves to be 'the King's poor cousin'. 'Nay,' Hal chimes in, 'they will be kin to us, or they will fetch it from Japhet' (II.ii.112–13, 117–18) – Japhet being the son of Noah from whom all Gentiles were thought to be descended. The pressure to dilute the prince's blue blood also dictates the ironic speculation about Hal marrying Poins's sister, Nell (II.ii.127–41). And by the end of the scene, the frail dyke of convention dividing Hal from the common tide of humanity has been breached by his compliance with Poins's scheme to disguise themselves in the 'leathern jerkins and aprons' of

Francis's calling: 'From a god to a bull? a heavy descension! it was Jove's case. From a prince to a prentice? a low transformation! that shall be mine' (II.ii.171, 173–5). The reincarnation of the heir apparent is complete two scenes later, when the prince-prentice answers Falstaff's 'Some sack, Francis' with his surrogate's remorseless 'Anon, anon, sir' (II.iv.281–2), directly echoing the corresponding scene in *Part 1*.

Nor is the razing of hierarchy the only effect sought by such confusions of identity. In the 'play extempore' of *Part 1* Falstaff plays Henry IV, reproving Hal 'in King Cambyses' vein' (II.iv.387); then he swaps places to play Hal to the prince's own impersonation of his father. The conscious theatricality of this parodic performance highlights both the rootlessness of the roles and the staged nature of the historical realities being burlesqued. The majesty of the English throne dwindles to a few tawdry props stripped of mystique: 'Thy state is taken for a join'd-stool, thy golden sceptre for a leaden dagger, and thy precious rich crown for a pitiful bald crown!' (II.iv.380–2). Falstaff s caricature of the admonishing monarch deploys an obsolete theatrical rhetoric persuasive enough to captivate his tavern audience: 'O Jesu, he doth it as like one of these harlotry players as ever I see!' (II.iv.395–6). But more important for the audience beyond the footlights is the scene's preemptive ironising of the serious clash of royal father and reprobate son in Act III. Their characters and their dialogue are marked out in advance as scripted creations, so that their impassioned appeals and protestations are mocked by their conformity to recognised postures and patterns of exchange.[12]

The spectators are encouraged to recognise majesty as a rehearsed production and reminded of the gulf between the performed events before their eyes and the remote past realities they presuppose. Henry IV himself activates this awareness by his frank confessions of using theatrical simulation and diversion as instruments of power:

And then I stole all courtesy from heaven,
And dress'd myself in such humility
That I did pluck allegiance from men's hearts,

(*1 Henry IV*, III.ii.50–2)

For all my reign hath been but as a scene
Acting that argument . . .
      . . . Therefore, my Harry,
Be it thy course to busy giddy minds
With foreign quarrels, that action, hence borne out,
May waste the memory of the former days.

(*2 Henry IV*, IV.v.197–8, 212–15)

The very battle fought at Shrewsbury to bolster the sovereign's unique authority involves the subterfuge of fielding noblemen 'Semblably furnish'd like the King himself' (*1 Henry IV*, V.iii.21). Advised by Hotspur that 'The King hath many marching in his coats', Douglas swears: 'Now by my sword, I will kill all his coats; / I'll murder all his wardrop, piece by piece, / Until I meet the King' (V.iii.25–8). But when he encounters the monarch in person, he remains understandably sceptical:

> *Douglas.* Another king? they grow like Hydra's heads.
> . . . What art thou
> That counterfeit'st the person of a king?
> *King.* The King himself, who, Douglas, grieves at heart
> So many of his shadows thou hast met
> And not the very King . . .
> *Douglas.* I fear thou art another counterfeit,
> And yet in faith thou bearest thee like a king.

(V.iv.25, 27–31, 35–6)

The action contrived to clinch the exclusive legitimacy of Bolingbroke's claim to the throne breeds a multiplicity of sovereigns. The ploy disperses Henry's singularity and blatantly insinuates that to bear oneself like a monarch and don the robes of royalty may be all there is to being royal for real – as Sir Walter Blunt discovers to his mortal dismay.

Detail and structure conspire throughout parts *1* and *2* to dismantle the scaffolding of dominion and unmask the fictive status of authorised social distinctions and moral oppositions. The factual coincidence of king and prince sharing their Christian name with the rebel Earl and his son is played up to the full in Shakespeare's phrasing to stimulate our apprehension of their covert equivalence:

> O that it could be prov'd
> That some night-tripping fairy had exchang'd
> In cradle-clothes our children where they lay,
> And call'd mine Percy, his Plantagenet!
> Then would I have his Harry and he mine.

(*1 Henry IV*, I.i.86–90)

> Harry to Harry shall, hot horse to horse,

(IV.i.122)

> Two stars keep not their motion in one sphere,
> Nor can one England brook a double reign
> Of Harry Percy and the Prince of Wales.

(V.iv.65–7)

Like Hal and Francis, or Hal and Falstaff when the latter takes the prince's part in the tavern, or ironically appropriates his promise of eventual contrition, the royal and the regicidal turn out to be Siamese twins. Indeed, as John Kerrigan has shown, both plays are obsessed with doubling and replication at every turn: from Falstaff with the dead Hotspur on his back, denying himself to be the 'double man' he seems (*1 Henry IV*, V.iv.138), or Shallow's cryptic query 'And is old Double dead?' (*2 Henry IV*, III.ii.43), down to the fine grain of speech rhythms, where duplication reigns in the mouths of foolish judge ('Certain, 'tis certain, very sure, very sure' [*2 Henry IV*, III.ii.36]) and majesty alike: 'Not Amurath an Amurath succeeds, / But Harry Harry' (*2 Henry IV*, V.ii.48–9). The rhetorical term for this figure of speech is *geminatio* or 'twinning'; and, as Kerrigan points out, quoting Thomas Wilson's definition in *The Arte of Rhetorique* (1553), 'In Tudor rhetoric, "doublet" translates *geminatio*: "when we rehearse one and the same word twice together", as in "Anon, Anon, sir!" '[13]

This recurrent local instruction in the art of gemination finds its global counterpart in the scenic composition of the plays. The structural principle of switching to and fro between king and conspirators, and from both to the Eastcheap empire of Falstaff, or the rural domain of Shallow and Silence, and back again, begins by obeying a logic of contrast and discrimination; but its cumulative impact transforms our initial acceptance of disparity into a dawning realisation of resemblance. The ceaseless commuting of the plays between diverse ranks and value systems discloses a primal appetite for consensus eating away at the ideology of difference and duality. The official scale of social worth, so graphically codified in the descending list of dramatis personae still fronting modern texts, is scrambled by these oscillations of perspective as surely as shuffling a new deck of cards confounds the fastidious decorum of each suit. The kaleidoscopic vision of *1* and *2 Henry IV* helps forge a prospect of egalitarian community which exposes the national and royal principles of union as frauds.

Nor can the teleological view of history conscripted by those principles survive the repeated sabotaging of inevitability and completion to which *Part 2*, as the expected resolution of questions left dangling in *Part 1*, is especially subject. A stubborn refusal of deterministic historiography is declared at the outset in the remarkable Induction and opening scene of the play. In a direct address to the audience, the personification of Rumour introduces himself as one upon whose tongues 'continual slanders ride, / The which in every language I pronounce, / Stuffing the ears of men with false reports' (*2 Henry IV*, Ind. 6–8). His present purpose, as he stands before the castle of Northumberland, is

> To noise abroad that Harry Monmouth fell
> Under the wrath of noble Hotspur's sword,
> And that the King before the Douglas' rage
> Stoop'd his anointed head as low as death.
>
> (Ind. 29–32)

The first scene then thrusts us into the midst of enacted history, as Lord Bardolph repeats Rumour's false account to Northumberland as 'certain news from Shrewsbury' (I.i.12). Northumberland needs convincing: 'How is this deriv'd?' (I.i.23). But the 'certain news' is rapidly unseated by Travers's revised report, which Morton's no less breathless arrival confirms: young Harry Percy's spur is cold indeed, and

> The sum of all
> Is that the King hath won, and hath sent out
> A speedy power to encounter you, my lord,
>
> (I.i.131–3)

For a moment the closed book of historical fact is reopened and rewritten. The fixity of the past surrenders to the flickering supposition that all might have been otherwise, that the chronicles could quite plausibly have been obliged to tell another tale. We are forewarned that this rival version is unfounded, and the upstart is, of course, swiftly deposed; but it is entertained and elaborated for long enough to stake its claim to likelihood and so restore the original fluidity of deep-frozen events. History is rewound and replayed with the subjunctive scenes spliced back in. We are called upon to witness the translation of once vital experience into a vulnerable narrative, refracted through this dramatic reconstruction in the lived present of performance: 'Open your ears; for which of you will stop / The vent of hearing when loud Rumour speaks?' (Ind. 1–2). History, it is plain, is not simply what happened, but what gets made, misconstrued, disputed and remodelled.[14]

Part 2 is riddled with double-takes, false starts and stops, rewrites and reversals of expectation: all of them calculated to resist, and thereby transform, the ultimate course things must take to climax in the defeat of the rebels and the coronation of the prodigal redeemed. The infectious doubling of identities is matched by a doubling of incident, in which the actual occurrence is unsettled by the sustained imagination of another possibility. Thus the achievement at Gaultree of a bloodless and just resolution, whereby the rebels' grievances will find redress and both sides enjoy the concord of 'restored love and amity' (IV.ii.65), is acted out convincingly up to the very last moment; at which point the apparent meaning of events is abruptly turned on its head by Prince John's icy duplicity. A similar effect is produced when King Henry envisions a persuasive future ruled by Hal's 'headstrong riot':

> The blood weeps from my heart when I do shape,
> In forms imaginary, th'unguided days
> And rotten times that you shall look upon,
> When I am sleeping with my ancestors.

> (IV.ii.58–61)

But these bleak predictions prove as mistaken as the abandoned future under Hal which excites Falstaff's fantasies, or the prophecy of the king's death in a Jerusalem which turns out to be the name of a palace chamber far from the Holy Land he hoped to wrest from the infidel.

Most disconcerting of all, perhaps, is the way the play trips Hal up on the threshold of his accession and moral resurrection. Having diagnosed his father's death with exemplary alacrity, he seizes the crown from the pillow and ceremoniously sets the 'polish'd perturbation' (IV.v.153) on his own head:

> My due from thee is this imperial crown,
> Which, as immediate from thy place and blood,
> Derives itself to me. [*Puts on the crown.*] Lo where it sits,
> Which God shall guard; and put the world's whole strength
> Into one giant arm, it shall not force
> This lineal honour from me. This from thee
> Will I to mine leave, as 'tis left to me. [*Exit.*]

> (IV.v.41–7)

Seconds later, the conclusive resonance of this speech is shattered as the king revives, denounces his son's precipitate, callous theft, and forces Hal to crawl back,

crown in hand, to convince him of the innocence of his motives and the genuine-
ness of 'The noble change' (IV.v.154) he keeps promising. Shakespeare's dramatisation of the episode exploits its disruptive impact to the full, compelling the
denouement to double back and restart from revised assumptions about Hal, and
with a refreshed feeling for the unpredictability of experience before the fact.

These backtracking devices allow the blood to flow once more through the
veins of chronicled history, flushing act and incident with the indeterminacy
denied them by the Medusan gaze of providential narrative. It comes as no surprise
to find the question of history on the overt agenda of *2 Henry IV*, with characters
speculating continually on the relation of the past to the future and on the possibility of foreknowledge:

> *King.*   O God, that one might read the book of fate
>   And see the revolution of the times . . .
> *Warwick.* There is a history in all men's lives,
>   Figuring the natures of the times deceas'd,
>   The which observ'd, a man may prophesy,
>   With a near aim, of the main chance of things
>   As yet not come to life, who in their seeds
>   And weak beginning lie intreasured.
>   Such things become the hatch and brood of time,
>
>   (III.i.45–6, 80–6)

'Jesus', exclaims Shallow, 'the days that we have seen!', confirming in his nostalgia for 'the times deceased', when he heard 'the chimes at midnight' (III.ii.219,
215), that a predilection for edited highlights of the past is not exclusive to great
lords. Such gentle guying of selective retrospection ('Lord, Lord, how subject we old
men are to this vice of lying!' [III.ii.303–4]) calls the whole project of the *Henry IV*
plays to account. For it keeps alive in the spectator's mind the distortions inevitably
entailed in the process of historiography, the gap which must always divorce long-
gone realities from the discursive representations in which alone they become intelligible. Not the least virtue of the Epilogue's appearance at the close of *Part 2*, to
promise that 'our humble author will continue the story' (Epil. 27–8), is its oblique
insistence that *as* a story, to quote Samuel Daniel's *Defence of Rhyme* (1603),

an Historie . . . is but a Mappe of Men, and dooth no otherwise acquaint us with the true
Substance of Circumstances then a superficiall Card dooth the Seaman with a Coast never
seene, which alwayes prooves other to the eye than the imagination forecast it . . .[15]

Both power and history are demystified, even as the plays complete their supposed contract with the presiding ideology. The prescribed royal reading of history
dictates the narrative shape of *1* and *2 Henry IV*. But the strategies of disenchant-
ment built into the dramatisation rob that narrative of its supremacy, breaking its
monopoly on what is thought to have happened. This critique of the approved
account is anchored in the utopian assumptions of an anticipated world. At the end
of *Part 1* and *Part 2* monarchy, hierarchy and the illusions that sustain them emerge
intact, even strengthened, *within* the world of the plays; but our understanding and

judgement of them has been changed completely by the way they have been portrayed. What the protagonists persist in believing, and what the spectators are encouraged to conclude from the standpoint they are obliged to adopt, are two quite different things. The perspectives of the denizens of *Henry IV* – high and low, urban and rural alike – must remain bound by the categories and limits of the imagined universe they inhabit; our assessment of them, however, is released from that bondage by our vantage-point as audience or readers, whose vision of their universe is filtered through the warped lens of defamiliarisation. As a result the plays liberate us to decipher 'the main chance of things / As yet not come to life' encoded in their depiction of 'the times deceas'd' (III.i.83–4, 81). They afford us a proleptic glimpse through their eyes of the future in the past.

'OF THINGS / AS YET NOT COME TO LIFE'

Reading the *Henry IV* plays in the light of Jameson's theory of interpretation explodes the common misconception of literary texts which prevents his most fertile insights from releasing the full potential of literature from the past. Jameson begins by blazing a trail towards viewing texts as active transfigurations of vanished realities, capable of vexing modern preconceptions and signposting the end of oppressive institutions. But this admirable enterprise soon shrivels into the extortion of progressive significance from works whose instinctive commitment to the legitimation of class society is taken as read. *Henry IV* testifies, however, to the historically evolved capacity of poetic language and dramatic form to undo the ideology of division from a standpoint beyond the reach of subjection. Jameson remains trapped in the historicist hermeneutics of suspicion from which his own sharpest insights offer an escape-route. To demonstrate this, moreover, is to pull the plug on a range of critical responses and a long tradition of theatrical productions, which have diminished or denied the power of the *Henry IV* plays to undercut the hegemonic narratives they stage.

Scott McMillin has recently traced the British performance history of *1* and *2 Henry IV* from the 1945 Old Vic production, starring Olivier and Richardson, to the 1986 touring version by the English Shakespeare Company, under the direction of Michael Bogdanov. His survey dwells on three benchmark productions, all of which put the plays on as part of a cycle sequence: the staging by the Shakespeare Memorial Theatre Company in 1951, directed by Anthony Quayle, which established the cycle mode as the standard modern format for the histories, and the RSC productions of 1964 and 1975, under the direction of Peter Hall and Terry Hands respectively. McMillin discerns an uncomfortably direct relationship between the politics of the institutionalised theatre and the political message all too predictably read into Hal's reformation:

The modern subsidised theatre helps cycles be staged and cycles make Falstaff a figure to be rejected. This is what happens to *1 Henry IV* in its modern cycle-oriented treatments: the Prince grows into royal authority by turning aside the old fat man, and it is government subsidy that provides the wherewithal . . . to let this lesson be dramatised.[16]

These major productions seem to have swallowed whole the hierarchical assumptions and the moralised conflation of personal and national destiny which the plays are not fooled by for a moment. For Peter Hall the world-view affirmed by the plays was plain: 'all Shakespeare's thinking, whether religious, political, or moral, is based on a complete acceptance of this concept of order. There is a just proportion in all things: man is above beast, king is above man, and God above king'; rebellion is monstrous because it 'destroys the order and leads to destructive anarchy'.[17] Terry Hands's production bent the drama into an ageless study in the growth of majesty, traced through the exemplary evolution of the adolescent male from callow disaffection to responsible maturity. For Hal, according to the programme note for the production, the stage 'is always the blank slate on which life writes its lessons', 'the bare metaphysical arena in which the soul of a royal Everyman discovers his destiny and true friends'.[18] As McMillin remarks: 'So long as Prince Hal is said to be caught up in such timeless and essential experience, his career will seem purified of the political and all the more agreeable to the managers of our affairs.'[19]

Given the opportunities for inculcating conformity afforded by suitably slanted productions, it leaves one less than astounded to learn that 'More than any other play, *1 Henry IV* is swung into position on occasions of dignity and ceremony in Stratford'.[20] After baptising the new Stratford Memorial Theatre in 1932 on the Bard's birthday, it was the birthday play during the history cycles of 1951, 1964 and 1975; and when the RSC opened at the Barbican in 1982 with another inevitable cycle of histories, the birthday production was once more *1 Henry IV*. 'The thinking of the RSC,' remarks McMillin wryly, 'had become so accustomed to taking the *Henrys* as curtain raisers for occasions of wealth and power that the venture could be predicted before some of the actors in the eventual production were out of secondary school.'[21] It is the cultural centrality and enormous influence of these imaginatively stunted versions of the *Henry IV* plays that make the development of readings that can do them justice so important. And this endeavour demands an approach fuelled by quite different assumptions about the relation of poetic writing to the enthroned prescriptions and stereotypes of the age.

That Tillyard's study of *Shakespeare's History Plays* (1944) directly and indirectly shaped the 1951 and 1964 cycle productions of *1* and *2 Henry IV* is no surprise. Tillyard's work has remained the cornerstone of the conventional view of the histories to this day, and the automatic antagonist of those seeking to contest the nationalistic and authoritarian attitudes he found sanctioned by these plays. According to Tillyard, Shakespeare

expressed successfully a universally held and still comprehensible scheme of history: a scheme fundamentally religious, by which events evolve under a law of justice and under the ruling of God's Providence, and of which Elizabeth's England was the acknowledged outcome.[22]

For Tillyard, therefore, the two parts of *Henry IV* exemplify the ideal education of the Christian prince for the office destiny has prepared for him. Tillyard's Hal 'is a man of large powers, Olympian loftiness, and high sophistication, who has acquired a thorough knowledge of human nature both in himself and in others. He is Shakespeare's studied picture of the kingly type.'[23] Hal's tormenting of Francis in *Part 1* clouds Tillyard's admiration for a moment, but the perfection of Hal's portrait is swiftly restored by the historian's appeal to the principle of degree: 'The sub-human element in the population must have been considerable in Shakespeare's day; that it should be treated almost like beasts was taken for granted.'[24] It is perhaps too easy to feel superior now to that telling rationalisation, whose offhand inhumanity has been highlighted in a recent study of the histories.[25] But it gives the measure of Tillyard's commitment to reading Shakespeare in *1* and *2 Henry IV* as the unquestioning advocate of a rigidly stratified society.

Reinforced by similar views of the histories promoted in John Dover Wilson's *The Fortunes of Falstaff* (1943), G. Wilson Knight's *The Olive and the Sword* (1944), and Lily B. Campbell's *Shakespeare's Histories: Mirrors of Elizabethan Policy* (1947),[26] this conception of *1* and *2 Henry IV* as a defence of the divine necessity of order and authority controlled discussion of the plays for decades. Its survival, in a subtly adapted, more appealing form, was guaranteed by C. L. Barber's classic study, *Shakespeare's Festive Comedy* (1959). Barber allows the saturnalian zest of Falstaff and the Eastcheap world much more play and purchase than most of the Tillyard camp tend to, but only because of its ulterior role as the negative pole in the moral schooling of the budding ruler. The temporary reign of misrule under Falstaff functions here as a kind of safety-valve, a cathartic release of anarchic energies and appetites, which Hal must finally reject to qualify as the governor of a stable, disciplined kingdom. The lawless threat to propriety is introduced in order to enhance the triumphant return of dutiful decorum with Hal's fulfilment of his royal vocation: 'the misrule works, through the whole dramatic rhythm, to consolidate rule'.[27]

Thirty years on, the same angle is still going strong: recycled in a still more sophisticated form and yoked now to a dissenting critical politics, but fundamentally unchanged. Thus, in the course of constructing his new-historicist Shakespeare in *Power on Display*, Leonard Tennenhouse maintains that

the various confrontations between licit and illicit authority comprising the *Henriad* more firmly draw the distinction between aristocracy and populace even as they appear to overturn this primary categorical distinction. . . . Criminalizing the popular figures of inversion is as necessary to the poetics of power as incorporating a certain popular vigor within the legitimate body of the state. . . . Legitimate order can come into being only through disruption. . . .[28]

This is also the position endorsed by Stephen Greenblatt, whose celebrated essay 'Invisible Bullets' takes *1* and *2 Henry IV* as ideal texts with which to bolster his belief that 'Shakespeare's plays are centrally, repeatedly concerned with the production and containment of subversion and disorder'.[29] In Greenblatt's view, power feeds off the transgression and sedition it needs in order to define its identity and authority. And by inoculating itself with a controlled symbolic dose of realisations which could destroy it, the body politic helps ward off actual insurrection. Hence, as theatrical instruments of the power of the Elizabethan state, 'the Henry plays confirm the Machiavellian hypothesis that princely power originates in force and fraud even as they draw their audience toward an acceptance of that power'.[30] Greenblatt's account of the relationship between drama and domination is more intricate than Tillyard's or Barber's, and its objective is demystification rather than occlusion, but the bottom line is the same: the *Henry IV* plays are the voice of Elizabethan orthodoxy, and never more so than when they mimic the accents of dissent.[31] This approach dovetails perfectly with Jameson's presumption that the masterpieces of the past cannot earn political salvation by their own merits, but must depend for redemption on the grace of the modern critic.

In *Shakespeare Recycled: The Making of Historical Drama* the cultural materialist Graham Holderness has attempted to overturn conservative readings of *1* and *2 Henry IV* by tying Falstaff into Bakhtin's concept of the carnivalesque and stressing his substantive function as

a constant focus of opposition to the official and serious tone of authority and power: his discourse confronts and challenges those of king and state. . . . His world is a world of ease, moral licence, appetite and desire; of humour and ridicule, theatricals and satire, of community, freedom and abundance; a world created by inverting the abstract society, the oppression and the hierarchy of the official world.[32]

But Falstaff can indeed merely invert; he cannot transcend that official world, which beholds in him its mirror image, its secret sharer, not its negation or displacement. Exhilarating as Holderness's sketch of him sounds, to champion the cause of Falstaff against the dour disciplines of authority and historical necessity simply reverses the poles of the orthodox view. Defecting to Eastcheap and elevating a sentimental idealisation of its ethos over the imperatives of duty and national destiny sells the plays short, because it leaves them caged within the system of social differences and moral dichotomies they seek to dismantle. To privilege the liberties of 'headstrong riot' (*2 Henry IV*, IV.iv.62) over 'The majesty and power of law and justice' (V.ii.78) is to repress the covert reciprocity of the royal and plebeian realms, whose values are in practice identical, and so leave the entrenched disparities of the status quo intact. This strategy plays straight into the hands of the new-historicist paradox whereby the upshot of subversion is to consolidate dominion and the rule of law.

As long as criticism of *Henry IV* keeps shuttling between the claims of the Crown and the lure of the taproom, it remains tangled in the spurious dilemma forged by Hal himself as he hesitates between his father and plump Jack. Whether the rejection of Falstaff is applauded, regretted or safely construed as ambivalent, the critic accepts the characters' perception of their world and the alternatives they confront at face value, as the terms on which we are supposed to interpret and evaluate the plays. But such readings must block out all the devices deliberately constructed to colour our vision and complicate our judgement; for the plays are designed to withdraw through formal implication what they avow through overt statement and action. Both parts of *Henry IV* employ techniques of framing, interruption and conflation, which weave a counterfactual perspective into their dramatisation of history, investing it with a buoyancy it would otherwise lack. By preventing our submersion in the mentality of the cast, they unravel the rationale of the standard interpretations. Far from enclosing the spectator in an Elizabethan perception of late medieval England, the *Henry IV* plays create a prospective climate of understanding, which invalidates the hierarchical terms in which the problems of the protagonists are posed and solved, even as it concedes the factual force and historical triumph of subjugation.

The inhabitants of *1* and *2 Henry IV* are doomed to dwell forever in 'the times deceas'd' (*2 Henry IV*, III.i.81) which, as one of them laments, 'Crowd us and crush us to this monstrous form' (IV.ii.34). But the plays' perspective on their lives reaches forward 'to sound the bottom of the after-times' (IV.ii.51) and anticipate the transfigured shape the 'hatch and brood' (III.i.86) of history might take. The opening speech of *Part 1* tunes us subliminally to this dual vision informing both plays:

> Those opposed eyes
> Which, like the meteors of a troubled heaven,
> All of one nature, of one substance bred,
> Did lately meet in the intestine shock
> And furious close of civil butchery,
> Shall now, in mutual well-beseeming ranks,
> March all one way, and be no more oppos'd
> Against acquaintance, kindred, and allies.

> (I.i.9–16)

The *Henry IV* plays are written in a way which allows us to behold a world ruled by fierce oppositions through the eyes of a world which has surrendered such barbarism to the co-operative sway of human solidarity.

Older and newer forms of historicist criticism share a notion of literature as the incurably anterior expression of an extinct reality. They evince a chronic aversion to the conjecture that Shakespeare's drama might be drawn as much towards a future beyond our own apprehension as back to its place of origin in the past. It is the virtue of Jameson's theoretical stance that it argues so effectively against such sterile historicism and so passionately for the activation of the utopian dimension of literature. Jameson's error, however, is to arrogate to the interpretive act alone that potent blend of critique and prescience which, as *Henry IV* attests, the most exacting literature of the past has always possessed, but which will remain inert and ineffectual if the prevalent accounts of that literature go unchallenged.

It is an error which Ernst Bloch, a major influence on Jameson, never made, mistaking as it does the power of the critic for the power of the work. For Bloch,

Every great work of art, above and beyond its manifest content, is carried out according to the latency of the page to come, or in other words, in the light of a future which has not yet come into being, and indeed of some ultimate resolution as yet unknown.[33]

And what lifts a work 'above and beyond its manifest content' and into the light of the future is the lever of form. As Adorno puts it: 'Perspectives must be fashioned that displace and estrange the world, reveal it to be, with its rifts and crevices, as indigent and distorted as it will appear one day in the messianic light.'[34] It is precisely such distortions that the *Henry IV* plays inflict on their age, which we are invited to see not as it was, but as it one day will *have been* for those no longer walled up in that kind of world. In these works we perceive Elizabethan realities transposed into the history of Henry IV, then filtered through the lens of futurity, which twists the plays out of line with convention and into their proleptic form. Parts *1* and *2* of *Henry IV* afford us nothing less than a preview of the past. They project us forward to a point where we can grasp Shakespeare's anachronistic version of his times as the eventual past of a still unfolding future.

NOTES

1. Reprinted from Kiernan Ryan, *Shakespeare* (Hemel Hempstead: Harvester, 2nd edition, 1995).

2. For fuller expositions and further commentary, see William C. Dowling, *Jameson, Althusser, Marx: An Introduction to 'The Political Unconscious'* (London, 1984); J. A. Berthoud, 'Narrative and ideology: a critique of Fredric Jameson's *The Political Unconscious*', in *Narrative: From Malory to Motion Pictures*, ed. Jeremy Hawthorn (London, 1985), pp. 101–16; Philip Goldstein, *The Politics of Literary Theory: An Introduction to Marxist Criticism* (Tallahassee, Fla., 1990), pp. 146–61; K. M. Newton, *Interpreting the Text* (Hemel Hempstead, 1990), pp. 111–19.

3. Fredric Jameson, *The Political Unconscious: Narrative as a Socially Symbolic Act* (Ithaca, N.Y., 1981), p. 18.

4. Fredric Jameson, 'Marxism and historicism', in his *The Ideologies of Theory: Essays 1971–1986. Volume 2: The Syntax of History* (London, 1988), p. 175.

5. Ibid., pp. 175, 176, 177.

6. Jameson, *The Political Unconscious*, p. 81.

7. See Stephen Greenblatt, 'Invisible Bullets: Renaissance Authority and its Subversion, *Henry IV* and *Henry V*', in Wilson and Dutton (1992), p. 97.

8. Jameson, *The Political Unconscious*, p. 81.

9. Ibid., p. 79.

10. Ibid., p. 287.

11. Ibid., p. 291.

12. On the issue of theatrical and verbal self-consciousness in *1* and *2 Henry IV*, see Sigurd Burckhardt, *Shakespeare's Meanings* (Princeton, N.J., 1968), pp. 144–205; James L. Calderwood, *Metadrama in Shakespeare's Henriad: Richard II to Henry V* (Berkeley, Calif., 1979); Graham Bradshaw, *Shakespeare's Scepticism* (Brighton, 1987), pp. 50–65; and Ronald R. Macdonald, 'Uneasy lies: language and history in Shakespeare's Lancastrian tetralogy', *Shakespeare Quarterly*, 35 (1984), pp. 22–39.

13. John Kerrigan, '*Henry IV* and the death of old Double', *Essays in Criticism*, XXXX (1990), pp. 24–53.

14. On the plays as dramatic historiography, see Catherine Belsey, 'Making histories then and now: Shakespeare from *Richard II* to *Henry V*', in *Uses of History: Marxism, Postmodernism and the Renaissance*, ed. Francis Barker, Peter Hulme and Margaret Iverson (Manchester, 1991), pp. 24–46; Graham Holderness, *Shakespeare Recycled: The Making of Historical Drama* (Hemel Hempstead, 1992), Ch. 4; and Phyllis Rackin, *Stages of History: Shakespeare's English Chronicles* (Ithaca, N.Y., 1990), pp. 137–48.

15. *Elizabethan Critical Essays*, ed. G. Gregory Smith, 2 vols (Oxford, 1904), 11, p. 370; quoted by Rackin, *Stages of History*, p. 143.

16. Scott McMillin, *Shakespeare in Performance: Henry IV, Part One* (Manchester and New York, 1991), pp. 11–12.

17. Quoted ibid., p. 57.

18. Quoted ibid., p. 83.
19. Ibid., p. 87.
20. Ibid., p. 85.
21. Ibid., p. 86.
22. E. M. W. TILLYARD, *Shakespeare's History Plays* (London, 1944), pp. 320–1.
23. Ibid., p. 269.
24. Ibid., p. 277.
25. Holderness, *Shakespeare Recycled*, p. 27.
26. JOHN DOVER WILSON, *The Fortunes of Falstaff* (Cambridge, 1943); G. WILSON KNIGHT, *The Olive and the Sword* (Oxford, 1944); LILY B. CAMPBELL, *Shakespeare's Histories: Mirrors of Elizabethan Policy* (San Marino, Calif., 1947).
27. C. L. BARBER, *Shakespeare's Festive Comedy* (Princeton, N.J., 1959), p. 226.
28. LEONARD TENNENHOUSE, *Power on Display: The Politics of Shakespeare's Genres* (London, 1986), pp. 83–4.
29. STEPHEN GREENBLATT, *Shakespearean Negotiations: The Circulation of Social Energy in Renaissance England* (Oxford, 1988), p. 40.
30. Ibid., p. 65.
31. For an intriguing variation on this line of argument, see STEVEN MULLANEY, *The Place of the Stage: License, Play, and Power in Renaissance England* (Chicago and London, 1988), pp. 76–87.
32. Holderness, *Shakespeare Recycled*, p. 138.
33. Quoted in FREDRIC JAMESON, *Marxism and Form* (Princeton, N.J., 1971), p. 149; translated by Jameson from [ERNST] BLOCH, *Das Prinzip Hoffnung* (Frankfurt, 1959), p. 110.
34. THEODOR ADORNO, *Minima Moralia*, trans. E. F. N. Jephcott (London, 1974), p. 247.

CHAPTER NINE

A Tale of Two Branaghs: *Henry V*, Ideology, and the Mekong Agincourt[1]

CHRIS FITTER

Chris Fitter, while responding to the attractiveness of Kenneth Branagh's 1989 film of *Henry V*, goes on to argue for a sceptical view of its conservative, sanctifying representation of monarchy. He seeks to expose the strategy by which the film smoothes the asperities of Shakespeare's narrative, making it conformable to the market requirements of Thatcher's Britain and Bush's USA.

Unlike Kiernan Ryan, Fitter sees Henry's attempts to bridge the gap between king and common soldier as a cynical attempt 'to overcome class disaffection by a rhetoric of demotic solidarity and class transcendence'. Athough Fitter, like Ryan, sees dramatic devices used to undercut ideology, their views of the King are far removed from each other. Fitter's view is also completely in contrast to that of David Baker in a later extract: for Baker, following Stephen Greenblatt, the play is an 'effort to intensify the power of the king and his war', whereas for Fitter, Shakespeare sets out to demystify those very things. Is Fitter justified in ascribing these qualities to the play (as opposed to particular productions)? In this, as in so much else, the debate about *Henry V* remains an intensely contested one.

We no longer are defensible (3.3.50)

Kenneth Branagh's 1989 film version of *Henry V*, darkly powerful in its primitive interiors of hewn oak in penumbra and its primordial Agincourt of morassed slugging, has been widely eulogized both for restoring the drama of Shakespearean drama, and for the intelligent candor of its tough realism. Reviewers have often defined the latter through contrast with Olivier's 1944 version, with its clowning (rather than conspiratorial) clerics in the opening scene, its excision of scenes that morally undercut Henry (Scroop and the conspirators, the Harfleur speech, Williams's challenge to the king over his responsibility for the war, the reference to Richard II and Henry's dubious title), and the pretty chivalry of its battle scene, all racing knights on caparisoned steeds, their pennants aflutter in brilliant sunshine. Branagh's *Henry*, we are told, restores the cuts and thus the honesty, gives us a credible, pained, demotic Henry, and an Agincourt that will not hide from us that war is hell.

This perspective, I will argue, is insupportable. It is credible – initially – only due to the film's contrast with two commanding legacies: the overtly (and dazzlingly successful) propagandist character of Olivier's film, which was structured to boost patriotic morale in the months prior to the D-Day offensive; and the deadening influence of the Victorian and Tillyardian tradition of Shakespeare as committed upholder of monarchical ideology ('The Tudor view of history'), which bequeaths here a Henry naively glorified as the 'mirror of all Christian kings.' (Among editions of *Henry* popularly used by students, John Russell Brown in the Signet writes of 'a simple plot . . . with an undoubted hero' [xxiv], while the Arden, edited by J. H. Walter, sings of 'Henry's perfection, physical, intellectual and spiritual', likening him to Aeneas. Matchless in its serene devotion to the English monarchy, this Arden can even claim, 'It is noteworthy that the French display degenerate breeding, disunity, dishonour and impiety in waging a "bellum impium" against Henry the rightful inheritor' [xxi; xxiv and xxix; xxx]. Clearly, moral duty lay in immediate abdication to a usurper's son, who didn't even speak the language.) Although many critics have disliked Henry, finding his character 'limited', his 'efficiency' instrumentalistic and deficient in human affection or depth, critics have nonetheless been overwhelmingly reluctant to concede that Shakespeare was deliberately writing an anti-imperialist drama critical of the monarchical system. It has become increasingly difficult to sustain in any version, however, the traditional, 'loyalist' reading of Shakespeare's political perspective, given the growing number of recent publications that recognize Henry's double standards and evasiveness, and the radical ambiguation of his stature within the drama.[2] Just such a riddling, demystifying reading has also in fact been staged recently, at the Royal Shakespeare Company; and it starred as Henry our new screen idol, Oscar nominee Kenneth Branagh (nominated in the categories of Best Actor and Best Director). There are thus two Branagh versions of *Henry V*, and we shall see that they are politically polar. Knowledge of the first – directed by Adrian Noble at Stratford in 1984 – casts transforming light on the supposed toughness and honesty of the second, directed by Branagh himself. This paper seeks to scrutinize the two productions, assessing each in the light of a close reading (my own) of the text the seventeenth century has left us; and to suggest that, at the level both of content and form, the 'new' film has in fact tenderly remodelled the critically exploded hagiography of the conservatives, restoring a fellowly, idealized Harry. Its narratological politics are carefully assimilated to those of the mainstream popular culture of the contemporary USA in such a way as to secure Branagh resounding personal success, a commercial Agincourt. Branagh, I suggest, like some literary Oliver North, has deliberately shredded vital documentation, provided by the text and the RSC production, and his Henry therefore emerges as a familiar figure: the handsome military hero and godly patriot at the heart of an establishment coverup.

Superficially, Branagh's movie much resembles the Stratford production. Branagh again is Henry, and Brian Blessed once more wonderful with his Exeter as ursine thane. Christopher Ravenscroft is again the refined, disdainful yet gradually impressed Montjoy, and Richard Easton the majestic, exasperated statesman, the Constable of France. The staging of Bardolph's execution at 3.6.109[3] directly before the eyes of the king, performed by Exeter in full armor, is borrowed from Noble's production (at Stratford, Bardolph is garroted from behind, in the film he is hanged from a woodland tree), as are deft moments of psychological highlighting: Henry collapsing, battle-worn but victorious, to be caught and supported by the massive Exeter, as a father cradles a son; Henry dragging Montjoy to the floor in an ecstasy of sudden savagery at his final appearance (4.7.70); Henry wavering, weakened, between exhausted tears and laughter after Agincourt at Fluellen's patriotic prattle over Welshness; the lengthy rendition of 'Non Nobis, Domine' as the soldiers exeunt from the battlefield (sung by the actors at the RSC). Also borrowed is the visual impact of the towering door in a blacked-out wall through whose strange light and primal immensity Henry enters, ominously, his council chamber. At Stratford, figures had exited rearstage through a normal door until, as Agincourt's sudden commencement, an unsuspected portal the height of an aerodrome hangar abruptly opened, looming overhead, to swallow the warriors in its swirling light as if into some monstrous apocalyptic plain.

Beyond the cast and such 'special effects', however, likeness ends.

Piece out our imperfections with your thoughts (Prologue, 23)

Interjacent between classes, Shakespeare problematized the ideology of each, and excelled in playing off against one another various groups in his audience. Adept at smuggling past the censor effects innocent on the page but explosive on the stage, he preserved a subversive subtext within dramas outwardly supportive of traditional authority and harmonic in finale. The 'hidden critique' of *Henry V* can be located, I suggest, in (among others) six crucial textual moments and devices, and it is by focusing these moments of political shibboleth that I wish to expose the operations of Branagh the shredder at work on the coverup. First crux is the treatment of the demystifying and satiric populist vignettes juxtaposed to the guiding narrative of regal idealism and nationalist solidarity; others consist of the nocturnal debate of Henry with Bates and Williams, the function of the Chorus, the presentation of Agincourt, the 'insulation' or otherwise of the final wooing scene; and finally the representational mode itself, and the political gains of collapsing artistic illusionism. In his treatment of each of these matters, I suggest, Adrian Noble's *Henry* is rendingly true to the sardonic exposures in Shakespeare's text.

Shakespeare's structural rotation of attention between the decision-making aristocratic class-fraction and the common people whose lives are convulsed by them (or the 'low-life' characters, as middle-class critics are in the habit of insultingly styling them) makes clear the human cost of imperial ambition; and likewise the insistent references to the outcast heartbreak and death of Falstaff ('the King has killed his heart'), capping and critiquing even the victory of Agincourt (4.7.40–54), obtrudes upon a thwarted Globe audience the cost of Henry's tactical moral *volte face*, to make in fact his fault glitter o'er his reformation. Noble squarely foregrounds the sufferings and terrors of the ordinary soldiers. Act 4, with the Chorus's lines on the 'poring dark' and 'foul womb of night', begins in absolute blackness and silence. Gradually the Chorus, whom we see to be wearing a First World War greatcoat, picks his way along a trench-like row of slumped, sleeping soldiers that spans the breadth of the set. His flashlight illuminates the taut, white faces of one soldier after another, who flinch, or stare hopelessly into the darkness and distance. Again, at the siege of Harfleur, the song into which Pistol's band breaks ('Would I were in an alehouse in London' [3.2.12–20])[4] is made a moving and spirited chorus, so that Fluellen's intervention to drive them into combat becomes a brutal act of class coercion. Howard Blake's musical setting of the song is a lifting, elegiac lament, whose naive, sorrowing cadences are thereafter used in a wordless soprano voiceover to haunt and highlight the carnage: the objectified consciousness of the play is thus a grieving proletarian consciousness. By contrast at the same siege the king's egotistic, rhetorical self-intoxication is underscored. Harfleur at 3.1 is a smooth, vast wall of gleaming grey steel that extends the breadth of the set, its apex soaring above view. Ascending this height are three parallel scaling ladders, onto the middle of which Henry throws himself after 'Once more unto the breach, dear friends, once more, / Or close the wall up with our English dead'. As soldiers swarm eagerly up the two flanking ladders, Henry abruptly freezes, three rungs up, and to the astonishment of the troops now above him, who exchange puzzled glances on their heights, Henry breaks into the lengthy and now redundant grandiloquence of a further thirty-two lines. At his ardent climax, crying 'God for Henry, England and St. George!' he throws up his arms in surrender to euphoria and topples stiffly backwards from the ladder into the arms of Exeter and his 'brothers'. His troops thus recommence the assault alone, Henry being below in fraternal delirium.

Politically companion masterstrokes of Noble are the decisions to make the commoners' sufferings visible, in bringing onstage the killings of Bardolph and the Boy. Bardolph kneels, hands tied, with the armored Exeter looming at his back, before the silent Henry some feet away – with a long, transfixing wordless gaze. When, at Henry's nod, he is abruptly garrotted, he offers no struggle. Gently, submissively, his head and shoulders sag forward onto his chest as he bows in death to become a kneeling corpse. The Boy, having at the conclusion of 4.4 interpreted Pistol's French knight, and delivered a second merry soliloquy to the audience, hoists the knight's double-handed sword over his shoulders. Hooking a hand casually over each end, he makes to exit. He is encircled suddenly by a knot of French soldiers, and frozen thus in a crucifixion Position, he is butchered. The lights dim over his corpse, as a distant boy's voice sings 'Would I were in an alehouse . . .'.

Henry's debate with Williams at 4.1 forms another site of decisive ideological construction, in the text's first inscription and in the reinscription of any subsequent production. In falling out with Pistol and then goading Williams into violent outrage, Henry's actions flatly contradict the Chorus's panegyric assurance that pining troops 'Beholding him, pluck comfort from his looks' (4 Chorus 42). Although the King's attempts to exculpate himself from responsibility for his troops' death (4.1.150–192) are, I submit, palpably contradictory and facile (although we lack space here to pursue this), clearer still is that Henry lapses thereafter into immediate contradiction of his own experience. His self-pitying soliloquy envies the peasant who 'can sleep so soundly' and 'never sees horrid night, the child of hell' only minutes after quitting lowly followers insomniac in nocturnal terror. Adrian Noble perhaps glances at the irony here, and in Henry's reference to the peasant's 'profitable labour' in the fields (4.1.283), by staging Williams, Bates and Court as clothed in indigent rags, and as equipped, with terrible poignancy, with nothing save simple agricultural implements to combat the French cavalry.

To the best of my knowledge no critic has commented on the strategic surplus of Alexander Court here. Guaranteed presence on stage through allocation of a single, opening line that could easily have gone to Williams or Bates ('Is not that the morning which breaks yonder?'), yet wordless thereafter throughout, Court constitutes, in an indeterminacy of role installed at the heart of a major debacle, a formidably unconstrained commentative resource. He may of course just sit; he may also sneer during the exchange, laugh derisively, turn his back on Henry, weep, or bite his thumb at the King. Such structural articulations of silence – where the dramatic conjuncture converts silence into disagreement, or compels directly involved protagonists into undisclosed framing action – link Court with the resolutely undeclarative Katharine in act five (from line 275, her final sentence being a furious rebuke: 'il n'est pas la coutume de France'); and with the pregnant onstage silences of such as Jessica in *The Merchant of Venice*, when in act 5 her father's death is merrily anticipated in racist terms. The deployment of such flexible, textually invisible resources to embarrass a textually dominant ideology is, I would suggest, a prime device of Shakespearean stagecraft for outwitting the Elizabethan censor. Although Noble does not articulate the densely potential silence of Court in terms of direct commentative gestures, his Alexander Court is yet visually eloquent throughout. Skeletal, ghastly in pallor, clad only in a thin grey vest and armed with a scythe, trembling incessantly and with dilated eyes, Court is silent because he is imbecile with terror.

The questionable function of the Chorus has consumed much ink, and still keeps word processors clacking. The Arden edition, as ever dazzlingly inept, noddingly accepts the Chorus's self-validation, and finds Shakespeare 'apologetic', cognizant that 'on the common stage he laid himself open to the scorn and censure of the learned and judicious' (xv). Other critics, less disposed to think Shakespeare a penitent theatrical ham embarrassedly playing sycophant to pedants, have looked beyond a surface meaning so pointedly contradictive of Shakespearean valuation of drama in *Hamlet* and elsewhere. In my view, the Chorus is indeed sycophantic, but toward Henry, not embryonic Arden editors of the late sixteenth century, and his propagandist, 'official' narrative of immaculate Henry provides Shakespeare with a respectable alibi which his staged action can then proceed to question, contradict and subvert. The Chorus is thus not the Bard enunciating *ex cathedra*, but is one of the *dramatis personae*; and, mindful of the many links of this play with *Hamlet*, I suggest that he is something of an anticipation of Polonius. Characterized as a courtly and high-minded flatterer (note the relentlessly insincere sycophancy toward the audience as 'gentles' (Prologue 8, 34; 2 Chorus 35) which conspires with the King's duplicitous class rhetoric: 'he . . . that sheds his blood with me . . . shall gentle his condition'), he is yet fatally out of touch with common people: his assurance, 'We'll not offend one stomach with our play' (2 Chorus 40) would disappoint or amuse a lusty audience, familiar with the bear-baiting pit across the grass, who have come to revel in a war play. In these aspects he resembles the pompous, misdiagnosing Polonius, who misconstrues Hamlet and stands alien to the sensibility of the common players. Polonial again is the repeated disruption of the drama: 'these tedious old fools' is precisely what the audience must have felt as he strode in yet again to shatter the racing momentum of the action. (One could imagine him listening stiffly at sidestage, peremptorily opining ' "half-achieved Harfleur" is good'.)

The disruptions are political. They constitute, I submit, deliberate frustrations and coolings of the audience by Shakespeare. The Chorus's foregroundings of the play's fictive devices disallow the audience self-transcendence and jingoistic fellowship with the King's 'brotherhood', and thereby they compel a 'Brechtian' alienation and critical relation to the action upon the disgruntled consciousness of an ineluctably 'exilic' audience.

Noble's production compromises here. His Chorus, Ian McDiarmid, is not given characterization, and he possesses quite magnetic subtleties and range of voice. Moreover, the disruptiveness of his speeches is reduced through his retention throughout on stage, as viewing from the sidelines, and through the maintenance of a swirl of preparatory activity around his speeches. Against this, however, he often kindles proletarian sympathies, when for instance his flashlight lingers tenderly, differentiatingly, on the slumped soldiers in the nocturnal 'trenches'. Whilst Henry's imperialism is not subjected to critical estrangement by the breaking of the spell, it yet is problematized by the mourning of its manifest costs, laid bare by an *exploratory* Chorus.

Equally prominent a frustration effect (and a point apparently unremarked in criticism hitherto) is that this play of Agincourt in fact refuses to stage a single scene of combat. At the close of the sixteenth century when the English monarchy had long lost its medieval military importance in Europe, Agincourt burned in the national memory as having ascended the brightest heaven of English martial pride and continental achievement. At least three other plays on Henry V were acted in London in the 1590s. Many among the Elizabethan genteel classes being trained in fencing, moreover, stage combats would be the more keenly relished for sleight of swordsmanship. Under such conditions, an Agincourt with no fighting was a phenomenon perilously close to a Rambo movie with no shootout for today's teenage audiences, or a *Rocky* sequel that skips the boxing. Shakespeare's combination of rapid-fire scene changes, French panic, confusion on both sides, and lushly narrated off-stage violence (Exeter on York's death, Montjoy on French steeds 'fetlock deep in gore') serve to substitute for combat and to contain audience disappointment, while the narrative shuffles on to the safety of comic gratifications with Fluellen's crooning Welshness and Henry's trick on Williams. The Shakespearean disallowance of a single duel or killing (though the chroniclers recount a personal duel with Alencon, to which the text draws our attention at 4.7.158) aims, I suggest, again to abort inebriated chauvinism, just as pronounced narrative details – the feral threats of mass rape and infanticide that Shakespeare invented for Henry at the Harfleur siege, the slitting of the French prisoners' throats in cold blood (mentioned twice, so as not to be missed [4.6.37; 4.7.10]), and the massacre of the boys – again steep our minds in the horrifying cost of Harry's imperialist 'honour'.

Integral to this logic is a humanization of the enemy – and during Agincourt itself – to the point where perversely we actually fear for his life. The Noble production projects just this logic, resisting the temptation to stage thrilling unscripted duels and easy heroics, and instead heightening the comedy and latent brutality of the scene between Pistol and the French knight. The latter, his head-piece ripped off, transpires to be middle-aged, balding and avuncular, hysterical with fear, and helplessly entombed inside a hundredweight of primrose-colored armour. At the scene's conclusion the Boy has to help lever him from his knees; and he exits, with melancholy clanking, on a comically excruciated 'Merci!'

Sensitive, too, to Shakespeare's planting of Fluellen, in 4.7, as a minefield of accidental arraignments of his sovereign, Noble sustains *across* the scene the incon-solable breakdown with which it opens ('Kill the poys and the luggage! 'tis expressly against the law of arms'). Fluellen's 'Alexander the Pig' and his analogy with Henry as one that 'killed his best friend' are the ramblings of a mind driven by horrors into an agnostic *metanoia*, questioning, in grieving stupor, the coherence of its founda-tions. 'There is a river in Macedon, and there is moreover a river at Monmouth', stumbles Fluellen, as one incapable of his own distress. 'It is called – Why?' The staggering pun on Wye trails downwards unanswerably along the mourning Welsh vowel into deadly silence. Henry, at his entry, shares in the collapse, sobs on Fluellen's shoulder at his address (from line 94). Fluellen, seeking finally to raise both their spirits, catastrophically reassures him: 'I *need not* be ashamed of your majesty, praised be God, so long as your majesty is an honest man . . . .' Agincourt has become infamy.

Adrian Noble's final *coup de théâtre* of ideological destabilization comes with his staging of act five. Shakespeare's wooing scene functions, of course, as a climax of triumphalist euphoria, the skilled and victorious duel with Katharine in part working on the audience as unconscious compensation for the austere interdiction of fighting action preceding it. (This aspect, naturally, is habitually lost on 'the learned and judicious': the indomitable Arden editor declares that 'The Christian prince to complete his virtues must be married. Bouvaisteau, following Aegidius Romanus, is most emphatic on this point.') Yet Shakespeare's scene offers also a characteristic, and virtuoso, split-level ending, the jubilation and romance of one plane repeatedly punctured and jabbed through by the upthrusts of a subtext always just beneath, like some shark's black fin breaking the surface of sunlit waters. Henry's 'love' of a Katharine he had refused earlier (3 Chorus 29–32), his 'plain' and 'downright' wooing as in reality a farce of juridical rape, constitute one such dark ambiguity, particularly as she is subsequently left aside for a rondo of collusive patriarchal smut between Henry and Burgundy. Retrospective to the action of the entire play, however, is that Henry's rhetoric now belittles the common man and celebrates monarchical autonomy in pointed contradiction of his earlier speeches, thus preserving to the end the play's political disquiet. Henry, always alert to the value of being a People's Prince (a lesson observed, no doubt, from the downfall of Richard II) has sought, following his disastrous encounter with Williams and Bates, to overcome class disaffection by a rhetoric of demotic solidarity and class tran-scendence (see especially the Crispian speech), thereby ironically repositioning his subjects in instrumental conformity and obedience. The scene in the French king's palace presents a glittering, sequestered, privileged finale, immediate upon the destitute Pistol's limping off bereaved, penniless, and assaulted by Henry's trusted officer. Safely out of his footsoldiers' earshot, Henry makes a snobbish joke about simple farmers (122–26), and asserts himself, like all 'great kings', the source, not follower, of behavioral norms (284–89). 'The liberty that follows our places stops the mouth of all find-faults' confesses a chilling truth, and this merriment over his power of life and death may uneasily remind us of the hanging of Bardolph and the royal intimidation and bribery of Michael Williams. Noble gives the split-level structure ingenious visual projection through bisecting the set. Just before the palace scene opens, the bodies of the wounded and murdered boys and troops are seen rearstage, laid out in a row as in a battlefield hospital. Amongst them, in low lighting, moves a female nurse in Victorian attire, pausing to set a candle beside each motionless body. She moves slowly, and her candle flickers quietly in the dusk, as a soprano voiceover sings once more at its most still and most lifting the wordless melody of 'Would I were in an alehouse'. As the nobility enter sumptuously attired for the gladding 'courtship', a thin gauze veil or 'scrim' falls midstage. Throughout the remaining action, as Henry, frontstage, jests and charms and celebrates his privilege, perceptible at rearstage through the scrim are the flickerings in twilight of testimonial candles.

> Never came reformation in a flood,
> With such a heady currance, scouring faults (1.1.3 3–34)

Turning to Branagh's own production of *Henry V* five years later, 'we must needs admit the means / How things are perfected', in Canterbury's cynical words (1.1.68–69). Branagh's film version expels almost every progressivist political gain from its RSC predecessor, triumphantly flattening down its multiple levels into a basic tale of sterling venture. Amputating the democratic limbs of the work, it excises the populist subtext out of effective existence. *Glasnost* it is not. Its opening omits the *facts* of the current parliamentary bill, and thus conceals the consequent structural antagonism established from the outset of the interests of the common people against those of state and church leaders, who conspire to strip the ill, aged and weak of 'A hundred almshouses right well supplied'. A long list of shredded textual 'secrets' further includes: excision of the praise (by Fluellen) of Pistol for courageous fighting, immediately prior to denying him Bardolph's life; the later assault on Pistol by Fluellen; Pistol's capture of a French soldier for ransom, and the subsequent dispossession of this ransom as the King orders all prisoners killed; the lines on 'Alexander the Pig'; the song of Pistol and friends, 'Would I were in an alehouse'; Henry's second argument to Williams, that many of the troops deserved their imminent deaths, as murderers, thieves, and pillagers; and the jolly colloquy between Henry and Burgundy over 'virgin crimson' and the future nakedness of Katharine. The Boy's two soliloquies (at 3.2 and 4.4) are also cut, news of his subsequent death thereby affecting us little. Henry's scheming deployment of Fluellen to quarrel with Williams is eradicated, along with Henry's buying off of Williams's criticisms with a gloveful of crowns: instead the film shows Henry wordlessly return the glove with a sardonic, hearty slap on Williams's shoulder, as he exits, in glory, to hear tally of the dead. Expurgated too is the final touch of Henry's ruthless coercion: he compels France to agree to his designation as French 'son and heir', an article the French king had avoided to the very last (353–65) – and a point used by Shakespeare to contradict certain chroniclers, who had written that Katharine's beauty made Henry soften his demands.

Another device tilting the movie away from involvement with Henry's victims and toward admiration of the King is Branagh's skillful recontextualizing of the fiendish Harfleur threats. Henry here delivers the speech in solitude from horse-back, his men having fled the breach in panic. It thereby functions as a brilliant trick to win a city apparently lost: through dazzling and solitary oratorical fiction he has won what his soldiers could not. A further royalist coup by Branagh is the class transference of an emotional crux he has remembered from the Noble pro-duction. The RSC vignette of the sudden French encirclement and hacking to death of the Boy is displaced in the movie onto the loyal Duke of York. The martyrolo-gical exaltation of the incident is thus transferred from the sphere of proletarian suffering and onto the heroized fidelity of the nobility.

It is the three flashbacks, however, that most would please an Arden editor (though they lack the authority of Bouvaisteau and Aegidius Romanus). The first, at 2.1, 'explains' Falstaff to the audience, as we see the fat knight revelling at the fireside with quips from *Henry IV*. He greets an entering Hal roaringly, and at once asks him not to banish plump Jack. The scene, however, elevates rather than subverts the Branagh Henry. Falstaff is hard and cold-eyed, witty but menacing. Henry's 'I know thee not, old man' is given only in voiceover, thought but not stated by a Hal dewy-eyed, grieving. Henry has thus an aching interiority opened up in him for us, begins a journey of sensitive, lonely inwardness. Far from being the royal machiavel, or relishing his status as 'maker of manners', he is here the silent sufferer, victim not origin of necessity.

For most viewers, the on-screen execution of Bardolph will appear a principal innovation of the film, and a locus of 'mature realism' concerning Henry. But the innovation, we have seen, was borrowed from Noble, and Branagh's own innova-tion – a second flashback at this point – works again to strengthen our identifica-tion with the King. Where the text gives us a stonily silent monarch (3.6.110), Branagh reopens a bravely agonized Henrician interiority, with a closeup on his tear-filled eyes as memory delves fondly back to carousals. In this vignette, like the last, Henry is set off from the drinkers, alone and watchful as if compassionately prescient – no inciting cheerleader of a close-knit band. The flashback's effect is to prioritize Henry's consciousness over that of Bardolph, simultaneously marginal-izing Bardolph while ennobling the King as a hero of pious discipline. Loyalty to staunch Henry is further rallied as, minutes later, conspicuous in a knot of soldiers, we see a non-alienated Pistol clearly enjoying Henry's rejoinder to Montjoy's contumely.

The final flashback comes during Burgundy's speech on battered France, as Henry's mind, patriotically impervious to it, recalls his own exhausted soldiers on the field of battle, then Falstaff, Mistress Quickly, Bardolph. Again the effect is to heroize, even sentimentalize, the King, his Romantic heart high-sorrowful, a mourning Mnemosyne, unrelapsing even here from an inner solidarity with loyal troops and beloved friends. The contrast with the RSC staging, with the scrim's ironic suggestion of amnesia and sequestration, could not be sharper in political polarization. Combined with its outright excision here of the bludgeoning of Pistol, the film preserves immaculate a blue-eyed People's Prince.

Branagh's gifted narratological intelligence similarly reconnotates and recuperates the nocturnal quarrel and soliloquy. This Williams, Bates and Court are well-clothed soldiers, with thick, dark jerkins. Untextually, this Williams jumps up to attack the King and must be hauled back by his companions, so that Henry becomes the wronged disputant. His lines on his army as harboring base criminals are cut – for they contradict earlier speeches, by himself and the Chorus, hymning the valor of his 'cull'd and choice-drawn cavaliers'. As Henry, now walking the dark alone, dispraises 'ceremony' – whose 'rents' and 'comings in' are in ample evidence in act 5 – Branagh transfigures the self-pity of privilege into objective oppression by having Henry pace here past a wagonload of pikes and helmets. His nonsense on the fortunate peasant, who never sees horrid night, is abruptly justified, as somnolent commoners heave suddenly into camera view. Where Shakespeare subverts, Branagh inventively validates.

The Chorus is easily made Branagh's ally. Entering below the feet of Bardolph lynched, he looks up and tut-tuts, before a truncated speech on cheerleading Henry and 'a little touch of Harry in the night'. Any alienation effect is easily removed by a systematic and massive reduction of his lines to a minimal narrative supply: at the opening of act 3, for instance, he is a mere voiceover as we follow a parchment map tracing English movement from Southampton to Calais and Harfleur. Rather than disrupt, intrude and problematize, this Chorus conversely adds momentum and coherence to the action. Branagh retains him perhaps as a technical problem for resourceful resolution, and he mainly succeeds; but this badly backfires, given the inherent naturalism of the cinematic medium, where Derek Jacobi deprecates 'four or five most vile and ragged foils' as scores of armed soldiers catapult in front and behind him, roaring to war, whilst he picks his way gingerly between huge wooden stakes jutting across an emerald meadow.

Only the battle scene appears to come close to an RSC-like questioning of all the King has set afoot. It is filmed for regret and sorrow, not battle-joy. We have slow motion, facial closeups of men in fatigue, laboriously swinging and reswinging broadswords as they slither in rain and mud. Their faces express doggedness, immense effortfulness, as they heave and pant, their actions rhythmically punctuated by the fall of horses and riders, of anonymous footsoldiers, into the spattering slush, in protracted, hopeless inevitability. Over the gruelling dying is elegiac, mourning music. Henry is seen open-mouthed in panting fatigue, transparently exhausted, but there are no individuated combats followed. All is mêlée, pain, reluctant duty; there is not even naturalistic sound. Instead is an eerie, distant simplification and magnification of key noises – the fall of Exeter's axe on a French shield comes as through a mist as a slow, torpid rhythm, reverberating and diffusing afar through the great emptiness.

Much in the tonality seems taken from a brutal British rugby match, yet 'the undefeated will' recalls Maldon. The tone of action could almost be mediated from Branagh's physique: this is a victory not of deft coordination or slender speed or intellectual strategy, but a triumph from dogged chunkiness, the bulldog's indomitable determination. Simplified and relentless, this doughty self-rootedness corresponds perfectly to Henry's cadencing:

We would not seek a battle as we are;
Nor, as we are, we say we will not shun it. (3.6.169–70)

But the structure also owes much, I suggest, to Vietnam movies of the 1980s, particularly its moral ambiguity: war is hell, but it heroizes. Far from antiheroic, the technique offers a different *style* of heroism: that of an ethical, courageous resolution. This is but heroism in a paradoxical garb. And it is illicit. We have, for example, only *honorific* blood in this film: virtually always a facial ornament, a red badge of courage, a thin, valorific smatter on cheekbone or jaw. Here is no gore of opened entrails or severed limbs, despite axes, double-handed swords and the specific enunciation of the text: 'When all those legs and arms and heads, chopped off in a battle . . .' (4.1.137). In Henry's triumphal march at the close, all the corpses he passes are unbloodied, with calmly closed eyes and sleeping faces. Not one rictus of death yawns on Branagh's Agincourt. The stakes we have seen driven in by mallets, which at the historical Agincourt spitted ranks of cavalry, are hygienically untenanted. (Contrast of the overall effect with Polansky's *Macbeth* will make my point very clearly.) Branagh, thus, has gorged us on the climactic battle which Shakespeare had doubly refused in denying his audience both staged combat and illusionist enablement. Yet this 'hellish' war will 'not offend one stomach' and imperil Henry's stature.

As the climax to this climax comes a long, and I think brilliantly innovative, four-minute scene (for which so much dialogue was cut – the excellent jokes in the French tent at 3.7, for instance), which we might refer to as the long path of grief. In it, Henry bears on his shoulder an anonymous dead boy far across the strewn field of battle, amongst the slain and the scavenging and the weary, to lay him on a wagon. Needless to say, the passage is an anthem of heroization, as, in this gesture of unity with the fallen, his simple followers gather to his path, move with him, while rich music swells over, and the corpses passed are each bloodless and clean. This is the apotheosis of the caring King, of whom the stoniest antimonarchist might relent to murmur, 'An honorable murderer, if you will . . .'. Structurally extraordinary, it is the precise opposite of a military march-past or a formal procession: it is a march *with*, and we have thus the final *frisson* of an authenticated solidarity in the weary, unassuming, democratic trudge of a King spontaneously at one with his people.

'He that sheds his blood with me . . . shall gentle his condition.' The long path of grief puts this into reverse. Constrained by text and sense from actualizing this instrumental bluff, Branagh must have Henry become a 'plain', 'good-hearted', 'downright' man, as he characterizes himself to Katharine while rhetorically outfoxing her. This 'downward' class transcendence lasts all the way to the Palace.

If it be a sin to covet honour,
I am the most offending soul alive (4.3.28–29)

Turning, finally, to observe the operations of ideology at the level of representational form, we must concede that any modern production of *Henry* is predestined from the outset to betray the first inscription of Shakespeare's play. The Elizabethan conditions of performance are irrecoverable, and probably beyond all modern analogy (although for bawdy anti-authoritarian relish, devoted attention to *ipsissima verba*, and jubilant audience participation, *The Rocky Horror Picture Show* staged at a North American student theater offers gusty points of comparison with feasts of misrule, and thus one dimension of affairs at Shakespeare's Globe). Yet it has been well observed that 'Elizabethan stage conditions are potentially productive of plurality of meaning: whereas films operate to close the plural work into a single dimension of significance'. The Elizabethan theater unfolds its spectacle across an apron stage, the audience surrounding it on three sides or more, and the consequent irreducibility of the action to a single visual perspective helps breed multiplicity of interpretive perceptions, impressions and meanings. Contrariwise, 'the introduction after 1660 of the proscenium theatre with perspective backdrops radically changed the relationship between the audience and the stage. . . . Film is the final realization of the project of perspective staging. The framed rectangle contains a world which is set out as the single object of the spectator's gaze, displayed in order to be known from a single point of view.'[5] Modern stage and film productions thus invite a 'tyranny' of directorial control of meaning, and encourage a relation of docile, passive empathy from an audience distanced from the plane of action in far-reaching tiers.

To disrupt monological meaning and 'parasitic' audience empathy in the modern playhouse, by the kind of Brechtian frustration effects that Shakespeare has built into *Henry V* through the Chorus, blundering pompously onstage to shatter the illusionism and repel us into skeptical detachment, is thus all the more urgent yet all the more dangerous an experiment in defamiliarization, if we are to try to be 'true' to this ambiguating and interrogative drama. The 1984 production took place in a divided RSC uncertain of its direction and politics. A prestigious, 'intellectual' theater granted experimental latitude within the security of national subsidy and a guaranteed audience of tourists and students, nonetheless its 'Royal' Charter, absence of proletarian audience, high prices and menace by Thatcherite cuts in arts spending towed it regularly toward the safe waters of naturalist drama. While Noble's production effected, as we have seen, a socialist restitution of political tensions, and resisted sensationalist possibilities at Agincourt and elsewhere, it opted against narrative disruptiveness and estrangements. The alienation effects of the Chorus were diminished by the continuation of action around his speeches, and the ungranted battle briefly adumbrated by turbulent lighting and a sudden violence of color lashed from the streaming of titanic banners. Illusionist excitements could not be entirely surrendered, nor linear drive arrested. Against this, however, the framing of the huge Stratford stage by tall, 'Victorian' red-brick walls, with doors into which characters in armor regularly vanished, as well as the use of the scrim in act 5, served as a mild, recurrent undercutting of the naturalism, and to activate the imagination toward associations with modern imperialist wars which the trench scene and the Florence Nightingale nurse confirmed.

Primitivist medieval *frissons* notwithstanding, Branagh's movie is a tamed tale, narratologically familiar, and sufficiently domesticated to thrive in the Oscar market in George Bush's USA. It slides away at every point from a Shakespearean interrogation of the action and liberation of the imagination, into the political and financial security of transparent and singular meaning. Deftly disambiguated by its director's hand, instantaneous intelligibility and firmly manipulated empathy are secured by supervening music-over at almost every scene, to aid a pulsing speech or moisten a baffled eye. (The closing music, to which the credits roll, is once more an endorsement of the noble King: the film's summation, its musical self-characterization, it is written in Henry's own major key, being the pious and majestic anthem 'Non nobis, domine'. No horror, indignation, skepticism or wit linger here to embarrass the final and regal record.)

That the Chorus's rupturing of the film's illusionism is reduced to a curiosity-value minimum ensures the continuous involvement of the audience at the emo-tive level; indeed its enveloping, even saturating, visual immediacies – its varied wardrobes, fall woodlands, brazier-lit interiors – help discourage 'thinking above the action'. (Testimony to its atmospheric seductions, the film won the Oscar for Best Costume.) The Elizabethan skeptical emphasis on the play as simulation is rejected, and along with it, critical plurality of meaning.

Furthermore, the very familiarity of the film's screen conventions works to naturalize ideology rather than interrogate and defamiliarize the action. By contrast with such films of Shakespeare as Peter Hall's *A Midsummer Night's Dream* and Grigori Kozintsev's *King Lear*, where normal habits of cinematic perception are sub-verted by mannered and disjunctive cinematography, this one assimilates itself at many points to the mainstream lineage of Vietnam movies. The rendering of Branagh's Agincourt owes much, for example, to Kubrick's *Full Metal Jacket*: the slow-motion silence as trainee marines stagger, topple and founder on through heavy rain together in swampish mud, or the reverberant stylized sound of the rifle shot within slow motion as the sniper's victim writhes on the ground. For the long, rich climax of cut-sound and elegiac music-over, the battle has much in common with the same devices in *Platoon* where Sergeant Elias (Willem Dafoe) is pursued and killed by Viet Cong in tragic slow motion. Henry's 'long path of grief' as he bears the dead boy in wide passage before the moving camera recalls the trium-phant end of *An Officer and a Gentleman* where Richard Gere carries forth Debra Winger in a similarly climactic and protracted ennobling rite. (The rearing of the Lone Ranger's white stallion before the walls of Harfleur we would prefer to forget.) Branagh's Henry, though thrilling entertainment, gives us a work whose center comprises, as in the tradition of United States versions of the Vietnam War, a young male rite-of-passage movie rather than a critique of institutional power and class injustice. Branagh's motto might almost have been Pistol's: 'Let senses rule, the word is "Pitch and Pay"' (2.3.50). And pitch and pay the masses have; Branagh, already famed in the United Kingdom, has successfully crafted a star-vehicle for himself, to conquer overseas the nation of Hollywood.

Shakespeare's play, however, satiric, ambiguating and interrogative, is clearly an exposé of imperialist rhetoric and a critique of the institution of monarchy. Compelled to provide panegyric and chauvinist surfaces to the play (the Chorus's encomia of Henry, the occasional moments of French-baiting) in order to please the royal censor and to secure the play commercial success, Shakespeare systematically proceeded, as we have seen, structurally to undercut such jingoism and hymning of royal authority through the action of the play. Monarchical interests, Shakespeare repeatedly shows, are inimical to those of the common people, whose support must thus be ideologically reinforced through oratorical inductions of false consciousness. As such, the play lays certain foundations of *Hamlet*. Hamlet is another People's Prince, but one, as it were, who has read *Henry V*: who knows that thrones are assumed in 'Polonial' courts, in the state-rooms of Canterbury and Ely and of royal machiavels, and that to ascend them is to pass inevitably into enmity and betrayal of Pistol and Mistress Quickly, of the Boy and the Players; that to assume monarchy is thus helplessly to inherit contamination: the contamination of a determinate location within a pre-existing and corruptive structure of class exploitation and rhetorical duplicity. His torn cry 'We are arrant knaves all, trust none of us' is a reinfusion of indignation into Pistol's steady cynicism: 'Trust none . . . Caveto be thy counsellor' (2.3.51, 54).

Kenneth Branagh has done us, as lovers of Shakespeare, a quite wonderful cultural service, in giving us a Shakespeare that is genuinely popular, intelligent and enthralling, unforgettable if also unfaithful. His screen persona is entirely winning, and his debut as film director certainly precocious. But he has done the ordinary people of the English-speaking world – which is coming to mean, at this time of global Anglophone hegemony, the majority of the citizens of the world – an irresponsible political disservice, in whitewashing traditional autocracy and the logic of imperialism. What Shakespeare has demystified, Branagh, persuasively, affably, immorally, has resanctified.

NOTES

1. Reprinted from Ivo KAMPS (ed.), *Shakespeare Left and Right* (New York and London: Routledge, 1991).
2. Critics who have disliked the character of Henry, while not reading the play as designedly subversive of authority or imperialism, include WILLIAM HAZLITT (chapter on *Henry V* in *Characters of Shakespeare's Plays*); A. C. BRADLEY ('The Rejection of Falstaff'); and MARK VAN DOREN (170–79). GERALD GOULD AND HAROLD C. GODDARD (215–68) appear the sole champions of the view that Shakespeare intentionally writes a mordant satire on imperialism and monarchical government: an interpretation with which I align myself. Other major accounts of the play that acknowledge its subversive dimensions and extend our perception of its terrible ironies, while recoiling nonetheless from the conclusion of a deeply anti-authoritarian Bard into the safety of a neutrally ambiguating Shakespeare, include NORMAN RABKIN (33–62), who sees Shakespeare producing ambiguity for its own sake, and critics who, like JOHN PALMER (*Political Characters* [1948] 180–249), GORDON ROSS SMITH AND KARL P. WENTERSDORF see Shakespeare simply holding the mirror up to nature as it was in those dark times. HONOR MATTHEWS (31–36, 51–66) posits the ambiguity of a reluctant machiavel, unable fully to repress his native good nature; ROY BATTENHOUSE ('*Henry V*') construes the play's satire as sympathetic and 'Chaucerian'; while JONATHAN DOLLIMORE AND ALAN SINFIELD ('History and Ideology') doubt the possibility of resolving whether the disunitary tendencies in the play override the harmonic.

STEPHEN GREENBLATT ('Invisible Bullets') argues the drama's registration of regal hypocrisy, ruthlessness and bad faith within the context of celebration and panegyric; while HAZELTON SPENCER billows ambiguity of his own in lauding a superlatively virtuous monarch whom he casually notes in his concluding paragraph to embody 'a semi-fascist ideal' (193–99).

3. All references to *Henry V* are to the Arden edition, ed. J. H. WALTER.

4. Blake's rendition incorporates Pistol's prose line preceding the song ('Would I were in an alehouse In London!') into the song itself as its first line (and ends it at line 17). I have accordingly referred to the song in this version.

5. [GRAHAM] HOLDERNESS ('Radical Potentiality') cites (183) and quotes (184) CATHERINE BELSEY, 'Shakespeare and Film', in *Literature/Film Quarterly*, vol. XI, no. 2 (1983).

CHAPTER TEN

Back by Popular Demand:
The Two Versions of *Henry V*[1]

ANNABEL PATTERSON

Annabel Patterson's book, *Shakespeare and the Popular Voice* (1989), aimed to challenge the widespread assumption that Shakespeare's attitude to the common people 'ranged from tolerant amusement to contempt'. Elements of her attempt to see Shakespeare as a moderate and enlightened progressive have been strenuously opposed by Richard Wilson (see the headnote to his essay earlier in this volume). The following extract, from Patterson's chapter on *Henry V*, illustrates a different aspect of study: the modern trend which combines textual criticism and bibliography with critical interpretation.

In many cases there are major differences between different early texts of the 'same' Shakespeare play, with no possible way of deciding which is the 'true' version. An older school of textual criticism sometimes accounted for such differences by assuming that so-called 'bad' quartos were texts corrupted or poorly reconstructed from a single, perfect 'original'. The modern movement in textual studies known as revisionism tries to explain these differences by the hypothesis that they may represent genuine alternative versions of the play, the result of revision by the author or the theatre company. This work has revolutionised modern understanding of several plays. It is now frequently accepted that there are two distinct versions of *King Lear*, and similar debate surrounds other plays where two or more early texts exist, including *Hamlet* and *Othello*. Another is *Henry V*, Patterson's subject here. She shows that there are major implications for our view of the play's politics depending on the textual issues. Patterson's theory has profound implications for any critical interpretation of the play: if, as she argues, we should recognise two distinct versions of the play with very different political effects, an interpretation which ignores the differences is likely to fall between two stools. The brief extract below serves to outline Patterson's argument but does not do full justice to the detail with which she supports her case.

or the fifth act in his history of the fifth Henry, Shakespeare suddenly required of his audience a shift in historical perspective. They are invited to imagine Henry's return, victorious from Agincourt, in terms of another anticipated return, presumably closer to their own immediate interest:

> now behold
> In the quick Forge and working-house of Thought,
> How London doth powre out her Citizens,
> The Maior and all his Brethren in best sort,
> Like to the Senatours of th'antique Rome,
> With the Plebeians swarming at their heeles,
> Goe forth and fetch their Conqu'ring Caesar in:
> As by a lower, but by loving likelyhood,
> Were now the Generall of our gracious Empresse,
> As in good time he may, from Ireland comming,
> Bringing Rebellion broached on his Sword,
> How many would the peacefull Citie quit,
> To welcome him?

> *(Folio*, TLN 2872–85)[2]

This Chorus, with its startling analogy between Elizabeth's most famous predecessor and her most notorious subject, Robert Devereux, second earl of Essex, currently in charge of the Irish campaign, demands that we juggle at least two meanings of 'history' as a category of thought: the fifteenth-century history that Shakespeare took over from Holinshed and others and rewrote to his own specifications, and the events in which he and his theater were environmentally situated in the late 1590s, and to some extent embroiled; while its *content* – the nature of popular leadership and the numerical signs of popularity ('How *many* would the peacefull Citie quit / to welcome him?') – requires a still more athletic intellectual response. Or rather, in Shakespeare's own terminology, the required activity is not so much athletic as artisanal, 'the quick Forge and working-house of Thought' associating the right imagination not with society's leaders but rather with that plebeian citizenry whose very breach of their normal workaday behavior is the sign of the extraordinary. And the fact that this Chorus did *not* appear in the only text of the play published in Shakespeare's lifetime raises still another issue – the relationship between 'history', 'popularity' and bibliography, or the story of how Shakespeare's playtexts were circulated in their own time and survived into ours. In the case of *Henry V* the story of the text is inseparable from the political history that is both its content and its context, as also from the thematics of the popular, here defined not as protest or festival but as the relationship of the many to the charismatic leader.

More than almost any other play of Shakespeare's, and certainly more than any other 'history', *Henry V* has generated accounts of itself that agree, broadly speaking, on the play's thematics – popular monarchy, national unity, militarist expansionism – but fall simply, even crudely, on either side of the line that divides belief from skepticism, idealism from cynicism, or, in contemporary parlance, legitimation from subversion. The most extreme example of the idealizing view, the film directed by Sir Laurence Olivier, was premiered in November 1944, in the context of the invasion of Normandy, and dedicated to the Commandos and Airborne Troops of Great Britain, 'the spirit of whose ancestors it has been humbly attempted to recapture'.[3] In the same year appeared E. M. W. Tillyard's influential study of the history plays, closely followed, in 1947, by Lily B. Campbell's, which to different degrees represented *Henry V* as the climax (successful or unsuccessful) of Shakespeare's own version of the Tudor myth, with Henry himself as Elizabeth's prototype.[4] As the nationalism of these projects was implicit, compared at least to Olivier's production, so their power to suggest an orthodoxy was greater.[5] Conversely, the age of nuclear deterrence and of ethically ambiguous geopolitical alliances has produced a criticism, both in England and in the United States, that looks rather at the tensions and contradictions in the Elizabethan ideology of ideal ruler, unified state, and providential history.[6]

The critical record, then, highlights the problem of intentionality, which will not be made to disappear by our focusing instead on the intentions of Shakespeare's readers; and any attempt to recuperate Shakespeare's own intentions must today grapple with the status of the texts that are all we have to work with. As it happens, the two surviving texts of *Henry V* point in different interpretive directions; the Folio can possibly sustain the hypothesis of ideological confusion or deliberate ambiguity; whereas the theses of Campbell and Tillyard could be better supported by *The Cronicle History of Henry the fifth*, the first Quarto version, which has long been ruled out of interpretive account by Shakespearean bibliographers, and placed in the evaluative category of the 'Bad Quartos', that is to say, beyond interpretive reach.[7] Though less textually unstable than *Hamlet* or *King Lear*, where the Quarto texts have strong claims to authorial cachet, *Henry V* therefore presents a unique challenge to the new textual studies, since its publication history is ineluctably connected to the major critical disagreements over the play's meaning and cultural function.

For the first Quarto version is not only shorter than the Folio but tonally different from it. Among the most striking absences in the Quarto are all five Choruses and the final Epilogue; hence, in the fifth Chorus, the non-appearance of the allusion to Essex's anticipated return from Ireland, which Gary Taylor has called 'the only explicit, extra-dramatic, incontestable reference to a contemporary *event* anywhere in the canon';[8] and with no epilogue, there is no final let-down, no admission that the legendary victory at Agincourt accomplished nothing, since in the following reign the regents for Henry VI 'lost France, and made his England bleed' (TLN 3379). These last lines, which subsume the heroic moment in the recursive patterns of history, were also excised from the Olivier production, which otherwise retained most of the Choruses;[9] and even in 1623 the Folio arrangement of the English histories by chronology of reign rather than of composition submerges the sceptical effect and makes Henry the center of the historical sweep through the fifteenth century rather than the last, inconclusive statement of the second tetralogy.

Also missing from the Quarto is Act 1, Scene 1, where the bishops cynically discuss how they are to motivate the war and distract the House of Commons from their plan to reclaim ecclesiastical property; the Hostess's claim in 2:1 that Falstaff is dying because 'The King has killed his heart'; almost all of the Harfleur episode, including the famous 'Once more unto the breach' speech by Henry, and most of his threats of violence upon the besieged citizens; much of the material in the scene before the battle of Agincourt, especially Henry's closing soliloquy on the hardships of kingship; several scenes in the French camp; all of Burgundy's speech on the damages suffered by France in the war; and much of the wooing scene between Kate and Henry. There is, however, nothing in the stage-historical records to refute the Quarto's claim that it represents the play as it was 'sundry times' acted by the Chamberlain's Company.[10] We simply do not know, in fact, what the performative version of *Henry V* was like; the Quarto may very well be closer than the Folio to what the London audiences actually saw on the stage at the absolute turn of the century.

The interest of the 1600 text has long been obscured by the theory of the Bad Quartos, a conception that took its authority from the piracy theory first circulated by the editors of the 1623 Folio, who referred to 'stolne, and surreptitious copies, maimed, and deformed by the frauds and stealthes of injurious impostors that exposed them' (A3r). And the piracy theory was in turn supported by that of memorial reconstruction, or dictation from memory by one or more actors complicit with a piratical printer.[11] These theories, rich in moral opprobrium, easily merged with subjective accounts of the *quality* of the differences observed, with the Folio versions of the plays being designated as 'artistically' superior. But this entire hypothesis is now in question. A more skeptical view is emerging of the claims made by John Heminge and Henry Condell in promoting their own edition; the theory of memorial reconstruction is under attack; and Peter Blayney, in rejecting the notion of piracy, draws our attention to Humphrey Moseley's own advertisement for the Beaumont and Fletcher Folio of 1647, where, in the course of explaining why he has taken the trouble to acquire authorial manuscripts, Moseley witnesses to an entirely reputable method of transmitting abridged playtexts to potential publishers:

When these Comedies and Tragedies were presented on the Stage, the Actours omitted some Scenes and Passages (with the Author's consent) as occasion led them; and when private friends desir'd a Copy, they then (and justly too) transcribed what they Acted.[12]

The parentheses here, 'with the author's consent' and 'justly too', speak to a theatrical practice of communal ownership of acting versions, and the open, legitimate exchange, commercial or otherwise, of transcriptions made by the actors of those versions.[13]

Memorial reconstruction may still be needed to explain those parts of a Quarto text (fewer than has been claimed) which are patently so garbled as to resist explanation by this new sociology of the theater. But we can now understand a feature of Quarto texts that memorial reconstruction could not account for – the omission of whole scenes or large blocks of material. In the case of *Henry V*, the omitted materials are so bulky and so crucial that other hypotheses have gradually emerged. The Arden edition admits at least three, each implying intention – the aesthetic ('cut for compression'), the political ('cut . . . possibly for censorship') and the

socioeconomic ('cut . . . for a reduced cast on tour in the provinces').[14] These suggestions, if not incompatible, derive from quite different critical assumptions and
agendas; and poised uncertainly between them is the inference that the style of the
Quarto version is more popular, in the sense of being lower and more *common*
than the Folio. As John Walter put it for the Arden edition, 'Generally there is a
lowering of pitch, a substitution of cliché and common currency of daily speech for
the more heightened style of the Folio.'

This notion was first proposed by Alfred Hart in 1942, in support of his own
version of the Bad Quarto theory. For him the Quartos were memorial reconstructions of previous abridgements of the plays prepared by Shakespeare's own
company in accordance with theatrical experience. The excisions, Hart thought,
were often theatrically intelligent but linguistically impoverished. The professional
abridger 'knew his audience loved an interesting story, packed with plenty of action
and told in simple language, and rid the play of similes, amplificatory passages,
platitudes, philosophic reflections, repetition, classical commonplaces, and literary
ornament'.[15] But even the best of the Bad Quartos (and *Henry V* is one of the best)
reveal reportorial incompetence incompatible with the work of 'an educated man':

Most of the [divergent] passages share certain characteristics in common – little elevation
of thought, a certain coarseness verging on vulgarity, almost complete lack of fancy or
imagination, dull, pedestrian and irregular verse, poor and over-worked vocabulary, frequent errors in grammar and syntax, and a primitive type of sentence-construction. King,
queen, cardinal, duchess, peer, soldier, lover, courtier, artisan, peasant, servant and child
all speak alike. . . . Essentially each of these and many other speeches exhibit all the marks
of garrulous illiteracy . . . (p. 104).

From the newly self-conscious posture that a critic in the 1980s is privileged to
adopt, one can see how deeply Hart's view of the Bad Quartos has collated the
moralism of his predecessors in the field of bibliography with a class consciousness
that distinguishes the 'educated' text (one that endorses social hierarchies) from the
'illiterate' reproduction that blurs them.

Hart's theory of the text was split – not only between contradictory notions
of good theater and good writing, but also between his wished-for separation of
Shakespeare from Badness and the knowledge that within the theatrical practice of
the Chamberlain's Men such separation was unlikely. Hart actually imagined a
scene in which Shakespeare, having previously, 'on fire with passion and emotions
. . . filled *Hamlet* with 1,600 lines of long speeches', later heard them read aloud. He
would then, Hart felt, 'have shaken his head in critical disapproval and accepted the
decision of his fellows to declaim less than a half of these speeches on the stage'
(p. 168). In this scenario, Shakespeare collaborates in the act of abridgment at least
to the point of authorizing major cuts; and the notion of Shakespeare's 'critical
disapproval' of his own longer first draft runs counter to Hart's own critical disapproval of the Bad Quartos in general.

Hart's confusions mark the transition from a Romantic aesthetics of genius to
a modern sociology of the theater. The notion that censorship was one motive for
the Quarto's reductions has different origins. In 1928, Evelyn May Albright argued
that the Folio 'represents the text of a play intended for use on a special occasion

at the Globe before an audience of statesmen and courtiers at the critical moment preceding the return of Essex from Ireland in the autumn of 1599'.[16] She saw the Folio as being broadly supportive of Essex and his policies, whereas the Quarto, intended for publication, was 'shorn of the most significant personal and political references' (p. 753). She thus keyed the play not into the history of printing, but into political history, specifically the history of Essex's rebellion, whose connection to Shakespeare's company has long been established. I refer to the special production on 5 February, 1601, the eve of the earl of Essex's rebellion, of 'the play . . . of Kyng Harry the iiijth, and of the kylling of Kyng Richard the second played by the L. Chamberlen's players'.[17] And while Albright's thesis of *another* special performance (of *Henry V* itself) is incapable of proof, that notorious production of *Richard II* is certainly part of the story of why and how the later play came into existence.

But before following up this lead, there is another theory that must first be described and then, to some extent, contested. For Hart's conclusions were eventually recruited by Gary Taylor to the services of the new textual criticism of Shakespeare, which in the 1970s sought to demonstrate that at least some of the Bad Quartos represent alternative *versions* of their plays, with the divergences explicable as authorial revision. Inspired, perhaps, by Hart's passing observation that the Quarto *Henry V* had 'heavier reductions of the cast' (p. 429) than any other, amounting to the disappearance of thirteen speaking characters (an observation which Hart subsumed under the category of blunder) Taylor developed a strenuous argument that abridgement was required not by the attention span of the London audiences but by the economic constraints on a company travelling (like the tragedians in *Hamlet*), in the less remunerative provincial towns.[18]

Taylor claimed that, once casting exigencies ruled, the Chorus could not be played by any of the other parts, who all appear in too close proximity for him to change costumes. Yet it is hard to believe that this distinctive, indeed, extraordinary feature of the Folio version, so essential in offering an epic view of the action, would simply be disposed of for practical reasons.[19] More importantly, Taylor himself admits that casting difficulties cannot explain the omission of the opening scene, which throws such a cynical light on the motives for the war against France (p. 80); of the Jamy and McMorris episode, which was either 'omitted to shorten the play or censored, because of King James's recently expressed irritation at dramatic ridicule of the Scots' (p. 85); that certain character substitutions were made for aesthetic reasons; and that some of the omissions in the Harfleur scene are evidence of 'deliberate and coherent' theatrical cutting 'in the interests of simplifying the play into patriotism' (p. 130).

This last suggestion could well be developed. For by this standard we might also comprehend the Quarto's omission of the cynical first scene with the bishops that undermines their case for the 'just war' against France; Burgundy's missing lament for the despoliation of the French countryside, for which Holinshed provides no mandate; and especially the radical alterations in the scene most crucial to Henry's characterization, the disguised visit to the common soldiers in the night before Agincourt. As Taylor himself observes, the Folio creates a striking contrast between the 'populist morale-building walk' *described* by the Chorus and what we actually see. Rather than building morale, Henry picks a fight with Pistol, enters the conversation with Bates and Williams disingenuously, putting them at a serious disadvantage in the discussion of the limits of military loyalty and the rectitude of the cause for which they fight, and then, after their departure, delivers a soliloquy on the hardship of his own condition, excruciating in its self-regard and completely lacking the egalitarian sympathies of his public military rhetoric (p. 88). In the Quarto text, bereft of the contrast between the idealized choric view of the occasion and its actual representation, the king's disguise loses some of its disingenuity, and without the closing soliloquy the scene concludes with 'good-natured Henry joking with his men, as they walk away'. 'What,' Taylor asks, 'was the impetus behind the series of alterations?' (p. 90). Given his own thesis, he is forced to propose that they were triggered by the prior decision to omit the Chorus for reasons of casting economy. We might rather feel in the Quarto a more coherent intention – to omit some of the most disturbing implications about Henry's character and motives.

As Taylor's struggles with the evidence reveal,[20] bibliographical arguments, when isolated from historical or cultural criticism, will tend, when the going gets tough, to fall back on subjective standards of value. The resistance of the textual evidence to bibliographical solution suggests that we need to consider other, more intentionalist explanations. Once one accepts the thesis that the Quarto text represents a theatrical abridgement, which has suffered some textual garbling in its passage from promptbook to printed text, it may fairly be asked what motivated *this* abridgement, these particular omissions. The notion of a *different*, more crudely patriotic Quarto is not, on its merits, implausible; and neither need it be seen as totally unShakespearean. Shakespeare's status as a working playwright is scarcely endangered if we posit abridgement as a tactical retreat from one kind of play to another, from a complex historiography that might have been misunderstood to a symbolic enactment of nationalistic fervor.

NOTES

1. Reprinted from ANNABEL PATTERSON, *Shakespeare and the Popular Voice* (Cambridge, MA and Oxford: Basil Blackwell, 1989).
2. In this chapter, where the history of the play-text and the divergences between Quarto and Folio are at the center of the argument, references are to the facsimile *First Folio of Shakespeare*, prepared by CHARLTON HINMAN (New York, 1968), and *Shakespeare's Plays in Quarto*, (eds) MICHAEL ALLEN AND KENNETH MUIR (Berkeley and Los Angeles, 1981).
3. See *Film Scripts One*, (eds) GEORGE P. GARRETT, O. B. HARDISON, JR, AND JANE R. GELFMAN (New York, 1971), p. 40. But compare also DOVER WILSON, (ed.), *Henry V* (Cambridge, 1947), viii: 'Happening to witness a performance by Frank Benson and his company at Stratford in August or September 1914, I discovered for the first time what it was all about. The epic drama of Agincourt matched the temper of the moment, when Rupert Brooke was writing *The Soldier* and the Kaiser was said to be scoffing at our "contemptible little army" which had just crossed the Channel, so exactly that it might have been written expressly for it.'
4. LILY B. CAMPBELL, *Shakespeare's 'Histories': Mirrors of Elizabethan Policy* (San Marino, Calif., 1947; repr. London, 1964), pp. 255–305; E. M. W. TILLYARD, *Shakespeare's History Plays* (New York, 1944; repr. 1947), pp. 304–14. Tillyard took a less sanguine view of *Henry V* than Campbell,

regarding it as a routine and formulaic performance without the energies invested in the two parts of *Henry IV*.

5. For a larger analysis and critique of the 'theme of England', as promoted by Tillyard and by Olivier's production, see GRAHAM HOLDERNESS, *Shakespeare's History* (New York, 1985), pp. 18–26, 184–200.

6. See, for instance, STEPHEN GREENBLATT, 'Invisible Bullets', in *Shakespearean Negotiations: The Circulation of Social Energy in Renaissance England* (Berkeley and Los Angeles, 1988), pp. 21–65; JONATHAN DOLLIMORE AND ALAN SINFIELD, 'History and Ideology: the Instance of *Henry V*', in *Alternative Shakespeares*, (ed.) JOHN DRAKAKIS (London, 1985), pp. 206–27; and LARRY S. CHAMPION, ' "What Prerogatives Meanes": Perspective and Political Ideology in *The Famous Victories of Henry V*', *South Atlantic Review*, 53 (1988), pp. 1–19, which provides an account of Shakespeare's most important source 'as either a glorification of monarchy or as an attack on its corruption, egocentricity, and militaristic monomania' (p. 14), depending on the spectator's own position. Earlier skeptical readings were primarily characterological in focus, including even that of GERALD GOULD, who in the immediate aftermath of World War I revolted against the 'more hideous "Prussianisms" with which Shakespeare has endowed his Henry'. See 'A New Reading of *Henry V*', *English Review* (1919), p. 42.

7. For the Quarto, I have used *Shakespeare's Plays in Quarto*, (eds) MICHAEL J. B. ALLEN AND KENNETH MUIR (Berkeley and Los Angeles, 1981); for the 1623 Folio, *The First Folio of Shakespeare* (New York, Norton Facsimile edition, 1968).

8. GARY TAYLOR, (ed.), *Henry V* (Oxford, 1984), p. 7 (italics added).

9. See *Film Scripts One*, p. 134: the film's final words are as follows:

> Small time: but in that small, most greatly lived
> This star of England: Fortune made his sword: and for his sake
> In your fair minds let this acceptance take.

10. It is sometimes assumed that the Folio text, though not deriving from a promptbook, represents an acting version, and that, on the basis of Choric references to staging, especially to the 'wooden O' of the fifth Chorus, it was designed for the new Globe theater built in 1599; but it is equally assumed in other instances (such as *Hamlet*) that the Folio text was sometimes or always abridged in actual performance.

11. See A. W. POLLARD, *Shakespeare's Folios and Quartos: A Study in the Bibliography of Shakespeare's Plays, 1594–1685* (London, 1909); W. W. GREG, (ed.), *The Merry Wives of Windsor* (Oxford, 1910); his theory was refined in *Two Elizabethan Stage Abridgements* (Oxford, 1923).

12. PETER BLAYNEY, 'Shakespeare's Fight', referring to FRANCIS BEAUMONT AND JOHN FLETCHER, *Comedies and Tragedies* (London, 1647), Sig. A2r.

13. Since Moseley did not in fact base his edition on these theatrical transcriptions, but rather, as he insists, on authorial manuscripts, he himself had nothing to gain by establishing the social legitimacy of the practices here described.

14. J. H. WALTER, (ed.), *King Henry V* (Cambridge, Mass., 1954), p. xxxv.

15. ALFRED HART, *Stolne and Surreptitious Copies: A Comparative Study of Shakespeare's Bad Quartos* (Melbourne, 1942), p. 130.

16. EVELYN MAY ALBRIGHT, 'The Folio Version of *Henry V* in relation to Shakespeare's Times', *PMLA*, 42 (1928), 722–56. This contributed to a long and intemperate argument between herself and RAY HEFFNER, who preferred to separate Shakespeare from politics. On Albright's side, see 'Shakespeare's *Richard II* and the Essex Conspiracy', *PMLA*, 42 (1927), 686–720; and

'Shakespeare's *Richard II*, Hayward's *History of Henry IV* and the Essex Conspiracy', *PMLA*, 46 (1931), 694–719; For Heffner's rebuttal, see 'Shakespeare, Hayward and Essex', *PMLA*, 45 (1930), 754–80, an essay which nevertheless contains invaluable information about Hayward's involvements with Essex.

17. See the confession of Sir Gilly Merrick, Essex's steward, on 5 March 1601, *Calendar of State Papers Domestic*, 1598–1601, Vol. 278, art. 78, p. 575.

18. In STANLEY WELLS AND GARY TAYLOR, *Modernizing Shakespeare's Spelling with Three Studies in the Text of Henry V* (Oxford, 1979). See also, for earlier versions of this theory, H. T. PRICE, *The Text of Henry V* (Newcastle-under-Lyme, 1920); GERDA OKERLUND, 'The Quarto Version of *Henry V* as a Stage Adaptation', *PMLA*, 49 (1934), 810–34; and W. W. GREG, *The Shakespeare First Folio* (Oxford, 1955).

19. For an alternative, unpersuasive explanation for the problem posed by a text without the Choruses, see W. D. SMITH, 'The *Henry V* Choruses in the first Folio', *Journal of English and Germanic Philology*, 53 (1954), 38–57, who sought to prove that the Choruses were a later addition, that the allusion in the fifth prologue was not to Essex but to Lord Mountjoy, who took over his commission. This argument was refuted by R. A. LAW, 'The Choruses in *Henry V*', *University of Texas Studies in English*, 35 (1956), 11–21.

20. In Taylor's single-volume edition of the play the casting hypothesis remains unqualified, but the 'simplification in the direction of patriotism' theory is greatly expanded to include a whole series of omissions. See *Henry V*, p. 12. The contradiction between this perceived pattern and its supposed motives – reducing the cast – is hereby exacerbated.

CHAPTER ELEVEN

'Wildehirissheman': Colonialist Representation in Shakespeare's *Henry V*[1]

DAVID J. BAKER

This extract from David Baker's essay on *Henry V* instances a post-colonial approach growing out of a New Historicist one. It starts in classic New Historicist manner, juxtaposing historical ancedote with literary text, and it continues by adopting Stephen Greenblatt's view of the play as a patriotic work designed 'to intensify the power of the king and his war'. Its challenge to Greenblatt is in giving more weight to voices other than those of monological power – a key move, since it opens up the post-colonial viewpoint. A focus on the clash of alien cultures was also a New Historicist speciality, but this essay, with its debt to Homi Bhabha, focuses directly on issues of colonisation and nationality. In this it typifies a number of recent discussions of the play.

I

On October 12, 1599, Christopher St. Lawrence, a captain of the Queen's army in Ireland, lately returned from that country, lifted his cup in a London tavern and made a toast. It was, under the circumstances, an impolitic gesture. Addressing the company, he 'drancke to the Health of my lord of *Essex*, and to the Confusion of his Ennemies'.[2] For this, St. Lawrence was officially rebuked and later summoned to the Privy Council to be interrogated by Robert Cecil for his 'vndecent Speaches'.[3] Invoking the name of Essex just two weeks after that commander had returned unbidden from his catastrophic Irish campaign was hazardous. Essex was in custody at that moment. But the troubling ambiguity of St. Lawrence's declaration lay, I think, not so much in what was said (his show of defiance was quickly apprehended – understood and contained – by the State), but in who said it. Before he left Essex had boasted that he would 'shake and sway the branches'[4] of Ireland, that 'tree which hath been the treasonable stock from which so many poisoned plants and grafts have been derived'.[5] But Christopher St. Lawrence, who toasted Essex, was himself an Irishman.

Or at least St. Lawrence could be named as an Irishman. Whether that name had any defining power was just what this incident calls into question. St. Lawrence had been born in Ireland, and had devoted himself to prosecuting England's wars against his homeland, but when he raised his cup, his status as a member of any 'nation' was a matter of anxious and irresolvable complexity. In fact, he later claimed before his questioners that he had made his 'vndecent' toast because someone had said that 'he was an *Irish* Man'. And 'I am sory', he went on to declare, 'that when I am in *England*, I shuld be esteemed an *Irish* Man, and in *Ireland*, an *English* Man; I haue spent my Blood, engaged and endangered my Liffe, often to doe her Majestie Service, and doe beseach to haue yt soe regarded.'[6] This soldier had drunk to the 'Confusion' of his commander's enemies, but his own situation and his own speech betray considerable confusion as well. Who was St. Lawrence? That is to say, how was he situated? Was his enemy the Irish rebel against whom he was ordered to fight, the same rebel with whom, it could be said, he shared a traitorous patrimony? Or was it rather his own sovereign, the English Queen who, in that year, had declared that she so distrusted the Irish in her army that she would henceforth deny them both commissions and companies. '[W]e command you', she wrote one officer, 'not onely to raise no more, [but] when these shall be decaid . . . to keepe them unsupplied that are already, and as they waste to Casse [strip] their bands.'[7] And the year before she had directed her council in Ireland to 'use all convenient means to clear our army of the Irish',[8] including, presumably, Captain St. Lawrence.

What this encounter in a tavern puts into question is the coherence of the colonialist discourse in which St. Lawrence tries to position himself. As an 'Irish' subject of an English queen, St. Lawrence was the product – quite literally – of the racial typology an imperial power had inscribed across its conquered colony. The very 'notion "Ireland"', it has been argued, 'is largely a fiction created by the rulers in England in response to [the] specific needs' of British colonialism.[9] And it is equally so, I would say, that the inhabitants of Ireland – the 'meere' Irish, the old English, the new English, all of them carefully categorized – are the creations of a power which requires rigid distinctions in kind. Colonial authority imposes a schema of essentialist categories on an apparently undifferentiated populace, and insists that the differences thus created inhere in the natives themselves. Thus in 1571 Edmund Campion could assure his readers that it was 'known that the simple Irish are utterly another people than our English in Ireland'. He presents them 'unfiled' – rough, authentic, absolutely and unchangeably themselves.[10] By such knowledge, a colonial regime produces the identity of the colonized, and does so of course in order that the colonizers might be defined; they are 'utterly another' people than their debased subjects.

Colonialist discourse would thus seem to be as fully hegemonic as any instrument of power can be. And yet the argument of this essay is that, as total as this colonial power is, it is not capable of insuring the stability of its own discourse. It is not capable of maintaining the distinctions it imposes.

Who, again, is Christopher St. Lawrence? His positioning within this discourse is anything but certain, and the problem he represents for colonialist typology is, I think, irresolvable and profoundly disruptive. St. Lawrence appears here as an emblem of what Homi Bhabha has called colonialist 'mimicry'. This arises, says

Bhabha, from the colonizers' 'desire for a reformed, recognizable Other, as *a subject of a difference that is almost the same, but not quite*',[11] a subject, that is, like St. Lawrence, who is English/Irish. He is enough like his masters to be identifiable, but unlike enough to be Other. St. Lawrence is a construct of colonial power, the result, as Bhabha says, of its 'production of differentiations, individuations, identity effects through which discriminatory practices can map out subject populations'. But in the difference colonial power creates there is also a danger for a colonial power, Bhabha insists. It lies in the 'but not quite' that it also generates, in the surplus of threatening and ungovernable significance that is produced in the very production of the differentiated Other. By imagining a figure – as it must – who is so Other that by 'definition' he violates the definitions imposed, colonialism introduces an instability within its own categories. These can never quite fix the subject of their classification, because then there would be nothing exorbitant about the Other, and it is just this that the colonizer needs to believe (and fears). Thus colonialism also 'requires modes of discrimination . . . that disallow a stable unitary assumption'[12] of identity. Colonial power, therefore, is *both* self-confirming and self-disrupting. It is always creating the schema which it itself will undo, a doubleness which Elizabethan writers on Ireland register again and again. We are told, often and at length, what the Irish are actually like, but in the same paragraph (sometimes in the same sentence) we read of the offensive mutability of everything Irish, and of the impossibility of maintaining proper difference. Campion complains: 'the very English of birth, conversant with the brutish sort of that people, become degenerate in short space and are quite altered into the worst sort of Irish rogues . . . living near them . . . [they are] transformed into them'.[13]

The hybrid – either the degenerate Englishman or the incompletely assimilated Irishman – could become, for colonial power, a figure of threatening ambiguity, and his language the site of unsettling contradictions. St. Lawrence and his 'vndecent Speaches' are a case in point. He does not merely 'rupture the discourse'; through him, it 'becomes transformed in . . . uncertainty'.[14] Since the authority St. Lawrence served both produced and disrupted the sharp distinctions that would have fixed his identity, he was left vulnerable to bewildering dislocations. He was an Englishman in Ireland, an Irishman in England, and whenever he spoke, wherever he spoke, there was a sense in which he was no *one* at all. The contradictions he represented as both colonizer and colonized could not be reconciled by anyone involved in this incident: not Lawrence's antagonists in the tavern, who (mis)-recognized him as a rebel, not his interrogators, who found themselves questioning a faithful servant of the Queen – whoever accused him, said St. Lawrence to Cecil, 'was a Villain, and that if he wold Name hym, he wold make him deny yt; I by God, that he wold'[15] – certainly not St. Lawrence himself, who was both (and/or neither) of these. His request, then, that he be 'regarded' as an identifiably English, incontrovertibly loyal adherent of the Crown is a plea for exactly that kind of stability of reference the discourse he inhabits cannot provide. When such ambiguities are produced *within* colonialist discourse, how can it be stable? How, for instance, is St. Lawrence's speech 'vndecent' except in its display, before the 'regard' of the authorities, of the indeterminacy of the discourse that (dis)locates both them and their witness? There was, we could say, a *doubleness* of vision in that interrogation.

195

What the authorities saw as they considered St. Lawrence did not confirm their sense that he was, as an Irishman, altogether Other. Instead, he was both obviously English and, it must have seemed, essentially alien. There was somehow a threatening difference in him, present but occluded, so that there in the Privy Council chamber they saw an outlandish rebel regarding them from the face of an English captain, and (to paraphrase Bhabha) 'the look of surveillance returned as the displacing gaze of the disciplined and the observer became the observed'.[16]

I have begun with this incident not only because, as several critics have noticed, it runs parallel in uncanny ways to a scene in Shakespeare's *Henry V*.[17] As I will show, when MacMorris, an Irish captain in Henry's army, asks his famous question, 'What ish my nation?', he is giving voice on stage to the contradictions that so split and tormented St. Lawrence before the Privy Council. But more generally, I cite it as an example of the incoherence of the imperial discourse *Henry V* articulates, an incoherence which is elided in many readings of the play. It is often argued that *Henry V* is a theatrical display of England's colonial power. Critics are right, I think, to emphasize that the play is an 'attempt to stage the ideal of a unified English Nation State'.[18] It is a patriotic work, written in time of colonial war to justify the expansionism and xenophobia of a nation consolidating an empire. Essex's campaign in Ireland is usually held up as a historical backdrop, and we are reminded of Shakespeare's invocation of him as 'the General of our gracious Empress / . . . from Ireland coming, / Bringing rebellion broache'd on his sword' (5.0.30–32). A powerful and theoretically interesting version of this traditional argument has been made by Stephen Greenblatt. *Henry V*, he tells us, 'originate[s] . . . in an effort to intensify the power of the king and his war'.[19] The play is thus an instrument of empire; it is, he says, pervasively, even totally organized by the discourse of sovereignty it articulates. But from the premise that English power is hegemonic Greenblatt draws this conclusion: that it is also univocal, that it speaks with one voice and one voice only. Although he allows that there are 'moments in which we hear voices that seem to dwell outside the realms ruled by the potentates of the land',[20] finally he seems unable to imagine other voices speaking in the place of English power. In *Henry V* the 'momentary sense of instability or plenitude – the existence of other voices – is produced by the monological power that ultimately denies the possibility of plenitude'.[21]

According to Greenblatt, then, power as it is articulated in *Henry V* works its way toward an end stage, a moment when it is homogeneous and undifferentiated. England's sense of herself as an imperial domain may have been produced at some earlier point by taking the conquered Irish (for instance) as Other, but eventually power excludes all traces of that Other, leaving power to address itself in its own self-confirming terms. But we can assume, I think, that in no discourse is identity established in the total absence of the Other. Identity is necessarily relational, a matter of differences, and this is especially so under colonialism, with its elaborate (and precarious) schemes of racial classification. In the colonies, as Benita Parry has put it, Self and Other are 'interdependent, conjunct, intimate'.[22] Definition is unstable and ongoing; the colonial equation requires the constant implication of a suppressed term. And if it is this discourse that 'speaks' in *Henry V*, the same discourse that failed to situate Christopher St. Lawrence, a self-divided voicing of ambivalent power pervaded by alien and disruptive traces that it generates and cannot (in principle) contain, then I think that we should expect to read that play differently. I do not deny that *Henry V* extends Elizabethan power; mine is not an argument against recuperation. This drama, I concur, is a voicing of imperial authority and *only* of that authority. I do deny, though, that English power itself is 'monological'. The recuperating discourse produces within itself, incessantly, its own disruption as echoes of voices not entirely its own. Certainly, as Shakespeare registers, those who speak for English colonialism represent it as self-identical and exclusive of all others. *Henry V* includes many declarations of the unbroken coherence of English power. In Act 1, for example, Canterbury prefigures Greenblatt's reading of the play in his well-known comparison of England's realm to a beehive. The honey bees, he tells Henry, are 'Creatures that by a rule in nature teach / The act of order to a peopled kingdom' (1.2.188–89) and therefore, he concludes, just as these insects are in 'continual motion' (1.2.185) for one purpose, 'many things, having full reference / To one consent, may work contrariously' (1.2.205–06). Like many later commentators, Canterbury insists that English power in this drama has an exalted integrity that contradictions only apparently violate. But we should notice, I think, that here the fullness of this authority, its splendid wholeness, depends for its very definition on partial traces of a presence, of a threatening Other that is always half-elided but never altogether eradicable. Canterbury's evocation of the beehive State is a response to the menace (which reveals itself in *Henry's* voice) of 'coursing snatchers' (1.2.143) on the borders, and especially of 'the Scot', who may, if England is left undefended, come 'pouring like the tide into a breach / With ample and brim fullness of his force / Galling the gleane'd land with hot assays' (1.2.149–51). To his listeners, Henry represents the Scots as a counter-hegemony, as a dangerous simulacrum of their own power. The violation they threaten will turn back on English might a version of itself, transforming England's 'pith and puissance' (3.0.21), at the point of entrance, into an emptiness to be filled with 'hot assays'. This rape (for that is what it is) can be defended against – 'Once more unto the breach, dear friends, once more' (3.1.1) – but its possibility cannot be forgotten.

II

Before I consider the larger implications of such a reading, I want to concentrate on a scene in which, we are told, England's imperial power is confirmed by those it dominates. My example is a locus classicus in Shakespeare's representation of the colonized. When this incident takes place in *Henry V*, it is the day before the battle of Agincourt, and MacMorris, an Irish captain in the King's army, finds himself engaged unwillingly in 'a few disputations' with Fluellen, a voluble Welshman. Their topic – or Fluellen's – is 'the disciplines of the war' (3.3.38–39), and although MacMorris holds that 'It is no time to discourse' (3.3.48), Fluellen persists; he must, as he puts it, 'maintain his argument' (3.3.24). But when MacMorris is told: 'I think, look you, under your correction, there is not many of your nation – ', the Welshman's sentence disintegrates under the force of the Irishman's enraged questions:

> Of my nation? What ish my nation? Ish a villain and a bastard and a knave and a
> rascal? What ish my nation? Who talks of my nation? (3.3.61–65)

To the other royal soldiers on stage, MacMorris' outburst is disquieting and incomprehensible. Fluellen can only respond lamely that MacMorris 'take[s] the matter otherwise than is meant' (3.3.66–67), and as the scene ends shortly thereafter, the feuding captains are warned by their English superior: 'Gentlemen both, you will mistake each other' (3.3.74). The 'communication' (3.3.41) Fluellen has forced on MacMorris has been exploded from within.

MacMorris' demand – 'Who talks of my nation?' – anticipates the question critics have asked about this passage. His question can be put in another way: when 'nations' are talked of, when the vocabulary of English sovereignty is invoked, who is it that is speaking? Do we hear in these oddly accented questions asked on an English stage the 'monological' voice of English authority, speaking through a kind of ventriloquism of power? Or do we hear the voice of the Irish, those Others on whom England imposed its power, whispering of their exclusion in a vocabulary not their own? Who *is* speaking in MacMorris' absurdly broken English? Some readers have in fact heard MacMorris as a representative of the historically brutalized Irish, and to them his questions speak of the predicament of subjugated identity. In part this is because, as an editor notes, 'the problems of the British in Ireland have continued to lend [him] . . . the thrill of topical interest'.[23] What does it mean, MacMorris seems to ask, to be 'of' a nation when you have no recognized nation, when those who insist that you are 'Irish' also deny the existence of something called 'Ireland', except perhaps as a colonial adjunct, a debased subsidiary to England, the only true nation? But for most readers this scene is a site triumphantly occupied by English power, and thus empty of any voice but one. Here, MacMorris the Irishman, along with Fluellen the Welshman and Jamy the Scotsman, those other ethnic 'types' whose accents are heard in *Henry V*, are entirely absorbed into the colonizers' racial typology and reduced to ludicrous caricatures. Greenblatt, as we might expect, thinks of such scenes as instances of 'recording' – the incorporation of other 'voices' into the discourse of power, the 'acknowledgement of the other [that] . . . issue[s] in the complete absorption of the other'.[24] In their individuality, these characters are 'curiously formal, a collection of mechanistic attributes'. Their accents are 'absurd'. (Note the metaphoric implications of 'recording': MacMorris sounds 'mechanistic' to Greenblatt because the voice he hears has been spliced into a tape loop circulating through power's recording machine. On perpetual playback, MacMorris cannot 'represent . . . what is alien but [only] what is predictable and automatic').[25] Typically, MacMorris and Fluellen both are said to be so assimilated that whatever they say reveals them as loyal subjects of the English crown. Many readers, for example, hear this Irishman as objecting to the implication that he is somehow different from other servants of the King. 'Who are you [Fluellen]', one critic imagines him protesting, 'a Welshman, to talk of the Irish as though they were a separate nation from you? I belong to this [English] family as much as you do'.[26] ' "What ish my nation?" ' agree others, 'is therefore a rhetorical question to which the answer is supplied by MacMorris' service in the English army'.[27]

But if, as I have argued, what speaks in MacMorris' questions is a discourse, and a troubled, often self-cancelling discourse, then I do not think we can be so certain that we know who is speaking or what loyalties his talk may have implied. 'Who . . . speaks when I do?' Jonathan Goldberg has asked. 'Do I speak or does something speak in me, something no smaller than the entire culture with all its multiple capacities?'[28] If this is so when one 'entire culture' voices itself, how 'multiple' will be the 'capacities' of discourse when, under colonialism, not one but several cultures at odds with one another meet and conflict within a 'single' voice? These disparities find their best register, I think, in the very criticism that tries to police this passage. In order to resolve the dispute between Fluellen and MacMorris into something like a civil 'communication', critics have resorted to finishing Fluellen's sentence for him,[29] to paraphrasing MacMorris' riposte,[30] and then to re-paraphrasing him.[31] 'When Fluellen persists in probing MacMorris's doubtful knowledge of warfare', one reader complains, 'the Irishman bursts out in a wholly unreasonable non-sequitur effectively prohibiting Fluellen from coming to the point.'[32] In fact, we could say that MacMorris' questions have the effect of preventing any final meaning – any discursive end 'point' – from emerging at all. Here, the voicing of imperial power gives way to a discursive heterogeneity, interrogates itself, and finds itself unable to sustain the distinctions on which it rests. As Christopher Miller has said in another context, 'the gesture of reaching out to . . . [an] unknown part of the world and bringing it back as language' – the appropriation of MacMorris' 'Irish' speech – brings colonial power 'face to face with nothing but itself, with the problems its own discourse imposes'.[33]

This (dis)ordering of power can be traced in the language of Fluellen's remark and MacMorris' response. Fluellen's observation ('I think, look you, under your correction, there is not many of your nation – ') is of course an act of linguistic colonialism. In Fluellen's remark, we catch colonialist discourse in the act of producing MacMorris as an 'Irish' subject. He implies that as an Irishman MacMorris can be named and categorized, that however few there might be of his kind, together they form a recognizable 'nation' within the colonizers' racial scheme. He assumes, that is, that this English word refers to the Irish, and thus he assigns MacMorris a distinct (although certainly subordinate) place in the grammar of imperial power. The Irish, like the Welsh, Fluellen implies, are 'under . . . correction', and he expects to be answered in the same terms he employs. As in the colonies themselves, the English language serves to define the colonized. In Ireland, for instance, the 'Act for the English order, habite and language' (1537) declared that the 'English tongue . . . [must] be from henceforth continually (and without ceasing or returning at any time to Irish . . . language) used by all men that will knowledge themselves according to their duties of allegiance, to be his Highness' true and faithful subjects'. Spoken English is to be the mark of 'knowledge'; such voices will be located, as the phrase goes, 'within the true'. While 'whosoever shall . . . not . . . use . . . the English tongue', the Act warns, 'his Majestie will repute them in his most noble heart as persons that esteeme not his most dread laws and commandements.'[34] They will be divided from true knowledge and from all civility because they do not speak English. As Edmund Spenser declared, 'it hath been ever the use of the conqueror to despise the language of the conquered, and to force him by all means to learn his'.[35]

And sometimes – as in Fluellen's remark – this strategy seemed to have had the effect of so organizing discourse that English hegemony was assured. Henry VIII, for example, was told by certain of Fluellen's countrymen petitioning for a union with England that 'Your highness will have but the more tongues to serve you'.[36]

But although the colonialist apparatus implied in Fluellen's jibe is reconstructed in MacMorris' response, its coherence is disrupted there. As with Christopher St. Lawrence, producing the 'Irishman' also produces the dangerous excess he is made to represent. It is not only that in this Irishman's speech English has been supplanted by a 'mingle mangle or gallimaufrie of both . . . languages',[37] as many travellers to Ireland itself complained. In MacMorris' queries, the assumptions undergirding the colonialist enterprise are dismantled, not because MacMorris rebuts them, but because, far more disruptively, he subjects them to a relentless interrogation which refuses to acknowledge that these premises could explain the subject – MacMorris himself – who asks them. What he 'represents' in this way is clearly *not* an alienated national identity, one which speaks through him and coherently declares itself. But his lines do stage a destabilizing disintegration of sense and reference within which ethnic identity is neither completely effaced nor altogether present, but displaced. Who, after all, 'ish' MacMorris? Who is this self-alienated character, a foreigner in an English army, and what does 'nation' mean when he says it? Has he borrowed an English term to denote an Irish synonym (which is?), or is he speaking now as an Englishman, fracturing a language other than his native dialect?

Even Renaissance authority may have found these questions difficult to resolve because, 'in Tudor parlance', we are told, 'each Gaelic clan was called a "nation": a clan chief', for example, 'when being recognized in his authority by the English, would be called "chief of his nation"'.[38] Within the language MacMorris tries to speak, then, there is a split in reference. Sometimes a 'nation' is what the English have; sometimes it is what they attribute to those whom they colonize, those to whom they deny a 'nation' while lending them the word. Which was MacMorris' usage? And if his language cannot be identified, how can his identity be fixed? His inability to utter the copula, to say 'is' as the English would have said it, becomes a sign of the ambiguity which invades assigned identity when MacMorris speaks their language. In the ontology of MacMorris' 'ish', there is no distinct presence or absence. When something 'ish', it both 'is' and it isn't. Like MacMorris himself, it is recognizable, but marked with an elusive difference. And this plurality of reference troubles each line MacMorris speaks. 'It is impossible to say', Philip Edwards has noted, 'precisely what Macmorris means by "Ish a villain and a bastard, and a knave, and a rascal". The subject of the sentence may be Ireland, Macmorris, or Fluellen.'[39] Or, he might have added, England. MacMorris' assertive voice shifts within the multidirectional terms of his speech. His vilification can attach itself to his antagonist, or turn back on himself, or the nation he serves, or even be directed at Ireland, so that the English violence inflicted on his homeland is, so to speak, revisited on it by himself in his own insistent but equivocal rhetoric. When MacMorris speaks in this tongue, he cannot be loyal or traitorous – not to England, not to Ireland, not to himself. Each of these is displaced within the language he speaks.

At issue, I want to insist, is not whether MacMorris articulates a genuine Irish identity (he doesn't), or whether he escapes being an ethnic stereotype (he can't).

In MacMorris, Shakespeare fashioned a colonialist caricature, and by doing so he 'helped to determine literary representation of the stock . . . Irishman . . . for centuries to come'.[40] As the prototypical stage Irishman, MacMorris is 'like a court jester'. He may 'challenge the audience's superiority', a critic reminds us, 'their national, English superiority over his Irishness', but he 'must . . . ultimately . . . confirm it, [and] be made to acknowledge the hierarchic order of things'.[41] Confronted by MacMorris, most Englishmen, I would suppose, left the theater with their sense of superiority intact. The 'order of things', in its larger outline, remained undisturbed. 'I am busied', wrote Essex from Ireland, 'in bringing all this chaos into order: in setting down every man's rank and degree, that those under me may not fall by the ears for precedence and place, and bounds, and limits.'[42] Essex's sentence multiplies restrictions meant to define. But as we saw, his concern for 'precedence and place', and the 'order of things' he imposed, could not make Christopher St. Lawrence, his own officer, a true-born Englishman. He was installed within that 'order', but he was also its disordering. Similarly, in MacMorris Shakespeare creates a character who is, in one sense, the dutifully assimilated Irishman most critics want him to be. But he is also, we remember, the character who looks for 'throats to be cut' (3.3.54) and swears to Fluellen, 'So Chrish save me, I will cut off your head' (3.3.73). He is thus not unlike the Irish rebels who horrify Fynes Moryson with their 'rude barbarous Cryes', 'terrible Executioners' who 'never [spare] any that yield to mercy', not 'beleeving them to be fully dead till they have cutt of their heads'.[43] MacMorris intimates a violence which is finally, I think, not so much the unmediated rage of the barbaric Other as the disorder intrinsic to the very 'order' by which the Other is fashioned. Nothing MacMorris says, therefore, is (or needs to be) oppositional; there is no 'before' in his speech which, as we watch, is transformed into the stuff of English sovereignty. Rather, his questions are repetitions of the controlling language. MacMorris iterates the terms of this discourse ('nation . . . nation . . . nation') until paradoxically we become aware of the almost effaced differences that are inscribed within them.[44] The discourse of his masters is attenuated so that its fault lines are exposed. Another way to put this is that, while Fluellen's half-sentence implies all the answers that make up colonialism's 'truth', MacMorris' outburst rephrases these answers as the questions they were designed to preclude. His queries are thus definitive for (and defined by) colonialist discourse. But by disordering the shape of the colonizer's 'knowledge', by stretching it in his repetition, he destabilizes its certainties. Something happens to change the form of the rhetoric from self-evident assertion to drawn-out interrogation. So if there is any point in this scene where 'subversion' occurs, it is not marked on the page. An unseen place of shift, it ties in the gap – the literal white space – between Fluellen's colonialist insult and the enraged reiterations that interrupt, rephrase, and question it.

III

I have offered this scene as a demonstration of the disruptive multiplicity which cannot be eradicated from even the most powerfully 'contained' and organized discourse. The scene has been called a 'furious repudiation of difference',[45] and in a way I think it is. Clearly, what agitates this moment in *Henry V* is the felt presence, just beyond the reach of colonialist power, of an Other so radically different that it cannot be represented in itself – that 'Wildehirissheman', who was written into the margins of a fifteenth-century text.[46] This barbarian must be absorbed and converted into the tropes of English colonial power; in this sense the threatening difference MacMorris represents is furiously repudiated. But difference is not simply a property of the Other that can be discarded. It is in fact inscribed within every act of othering, every difference colonial power marks. Difference is of power's own making, therefore, and is all the more persistent for being repudiated. Thus the attempts of colonial power to rid itself of its 'mimic' only bring it closer, until like Christopher St. Lawrence or MacMorris, the Other stands within the discourse, a figure in whom the very excess that was meant to be excluded is manifest. 'The *menace* of mimicry', as Bhabha puts it, 'is in its *double* vision which in disclosing the ambivalence of colonial discourse also disrupts its authority.'[47] Look at *Henry V* and something unnamed looks back.

NOTES

1. Reprinted from *English Literary Renaissance* 22 (1992).
2. *Letters and Memorials of State*, ed. Arthur Collins (1746), p. 133. This incident is discussed in Paul A. Jorgensen, *Shakespeare's Military World* (Berkeley, 1956), p. 80, and in Philip Edwards, *Threshold of a Nation: A Study in English and Irish Drama* (Cambridge, Eng., 1979), pp. 76–77.
3. *Letters*, p. 137. Cecil objected most to the 'Speaches' regarding himself; he told St. Lawrence that he 'tooke hym to be his professed Ennemy' – a charge the witness denied.
4. Quoted in Cyril Falls, *Elizabeth's Irish Wars* (London, 1950), p. 232.
5. Elizabeth I, quoted in Falls, p. 239.
6. Letters, p. 137.
7. Perhaps it was this policy which led St. Lawrence to complain, when directed 'to return to his Charge . . . that he had but a poore Command there'. *Letters*, p. 137.
8. Quoted in Jorgensen, p. 79.
9. Declan Kiberd, quoted in David Cairns and Shaun Richards, *Writing Ireland: Colonialism, Nationalism and Culture* (Manchester: Manchester University Press, 1988), p. 8.
10. [Edmund Campion], *A History of Ireland* in *Elizabethan Ireland: A Selection of Writings by Elizabethan Writers on Ireland*, ed. James P. Myers, Jr. (Hamden, Conn., 1983) p. 25.
11. 'Of Mimicry and Man: The Ambivalence of Colonial Discourse', *October* no. 28 (1984), 126. Emphasis Bhabha's. For [Homi] Bhabha's investigation of colonialism's internal divisions, see also 'The Other Question – The Stereotype and Colonial Discourse', *Screen* 24 (1983), 18–36, 'Signs Taken For Wonders: Questions of Ambivalence and Authority under a Tree Outside Delhi, May 1817', *Critical Inquiry* 12 (1985), 144–65, and 'Sly Civility', *October* no. 34 (1985), 71–80. My essay has been influenced throughout by what Sara Suleri has called Bhabha's 'powerful and impacted reading' of the colonial situation.
12. 'Signs Taken For Wonders', p. 153.
13. Campion, p. 25.
14. 'Mimicry and Men', p. 127.
15. *Letters*, p. 137.

16. As Homi Bhabha has argued, a 'repertoire of conflictual positions constitute the subject in colonial discourse. The taking up of *any one position*, within a specific discursive form, in a particular historical conjunction, is always thus problematic'. See 'Of Mimicry and Man', p. 129.

17. All citations are from *Henry V*, ed. Gary Taylor (Oxford, 1982).

18. Cairns and Richards, p. 11.

19. Stephen Greenblatt, *Shakespearean Negotiations: The Circulation of Social Energy in Renaissance England* (Berkeley, 1988), p. 63.

20. *Shakespearean Negotiations*, p. 43.

21. *Shakespearean Negotiations*, p. 37. Emphasis mine.

22. [Benita Parry], 'Problems in Current Theories of Colonial Discourse', *Oxford Literary Review* 9 (1987), 29.

23. Gary Taylor, introduction, *Henry V*, p. 67.

24. *Shakespearean Negotiations*, p. 59.

25. *Shakespearean Negotiations*, p. 56. Even Jonathan Dollimore and Alan Sinfield, whose reading of *Henry V* is a tacit critique of Greenblatt's, concur that the 'issue of English domination [over its colonies] . . . appears in the play to be more containable'. See their 'History and ideology: the instance of *Henry V*', in *Alternative Shakespeares*, ed. John Drakakis (London, 1985), p. 224.

26. Edwards, pp. 75–76.

27. Cairns and Richards, p. 10.

28. [Jonathan Goldberg], 'Shakespearean Inscriptions: the voicing of power' in *Shakespeare and the Question of Theory* ed. Patricia Parker and Geoffrey Hartman (London: Methuen), pp. 118–19.

29. Jorgensen, p. 78.

30. See the paraphrase of W. J. Craig quoted in Edwards, p. 75.

31. Edwards, pp. 75–76.

32. Joseph Th. Leerssen, *Mere Irish & Fíor-Ghael: Studies in the Idea of Irish Nationality, its Development and Literary Expression Prior to the Nineteenth Century* (Amsterdam: John Benjamins, 1986), p. 95.

33. [Christopher Miller], *Blank Darkness: Africanist Discourse in French* (Chicago, 1985), p. 5.

34. Quoted in Leerssen, p. 41.

35. [Edmund Spenser], *A View of the Present State of Ireland*, ed. W. L. Renwick (Oxford, 1970), p. 67.

36. Quoted in Edwards, p. 86.

37. Quoted in Nicholas Canny, *The Formation of the Old English Elite in Ireland* (Dublin, 1975), p. 4.

38. Leerssen, p. 25. Emphasis mine.

39. Edwards, pp. 248–49.

40. *Shakespearean Negotiations*, p. 57.

41. Leerssen, p. 87.

42. Quoted in Jorgensen, p. 60.

43. Quoted in Jorgensen, p. 79. The comparison between MacMorris and these ferocious Irishmen is Jorgensen's.

44. Another point at which repetition restates and undermines the order of English authority is the wooing scene in Act V. Katherine is doubly Other, once because she is French, again because she is a woman. I would argue that her French/English has the same function as MacMorris' Irish/English: both mark the differences that persist within assimilating power.

45. Edwards, p. 76.

46. Quoted in Leerssen, p. 39.

47. 'Of Mimicry and Man', p. 129. Emphasis Bhabha's.

CHAPTER TWELVE

History and Ideology, Masculinity and Miscegenation: The Instance of *Henry V*[1]

ALAN SINFIELD AND JONATHAN DOLLIMORE

Sinfield and Dollimore are two leading cultural-materialist critics. This essay was originally written in shorter form for the influential volume *Alternative Shakespeares* (Drakakis, 1985). The intention was to explore the complex topic of ideology and, as Dollimore put it elsewhere, 'conflict between class fractions within the State and, correspondingly, the importance of a non-monolithic conception of power'. The discussion of gender roles was added later for the essay's reappearance in Alan Sinfield's book *Faultlines* (1992). In its extended form, as excerpted here, it remains one of the most comprehensive and intellectually agile modern accounts of *Henry V*. The 'faultlines' of Sinfield's title are those points at which the dominant discourses of a culture can be revealed as contradictory, so allowing the prising apart of ideology from power and giving a hearing to voices which challenge the culturally dominant forces. Sinfield and Dollimore see insurrection as the play's 'obsessive preoccupation', but in clear distinction to the New Historicists, they do not 'assume inevitable success' for 'strategies of containment'.

WARRING IDEOLOGIES

. . . Theories of the ultimate unity of both history and the human subject derive from a Western philosophical tradition where, moreover, they have usually implied each other: the universal being seen as manifested through essences that in turn presuppose universals. Often unawares, idealist literary criticism has worked within or in the shadow of this tradition, as can be seen for example in its insistence that the universal truths of great literature are embodied in coherent and consistent 'characters'.

The alternative to this is not to become fixated on its negation – chaos and subjective fragmentation – but rather to understand history and the human subject in terms of social and political process. Ideology is composed of those beliefs, practices, and institutions that work to legitimate the social order – especially by the process of representing sectional or class interests as universal ones.[2] This process presupposes that there are other, subordinate cultures that, far from sharing the interests of the dominant one, are in fact being exploited by it. This is one reason why the dominant tend not only to 'speak for' the subordinate but actively to repress it as well. This repression operates coercively but also ideologically (the two are in practice inseparable). So, for example, at the same time that the Elizabethan ruling fraction claimed to lead and speak for all, it not only persecuted those who did not fit in, but even blamed them for social instability that originated in its own policies. This is an instance of a process of displacement crucial then (and since) in the formation of dominant identities – class, cultural, racial, and sexual.

Ideology is not just a set of ideas; it is material practice, woven into the fabric of everyday life. At the same time, the dominant ideology is realized specifically through the institutions of education, the family, the law, religion, journalism, and culture. In the Elizabethan state, all these institutions worked to achieve ideological unity – not always successfully, for conflicts and contradictions remained visible at all levels, even within the dominant class fraction and its institutions. The theater was monitored closely by the state – both companies and plays had to be licensed – and yet its institutional position was complex. On the one hand, it was sometimes summoned to perform at Court and as such may seem a direct extension of royal power;[3] on the other hand, it was the mode of cultural production in which market forces were strongest, and as such it was especially exposed to the influence of subordinate and emergent classes. We should not, therefore, expect any straightforward relationship between plays and ideology: on the contrary, it is even likely that the topics that engaged writers and audiences alike were those where ideology was under strain. We shall take as an instance for study *Henry V*, and it will appear that even in this play, which is often assumed to be the one where Shakespeare is closest to state propaganda, the construction of ideology is complex – even as it consolidates, it betrays inherent instability.

The principal strategy of ideology is to legitimate inequality and exploitation by representing the social order that perpetuates these things as immutable and unalterable – as decreed by God or simply natural. Since the Elizabethan period, the ideological appeal to God has tended to give way to the equally powerful appeal to the natural. But in the earlier period, both were crucial: the laws of degree and order inferred from nature were further construed as having been put there by God. One religious vision represented ultimate reality in terms of unity and stasis: human endeavor, governed by the laws of change and occupying the material domain, is ever thwarted in its aspirations, ever haunted by its loss of an absolute that can only be regained in transcendence, the move through death to eternal rest, to an ultimate unity inseparable from a full stasis, 'when no more *Change* shall be' and 'all shall rest eternally' (Spenser, *Faerie Queene* 7.2). The metaphysical vision has its political uses, especially when aiding the process of subjection by encouraging renunciation of the material world and a disregard of its social aspects such that oppression is experienced as a fate rather than an alterable condition. Protestantism tended to encourage engagement in the world rather than withdrawal from it; most of the *Faerie Queene* is about the urgent questing of knights and ladies. The theological underpinning of this activist religion was the doctrine of callings: 'God bestows his gifts upon us . . . that they might be employed in his service and to his glory, and that in this life.'[4] This doctrine legitimated the expansive assertiveness of a social order that was bringing much of Britain under centralized control, colonizing parts of the New World and trading vigorously with most of the Old, and that was to experience revolutionary changes. At the same time, acquiescence in an unjust social order (like that encouraged by a fatalistic metaphysic of stasis) seemed to be effected, though less securely, by an insistence that 'whatsoever any man enterpriseth or doth, either in word or deed, he must do it by virtue of his calling, and he must keep himself within the compass, limits or precincts thereof'.[5] This ideology was nonetheless metaphysical.

Such an activist ideology is obviously appropriate for the legitimation of warfare. It is offered by the Archbishop of Canterbury in *Henry V*, and as the Earl of Essex set off for Ireland in 1599, Lancelot Andrewes assured the queen in a sermon that it was 'a war sanctified'.[6] In the honeybees speech in *Henry V*, human endeavor is not denigrated but harnessed in an imaginary unity quite different from that afforded by stasis: 'So may a thousand actions, once afoot / End in one purpose.'[7] Like so many political ideologies, this one shares something essential with the overtly religious metaphysic it appears to replace – namely a teleological explanation of its own image of legitimate power, based on the assertion that such power derives from an inherent natural and human order encoded by God. Thus the 'one purpose' derives from an order rooted in 'a rule of nature' (1.2.188), itself a manifestation of 'heavenly' creation, God's regulative structuring of the universe. What this inherent structure guarantees above all is, predictably, obedience:

> Therefore doth heaven divide
> The state of man in divers functions,
> Setting endeavour in continual motion;
> To which is fixed, as an aim or butt,
> Obedience.
>
> (1.2.183–87)

And what in turn underpins obedience is the idea of one's job or calling – in effect one's beelike *function* – as following naturally from a God-given identity: soldiers,

> armed in their stings,
> Make boot upon the summer's velvet buds;
> Which pillage they with merry march bring home
> To the tent-royal of their emperor.
>
> (1.2.193–96)

The activist ideology thus displaces the emphasis on stasis yet remains thoroughly metaphysical nonetheless. More generally, in this period, perhaps more than any since, we can see a secular appropriation of theological categories to the extent that it may be argued that Reformation theology actually contributed to secularization;[8] nevertheless, it was an appropriation that depended upon continuities, the most important of which, in ideological legitimation, is this appeal to teleology.

Not only the justification of the war but, more specifically, the heroic representation of Henry works in such terms. His is a power rooted in nature – blood, lineage, and breeding: 'The blood and courage that renowned them / Runs in your veins' (1.2.118) – but also deriving ultimately from God's law as it is encoded in nature and, by extension, society: France belongs to him 'by gift of heaven, / By law of nature and of nations' (2.4.79). Conversely, the French king's power is construed in terms of 'borrowed glories', 'custom' and 'mettle . . . bred out' (2.4.79, 83; 2.5.29). With this theory of legitimate versus illegitimate power, the responsibility for aggression is displaced onto its victims. Thus does war find its rationale, injustice its justification.

There are two levels of disturbance in the state and the ideology that legitimates it: contradiction and conflict.[9] Contradiction is the more fundamental, in the sense of being intrinsic to the social process as a whole – when for example the dominant order negates what it needs or, more generally, in perpetuating itself produces also its own negation. Thus, for example, in the seventeenth century, monarchy legitimated itself in terms of religious attitudes that themselves came to afford a justification for opposition to monarchy. We shall be observing contradiction mainly as it manifests itself in the attempts of ideology to contain it. Conflict occurs between opposed interests, either as a state of disequilibrium or as active struggle; it occurs along the structural faultlines produced by contradictions. Moreover, ideology is destabilized not only from below but by antagonisms within and among the dominant class or class fraction (high, as opposed to popular, literature will often manifest this kind of destabilization).

Ideologies that represent society as a spurious unity must of necessity also efface conflict and contradiction. How successful they are in achieving this depends on a range of complex and interrelated factors, only a few of which we have space to identify here. One such will be the relative strength of emergent, subordinate, and oppositional elements within society.[10] The endless process of contest and negotiation between these elements and the dominant culture is often overlooked in the use of some structuralist perspectives within cultural analysis. A further factor militating against the success of ideological misrepresentation involves a contradiction fundamental to ideology itself (and this will prove especially relevant to *Henry V*): the more ideology (necessarily) engages with the conflict and contradiction that it is its *raison d'être* to occlude, the more it becomes susceptible to incorporating them within itself. It faces the contradictory situation whereby to silence dissent, one must first give it a voice; to misrepresent it, one must first present it.

These factors make for an inconsistency and indeterminacy in the representation of ideological harmony in writing: the divergencies have to be included if the insistence on unity is to have any purchase, yet at the same time their inclusion invites skeptical interrogation of the ideological appearance of unity, of the effacements of actual conflict. There may be no way of resolving whether one, or which one, of these tendencies (unity versus divergencies) overrides the other in a particular play, but in a sense it does not matter: there is here an indeterminacy which alerts us to the complex but always significant process of theatrical representation and, through that, of political and social process.

AESTHETIC COLONIZATIONS

It is easy for us to assume, reading *Henry V*, that foreign war was a straightforward ground upon which to establish and celebrate national unity. In one sense this is so, and it is the basic concern of the play. But in practice foreign war was the site of competing interests, material and ideological, and the assumption that the nation must unite against a common foe was shot through with conflict and contradiction. Such competition occurred equally in the hegemonic class fraction, though it was they who needed, urgently, to deny divisions and insist that everyone's purpose was the same. Queen Elizabeth feared foreign war because it was risky and expensive and threatened to disturb the fragile balance on which her power was founded. Members of the Privy Council favored it – in some cases because it would strengthen their faction (puritans continually urged military support for continental protestants), in other cases because it would enhance their personal, military, and hence political, power. The church resented the fact that it was expected to help finance foreign wars; but in 1588 Archbishop John Whitgift encouraged his colleagues to contribute generously towards resistance to the Armada on the grounds – just as in *Henry V* – that it would head off criticism of the church's wealth.[11]

For the lower orders, war meant increased taxation, which caused both hardship and resentment, as Francis Bacon testified in Parliament in 1593. On the other hand, war profited some people, though in ways that hardly inspired national unity. Some officers took money in return for discharging mustered men and enlisting others instead. Essex complained in Star Chamber in 1596 that 'the liege and free people of this realm are sold like cattle in a market'.[12] In 1589 Sir John Smith overheard two gentlemen joking that the recent military expedition against Spain 'would be worth unto one of them above a thousand marks and to the other above £400 . . . by the death of so many of their tenants that died in the journey: that the new fines for other lives would be worth that or more'. War, in these aspects, must have tended to discredit ideas of shared national purpose. Indeed, there are a number of reports of mutinous individuals asserting that poor people would do better under the king of Spain.[13] This desperate or perverse inversion, whereby the demonized other of state propaganda was perceived as preferable, indicates both the failure of that propaganda and its success. For the perceived alternative was only another version of the existing power structure – the Spanish monarchy, of course, behaved broadly like the English one.

In fact, *Henry V* only in one sense is 'about' national unity: its obsessive preoccupation is insurrection. The king is faced with actual or threatened insurrection from almost every quarter: the church, 'treacherous' fractions within the ruling class, slanderous subjects, and soldiers who undermine the war effort, either by exploiting it or by skeptically interrogating the king's motives. All these areas of possible resistance in the play had their counterparts in Elizabethan England, and the play seems, in one aspect, committed to the aesthetic colonization of such elements in Elizabethan culture; systematically, antagonism is reworked as subordination or supportive alignment. It is not so much that these antagonisms are openly defeated but rather that they are represented as inherently submissive. Thus the

Irish, Welsh, and Scottish soldiers manifest, not their countries' centrifugal relationship to England, but an ideal subservience of margin to center. Others in the play are seen to renounce resistance in favor of submission. Perhaps the most interesting instance of this is the full and public repentance of the traitors, Cambridge, Grey, and Scrope. Personal confession becomes simultaneously a public acknowledgment of the rightness of that which was challenged. It is, of course, one of the most authoritative ideological legitimations available to the powerful: to be sincerely validated by former opponents – especially when their confessional self-abasement is in excess of what might be expected from the terms of their defeat.

Nevertheless, we should not assume inevitable success for such strategies of containment; otherwise how could there have been Catholic recusants, the Essex rebellion, enclosure riots? *Henry V* belongs to a period in which the ideological dimension of authority – that which helps effect the internalization rather than simply the coercion of obedience – is recognized as imperative and yet, by that selfsame recognition, rendered vulnerable to demystification. For example, the very thought that the actual purpose of the war might be to distract attention from troubles at home would tend to undermine the purposed effect. The thought is voiced twice in *2 Henry IV*: it is part of the advice given to Hal by his father (4.5.212–15) and John of Lancaster envisages it in the final speech. It is suppressed in *Henry V* yet it twice surfaces obliquely (2.1.90–92; 4.1.228–29).

At the height of his own program of self-legitimation, Henry 'privately' declares his awareness of the ideological role of 'ceremony' (4.1.242–45). In the same soliloquy, Henry speaks his fear of deceptive obedience – masking actual antagonism. It is a problem of rule that the play represses and resolves and yet reintroduces here in a half-rationalized form, as the 'hard condition, / Twin born with greatness' is presented initially as the sheer burden of responsibility carried by the ruler, the loneliness of office, but then as a particular kind of fear. As the soliloquy develops, its subtext comes to the fore, and it is the same subtext as that in the confrontation with Bates and Williams: the possibility, the danger of subjects who disobey. What really torments Henry is his inability to ensure obedience. His 'greatness' is 'subject to the breath / Of every fool', 'instead of homage sweet', he experiences 'poisoned flattery', and although he can coerce the beggar's knee he cannot fully control it (4.1.240–41, 256–57). Not surprisingly, he has bad dreams. The implication is that subjects are to be envied not because, as Henry suggests, they are more happy in fearing than (like him) being feared, but almost the reverse: because, as subjects, they cannot suffer the king's fear of being disobeyed and opposed. Henry indicates a paradox of power, only to misrecognize its force by mystifying both kingship and subjection. His problem is structural, since the same ceremony and role-playing that constitute kingship are the means by which real antagonisms can masquerade as obedience – 'poisoned flattery'. Hence, perhaps, the slippage at the end of the speech from relatively cool analysis of the situation of the laboring person (referred to initially as 'private men', lines 243–44) into an attack on him or her as 'wretched slave . . . vacant mind . . . like a lackey' (274–79), and finally 'slave' of 'gross brain' (287–88).

The play circles obsessively around the inseparable issues of unity and division, inclusion and exclusion. Before Agincourt, the idea of idle and implicitly disaffected people at home is raised (4.3.16–18), but this is converted into a pretext for the king to insist upon his army as a 'band of brothers' (4.3.60). Conversely, unity of purpose may be alleged and then undercut. The act 3 Chorus asks:

> For who is he, whose chin is but enrich'd
> With one appearing hair, that will not follow
> These cull'd and choice-drawn cavaliers to France?
>
> (lines 22–24)

But within fifty lines Nym, the Boy, and Pistol are wishing they were in London.

However, the threat of disunity did not involve only the common people. That the king and the aristocracy have more interest in foreign wars and in the area of 'England' produced by them than do the common people is easy enough for us to see now. But such a straightforward polarization does not yield an adequate account of the divergent discourses informing *Henry V*; on the contrary, it accepts uncritically a principal proposition of Elizabethan state ideology, namely that the ruling class was coherent and unified in its purposes, a proposition necessary to the idea that the state could be relied upon to secure the peace of all its subjects. Evidence to the contrary was dangerous, helping to provoke the thought that most violence stemmed from the imposition of 'order'.

In practice, while the aristocracy helped to sponsor the ideology of the monarch's supreme authority, it actually retained considerable power itself, and the power of the Crown probably decreased during Elizabeth's reign.[14] Elizabeth could maintain her position only through political adroitness, patronage, and force – and all these, the latter especially, could be exercised only by and through the aristocracy itself. Elizabeth could oppose the Earl of Leicester if supported by Burghley, or vice versa, but she could not for long oppose them both. After the death of Leicester in 1589, the power struggle was not so symmetrical. The rise of the youthful, charismatic, and militarily impressive Earl of Essex introduced a new element: he rivaled the queen herself, as Burghley and Leicester never did. The more service, especially military, Essex performed, the more he established a rival power base, and Elizabeth did not care for it.[15] The Irish expedition was make or break for both; Essex would be away from court and vulnerable to schemes against him, but were he to return with spectacular success he would be unstoppable. In the event he was not successful, and thus found himself pushed into a corner where he could see no alternative but direct revolt. The exuberance of *Henry V* leads most commentators to link it with the early stages of the Irish expedition, when a successful return could be anticipated; the Chorus of act 5 (lines 29–35) actually compares Henry's return to England with it, and there are indeed parallels between Henry and Essex. Both left dangers at home when they went to war, besieged Rouen, sacked foreign towns, were taken to represent a revival of chivalry and national purpose; Essex was already associated with Bolingbroke.[16] The crucial difference, of course, is that Essex was not the monarch. That is why Henry must be welcomed 'Much more, and much more cause'. Henry is both general and ruler, and therefore the structural problem of the over-mighty subject – the repeated theme of other plays – does not present itself.

Henry V was a powerful Elizabethan fantasy simply because nothing is allowed to compete with the authority of the king. The noblemen are so lacking in distinctive qualities that they are commonly reorganized or cut in production. And the point where the issue might have presented itself – the plot of Cambridge, Scrope, and Grey – is hardly allowed its actual historical significance. Holinshed makes it plain that Cambridge's purpose in conspiring against Henry was to exalt to the crown Edmund Mortimer, and after that himself and his family; that he did not confess this because he did not want to incriminate Mortimer and cut off this possibility; that Cambridge's son was to claim the crown in the time of Henry VI, and that this Yorkist claim was eventually successful.[17] Cambridge makes only an oblique reference to this structural fault in the state (2.2.151–53). The main impression we receive is that the conspirators were motivated by greed and incomprehensible evil – according to Henry, like 'Another fall of man' (line 142). Such arbitrary and general 'human' failings obscure the kind of instability in the ruling fraction to which the concurrent career of Essex bore witness.

That the idea of a single source of power in the state was, if not a fantasy, a rare and precarious achievement is admitted in the Epilogue. The infant Henry VI succeeded, 'Whose state so many had the managing / That they lost France and made his England bleed' (lines 11–12). Many managers disperse power, and unity falls apart.

The aristocracy is the most briskly handled of the various agents of disruption. Whether this is because it was the least or the most problematic is a fascinating question, but one upon which we can only speculate. *Henry V* far more readily admits of problems in the role of the church, though the main effect of this is again to concentrate power, now spiritual as well as secular, in the king. The archbishop's readiness to use the claim to France to protect the church's interests tends to discredit him and the church, but this allows the king to appropriate their spiritual authority. Thus power, which in actuality was distributed unevenly across an unstable fraction of the hegemonic class, is drawn into the person of the monarch; he becomes its sole source of expression, the site and guarantee of ideological unity. This is a crucial effect of a process already identified – namely a complex, secular appropriation of the religious metaphysic in the legitimation of war:

> his wildness, mortified in him,
> Seem'd to die too; yea, at that very moment,
> Consideration like an angel came,
> And whipp'd th'offending Adam out of him.
>
> (1.1.26–29)

The language is that of the Prayer Book service of baptism: Henry takes over from the church sacramental imagery that seems to transcend all worldly authority. Thus he is simultaneously protected from any imputation of irreligion that might seem to arise from his preparedness to seize church property and becomes the representative of personal piety, which adhered only doubtfully to the bishops. In him, contradictions are resolved or transcended. This presumably is why the clerics are not needed after act 1. From the beginning, and increasingly, Henry's appeals to God, culminating in the insistence that 'God fought for us' (4.8.118), enact the priestly role as Andrewes identified it in his sermon on the Essex expedition, where he observed that in successful Old Testament wars 'a captain and a Prophet sorted together'. The two roles are drawn into the single figure of Henry V.[18]

On the eve of Agincourt, Henry gives spiritual counsel to his soldiers:

> Every subject's duty is the king's; but every subject's soul is his own. Therefore should every soldier in the wars do as every sick man in his bed, wash every mote out of his conscience; and dying so, death is to him advantage; or not dying, the time was blessedly lost wherein such preparation was gained.
>
> (4.1.182–89)

It is the high point of Henry's priestly function, the point at which the legitimation religion could afford to the state is most fully incorporated into a single ideological effect. Yet Henry is defensive and troubled by the exchange, and Williams is not satisfied. What has happened, surely, is that the concentration of ideological power upon Henry seems to amount also to a concentration of responsibility:

> Upon the king! let us our lives, our souls,
> Our debts, our careful wives,
> Our children, and our sins, lay on the king!
>
> (4.1.236–38)

In the play the drive for ideological coherence has systematically displaced the roles of church and aristocracy, and nothing seems to stand between the king and the souls of his subjects who are to die in battle.

Henry handles the issue in two main ways. First, he reduces it to the question of soldiers who have committed serious crimes, for which Henry can then refuse responsibility; initial questions about widows and orphans (4.1.141–43) slip out of sight. Second, the distinction between him and his subjects is effaced by his insistence that 'the King is but a man' (4.1.101–2) and that he himself gains nothing, indeed loses, from the power structure:

> O ceremony, show me but thy worth!
> What is thy soul of adoration?
> Art thou aught else but place, degree, and form,
> Creating awe and fear in other men?
> Wherein thou art less happy, being fear'd,
> Than they in fearing.
>
> (4.1.250–55)

Here the king himself is collapsed, syntactically, into the mere shows of ceremony: 'thou' in the third line quoted refers to 'ceremony', in the fifth to Henry, and he slips from one to the other without the customary formal signals.[19] The effect, if we credit it, is to leave 'place, degree, and form', 'awe and fear' standing without the apparent support of human agency: Henry engrosses in himself the ideological coherence of the state and then, asked to take responsibility for the likely defeat at Agincourt, claims to be an effect of the structure he seemed to guarantee.

The act 2 Chorus wants to proclaim unity: 'honour's thought / Reigns solely in the breast of every man' – but is rapidly obliged to admit treachery: 'O England . . . Were all thy children kind and natural' (lines 3–4, 16, 19). The following scene is not, however, about Cambridge, Scrope, and Grey, but about Nym, Bardolph, and Pistol. This disputatious faction proves much more difficult to incorporate than the rebel nobility. Increasingly, since 2 Henry IV, sympathy for these characters has been withdrawn; from this point on there seems to be nothing positive about them. It is here that Fluellen enters, offering an alternative to Falstaff among the lesser gentry and an issue – the control of England over the British Isles – easier to cope with. Fluellen may be funny, old-fashioned, and pedantic, but he is totally committed to the king and his purposes, as the king recognizes (4.1.83–84). The low characters are condemned not only to death but also to exclusion from national unity; it is as if they have had their chance and squandered it. Gower describes Pistol as 'a gull, a fool, a rogue, that now and then goes to the wars, to grace himself at his return into London under the form of a soldier' (3.6.68–70), and Bardolph endorses the identification:

Well, bawd I'll turn,
And something lean to cut-purse of quick hand.
To England will I steal, and there I'll steal:
And patches will I get unto these cudgell'd scars,
And swear I got them in the Gallia wars.

(5.1.89–93)

This group, disbanded soldiers, was a persistent danger and worry in Elizabethan society; William Hunt suggests that 'embittered veterans and deserters brought back from the Low Countries the incendiary myth of an army of avengers'. Two proclamations were issued in 1589 against 'the great outrages that have been, and are daily committed by soldiers, mariners and others that pretend to have served as soldiers, upon her Highness' good and loving subjects'; martial law was instituted to hang offenders.[20] The Elizabethan state was prepared to exclude such persons from its tender care, perhaps exemplifying the principle whereby dominant groups identify themselves by excluding or expelling others; not only are the virtues necessary for membership identified by contrast with the vices of the excluded but, often, the vices of the dominant are displaced onto the excluded. That Pistol has this degree of significance is suggested by the play's reluctance to let him go. He is made to discredit himself once more at Agincourt (4.4), and in his final confrontation with Fluellen he is clumsily humiliated (5.1).

Despite the thorough dismissal of Bardolph, Nym, and Pistol, Henry V does not leave the issue of lower-class disaffection. If those characters must be abandoned because unworthy or incapable of being incorporated into the unified nation, others must be introduced who will prove more tractable.

The issue of the English domination of Wales, Scotland, and Ireland appears in the play to be more containable, though over the centuries it may have caused more suffering and injustice than the subjection of the lower classes. The scene of the four captains (3.3) seems to effect an effortless incorporation, one in which, as

Philip Edwards has pointed out, the Irish Macmorris is even made to protest that he does not belong to a distinct nation.[21] The English captain, of course, is more sensible than the others. Most attention is given to Fluellen – Wales must have seemed the most tractable issue, for it had been annexed in 1536, and the English church and legal system had been imposed; Henry V and the Tudors could indeed claim to be Welsh. The jokes about the way Fluellen pronounces the English language have, apparently, for Elizabethan audiences and many since, been an adequate way of handling the repression of Welsh language and culture; the annexation of 1536 permitted only English speakers to hold administrative office in Wales.[22]

Ireland was the great problem – the one Essex was supposed to resolve. The population was overwhelmingly Catholic and liable to support a continental invader, and resistance to English rule proved irrepressible, despite or, more probably, because of the many atrocities committed against the people – such as the slaughter of all the six hundred inhabitants of Rathlin Island by John Norris and Francis Drake in 1575. The assumption that the Irish were a barbarous and inferior people was so ingrained in Elizabethan England that it seemed no more than a natural duty to subdue them and destroy their culture. Indeed, at one level, their ideological containment was continuous with the handling of the disaffected lower-class outgroup (a proclamation of 1594 dealt together with vagabonds who begged 'upon pretense of service in the wars without relief' and 'men of Ireland that have these late years unnaturally served as rebels against her majesty's forces beyond the seas').[23] But much more was at stake in the persistent Irish challenge to the power of the Elizabethan state, and it should be related to the most strenuous challenge to English unity in *Henry V*: like Philip Edwards, we see the attempt to conquer France and the union in peace at the end of the play as a representation of the attempt to conquer Ireland and the hoped-for unity of Britain.[24] The play offers a displaced, imaginary resolution of one of the state's most intractable problems.

Indeed, the play is fascinating precisely to the extent that it is implicated in and can be read to disclose both the struggles of its own historical moment and their representations. To see the play in such terms is not at all to conclude that it is merely a deluded and mystifying ideological fantasy. We have observed that the king finally has difficulty, on the eve of Agincourt, in sustaining the responsibility that seems to belong with the ideological power that he has engrossed to himself: thus the fantasy of establishing ideological unity in the sole figure of the monarch arrives at an impasse that it can handle only with difficulty. As we have argued, strategies of containment presuppose centrifugal tendencies, and how far any particular instance carries conviction cannot be resolved by literary criticism. If we attend to the play's different levels of signification rather than its implied containments, it becomes apparent that the question of conviction is finally a question about the diverse conditions of reception. How far the king's argument is to be credited is a standard question for conventional criticism, but a materialist analysis takes several steps back and reads real historical conflict in and through his ambiguities. Relative to such conflict, the question of Henry's integrity becomes less interesting.

[From the preceding two paragraphs as originally published, Richard Levin has drawn the assertion that 'according to Jonathan Dollimore and Alan Sinfield, the project of *Henry V* is the 'establishing [of the] ideological unity' of the state and its class system and the 'ideological containment' of threats to it'.[25] The words in quotation marks have indeed just appeared; the reader may judge whether in context they mean what Levin says they mean.]

If *Henry V* represents the fantasy of a successful Irish campaign, it also offers, from the very perspective of that project, a disquietingly excessive evocation of suffering and violence:

> If not, why, in a moment look to see
> The blind and bloody soldier with foul hand
> Defile the locks of your shrill-shrieking daughters;
> Your fathers taken by the silver beards,
> And their most reverend heads dash'd to the walls;
> Your naked infants spitted upon pikes,
> Whiles the mad mothers with their howls confus'd
> Do break the clouds, as did the wives of Jewry
> At Herod's bloody hunting slaughtermen.
>
> (3.3.33–41)

This reversal of Henry's special claim to Christian imagery – now he is Herod against the Innocents – is not actualized in the play (contrary to the sources, in which Harfleur is sacked), but its rhetoric is powerful, and at Agincourt the prisoners are killed (4.6.37). Here and elsewhere, the play dwells upon imagery of slaughter to a degree that disrupts the harmonious unity towards which ideology strives. So it was with Ireland: even those who, like the poet Edmund Spenser, defended torture and murder expressed compunction at the effects of English policy: '[The Irish] were brought to such wretchedness, as that any stony heart would have rued the same. Out of every corner of the woods and glens they came creeping forth upon their hands, for their legs would not bear them. . . . They did eat of the dead carions.'[26]

The human cost of imperial ambition protruded through even its ideological justifications, and the government felt obliged to proclaim that its intention was not 'an utter extirpation and rooting out of that nation'.[27] The claim of the English state to be the necessary agent of peace and justice was manifestly contradicted. Ireland was, and remains, its bad conscience.

Henry V can be read to reveal not only the rulers' strategies of power, but also the anxieties informing both them and their ideological representation. In the Elizabethan theater, to foreground and even to promote such representations was not to foreclose on their interrogation. We might conclude from this that Shakespeare was indeed wonderfully impartial on the question of politics (as the quotations in our opening paragraph claim); alternatively, we might conclude that the ideology that saturates his texts, and their location in history, are the most interesting things about them.

MASCULINITY

Sexualities and genders constitute a further ground of disturbance in the England of *Henry V*, overlapping the preceding discussion at virtually every point. Of course, critics have discovered ideal unities here also. To old historicists, the marriage of Henry to Princess Katharine is the key embodiment of the harmony supposedly attained at the play's closure. This attitude is still active; for George L. Geckle, Henry's wooing of Katharine is 'a microcosmic reflection of the macrocosmic conflict between the two nations of England and France with the English representing masculine aggressiveness and the French representing feminine passivity'. Fortunately the princess, as her 'bawdy English lesson' proves, 'is a normal young woman in her private life and worthy of England's finest'. So the king manifests 'a truly integrated personality' and brings 'political order out of disorder and sexual unity out of an aggressive courtship'.[28] The feminist challenge to such genial complacency has sometimes taken a psychoanalytic perspective that regards sexuality as mainly an individual matter. Linda Bamber believes that 'by refusing the simple code of manliness [Hal/Henry] becomes more of a man than he would by accepting it'; Peter Erickson holds that 'the ending of *Henry V* proposes to round out the king's character by providing him with a woman, but this proposal cannot be enacted because his character is too entrenched in a narrow masculinity. All emotional depth is concentrated in male relations.'[29] Both these psychoanalytic readings depend on a binary composed of the individual psyche and a normative curve of maturation that the individual is supposed to achieve. Thus they reconstitute a metaphysic of teleological integration comparable to that supposed in earlier criticism; they relocate it for literary intellectuals of our time, for whom notions like God and national unity are problematic, in the individual psyche.

Rather, sexualities, genders, and the norms proposed for them are principal constructs through which ideologies are organized, diversely in diverse cultures but always with reference to power structures that are far wider than individuals and their psyches. They are major sites of ideological production upon which meanings of very diverse kinds are established and contested. That the ideological maneuverings already addressed in *Henry V* are continuous in scope and relevance with sexualities and genders is evident from the way they present similar patterns: potentially insubordinate features are expelled after being demonized, or incorporated after being represented as inherently submissive. Even so, again, state orthodoxy proves unable entirely to banish the specter of revolt. This is not to say that sexuality produces some pure, unmediated revolt of the body against ideology, in the manner suggested by some followers of Bakhtin.[30] But genders and sexualities, like other ideological formations, cannot but allow skeptical interrogation as well as acquiescence. Even the marriage of Henry and Katharine, which has often seemed a triumphant achievement of state and individual integration, proves in its historical context to hold a specific residuum of anxiety.

It is often said that women have little place in the history plays because the men there define themselves against other men.[31] In a way, this is true, but the men do this through constant reference to ideas of the feminine and the female (once again, the matter is not adequately addressed at the level of individuality alone). At the start of the play, the feminine and the female are invoked only to be set aside as the state gears itself for war: 'Silken dalliance in the wardrobe lies', the Chorus says at the start of act 2; and Mistress Quickly is brought in to marry Pistol so that, like the wives of Hotspur and Mortimer in *I Henry IV*, she can be abandoned for war (2.3). This is the pattern we have observed with other disorderly elements: genders and sexualities are among the potential disruptions that Henry must incorporate or expel in order to appear the undivided leader of an undivided kingdom. However, as it transpires, this exclusion of sexual disruption has to be repeated all through the play: banishment of the feminine and the female, even as these are conceived of by the masculine and the patriarchal, cannot easily be achieved. One reason is that Henry's title to the lands of France depends on Edward III's mother – Isabella, daughter of Philip IV of France. The French declare that their Salic law bars such succession through the female line: 'they would hold up this Salic law / To bar your highness claiming from the female'.[32] The archbishop counters that Salic law is not properly applied to the lands of France (1.2.32–64), and that diverse claims through the female line have already been asserted there. However, this latter argument contributes to the play's nervousness about the female, for the claims of Pepin, Hugh Capet, and Lewis X through the female line seem, in the archbishop's presentation, to have involved continuous quarreling and uncertainty (1.2.64–95).

In fact, this dependence upon female influence over inheritance, legitimacy, and the state produces so much anxiety that the English can hardly bring themselves to name it. The crucial fact that Isabella was daughter of Philip IV and mother of Edward III is not actually stated by the archbishop. Gary Taylor suggests in his Oxford edition of the play that 'Shakespeare assumes his audience's familiarity with this fact, as Canterbury assumes Henry's' (p. 102). Perhaps. But Henry's *male* lineage, which was certainly more familiar, is repeatedly reasserted. The archbishop, enthusiastic as he is about Henry's pedigree, does not invite him to dwell upon Isabella, his great-great grandmother:

> Look back into your mighty ancestors:
> Go, my dread lord, to your great-grandsire's tomb,
> From whom you claim; invoke his warlike spirit,
> And your great-uncle's, Edward the Black Prince . . .

> (1.2.102–5)

The more important the female influence, the more the masculinity of the English must be stressed. This is perhaps why the archbishop's speech has so often been found problematic in the theater, and may even be played for laughs as the foolish jargon of a legalistic mind: the speech is unfocused because it cannot admit its central concern. Even the pedigree Exeter presents to the French shows Henry 'evenly deriv'd / From his most fam'd of famous ancestors, / Edward the Third' (2.4.911–13), apparently not mentioning the source of the claim, the maternal lineage of Edward himself. Phyllis Rackin has shown how this topic informs *King John*: 'The son's name and entitlement and legitimacy all derived from the father, and only the father was included in the historiographic text. But only the mother could guarantee that legitimacy. As bearers of the life that names, titles, and historical records could never fully represent, the women were keepers of the unspoken and unspeakable reality that always threatened to belie the words that pretended to describe it.'[33]

In *Henry V*, the superior manliness of the English is so insisted upon that it comes to appear the main validation of their title: because they are more manly than the French, they are more fit to rule anywhere. Before Harfleur, the king exhorts his army in these terms:

> On, on, you noblest English!
> Whose blood is fet from fathers of war-proof;
> Fathers that, like so many Alexanders,
> Have in these parts from morn till even fought,
> And sheath'd their swords for lack of argument.
> Dishonour not your mothers; now attest
> That those whom you call'd fathers did beget you.

> (3.1.17–23)

The danger Henry disavows is that his men might not be truly descended from their warlike fathers; their mothers' contribution is envisaged as either facilitating the transmission of English male qualities or impeding them by cuckolding their husbands. Hence Henry's ready threatening of the citizens of Harfleur, three times in his speech before the town, with rape: 'What is't to me', he asks, 'If your pure maidens fall into the hand / Of hot and forcing violation?' (3.3.20–21). On the one hand, this shows that Henry is too much of a man to worry if the lads go a bit too far; in fact, his scopophilic anticipation is disconcertingly fulsome. On the other, the speech exhibits an uneasy identification with the fear he attributes to the men of Harfleur, that women's sexuality is a likely ground of male humiliation.

The most persistent alarm is not that women will intrude upon the state and its wars, but that the men will prove inadequate. The 'feminine' and the 'effeminate' appear, alongside the female, fatally tainted by it, and as attributes applicable to men. The opposition is starkly presented in *1 Henry IV* through Hotspur's dismissal of the 'popinjay' who upset him after the real men had been having one of their battles by being 'perfumed like a milliner' and talking 'like a waiting-gentlewoman'.[34] But suppose 'effeminacy' gets into the mainstream of the state? – already the popinjay positions the Court as effete center versus manly margin. At the margins of the city, Bolingbroke complains at the end of *Richard II*, the Prince of Wales is in the taverns with 'unrestrained loose companions':

> he, young wanton, and effeminate boy,
> Takes on the point of honour to support
> So dissolute a crew.[35]

'Effeminacy' in early modern England included virtually everything that was not claimed as distinctively masculine. In *Richard III*, the king is credited (falsely) with 'gentle, kind, effeminate remorse' in being reluctant to depose his brother's son – it is implied that he will have to overcome it for the good of the commonwealth. Too much devotion to women produces effeminacy (I cease the quotation marks, but it should be remembered that this is a coercive construct, not a natural category).

Romeo, distressed at his failure to defend Mercutio, complains that Juliet's beauty 'hath made me effeminate'.[36] Effeminacy is any male falling away from the proper totality of masculine essence. Hence the banishment of Falstaff in *2 Henry IV* and, more decisively, his death in *Henry V*. Falstaff represents in part effeminate devotion to women (though there is far more talk of that than action), and in part male bonding with the 'wrong' person (interpreted lately as homosexuality, since that has become the most prominent kind of 'wrong' male bonding). The relation between these two aspects of effeminacy will appear shortly. But above all, with his drinking, eating, jesting, and fatness, Falstaff embodies unmasculine *relaxation* – loosening, softening, languishing, letting go. He is 'fat-witted with drinking of old sack, and unbuttoning thee after supper, and sleeping upon benches after noon'; if his girdle breaks, his guts will fall about his knees. Bolingbroke defined the prince's effeminacy as consorting with 'unrestrained loose companions'.[37] The masculine, conversely, is represented as *taut*, often with phallic connotation: 'Stiffen the sinews', Henry urges before Harfleur, 'Now set the teeth and stretch the nostril wide, / Hold hard the breath, and bend up every spirit / To his full height! . . . I see you stand like greyhounds in the slips, / Straining upon the start' (3.1.7, 15–17, 31–32). Rachel Blau DuPlessis, in her essay 'For the Etruscans', quotes Frances Jaffer on gendering in the customary language of criticism: ' "lean, dry, terse, powerful, strong, spare, linear, focused, explosive" – god forbid it should be "limp"!! But – "soft, moist, blurred, padded, irregular, going round in circles", and other descriptions of *our* bodies – the very *abyss* of aesthetic judgment.'[38] 'Screw your courage to the sticking-place', Lady Macbeth says, wanting her husband to be a man; he says he will 'bend up / Each corporal agent' (1.7.61, 80–81). Prince Hal worries his father because effeminate behavior means a general failure to remain lean and taut for active male responsibility – though in fact the king is nearer the truth when he describes the prince as having his feminine qualities under proper restriction:

> He hath a tear for pity, and a hand
> Open as day for melting charity:
> Yet notwithstanding, being incens'd, he's flint.

The dominance of the latter quality in the reign of Henry V is demonstrated when Mistress Quickly and Doll Tearsheet are taken to be whipped as accessories to manslaughter ('for the woman is dead that you and Pistol beat'). Prostitution and motherhood – ultimate marks of male dependence upon the female – coincide in Doll's fake or real pregnancy; and the beadles are said to be notably thin.[39]

Both the English and French men figure their countries as women requiring masculine control. In the French view, Henry's effeminacy renders him an unlikely challenger for the female French body:

> there's nought in France
> That can be with a nimble galliard won;
> You cannot revel into dukedoms there.

> (1.2.251–53)

The effeminate virtues of courtship are irrelevant, France has to be taken by force – and, indeed, we do not see Henry trying to win the hearts of French citizens. Nor is it only that the monarch would need masculine vigor. As Jean Howard observes, 'the legitimacy of the monarch is always a question in the history play, and the impression of legitimacy depends in part both on the monarch's production of gender difference and on the powerful subordination of the feminine to masculine authority'.[40] The Dauphin believes Henry has not the male charisma to dominate France – England

>   is so idly king'd
> Her sceptre so fantastically borne
> By a vain, giddy, shallow, humorous youth,
> That fear attends her not.

> (2.4.26–29)

In fact the charge of effeminacy is made by both sides – by the French against the English and by the play against the French. The latter seek to establish their superiority by bragging continually of their manly strength. 'My horse is my mistress', declares the Dauphin, 'I once writ a sonnet in his praise' (3.7.41–42, 45). A series of misogynist puns follows. However, the French overdo it and appear florid and effete; the Dauphin's horse is referred to as a 'palfrey', suggesting a lady's mount.[41] At Agincourt, the French are wearing 'gay new coats' while the English have 'not a piece of feather in our host' (4.3.112, 118). The English are the real men, and this masculinity seems to legitimate their war effort. When the French realize this, they apprehend it at once in terms of power over women:

> Our madams mock at us, and plainly say
> Our mettle is bred out; and they will give
> Their bodies to the lust of English youth
> To new-store France with bastard warriors.

> (3.5.28–31)

These attitudes run through the English too: Nym and Pistol dispute over Mistress Quickly (2.1), and even the deferential Fluellen has to prove his manhood against Macmorris and Pistol (3.2.132–35; 3.6.84–86; 5.1). There seems nothing else to talk about. However, Henry's manhood is supposed to be effortless – when he finds himself boasting of English superiority, he quickly attributes such vaunting to the air of France (3.6.155–58).

In all this, women are the losers, as Henry readily acknowledges when throwing back the French challenge: 'many a thousand widows / Shall this his mock mock out of their dear husbands; / Mock mothers from their sons' (1.2.284–86). The terms get even more unpleasant when defeat is likely. Bourbon says of the Frenchman who will not return with him to the field at Agincourt,

> Let him go hence, and with his cap in hand,
> Like a base pandar, hold the chamber-door
> Whilst by a slave, no gentler than my dog,
> His fairest daughter is contaminated.

> (4.5.13–16)

The price of male failure is greater oppression of women. The other losers are men who do not relish such adventures. The Chorus at the start of act 3 says England is left

> Guarded with grandsires, babies, and old women,
> Either past or not arriv'd to pith and puissance:
> For who is he, whose chin is but enrich'd
> With one appearing hair, that will not follow
> These cull'd and choice-drawn cavaliers to France?

(lines 20–24)

Who indeed? There may be such men, but they are obviously under considerable coercion to conform. The king at Agincourt says those not present may 'hold their manhoods cheap whiles any speak / That fought with us upon Saint Crispin's day' (4.3.66–67). No space is left for a kind of manhood that would not be fighting. Of course, all strongly held convictions tend to place pressure upon those who disagree, but assertive masculinity is oppressive in principle, for it justifies itself by its success in intimidating others.

Plainly we are on the territory of the homosocial, as Eve Sedgwick has identified it: 'the status of women, and the whole question of arrangements between genders, is deeply and inescapably inscribed in the structure even of relationships that seem to exclude women – even in male homosocial/homosexual relationships'. The English and French men fight over the bodies of France and French women, giving great attention to their standing with each other and precious little to the welfare of their peoples. However, the cement of their homosocial rivalry is not, in this version, hostility towards homosexuality, as Sedgwick finds it to be in our modern cultures. As she and others have shown, the place of same-sex love was not the same in early modern England as now, and hence 'the structure of homosocial continuums [must be] culturally contingent, not an innate feature of either "maleness" or "femaleness" '.[42] In *Henry V*, I see no sign that homosexuality is distinctly apprehended as a category. Effeminacy, as constructed in the play, is not specifically linked to same-sex physical passion; its stigma is, more directly, associated with regression towards the female. This is compatible with a major strand in early modern gender theory, which has been shown to derive from Galen and Aristotle. In brief, it was held that women and men were not essentially different biologically; rather, women were taken to be incomplete versions of men, falling short of the highest kind of creation.[43] Conversely, the danger for the male was effeminacy – the disastrous slide back into the female; and same-sex passion was relatively unimportant. Masculine qualities in a female might be even admired, at least in some circumstances, as an upward movement. England did well in a manly way when previously her menfolk were fighting in France:

> When all her chivalry hath been in France
> And she a mourning widow of her nobles,
> She hath herself not only well defended,
> But taken and impounded as a stray
> The King of Scots.

(1.2.157–61)

Queen Elizabeth at the time of the Armada might declare, 'I know I have the body of a weak and feeble woman, but I have the heart and stomach of a king'.[44] But the idea of the male regressing to the female always made for anxiety. Patroclus warns Achilles in *Troilus and Cressida*, in respect of Achilles' devotion to Hector's sister, Polyxena,

> A woman impudent and mannish grown
> Is not more loath'd than an effeminate man
> In time of action.

Those are the priorities; and the relationship between Achilles and Patroclus is not in question, because it does not undermine warrior values – Patroclus, although he has 'little stomach to the war', is urging Achilles to fight. Stephen Orgel summarizes: 'The fear of effeminization is a central element in all discussions of what constitutes a "real man" in the period, and the fantasy of the reversal of the natural transition from woman to man underlies it.'[45] How precarious, and how cultural, masculinity might be is illustrated by an instance offered in Spenser's *View of the Present State of Ireland*:

Then when Cyrus had overcome the Lydians that were a warlike nation, and devised to bring them to a more peacable life, he changed their apparel and music, and instead of their short warlike coats, clothed them in long garments like wives, and instead of their warlike music, appointed to them certain lascivious lays and loose gigs, by which in short space their minds were so mollified and abated that they forgot their former fierceness and became most tender and effeminate.[46]

The most surprising passage in *Henry V* – one that, because it is hard to handle in our cultures, has attracted little comment – is the love-death of Suffolk and York at Agincourt:

> Suffolk first died; and York, all haggled over,
> Comes to him, where in gore he lay insteep'd,
> And takes him by the beard, kisses the gashes
> That bloodily did yawn upon his face;
> And cries aloud, 'Tarry, my cousin Suffolk!
> My soul shall thine keep company to heaven;
> Tarry, sweet soul, for mine, then fly abreast,
> As in this glorious and well-foughten field
> We kept together in our chivalry!'
> Upon these words I came and cheer'd him up –,
> He smil'd me in the face, taught me his hand,
> And, with a feeble gripe, says, 'Dear my lord,
> Commend my service to my sovereign.'
> So did he turn, and over Suffolk's neck
> He threw his wounded arm, and kiss'd his lips;
> And so espous'd to death, with blood he seal'd
> A testament of noble-ending love.

The pretty and sweet manner of it forc'd
These waters from me which I would have stopp'd;
But I had not so much of man in me,
And all my mother came into mine eyes
And gave me up to tears.

(4.6.11–32)

York kisses Suffolk twice, on the gashes on his face and on the lips; Gary Taylor notes uneasily that 'Shakespeare's contemporaries were less squeamish than we about men kissing men' (p. 241), but that hardly addresses the emotional weight of the scene. Suffolk is called 'sweet soul', embraced, 'espous'd' (I think – the referent is uncertain). Their 'testament of noble-ending love' is called 'pretty and sweet'. And Exeter's response is to weep, to lose manly control, to surrender himself to the feminine response inherited from his mother. In this play, no behavior could be more highly charged, and the episode is placed at the point where the battle is still in question, where its particular emotions may be most finely apprehended. What is apparent is that same-sex passion, when sufficiently committed to masculine warrior values, is admired, even at the point where it slides towards the feminine. 'In this glorious and well-foughten field / We kept together in our chivalry! . . . Commend my service to my sovereign.' In such a context of devotion to the state, its fighting and its command structure, there is no damaging effeminacy in same-sex passion; it is women and popinjays that are the danger (the same considerations apply to Coriolanus and Aufidius). Intense emotion between men, so long as it is associated with something manly like trying to kill people, is not a drawback; on the contrary, it is the implicit goal and ultimate expression of their efforts.[47] There is a deal of this in the rage against the treacherous noblemen in act 2 scene 2. Over Suffolk and York, Henry finds himself moved to 'mistful eyes', but only for a moment: news that the French have reinforced their men recalls him to manly matters and he orders, unsentimentally, the killing of prisoners (4.6.33–37).

MISCEGENATION

It should not now need demonstrating that Princess Katharine is planted in the play as the reward for and final validation of Henry's manliness, the symbol of enforced French submission.[48] She is reported to be on offer to the English in the act 3 Chorus – directly before Henry's rape speech at Harfleur. Immediately after the entering of Harfleur, she is shown learning how to translate her body into language accessible to the English (3.4). In Henry's 'wooing', he does not disguise that she is under compulsion. When she asks if she could possibly love the enemy of France, he finds opportunity for a joke: 'I love France so well that I will not part with a village of it'; when she says it must be as it pleases her father, he replies 'Nay, it will please him well, Kate; it shall please him, Kate'. The deal has already been struck, and she is 'our capital demand' (5.2.178–80, 261–63, 96). Nevertheless, critics have shied away from the thought that, after the princess's initial refusal to submit to the pretense that Henry is a courtly wooer, the king resorts to a sadistic exercise of power over her. The scene may certainly be played in that way. Henry is only too ready to repudiate once more the effeminate virtues of men who can dance and 'rhyme themselves into ladies' favours' for those of the 'plain soldier' (lines 134–73). The princess's inability to respond fluently leaves her vulnerable to long, cajoling speeches in which she is overwhelmed, like France before her, by the power of England. 'It is as easy for me, Kate, to conquer the kingdom as to speak so much more French', Henry says (lines 191–92), but since he is the conqueror, he can use English when he wants to. For it doesn't really matter whether the princess understands him, though she must realize well enough that she is being browbeaten. Calling her so insistently 'Kate' (twenty-eight times in the interview) is part of the humiliation: she cannot prevent the anglicization or the intimacy – Gary Taylor points out that the name was 'associated with promiscuous women'.[49] To be sure, an arranged marriage is only what one should expect; there is no precedent in the chronicles for any personal interaction. What complicates the betrothal ideologically is the attempt of the king to throw some kind of romantic veil over his conquest (as if they were Beatrice and Benedick just looking for an excuse to get together), and without even questioning male dominance (unlike Beatrice and Benedick). In *The Famous Victories of Henry the Fift*, from which the betrothal scene derives (printed in Walter's edition, pp. 165–67), the king is represented as falling genuinely in love with Katheren, to the point where he regards his defeat of the French as a disadvantage (likely to prejudice her against him), and she persuades him to abate his demands for territory; she has as many lines as he. In this scenario feminine values are made to win out, perhaps at a cost in plausibility. But in *Henry V* they tangle inconclusively: the text wants the king to display excellence in this skirmish as he has in all the others, but shrinks from allowing him to become contaminated with the effeminacy of wooing. (Of course, this is not Henry's individual failure, but another instance of the faultline, identified in chapter 2, whereby marriage was supposed to be both the means through which property and inheritance were arranged and also a fulfilling personal relationship.) Only when he has dominated Katharine by kissing her does Henry discover an element of yielding to her in himself; ominously enough, he attaches it to the most potent and demonized image for illegitimate female wiles: 'You have witchcraft in your lips, Kate' (line 292). The peak of personal emotion in the play remains the love-death of Suffolk and York.

Commentators have said that Katharine is submissive,[50] but she need not be played quite like that. In fact, she may be seen as avoiding collusion with Henry's approaches through a minimalist strategy of one-line replies – the least that courtesy requires. 'I cannot tell', she says three times. 'I do not know', her father must decide. She declines to join in the pretense that her preferences matter – it is as much resistance as she can manage. In the customary masculine manner, Henry decides that her reluctance means yes: 'Come, I know thou lovest me' (line 205). But there is no reason (only sexist assumptions) to believe that Katharine is coy or teasing. When she objects to the king kissing her hand – insisting on the power relations – that it is inappropriate for a conqueror ('mon très puissant seigneur') to abase his grandeur and kiss the hand of 'votre seigneurie indigne serviteur' – he takes it as a pretext to kiss her lips. She objects that this is not the custom in France, but he overrides her ('nice customs curtsy to great kings'), stops her mouth (as such men like to say), and forces her: 'therefore, patiently and yielding . . .' (lines 265–91).

I am not saying that this is the 'right' way to play the scene. Rather, as was argued earlier, the text is implicated, necessarily, in the complexities of its culture, and manifests not only the strategies of power but also the anxieties that protrude through them, making it possible always to glimpse alternative understandings. The traditional reading – the triumph of personal and international peace and harmony through the betrothal of Henry and Katharine – is not a different scene from the one I propose, in which she is recognized as one figure in a far larger ideological structure of sexualities and genders. It is an alternative reading of the same scene, one the text cannot but license in some measure. As Lance Wilcox puts it in his essay on the play, with evident reference to the current state of the law in many countries, 'When is a rapist not a rapist? When he's a husband.'[51] Whether the betrothal of Katharine appears delightful or oppressive depends on the framework of assumptions readers and audiences bring to it. Even so, my story of Katharine's recalcitrance gains support from Henry's complaint when the others return: 'I cannot so conjure up the spirit of love in her, that he will appear in his true likeness.' She has not performed properly to his script, so he threatens to demand more French cities (lines 306–8, 334–37). Burgundy's solution is to engage Henry in a sequence of bawdy innuendoes that positions Katharine, apparently in her hearing, as the merest object of male use. Cities and maids, it is said once more, are the same: 'for they are all girded with maiden walls that war hath never entered' (lines 339–41). The princess, Burgundy means, must be forced, and Henry will get the cities eventually through the marriage. They drop the pretense of seeking Katharine's consent; she does not speak again.

Despite the bullying of Henry and the other men – and this is the kind of point of ideological contradiction against which no text can entirely protect itself – the state cannot be secured against female influence. The betrothal, of course, is witness to that: it is to confirm his claim to France that Henry marries the French king's daughter. English unease at this is evident in the demand that the French king name Henry 'Notre très cher filz Henry, Roy d'Angleterre, Héritier de France' (5.2.357–58). It sounds as if Henry is the lineal son of the French monarch, but actually such nomination depends on his wife. Henry is following the precedent of Edward III's father at the start of the story, inviting once more the embarrassment of the royal title passing through the female. In fact, fear of miscegenation – always a complication in imperialism – has been a major preoccupation all through the play; xenophobia and racism often accompany male homosocial insecurity. The archbishop's explanation of Salic law is that it was devised to prevent conquerors from marrying local women:

> Charles the Great having subdued the Saxons,
> There left behind and settled certain French;
> Who, holding in disdain the German women
> For some dishonest manners of their life,

Establish'd then this law; to wit, no female
Should be inheritrix in Salic land.

(1.2.46–51)

The French draw upon this attitude to dismiss the English, regarding them as degenerate consequences of their men mating with native women after the Norman conquest of 1066 (it is another way of blaming women):

O Dieu vivant! shall a few sprays of us,
The emptying of our fathers' luxury,
Our scions, put in wild and savage stock,
Spirt up so suddenly into the clouds,
And overlook their grafters?

(3.5.5–9)

If this is a danger, Henry is courting it by grafting English virtues onto French stock. The French queen welcomes the prospect 'That English may as French, French Englishmen, / Receive each other' (5.2.385–86). But such sexual mingling, in the terms the play has established, involves contamination of English masculinity with French effeminacy. Henry has hopes of a soldier son, he tells Katharine, typically writing a script for her:

If ever thou beest mine, Kate, as I have a saving faith within me tells me thou shalt, I get thee with scambling, and thou must therefore needs prove a good soldier-breeder. Shall not thou and I, between Saint Denis and Saint George, compound a boy, half French, half English, that shall go to Constantinople and take the Turk by the beard? shall we not? what sayest thou, my fair flower de-luce?

(5.2.211–18)

But the ideology of the play has made this unlikely, for it has maintained that the French (whom the princess is made to personify in the last phrase quoted) are *not* good soldier-breeders. The point is evidently in Henry's mind when he adds: 'do but now promise, Kate, you will endeavour for your French part of such a boy, and for my English moiety take the word of a king and a bachelor' (lines 223–26). There is no problem (of course) about Henry's capacity, but Katharine must promise to make a special effort. 'Take her, fair son', says the French king, 'and from her blood raise up / Issue to me' (lines 366–67). The issue have to be French to strengthen the English claim to French territory, but by just so much, the rhetoric of the play has been saying, they will be effeminate, French-style men, and hence unable to defend that territory. Henry V cannot secure his imperial inheritance without putting it at risk from female influence. So the unfortunate reign of Henry VI, with its 'weak' king and dangerous women, is biologically encoded through a kind of Social Darwinism. Immediately at the opening of 1 *Henry VI* the son of Katharine and Henry V is called 'an effeminate prince'; a campaign over the French cities ensues, concluding with their loss through an 'effeminate peace'.[52]

All this was important because contemporary monarchs, including Elizabeth and her presumed successor, James VI, relied on claims through the female line, albeit reluctantly. But the attribution of military failure to female influence through miscegenation found its most immediate current shape in respect of anxieties about the current imperial project in Ireland. The devastation of France described at length by Burgundy (once more in terms of a need for sexual control [5.2.29–67]) sounds much too extensive to be the outcome of Henry V's relatively limited operations along the coast of Normandy; far more like the consequences of English policy in Ireland as it was described in many contemporary accounts, with agriculture destroyed and the people grown 'like savages' (line 59). In his *View of the Present State of Ireland*, Spenser laments that the English who have been settled there identify with Irish rather than English interests, to the point of preferring to speak Erse: 'It seemeth strange to me that the English should take more delight to speak that language than their own, whereas they should (methinks) rather take scorn to acquaint their tongues thereto, for it hath been ever the use of the conquerer to despise the language of the conquered, and to force him by all means to learn his.' This latter, of course, is the tendency manifested by Henry. The reason it did not work out in Ireland, Spenser says, is 'fostering and marrying with the Irish'. In Spenser's view, such intermingling is extremely undesirable; because of it 'great houses . . . have degendered from their ancient dignities and now are grown as Irish as O'Hanlan's breech, (as the proverb there is)'. Though some great men have successfully made 'such matches with their vassals, and have of them nevertheless raised worthy issue . . . yet the example is so perilous as it is not to be adventured'. For 'how can such matching but bring forth an evil race, seeing that commonly the child taketh most of his nature of the mother, besides speech, manners, inclination, which are for the most part agreeable to the conditions of their mothers?' Henry VII and Elizabeth passed acts against intermarriage in Ireland, and other commentators confirmed the dangers – Richard Stanyhurst, Barnaby Rich, and William Herbert.[53] By this analysis, Henry's marriage is a considerable blunder. He tells Katharine: 'England is thine, Ireland is thine, France is thine, and Henry Plantagenet is thine' (5.2.252–53). But each of those four imperial claims is fraught with the seeds of its own falsification. The dominant again proves inseparable from that which it seeks to control.

In some respects, my account has produced distinctions between ideas of genders and sexualities in early modern England and today. Nevertheless, there are also continuities: imperialist, xenophobic, and male homosocial ideologies still often reinforce each other, demonizing the female, the feminine, and the effeminate. The dominance of masculine attributes is represented as 'order', and the answer when that order fails to carry conviction is said to be more order (rulers should be more manly). But because the order was of a kind that produces its own concomitant disorder, as the bellicosity of the English and French produces war, that answer must be futile. Nor, as critics have hoped, is a convenient resolution available in the 'softening' or 'balancing' of manly attributes such as appear in Henry V by placing him in negotiation with the French princess, or even with the love-death of Suffolk and York. For the terms of such negotiations still presuppose, not only the oppressive initial construction of genders and sexualities, but also the anxieties and power assumptions that remain inscribed within them. Critics who believe that Henry becomes more fully human through interaction with the feminine qualities of the princess do not dream of suggesting that the effeminate as such might in any way be redeemed: that remains the 'wrong' kind of femininity, the 'wrong' kind of compromise. The dominant, characteristically, takes from its others what it can incorporate, leaving the remainder more decisively repudiated.

NOTES

1. Reprinted from ALAN SINFIELD, *Faultlines: Cultural Materialism and the Politics of Dissident Reading* (Oxford: Clarendon Press, 1992).

2. A materialist criticism will be concerned with aspects of ideology additional to those dealt with here, and our emphasis on ideology as legitimation, though crucial, should not be taken as an exhaustive definition of the topic. For a fuller discussion of ideology and subjectivity, see [JONATHAN] DOLLIMORE, *Radical Tragedy* (Hemel Hempstead: Harvester, 1984), esp. chs. 1, 10, 16; [JONATHAN] DOLLIMORE AND [ALAN] SINFIELD, eds., *Political Shakespeare: New Essays in Cultural Materialism* (Manchester: Manchester University Press, 1985); and, more generally, JANET WOLFF, *The Social Production of Art* (London: Macmillan, 1981), esp. ch. 3.

3. See STEPHEN ORGEL, 'Making Greatness Familiar', in Stephen Greenblatt, ed., *The Power of Forms in the English Renaissance* (Norman, Okla.: Pilgrim Books, 1982).

4. IAN BREWARD, ed., *The Work of William Perkins* (Abingdon: Sutton Courtenay Press, 1970), p. 150.

5. Ibid., p. 449.

6. LANCELOT ANDREWES, *Works* (Oxford: Clarendon Press, 1841), 1:325.

7. Shakespeare, *Henry V*, ed. JOHN H. WALTER (London: Methuen, 1954), 1.2.211–12.

8. See pp. 175–81, 199–200, and ALAN SINFIELD, *Literature in Protestant England, 1550–1660* (London: Croom Helm, 1983), ch. 7.

9. This distinction derives from (but also differs from) ANTHONY GIDDENS, *A Contemporary Critique of Historical Materialism* (London: Macmillan, 1981), 1:231–37.

10. See RAYMOND WILLIAMS, *Marxism and Literature* (Oxford: Oxford Univ. Press, 1977), pp. 121–27.

11. JOHN STRYPE, *The Life and Acts of John Whitgift* (Oxford: Oxford Univ. Press, 1822), 1:524–26. See further FELICITY HEAL, *Of Prelates and Princes* (Cambridge: Cambridge Univ. Press, 1980).

12. J. E. NEALE, *Elizabeth I and Her Parliaments, 1584–1601* (London: Cape, 1957), pp. 309–10; LUCY DE BRUYN, *Mob-Rule and Riots* (London: Regency, 1981), p. 36.

13. WILLIAM HUNT, *The Puritan Moment* (Cambridge, Mass.: Harvard Univ. Press, 1983), pp. 33, 60–61.

14. See PERRY ANDERSON, *Lineages of the Absolute State* (London: New Left Books, 1974), pp. 16–59, 113–42; W. T. MACCAFFREY, 'England: The Crown and the New Aristocracy, 1540–1600', *Past and Present* 30 (1965): 52–64.

15. G. B. HARRISON, *The Life and Death of Robert Devereux, Earl of Essex* (London: Cassell, 1937), p. 102 and chs. 9–12.

16. Ibid., pp. 214–15.

17. GEOFFREY BULLOUGH, *Narrative and Dramatic Sources of Shakespeare*, vol. 4, *Later English History Plays* (London: Routledge, 1966), p. 386.

18. Andrewes, *Works*, 1:326.

19. See GARY TAYLOR's note to these lines in his Oxford edition of *Henry V* (Oxford: Oxford Univ. Press, 1982).

20. Hunt, *Puritan Moment*, p. 60; de Bruyn, *Mob-Rule*, p. 62; for further instances see Hunt, p. 50; and de Bruyn, p. 26.

21. PHILIP EDWARDS, *Threshold of a Nation* (Cambridge: Cambridge Univ. Press, 1979), pp. 75–78, referring to *Henry V* 3.2.125–27. Edwards shows how an Irish captain who had been in Essex's army made a protest similar to that of Macmorris.

22. DAVID WILLIAMS, *A History of Modern Wales*, 2d ed. (London: John Murray, 1977), ch. 3.

23. PAUL L. HUGHES AND JAMES F. LARKIN, *Tudor Royal Proclamations* (New Haven: Yale Univ. Press, 1969), 3:134–35.

24. Edwards, *Threshold*, pp. 74–86. See DAVID BEERS QUINN, *The Elizabethans and the Irish* (Ithaca, N.Y.: Cornell Univ. Press, 1966), chs. 4, 5, and 7.

25. RICHARD LEVIN, 'The Poetics and Politics of Bardicide', *PMLA* 105 (1990): 491–504.

26. EDMUND SPENSER, *A View of the Present State of Ireland*, ed. W. L. Renwick (Oxford: Clarendon Press, 1970), p. 104.

27. Hughes and Larkin, *Tudor Royal Proclamations*, 3:201.

28. GEORGE L. GECKLE, 'Politics and Sexuality in Shakespeare's Second Tetralogy', in H. W. Matalene, *Romanticism and Culture: A Tribute to Morse Peckham* (Columbia, S.C.: Camden House, 1984), pp. 130–31. The second half of the present chapter is new; Jonathan Dollimore and I have sometimes been asked why we did not address the sexual politics of *Henry V* in this essay as it appeared in *Alternative Shakespeares*, edited by John Drakakis. The answer is that other essays in *Alternative Shakespeares* were to do that (see the fine contributions of Jacqueline Rose and Catherine Belsey), and we had a strict word limit in which to attempt the complex topic of ideology.

29. LINDA BAMBER, *Comic Women, Tragic Men* (Stanford: Stanford Univ. Press, 1982), p. 152; PETER ERICKSON, *Patriarchal Structures in Shakespeare's Drama* (Berkeley: Univ. of California Press, 1985), p. 62. This is like Wilbur Sanders's centering of individuals in the history plays (see Wilbur Saunders, *The Dramatist and the Received Idea* (Cambridge: Cambridge University Press, 1968), pp. 157, 166 and also p. 190).

30. See Dollimore, in Dollimore and Sinfield, eds., *Political Shakespeare*, pp. 72–80.

31. COPPÉLIA KAHN, *Man's Estate* (Berkeley: Univ. of California Press, 1981), p. 47; Bamber, *Comic Women*, pp. 135,164–65; Erickson, *Patriarchal Structures*, pp. 61–62. However, PHYLLIS RACKIN argues that women are potentially subversive in Shakespearean history plays, that this subversion works only momentarily in *1 Henry VI*, and that it is effective in *King John* (Rackin, *Stages of History* [Ithaca, N.Y.: Cornell Univ. Press, 1990], ch. 4). See also JEAN HOWARD, ' "Effeminately Dolent": Gender and Legitimacy in Ford's *Perkin Warbeck*', in Michael Neill, ed., *John Ford: Critical Re-Visions* (Cambridge: Cambridge Univ. Press, 1988), pp. 263, 278, et passim.

32. 1.2.91–92. Here, no doubt significantly, but I am no Freudian, Coppélia Kahn slips, and says, 'Henry bases his claim to the French crown on the Salic Law, which forbids inheritance through the female' (*Man's Estate*, p. 79). It is the other way round: Henry's title depends on denying that Salic law applies, he claims to inherit through the female line.

33. Rackin, *Stages of History*, p. 191; also pp. 167–68.

34. Shakespeare, *1 Henry IV*, ed. A. R. HUMPHREYS (London: Methuen, 1960), 1.3.28–68.

35. Shakespeare, *Richard II*, ed. PETER URE (London: Methuen, 1966), 5.3.7, 10–12.

36. *Richard III*, ed. ANTONY HAMMOND (London: Methuen, 1981), 3.7.210; *Romeo and Juliet*, ed. BRIAN GIBBONS (London: Methuen, 1980), 3.1.116.

37. *1 Henry IV* 1.2.2–4, 3.3.150–52; *Richard II* 5.3.7. In an essay forthcoming in *Renaissance Drama* (1991), 'Wales, Ireland, and *1 Henry IV*', CHRISTOPHER HIGHLEY shows how *1 Henry IV*, like other contemporary documents, imagines the threat from the Celtic fringe in terms of the overthrow of a masculine English identity through castration.

38. In ELAINE SHOWALTER, ed., *The New Feminist Criticism* (London: Virago, 1986), p. 278. Coppélia Kahn, partly following W. H. AUDEN in *The Dyer's Hand* (New York: Random House, 1963), p. 196, says Falstaff avoids 'sexual maturity', desires food and drink more than women, and gives 'his

own deepest affections to a boy' (Kahn, *Man's Estate*, pp. 72–73). Of course, Auden and Kahn are hinting, darkly, at homosexuality.

39. Shakespeare, *2 Henry IV*, ed. A. R. HUMPHREYS (London: Methuen, 1966), 4.4.31–33; 5.4.

40. Howard, ' "Effeminately Dolent",' p. 275. Howard argues that Perkin Warbeck in John Ford's play of that name (c. 1632) is ' "contaminated" by traffic with the feminine', that his courtship is unlike that of Henry V, and that it all shows 'the faltering, but hardly the collapse, of the machinery of patriarchal absolutism' (pp. 272, 276).

41. In the New Arden edition, John H. Walter says 'the effeminate Dauphin is riding a lady's horse' (p. 84), but Gary Taylor in the Oxford edition says this need not be so, discerning no 'signs of effeminacy in the Dauphin' (p. 197). Erickson says the Dauphin is 'a travesty of masculinity' (*Patriarchal Structures*, p. 55).

42. EVE KOSOFSKY SEDGWICK, *Between Men: English Literature and Male Homosocial Desire* (New York: Columbia Univ. Press, 1985), pp. 25, 5, and pp. 1–27, passim. See STEPHEN ORGEL, 'Nobody's Perfect: Or Why Did the English Stage Take Boys for Women?' *South Atlantic Quarterly* 88 (1989): 7–29; ALAN BRAY, *Homosexuality in Renaissance England* (London: Gay Men's Press, 1982); and ALAN BRAY's important new article: 'Homosexuality and the Signs of Male Friendship in Elizabethan England', *History Workshop* 29 (1990): 1–19.

43. See IAN MACLEAN, *The Renaissance Notion of Women* (Cambridge: Cambridge Univ. Press, 1980); THOMAS LAQUEUR, 'Orgasm, Generation, and the Politics of Reproductive Biology', *Representations* 14 (1986): 1–41; GREENBLATT, 'Fiction and Friction', in STEPHEN GREENBLATT, *Shakespearean Negotiations* (Oxford: Clarendon Press, 1988), pp. 73–86.

44. J. E. NEALE, *Queen Elizabeth* (London: Cape, 1934), p. 279.

45. *Troilus and Cressida*, ed. KENNETH PALMER (London: Methuen, 1982), 3.3.216–19; Orgel, 'Nobody's Perfect', pp. 14–15. REBECCA W. BUSHNELL observes that tyrants were said to be 'effeminate' – subject to their lusts, mainly in respect of women (*Tragedies of Tyrants* [Ithaca, N.Y.: Cornell Univ. Press, 1990], pp. 63–69).

46. Spenser, *View*, ed. Renwick, pp. 69–70. Spenser says he is quoting Aristotle, but Renwick says it is an elaboration of Herodotus (p. 206).

47. For Erickson, this 'set piece is a microcosm of the historical as well as psychological escapism implicit in Henry V's heroic impulse' (*Patriarchal Structures*, p. 54).

48. See NORMAN RABKIN, 'Rabbits, Ducks and *Henry V*', *Shakespeare Quarterly* 28 (1977): 279–96; Kahn, *Man's Estate*, pp. 79–80; COLIN MACCABE, 'Towards a Modern Trivium – English Studies Today', *Critical Quarterly* 26 (1984): 69–82, p. 72; LEONARD TENNENHOUSE, *Power on Display* (New York: Methuen, 1986), p. 71; Erickson, *Patriarchal Structures*, pp. 59–63; LANCE WILCOX, 'Katherine of France as Victim and Bride', *Shakespeare Studies* 17 (1985): 61–76.

49. Taylor, ed., *Henry V* (Oxford ed.), p. 270.

50. Kahn, *Man's Estate*, p. 79; Bamber, *Comic Women*, p. 146.

51. Wilcox, 'Katherine of France', p. 66.

52. Shakespeare, *1 Henry VI*, ed. ANDREW S. CAIRNCROSS (London: Methuen, 1962), 1.1.35, 5.4.107. Coppélia Kahn quotes the prophecy that there will be 'none but women left to wail the dead' (*1 Henry VI* 1.1.51) and observes 'the fear that without the masculine principle of succession the race will become impotent and feminized' (Kahn, *Man's Estate*, p. 62).

53. Spenser, *View*, ed. Renwick, pp. 66–68. See also the notes in RUDOLF GOTTFRIED, ed., *Spenser's Prose Works*, in Edwin Greenlaw, Charles Grosvenor Osgood, Frederick Morgan Padelford, and Ray Heffner, eds., *The Works of Edmund Spenser: A Variorum Edition* (Baltimore: Johns Hopkins Press, 1949), pp. 349–51.

Bibliography

ALTMAN, JOEL B., ' "Vile Participation": The Amplification of Violence in the Theater of *Henry V'*, *Shakespeare Quarterly* 42 (1991), pp. 1–32

BAMBER, LINDA, *Comic Women, Tragic Men: A Study of Gender and Genre in Shakespeare* (Stanford, CA: Stanford University Press, 1982)

BARBER, C. L., *Shakespeare's Festive Comedy: A Study of Dramatic Form and its Relation to Social Custom* (Princeton, NJ: Princeton University Press, 1959)

BARKER, DEBORAH E. AND KAMPS, IVO (eds), *Shakespeare and Gender: A History* (London and New York: Verso, 1995)

BARROLL, LEEDS, 'A New History for Shakespeare and His Time', *Shakespeare Quarterly* 39 (1988), pp. 441–64

BASSNETT, SUSAN, *Shakespeare: The Elizabethan Plays* (Basingstoke: Macmillan, 1993)

BATCHELOR, JOHN, CAIN, TOM AND LAMONT, CLAIRE (eds), *Shakespearean Continuities: Essays in Honour of E.A.J. Honigmann* (Basingstoke: Macmillan, 1997)

BATTENHOUSE, ROY, '*Henry V* as Heroic Comedy' in *Essays on Shakespeare and Elizabethan Drama in Honor of Hardin Craig*, ed. Richard Hosley (Columbia, MO: University of Missouri Press, 1962), pp. 163–82

BELSEY, CATHERINE, *Critical Practice* (London: Methuen, 1980)

BELSEY, CATHERINE, 'Making Histories Then and Now: Shakespeare from *Richard II* to *Henry V'*, in Francis Barker, Peter Hulme and Margaret Iverson (eds), *Uses of History: Marxism, Postmodernism and the Renaissance* (Manchester: Manchester University Press, 1991)

BERGER, JR., HARRY, 'Psychoanalysing the Shakespeare Text: the First Three Scenes of the *Henriad'*, in Patricia Parker and Geoffrey Hartman (eds), *Shakespeare and the Question of Theory* (New York and London: Methuen, 1985)

BERGERON, DAVID M., '*Richard II* and Carnival Politics', *Shakespeare Quarterly* 42 (1991), pp. 33–43

BERGERON, DAVID M. (ed.), *Reading and Writing in Shakespeare* (Newark, NJ and London: University of Delaware Press, 1996)

BERKOWITZ, GERALD, '*Richard II'*, *Shakespeare Bulletin: A Journal of Performance Criticism and Scholarship* 14 (1996), p. 9

BLOOM, HAROLD (ed.), *William Shakespeare: Histories and Poems* (New York: Chelsea House Publishers, 1986)

BOOSE, LYNDA E. AND Burt, Richard (eds), *Shakespeare, the Movie: Popularizing the Plays on Film, TV, and Video* (London and New York: Routledge, 1997)

BRADLEY, A. C., 'The Rejection of Falstaff', in *Oxford Lectures on Poetry*, 2nd edn. (London: Macmillan, 1909), pp. 256–8

BRAY, ALAN, *Homosexuality in Renaissance England*, 2nd edn. (London: Gay Men's Press, 1988)

BREDBECK, GREGORY W., *Sodomy and Interpretation: Marlowe to Milton* (Ithaca, NY: Cornell University Press, 1991)

BREIGHT, CURTIS, 'Branagh and the Prince, or a "Royal Fellowship of Death"', *Critical Quarterly* 33 (1991); reprinted in Shaughnessy (1998)

BURNETT, MARK THORNTON AND WRAY, RAMONA (eds), *Shakespeare and Ireland: History, Politics, Culture* (Basingstoke: Macmillan, 1997)

CALDERWOOD, JAMES L., *Shakespearian Metadrama: The Argument of the Play in 'Titus Andronicus', 'Love's Labour's Lost', 'Romeo and Juliet', 'A Midsummer Night's Dream' and 'Richard II'* (Minneapolis, MN: University of Minnesota Press, 1971)

CALDERWOOD, JAMES L., *Metadrama in Shakespeare's Henriad: 'Richard II' to 'Henry V'* (Berkeley, CA: University of California Press, 1979)

CARTELLI, THOMAS, *Repositioning Shakespeare: National Formations, Postcolonial Appropriations* (London and New York: Routledge, 1999)

CHAMPION, LARRY S., *'The Noise of Threatening Drum': Dramatic Strategy and Political Ideology in Shakespeare and the English Chronicle Plays* (Newark, NJ: University of Delaware Press, 1990)

CLARE, JANET, 'The Censorship of the Deposition Scene in *Richard II*', *Review of English Studies* XLI (1990), pp. 89–95

COHEN, DEREK, *Shakespeare's Culture of Violence* (Basingstoke: Macmillan, 1993)

COLLEY, SCOTT, *Richard's Himself Again: A Stage History of* Richard III (New York: Greenwood Press, 1992)

COUSIN, GERALDINE, *King John* (Manchester: Manchester University Press, 1994) Shakespeare in Performance series

COX, J. D., *Shakespeare and the Dramaturgy of Power* (Princeton, NJ: Princeton University Press, 1989)

CURREN-AQUINO, DEBORAH T. (ed.), *King John: New Perspectives* (Newark, NJ: University of Delaware Press, 1989)

DAVIES, ANTHONY, *Filming Shakespeare's Plays: The Adaptations of Laurence Olivier, Orson Welles, Peter Brook and Akira Kurosawa* (Cambridge: Cambridge University Press, 1988)

DAVIES, ANTHONY AND WELLS, STANLEY (eds), *Shakespeare and the Moving Image: The Plays on Film and Television* (Cambridge: Cambridge University Press, 1994)

DE SOMOGYI, NICK, *Shakespeare's Theatre of War* (Aldershot: Ashgate Publishing, 1998)

DE SOUSA, GERALDO U., *Shakespeare's Cross-Cultural Encounters* (Basingstoke: Macmillan, 1999)

DEAN, PAUL, 'Shakespeare's *Henry VI* Trilogy and Elizabethan "Romance" Histories: the Origins of a Genre', *Shakespeare Quarterly* 33 (1982), pp. 34–48

DEAN, PAUL, 'Forms of Time: Some Elizabethan Two-Part History Plays', *Renaissance Studies* 4 (1990), pp. 410–30

DOLLIMORE, JONATHAN, *Radical Tragedy: Religion, Ideology and Power in the Drama of Shakespeare and his Contemporaries* (Hemel Hempstead: Harvester, 1984)

DOLLIMORE, JONATHAN AND SINFIELD, ALAN (eds), *Political Shakespeare: New Essays in Cultural Materialism* (Manchester: Manchester University Press, 1985)

DRAKAKIS, JOHN (ed.), *Alternative Shakespeares* (London and New York: Methuen, 1985)

DUBROW, HEATHER AND STRIER, RICHARD (eds), *The Historical Renaissance: New Essays on Tudor and Stuart Literature and Culture* (Chicago and London: University of Chicago Press, 1988)

DUSINBERRE, JULIET, '*King John* and Embarrassing Women', *Shakespeare Survey* 42 (1990), pp. 37–51

DUTTON, RICHARD, *Mastering the Revels: The Regulation and Censorship of English Renaissance Drama* (Basingstoke: Macmillan, 1991)

FERGUSON, MARGARET W., QUILLIGAN, MAUREEN AND VICKERS, NANCY J. (eds), *Rewriting the Renaissance: The Discourses of Sexual Difference in Early Modern Europe* (Chicago and London: University of Chicago Press, 1986)

FERRIS, DIANE, 'Elizabeth I and *Richard II*: Portraits in 'Masculine' and 'Feminine' Princes,' *International Journal of Women's Studies* 4 (1981), pp. 10–18

FREY, DAVID L., *The First Tetralogy. Shakespeare's Scrutiny of the Tudor Myth: A Dramatic Exploration of Divine Providence* (The Hague: Mouton, 1976)

GARBER, MARJORIE, *Shakespeare's Ghost Writers: Literature as Uncanny Causality* (New York and London: Methuen, 1987)

GODDARD, HAROLD C., *The Meaning of Shakespeare* (Chicago: University of Chicago Press, 1951)

GOLDBERG, JONATHAN, *Sodometries: Renaissance Texts, Modern Sexualities* (Stanford, CA: Stanford University Press, 1992)

GRADY, HUGH, *The Modernist Shakespeare: Critical Texts in a Material World* (Oxford: Clarendon Press, 1991)

GOULD, GERALD, 'A New Reading of *Henry V*', *English Review* 29 (1919), pp. 42–55

GREENBLATT, STEPHEN J., *Renaissance Self-fashioning: From More to Shakespeare* (Chicago and London: University of Chicago Press, 1980)

GREENBLATT, STEPHEN J., *Shakespearean Negotiations: The Circulation of Social Energy in Renaissance England* (Oxford: Clarendon Press, 1988)

GREENBLATT, STEPHEN, 'Invisible Bullets: Renaissance Authority and its Subversion, *Henry IV* and *Henry V*' in Wilson and Dutton (1992)

GREENBLATT, STEPHEN J., 'Murdering Peasants: Status, Genre, and the Representation of Rebellion', in Stephen Greenblatt (ed.), *Representing the English Renaissance* (Berkeley, CA: University of California Press, 1988)

GREENBLATT, STEPHEN J., *Learning to Curse: Essays in Early Modern Culture* (New York and London: Routledge, 1990)

HALPERN, RICHARD, *The Poetics of Primitive Accumulation: English Renaissance Culture and the Genealogy of Capital* (Ithaca, NY: Cornell University Press, 1991)

HAMILTON, DONNA B., *Shakespeare and the Politics of Protestant England* (Hemel Hempstead: Harvester, 1992)

HAMILTON, DONNA B. AND STRIER, RICHARD (eds), *Religion, Literature, and Politics in Post-Reformation England, 1540–1638* (Cambridge: Cambridge University Press, 1996)

HANKEY, JULIE, *Plays in Performance: Richard III* (Bristol: Bristol Classical Press, 2nd edition, 1988)

HARDIN, RICHARD F., 'Chronicles and Mythmaking in Shakespeare's Joan of Arc', *Shakespeare Survey* 42 (1990), pp. 25–36

HARRISON, WILLIAM, *The Description of England* (1587); ed. Georges Edelen (Washington, D.C. and New York: The Folger Shakespeare Library and Dover Publications, 1994)

HAWKES, TERENCE (ed.), *Alternative Shakespeares: Volume 2* (London and New York: Routledge, 1996)

HAZLITT, WILLIAM, *Characters of Shakespeare's Plays* (London, 1817)

HEADLAM WELLS, ROBIN, *Shakespeare, Politics and the State* (Basingstoke: Macmillan, 1986)

HEINEMANN, MARGOT, 'Political Drama', in *The Cambridge Companion to English Renaissance Drama*, ed. A. R. Braunmuller and Michael Hattaway (Cambridge: Cambridge University Press, 1990)

HELGERSON, RICHARD, *Forms of Nationhood: The Elizabethan Writing of England* (Chicago: University of Chicago Press, 1992)

HIGHLEY, CHRISTOPHER, *Shakespeare, Spenser, and the Crisis in Ireland* (Cambridge: Cambridge University Press, 1997)

HODGDON, BARBARA, *The End Crowns All: Closure and Contradiction in Shakespeare's History* (Princeton, NJ: Princeton University Press, 1991)

HODGDON, BARBARA, *Henry IV, Part Two* (Manchester: Manchester University Press, 1993) Shakespeare in Performance series

HOLDERNESS, GRAHAM, *Shakespeare's History* (Dublin: Gill and Macmillan, 1985)

HOLDERNESS, GRAHAM, 'Radical Potentiality and Institutional Closure: Shakespeare in Film and Television' in Dollimore and Sinfield (1985)

HOLDERNESS, GRAHAM (ed.), *The Shakespeare Myth* (Manchester: Manchester University Press, 1988)

HOLDERNESS, GRAHAM, POTTER, NICK AND TURNER, JOHN, *Shakespeare: The Play of History* (Basingstoke: Macmillan, 1988)

HOLDERNESS, GRAHAM, '"What Ish my Nation?": Shakespeare and National Identities', *Textual Practice* 5 (1991), pp. 74–93; reprinted in Kamps (1995)

HOLDERNESS, GRAHAM (ed.), *Shakespeare's History Plays: Richard II to Henry V* (Basingstoke: Macmillan, 1992)

HOLDERNESS, GRAHAM, *Shakespeare Recycled: The Making of Historical Drama* (New York and London: Harvester Wheatsheaf, 1992)

HOLDERNESS, GRAHAM, *Shakespeare: The Histories* (Basingstoke: Macmillan, 2000)

HOLINSHED, RAPHAEL, *Chronicles of England, Scotland, and Ireland* (1587); 2nd edn. (London, 1808)

HONIGMANN, E. A. J., *Shakespeare: The 'Lost Years'* (Manchester: Manchester University Press, 1985)

HOPKINS, LISA, 'Neighbourhood in *Henry V*', in Burnett and Wray (1997)

HOPKINS, LISA, *The Shakespearean Marriage: Merry Wives and Heavy Husbands* (Basingstoke: Macmillan, 1998)

HOWARD, JEAN E. AND O'CONNOR, MARION F. (eds), *Shakespeare Reproduced: The Text in History and Ideology* (London and New York: Methuen, 1987)

HOWARD, JEAN E. AND RACKIN, PHYLLIS, *Engendering a Nation: A Feminist Account of Shakespeare's English Histories* (London and New York: Routledge, 1997)

ISER, WOLFGANG, *Staging Politics: The Lasting Impact of Shakespeare's Histories*, translated by David Henry Wilson (New York: Columbia University Press, 1993)

JAMESON, FREDRIC, 'Religion and Ideology: *Paradise Lost*', in Francis Baker et al. (eds), *Literature, Politics and Theory: Papers from the Essex Conference 1976–84* (London: Methuen, 1986), pp. 38–9

JARDINE, LISA, *Reading Shakespeare Historically* (London and New York: Routledge, 1996)

JONES, EMRYS, *The Origins of Shakespeare* (Oxford: Clarendon Press, 1977)

KAHN, COPPÉLIA, *Man's Estate: Masculine Identity in Shakespeare* (Berkeley, CA: University of California Press, 1981)

KAMPS, IVO (ed.), *Shakespeare Left and Right* (New York and London: Routledge, 1991)

KAMPS, IVO (ed.), *Materialist Shakespeare: A History* (London and New York: Verso, 1995)

KANTOROWICZ, ERNST H., *The King's Two Bodies: A Study in Medieval Political Theology* (Princeton, NJ: Princeton University Press, 1957)

KASTAN, DAVID SCOTT, 'Proud Majesty Made a Subject: Shakespeare and the Spectacle of Rule', *Shakespeare Quarterly* 37 (1986), pp. 459–75

KELLY, H. A., *Divine Providence in the England of Shakespeare's Histories* (Cambridge, MA: Harvard University Press, 1970)

KINNEY, ARTHUR F., 'Essex and Shakespeare versus Hayward', *Shakespeare Quarterly* 44 (1993), pp. 464–6

KNOWLES, RONALD (ed.), *Shakespeare and Carnival: After Bakhtin* (Basingstoke: Macmillan, 1998)

KOLIN, PHILIP C., *Shakespeare and Feminist Criticism: An Annotated Bibliography and Commentary* (New York: Garland, 1991)

LEGGATT, ALEXANDER, *Shakespeare's Political Drama: The History Plays and the Roman Plays* (London and New York: Routledge, 1988)

LENZ, CAROLYN RUTH SWIFT, GREENE, GAYLE and NEELY,. CAROL THOMAS, *The Woman's Part: Feminist Criticism of Shakespeare* (Urbana, IL: University of Illinois Press, 1983)

LEVEY, CHRISTINE, 'A Bibliography of Psychological and Psychoanalytic Shakespeare Criticism: 1979–1989', in B. J. Sokol (ed.), *The Undiscover'd Country: New Essays on Psychoanalysis and Shakespeare* (London: Free Association Books, 1993)

LIEBLER, NAOMI CONN, 'King of the Hill: Ritual and Play in the Shaping of *3 Henry VI*' in Velz (1997)

LOEHLIN, JAMES N., *Henry V* (Manchester: Manchester University Press, 1996) Shakespeare in Performance series

LOOMBA, ANIA AND ORKIN, MARTIN (eds), *Post-Colonial Shakespeares* (London and New York: Routledge, 1998)

MARCUS, LEAH S., *Puzzling Shakespeare: Local Reading and its Discontents* (Berkeley, CA: University of California Press, 1988)

MARX, STEVEN, 'Holy War in *Henry V*' in Wells (1995)

MATTHEWS, HONOR, *Character and Symbol in Shakespeare's Plays* (Cambridge: Cambridge University Press, 1962)

MAUS, KATHARINE EISAMAN, *Inwardness and Theater in the English Renaissance* (Chicago and London: University of Chicago Press, 1995)

MCALINDON, TOM, 'Pilgrims of Grace: *Henry IV* Historicised' in Wells (1995)

MCALINDON, TOM, 'Testing the New Historicism: "Invisible Bullets" Reconsidered', *Studies in Philology* 92 (1995), pp. 411–38

MCEACHERN, CLAIRE, *The Poetics of English Nationhood, 1590–1612* (Cambridge: Cambridge University Press, 1996)

MCMILLIN, SCOTT, 'Shakespeare's *Richard II*: Eyes of Sorrow, Eyes of Desire', *Shakespeare Quarterly* 35 (1984), pp. 40–52

MCMILLIN, SCOTT, *Henry IV, Part One* (Manchester: Manchester University Press, 1991) Shakespeare in Performance series

MELCHIORI, GIORGIO, *Shakespeare's Garter Plays: Edward III to Merry Wives of Windsor* (Newark, NJ: University of Delaware Press, 1994)

MERON, THEODOR, *Henry's Wars and Shakespeare's Laws: Perspectives on the Law of War in the Later Middle Ages* (Oxford: Clarendon Press, 1993)

MONTROSE, LOUIS A., '"Shaping Fantasies": Figurations of Gender and Power in Elizabethan Culture', *Representations* 1 (1983), pp. 61–94

MOULTON, IAN FREDERICK, 'A Monster Great Deformed: the Unruly Masculinity of Richard III', *Shakespeare Quarterly* 47 (1996), pp. 251–68

MULLANEY, STEVEN, *The Place of the Stage: License, Play, and Power in Renaissance England* (Ann Arbor, MI: University of Michigan Press, 1988)

MURPHY, ANDREW, *But the Irish Sea Betwixt Us: Ireland, Colonialism and Renaissance Literature* (Lexington, KY: University Press of Kentucky, 1999)

NEVO, RUTH, *Comic Transformations in Shakespeare* (London: Methuen, 1980)

NEWMAN, KAREN, *Fashioning Femininity and English Renaissance Drama* (Chicago: University of Chicago Press, 1991)

NEWTON, K. M. (ed.), *Twentieth-Century Literary Theory: A Reader* (Basingstoke: Macmillan, 2nd edition, 1997)

NORBROOK, DAVID, '"A Liberal Tongue": Language and Rebellion in *Richard II*', in John M. Mucciolo, Steven J. Doloff and Edward A. Rauchut (eds), *Shakespeare's Universe: Renaissance Ideas and Conventions. Essays in Honour of W. R. Elton* (Aldershot: Scolar Press, 1996)

NORWICH, JOHN JULIUS, *Shakespeare's Kings* (Harmondsworth: Penguin, 2000)

NUTTALL, A. D., *A New Mimesis: Shakespeare and the Representation of Reality* (London: Methuen, 1983)

NUTTALL, A. D., 'Ovid's Narcissus and Shakespeare's *Richard II*: the Reflected Self', in Charles Martindale (ed.), *Ovid Renewed: Ovidian Influences on Literature and Art from the Middle Ages to the Twentieth Century* (Cambridge: Cambridge University Press, 1988)

ORNSTEIN, ROBERT, *A Kingdom for a Stage: The Achievement of Shakespeare's History Plays* (Cambridge, MA: Harvard University Press, 1972)

PALMER, JOHN, *Political Characters of Shakespeare* (London: Macmillan, 1945)

PARKER, PATRICIA, *Literary Fat Ladies: Rhetoric, Gender, Property* (London: Methuen, 1987)

PATEMAN, CAROLE, *The Sexual Contract* (Stanford, CA: Stanford University Press, 1988)

PATTERSON, ANNABEL, *Shakespeare and the Popular Voice* (Cambridge, MA and Oxford: Basil Blackwell, 1989)

PATTERSON, ANNABEL, *Reading Holinshed's Chronicles* (Chicago: University of Chicago Press, 1994)

PILKINGTON, ACE G., *Screening Shakespeare from* Richard II *to* Henry V (Newark, NJ: University of Delaware Press, 1991)

PUGLIATTI, PAOLA, *Shakespeare the Historian* (Basingstoke: Macmillan, 1996)

RABKIN, NORMAN, *Shakespeare and the Problem of Meaning* (Chicago: University of Chicago Press, 1981)

RACKIN, PHYLLIS, *Stages of History: Shakespeare's English Chronicles* (London: Routledge, 1991)

RACKIN, PHYLLIS, 'Historical Difference/Sexual Difference' in *Privileging Gender in Early Modern Britain*, ed. Jean R. Brink (Kirksville, MO: Sixteenth-Century Journal Publishers, 1992), pp. 37–63

RIBNER, IRVING, *The English History Play in the Age of Shakespeare* (London: Oxford University Press, 1957)

RICHMOND, HUGH M., *King Richard III* (Manchester: Manchester University Press, 1989) Shakespeare in Performance series

RICHMOND, HUGH M., *King Henry VIII* (Manchester: Manchester University Press, 1994) Shakespeare in Performance series

ROSSITER, A. P., *Angel with Horns* (London and New York: Longman, 1961)

RYAN, KIERNAN, *Shakespeare* (Hemel Hempstead: Harvester, 1989; 2nd edition, 1995)

SACCIO, PETER, *Shakespeare's English Kings: History, Chronicle and Drama* (London: Oxford University Press, 1977)

SHAKESPEARE, WILLIAM, *Henry V*, ed. J.H. Walter (The Arden Shakespeare. London: Methuen, 1983)

SHAKESPEARE, WILLIAM, *King Henry V*, ed. T.W. Craik (The Arden Shakespeare. London: Routledge, 1995)

SHAKESPEARE, WILLIAM, *Richard II*, ed. Peter Ure (The Arden Shakespeare. London: Methuen, 1961)

SHAUGHNESSY, ROBERT (ed.), *Shakespeare on Film* (Basingstoke: Macmillan, 1998)

SHEWRING, MARGARET, *King Richard II* (Manchester: Manchester University Press, 1996) Shakespeare in Performance series

SIMMONS, J. L., 'Masculine Negotiations in Shakespeare's History Plays: Hal, Hotspur, and "the foolish Mortimer"', *Shakespeare Quarterly* 44 (1993), pp. 440–63

SINFIELD, ALAN, *Faultlines: Cultural Materialism and the Politics of Dissident Reading* (Oxford: Clarendon Press, 1992)

SMIDT, KRISTIAN, *Unconformities in Shakespeare's History Plays* (Basingstoke: Macmillan, 1982)

SMITH, GORDON ROSS, 'Shakespeare's *Henry V*: Another Part of the Critical Forest', *Journal of the History of Ideas* 37 (1976), pp. 3–26

SPENCER, HAZELTON, *The Art and Life of William Shakespeare* (New York: Harcourt, 1940)

SPRAGUE, A. C., *Shakespeare's Histories: Plays for the Stage* (London: Society for Theatre Research, 1964)

SPRENGNETHER, MADELON, *The Spectral Mother: Freud, Feminism and Psychoanalysis* (Ithaca, NY: Cornell University Press, 1990)

TAYLOR, MICHAEL, *Shakespeare Criticism in the Twentieth Century* (Oxford: Oxford University Press, 2001)

TENNENHOUSE, LEONARD, *Power on Display: The Politics of Shakespeare's Genres* (New York and London: Methuen, 1986)

THAYER, C. G., *Shakespearean Politics: Government and Misgovernment in the Great Histories* (Athens, OH: Ohio University Press, 1983)

TILLYARD, E. M. W., *The Elizabethan World Picture* (1943); 2nd edn. (Harmondsworth: Penguin, 1976)

TILLYARD, E. M. W., *Shakespeare's History Plays* (1944); 2nd edn. (Harmondsworth: Penguin, 1966)

TRAUB, VALERIE, *Desire and Anxiety: Circulations of Sexuality in Shakespearean Drama* (London and New York: Routledge, 1992)

UNDERDOWN, DAVID E., 'The Taming of the Scold: The Enforcement of Patriarchal Authority in Early Modern England' in *Order and Disorder in Early Modern England*, ed. Anthony Fletcher and John Stevenson (Cambridge: Cambridge University Press, 1985), pp. 116–36

VAN DOREN, MARK, *Shakespeare* (New York: Holt, 1939)

VELZ, JOHN W. (ed.), *Shakespeare's English Histories: A Quest for Form and Genre* (Tempe, AZ: Mediaeval and Renaissance Texts and Studies, 1997)

VICKERS, BRIAN, *Appropriating Shakespeare: Contemporary Critical Quarrels* (New Haven, CT, and London: Yale University Press, 1993)

WALCH, GÜNTER, '*Henry V* as Working-house of Ideology', *Shakespeare Survey* 40 (1988), pp. 63–8

WATSON, DONALD G., *Shakespeare's Early History Plays: Politics at Play on the Elizabethan Stage* (Basingstoke: Macmillan, 1990)

WEIMANN, ROBERT, 'Bifold Authority in Shakespeare's Theatre', *Shakespeare Quarterly* 39 (1988), pp. 401–17

WELLS, STANLEY (ed.), *Shakespeare Survey* 48 (Cambridge: Cambridge University Press, 1995)

WENTERSDORF, KARL P., 'The Conspiracy of Silence in *Henry V*', *Shakespeare Quarterly* 27 (1976), pp. 264–87

WILDERS, JOHN, *The Lost Garden: A View of Shakespeare's English and Roman History Plays* (Basingstoke: Macmillan, 1978)

WILLIAMS, RAYMOND, *Marxism and Literature* (Oxford: Oxford University Press, 1977)

WILSON, RICHARD, *Will Power: Essays on Shakespearean Authority* (New York and London: Harvester, 1993)

WILSON, RICHARD, 'Shakespeare and the Jesuits', *Times Literary Supplement*, 19 December 1997, pp. 11–13

WILSON, RICHARD AND DUTTON, RICHARD (eds), *New Historicism and Renaissance Drama* (London and New York: Longman, 1992)

WOOD, NIGEL (ed.), *Henry IV Parts One and Two* (Buckingham: Open University Press, 1995)

WOODBRIDGE, LINDA AND BERRY, EDWARD (eds), *True Rites and Maimed Rites: Ritual and Anti-Ritual in Shakespeare and his Age* (Urbana, IL: University of Illinois Press, 1992)

Index